NATIONAL SECURITY

ISSN 1543-5407

NATIONAL SECURITY

Kim Masters Evans

INFORMATION PLUS® REFERENCE SERIES
Formerly Published by Information Plus, Wylie, Texas

Detroit • New York • San Francisco • New Haven, Conn • Waterville, Maine • London

National Security

Kim Masters Evans
Paula Kepos, Series Editor

Project Editors: Elizabeth Manar, Kathleen J. Edgar

Rights Acquisition and Management: Jennifer Altschul, Kelly Quin

Composition: Evi Abou-El-Seoud, Mary Beth Trimper

Manufacturing: Cynde Bishop

Product Management: Carol Nagel

Gale
27500 Drake Rd.
Farmington Hills, MI 48331-3535

ISBN-13: 978-0-7876-5103-9 (set) ISBN-10: 0-7876-5103-6 (set)
ISBN-13: 978-1-4144-3380-6 ISBN-10: 1-4144-3380-8

ISSN 1543-5407

This title is also available as an e-book.
ISBN-13: 978-1-4144-5756-7 (set)
ISBN-10: 1-4144-5756-1 (set)
Contact your Gale sales representative for ordering information.

Printed in the United States of America
1 2 3 4 5 6 7 13 12 11 10 09

TABLE OF CONTENTS

PREFACE

National Security is part of the *Information Plus Reference Series*. The purpose of each volume of the series is to present the latest facts on a topic of pressing concern in modern American life. These topics include today's most controversial and studied social issues: abortion, capital punishment, care for the elderly, crime, the environment, gambling, health care, immigration, minorities, national security, social welfare, women, youth, and many more. Even though this series is written especially for high school and undergraduate students, it is an excellent resource for anyone in need of factual information on current affairs.

By presenting the facts, it is the intention of Gale, a part of Cengage Learning, to provide its readers with everything they need to reach an informed opinion on current issues. To that end, there is a particular emphasis in this series on the presentation of scientific studies, surveys, and statistics. These data are generally presented in the form of tables, charts, and other graphics placed within the text of each book. Every graphic is directly referred to and carefully explained in the text. The source of each graphic is presented within the graphic itself. The data used in these graphics are drawn from the most reputable and reliable sources, in particular from the various branches of the U.S. government and from major independent polling organizations. Every effort was made to secure the most recent information available. Readers should bear in mind that many major studies take years to conduct, and that additional years often pass before the data from these studies are made available to the public. Therefore, in many cases the most recent information available in 2009 is dated from 2006 or 2007. Older statistics are sometimes presented as well, if they are of particular interest and no more-recent information exists.

Even though statistics are a major focus of the *Information Plus Reference Series*, they are by no means its only content. Each book also presents the widely held positions and important ideas that shape how the book's subject is discussed in the United States. These positions are explained in detail and, where possible, in the words of their proponents. Some of the other material to be found in these books includes historical background, descriptions of major events related to the subject, relevant laws and court cases, and examples of how these issues play out in American life. Some books also feature primary documents, or have pro and con debate sections giving the words and opinions of prominent Americans on both sides of a controversial topic. All material is presented in an even-handed and unbiased manner; readers will never be encouraged to accept one view of an issue over another.

HOW TO USE THIS BOOK

National security has been foremost on the minds of many Americans since the September 11, 2001, terrorist attacks. The United States has taken many major steps since that time, including the formation of the U.S. Department of Homeland Security, increased security measures at airports, the enactment of the Patriot Act of 2001, and the invasions of Afghanistan and Iraq. This book covers all these topics and more, providing the history of national security in the United States, descriptions of the various conventional and nonproliferation treaties and regimes, and information on countries of concern to the United States. Nuclear, chemical, and biological weapons are discussed in detail, as are domestic and international terrorism and Americans' feelings regarding national security after the September 11, 2001, terrorist attacks.

National Security consists of ten chapters and three appendixes. Each of the chapters is devoted to a particular aspect of U.S. national security. For a summary of the information covered in each chapter, please see the synopses provided in the Table of Contents at the front of the book. Chapters generally begin with an overview of the basic facts and background information on the chapter's topic, then proceed to examine subtopics of particular interest. For example, Chapter 6: Countries of Concern begins by briefly discussing the United States' history and relationship with Russia, Communist China, and the Middle East. Then the chapter examines in detail the United States' biggest enemies: Iran and North Korea. A brief history of Iran is provided, and then its foreign relations with the Middle East and the United States are examined. Among the topics that are addressed are its nuclear program and whether it is really developing nuclear weapons, United Nations resolutions calling on it to suspend its nuclear activities, and the future of U.S.-Iranian relations. A short history is given for North Korea, and then the chapter examines its foreign relations with the Soviet Union and Communist China, its nuclear program, and the international efforts to stop this program. The chapter concludes by discussing other countries of concern: Cuba, Syria, and Sudan. Readers can find their way through a chapter by looking for the section and subsection headings, which are clearly set off from the text. Or, they can refer to the book's extensive index, if they already know what they are looking for.

Statistical Information

The tables and figures featured throughout *National Security* will be of particular use to readers in learning about this topic. These tables and figures represent an extensive collection of the most recent and valuable statistics on national security, as well as related issues—for example, graphics cover common chemical warfare agents, U.S. State Department–designated foreign terrorist organizations, suggested items for a home emergency supply kit, and the number of nuclear warheads in the U.S. stockpile. Gale, a part of Cengage Learning, believes that making this information available to readers is the most important way to fulfill the goal of this book: to help readers understand the issues and controversies surrounding national security in the United States and reach their own conclusions.

Each table or figure has a unique identifier appearing above it, for ease of identification and reference. Titles for the tables and figures explain their purpose. At the end of each table or figure, the original source of the data is provided.

To help readers understand these often complicated statistics, all tables and figures are explained in the text. References in the text direct readers to the relevant statistics. Furthermore, the contents of all tables and figures are fully indexed. Please see the opening section of the index at the back of this volume for a description of how to find tables and figures within it.

Appendixes

Besides the main body text and images, *National Security* has three appendixes. The first is the Important Names and Addresses directory. Here, readers will find contact information for a number of government and private organizations that can provide further information on aspects of national security. The second appendix is the Resources section, which can also assist readers in conducting their own research. In this section, the author and editors of *National Security* describe some of the sources that were most useful during the compilation of this book. The final appendix is the index.

ADVISORY BOARD CONTRIBUTIONS

The staff of Information Plus would like to extend its heartfelt appreciation to the Information Plus Advisory Board. This dedicated group of media professionals provides feedback on the series on an ongoing basis. Their comments allow the editorial staff who work on the project to continually make the series better and more user-friendly. Our top priorities are to produce the highest-quality and most useful books possible, and the Advisory Board's contributions to this process are invaluable.

The members of the Information Plus Advisory Board are:

- Kathleen R. Bonn, Librarian, Newbury Park High School, Newbury Park, California
- Madelyn Garner, Librarian, San Jacinto College–North Campus, Houston, Texas
- Anne Oxenrider, Media Specialist, Dundee High School, Dundee, Michigan
- Charles R. Rodgers, Director of Libraries, Pasco-Hernando Community College, Dade City, Florida
- James N. Zitzelsberger, Library Media Department Chairman, Oshkosh West High School, Oshkosh, Wisconsin

In addition, Information Plus staff owe special thanks to Dr. Harold Molineu, Professor of Political Science at Ohio University, for his particular assistance as an acting adviser on *National Security*. Dr. Molineu's substantial background in the field allowed him to provide expert advice and indispensable recommendations on content and organization.

COMMENTS AND SUGGESTIONS

The editors of the *Information Plus Reference Series* welcome your feedback on *National Security*. Please direct all correspondence to:

Editors
Information Plus Reference Series
27500 Drake Rd.
Farmington Hills, MI 48331-3535

CHAPTER 1
A HISTORICAL OVERVIEW

Throughout its existence, the United States has faced several major external threats to its national security. The first and most enduring threat was the quest for land by other nations desiring to expand their empires. This threat persisted through the 1940s, culminating in World War II (1939–1945). Following the war, U.S. security was threatened by the spread of communism—an economic and political system completely in opposition to the principles of democracy and capitalism embraced by the United States. The cold war period lasted into the early 1990s and pitted the United States against the world's only other superpower of the time: the Soviet Union. The U.S. government made many foreign policy decisions during the cold war that affected its future national security.

Even before the cold war ended, a new threat arose from political and ideological forces sweeping the planet. International terrorism gained prominence as a means for individuals with common grievances to challenge national governments. The United States has become a target for terrorist groups bent on destroying the military, political, economic, and social factors that have catapulted the United States to a position of dominance. At the same time, technological advances have allowed unfriendly nations to acquire new weapons that could inflict mass destruction on the United States. There is a real threat that such weapons could fall into the hands of terrorist groups that would not hesitate to use them against the United States.

Protecting U.S. national security means protecting its key assets: people, territory, infrastructure, economy, and sovereignty (supreme and independent political authority). Since its birth as a nation in 1776, the United States has developed a massive array of systems, tools, and weapons to safeguard these assets. However, national security is not just about defending the homeland and reacting to attacks. The U.S. government also takes a proactive approach, meaning that it anticipates future threats and uses its power to try to manipulate world affairs to its own political and economic benefit. U.S. goals for self-preservation and prosperity in the twenty-first century revolve around maintaining military supremacy, eliminating terrorism and weapons of mass destruction, and spreading democratic principles throughout the world. To understand how the United States arrived at this juncture, it is necessary to review the historical factors that have shaped U.S. foreign policy since the nation was founded.

COLONIALISM AND EMPIRE BUILDING

The United States was born in 1776 in a world consumed with colonialism and empire-building. For several centuries, European superpowers—primarily Britain, Portugal, France, and Spain—had colonized territories throughout the Western Hemisphere by military force or gradual settlement. Russia had expanded its own empire throughout eastern Europe. In China the Ch'ing dynasty had conquered large parts of southern Asia. The Turkish Ottoman Empire controlled a long swath of land around the Mediterranean Sea encompassing parts of the Middle East, northern Africa, and southern Europe.

When European colonists first came to the "New World," they found a vast expanse of land inhabited by indigenous peoples that the new settlers called Indians. Many of the first colonies were business ventures financed by wealthy English businessmen and landowners. The king of England granted limited political rights to these colonies, but exerted heavy taxation on them. During the late 1700s the colonists' desire for self-governance and tax relief drove them to seek independence from Britain and establish a new nation: the United States of America.

REVOLUTIONARY WAR

Even before the Revolutionary War (1775–1783), the North American colonies had formed militias (groups of private citizens devoted to military missions). Some militias were relatively well trained and equipped, whereas others were not. Among the militia members were minutemen—named for their claim that they could be ready to fight in a minute. Some of the colonial militias gained valuable military experience fighting with the British against French and Native American forces during the French and Indian War (1754–1763). Among these fighters was a young officer named George Washington (1732–1799), who would be named commander in chief of the colonists' Continental army at the onset of the Revolutionary War.

The Continental army overcame enormous obstacles to defeat the professional British army, which was supplemented with thousands of Hessians (German mercenary soldiers). The colonists were aided in their struggle by a variety of European nations, particularly France, Britain's longtime enemy. In 1778 the colonists signed the Treaty of Alliance with France; it was the last bilateral (two-party) military agreement the United States would make for nearly two centuries. The military operations of the Revolutionary War ended in 1781, when the last British troops surrendered. The war was officially declared over two years later with the signing of the Treaty of Paris.

THE 1800s

During the 1800s the new United States grew tremendously in terms of territory, population, and economic might. More than two dozen states were added to the Union. Expansionism was accompanied by violent conflicts with Britain (the War of 1812), Mexico (the Mexican War, 1846–1848), and Spain (the Spanish-American War, 1898). In addition, the so-called Indian Wars were waged for many years against Native American tribes.

The U.S. military matured throughout the nineteenth century to secure and seize territory from Europe's colonial powers and Mexico. The growth of the U.S. Navy was driven in part by threats from the Barbary pirates—bands of pirates positioned around the Mediterranean Sea, primarily in North Africa, who terrorized and captured sailing ships and demanded ransom payments from the hostages' governments for their safe return. Some nations, including the United States, paid annual fees to the pirates to ensure the safe passage of their ships through the area. However, the U.S. government tired of this arrangement in 1801 and launched military attacks against the pirates. The U.S. Navy eventually prevailed and a treaty ended the threat to U.S. sailing ships.

Meanwhile in the United States, deep divisions developed between northern and southern factions on the morality of slavery and associated political and economic issues. In 1861 a devastating civil war erupted between Union (northern) and Confederate (southern) forces. When the war ended in 1865, hundreds of thousands of military personnel had died. (See Table 1.1.) Over the following decades the nation was consumed with reconstruction and internal affairs. The government vowed to stay out of territorial disputes simmering in Europe and the rest of the world.

THE WORLD WARS

In 1914 World War I began in Europe. It pitted the forces of Britain, France, Italy, and Russia (collectively known as the Allied powers) against Germany, Austria-Hungary, and the Ottoman Empire (collectively known as the Central powers). The United States was reluctant to get involved, but it eventually entered the war in April 1917 on the side of the Allies and fought until the war ended in November 1918. The Allies were victorious: Austria-Hungary and the Ottoman Empire were divided into a number of separate nations, and severe economic sanctions were imposed against Germany. Reacting to the tremendous loss of life and devastation caused by the war, in the 1920s the United States developed an isolationist stance, determined to stay out of any future European conflicts. This position was to be short lived.

During the 1930s Japan, Germany, and Italy began aggressive military campaigns against their neighbors. In 1939, after years of aggressive expansion, Germany invaded Poland. In response, Britain, France, and Canada declared war on Germany, thereby marking the beginning of World War II. The German blitzkrieg (lightning-fast war) was incredibly successful. By 1941 German forces had defeated and occupied France and invaded the Soviet Union. War had spread throughout Europe, North Africa, parts of China, and the North Atlantic and South Pacific oceans. In the United States President Franklin D. Roosevelt (1882–1945) publicly adhered to the isolationist sentiment of the American public; however, as early as 1939 he began quietly expanding the nation's military capabilities.

On December 7, 1941, Japanese forces staged a surprise attack on the U.S. naval base at Pearl Harbor, Hawaii. Within days, the United States was at war with Japan, Germany, and Italy. A flood of U.S. goods and military might turned the tide of the war. By early 1945 Germany and Italy had been defeated. In August of that year Japan surrendered after suffering two devastating hits by U.S. atomic bombs. World War II was over, and a new world order had been established. The United States abandoned its isolationist stance and assumed an active role in international affairs.

TABLE 1.1

U.S. military personnel and casualties in major wars, 1775–1991

War/conflict	Branch of service	Number serving	Casualties: Total deaths	Battle deaths	Other deaths[a]	Wounds not mortal[a]
Revolutionary War 1775–1783	Total	—[b]	4,435	4,435	—	6,188
War of 1812 1812–1815	Total	286,730[c]	2,260	2,260	—	4,505
Mexican War 1846–1848	Total	78,718[c]	13,283	1,733	11,550	4,152
Civil War (Union Forces only)[d] 1861–1865	Total	2,213,363	364,511	140,414	224,097	281,881
Spanish-American War	Total	306,760	2,446	385	2,061	1,662
World War I 1917–1918	Total	4,734,991	116,516	53,402	63,114	204,002
World War II 1941–1946[e]	Total	16,112,566	405,399	291,557	113,842	670,846
Korean War 1950–1953[f]	Total	5,720,000	36,574	33,739	2,835	103,284
Vietnam conflict 1964–1973[g]	Total	8,744,000	58,220	47,434	10,786	Hosp. care reqd. 153,303 No hospital care 150,341
Persian Gulf War 1990–1991[h]	Total	2,225,000	382	147	235	467

Notes: Data prior to World War I are based on incomplete records in many cases. Casualty data are confined to dead and wounded and, therefore, exclude personnel captured or missing in action who were subsequently returned to military control.

[a]Marine Corps data for World War II, the Spanish-American War, and prior wars represent the number of individuals wounded, whereas all other data in this column represent the total number (incidence) of wounds.

[b]Not known, but estimates range from 184,000 to 250,000.

[c]As reported by the Commissioner of Pensions in the annual report for fiscal year 1903.

[d]Authoritative statistics for the Confederate forces are not available. Estimates of the number who served range from 600,000 to 1,500,000. The final report of the Provost Marshal General, 1863–1866, indicated 133,821 Confederate deaths (74,524 battle and 59,297 other) based upon incomplete returns. In addition, an estimated 26,000 to 31,000 Confederate personnel died in Union prisons.

[e]Data are for the period December 1, 1941, through December 31, 1946, when hostilities were officially terminated by Presidential Proclamation, but a few battle deaths or wounds not mortal were incurred after the Japanese acceptance of the Allied peace terms on August 14, 1945. Number serving from December 1, 1941, through August 31, 1945, were: Total–14,903,213.

[f]Worldwide military deaths during the Korean War totaled 54,246. In-theater casualty records are updated annually.

[g]Number serving covers the period August 5, 1964 ("Vietnam era" begins) through January 27, 1973 (date of cease-fire). Deaths include the period November 1, 1955 (commencement date for the Military Assistance Advisory Group) through May 15, 1975 (date last American servicemember left Southeast Asia). Casualty records are updated annually, including current deaths that are directly attributed to combat in the Vietnam Conflict. Additional detail now on table shows number of WIA servicemembers not requiring hospital care.

[h]Report does not include one POW (Speicher). Casualty records are updated annually.

SOURCE: Adapted from "Principal Wars in Which the United States Participated: U.S. Military Personnel Serving and Casualties," in *DoD Personnel and Military Casualty Statistics: Military Casualty Information*, U.S. Department of Defense, May 2008, http://siadapp.dmdc.osd.mil/personnel/CASUALTY/WCPRINCIPAL.pdf (accessed August 9, 2008)

THE UNITED NATIONS

Only months after World War II ended, the representatives of dozens of nations met in the United States and drafted a constitution for a new world organization called the United Nations (UN). The UN's purpose was twofold. First, it was to provide a medium through which international disagreements could be settled peacefully. Second, the UN would tackle vexing humanitarian issues, such as world hunger and disease. A similar organization, called the League of Nations, had sprung up after World War I, but fell apart soon afterward because it received little support in the United States. However, the ravages of World War II had convinced Americans that such a body was needed. In late 1945 Congress overwhelmingly ratified the UN Charter. The UN Security Council would play a major role in determining the course of future conflicts around the world. The Security Council was set up so that five nations (the so-called permanent members) have special veto powers over UN resolutions. The permanent members are the United States, France, Great Britain, China, and Russia (formerly the Soviet Union).

UN programs are funded through assessed and voluntary contributions by member countries. Assessments are based on each country's financial assets. In *United Nations System Funding: Congressional Issues* (February 1, 2008, http://www.fas.org/sgp/crs/row/RL33611.pdf), Marjorie Ann Browne and Kennon Nakamura of the Congressional Research Service (CRS) note that the United States has been the single largest financial contributor since the UN was founded. Table 1.2 shows the

TABLE 1.2

Top ten contributors to the United Nations (UN) regular budget, by member state, 2008

Member state	Percentage of budget	Assessments for 2008 in U.S. $
United States*	22.00	453,338,391
Japan	16.624	342,558,973
Germany	8.577	176,740,154
United Kingdom*	6.642	136,866,982
France*	6.301	129,840,236
Italy	5.079	104,659,349
Canada	2.977	61,344,927
Spain	2.968	61,159,470
China*	2.667	54,956,977
Mexico	2.257	46,508,398

*Permanent members of the U.N. Security Council.

SOURCE: Adapted from Marjorie Ann Browne and Kennon H. Nakamura, "Table 3. Top 10 U.N. Regular Budget Contributors for 2008," in *United Nations System Funding: Congressional Issues*, Congressional Research Service, February 1, 2008, http://assets.opencrs.com/rpts/RL33611_20080201.pdf (accessed July 26, 2008)

top ten contributors to the UN regular budget (excluding special programs) for 2008. The U.S. assessment was $453.3 million, or 22% of the total.

COMMUNISM AND THE COLD WAR

The Soviet Union had been a wartime ally of the United States, but relations became strained after World War II ended. During the war the Soviet army "liberated" a large part of eastern Europe from Nazi occupation. Through various means, the Union of Soviet Socialist Republics (USSR) assumed political control over these nations. The USSR assumed a major role in international affairs, placing it in direct conflict with the only other superpower of the time: the United States. A "cold" war began between two rich and powerful nations with completely different political, economic, and social goals for the world. The war was called "cold" because it was fought mostly by politicians and diplomats. A direct and large-scale military conflict (or "hot" war) between U.S. and Soviet forces never occurred.

Even though the cold war began in the 1940s, its roots actually lie in the late 1910s. In 1917 a group called the Bolsheviks seized power in Russia during the October Revolution and installed a socialist government. Socialism, and its more radical form—communism—also appealed to some people in Europe and the United States. In 1919 the home of the U.S. attorney general Alexander Mitchell Palmer (1872–1936) was bombed, and postal inspectors intercepted nearly forty mail bombs before they reached their intended targets. A "Red Scare" swept through the United States (so-named because red was the color associated with the October Revolution and the new Russian flag). The Bureau of International Information Programs notes in *Outline of U.S. History* (2005, http://www.america.gov/media/pdf/books/historytln.pdf#popup) that the federal government rounded up communist radicals in the United States and deported those who were not U.S. citizens. The incident left feelings of deep mistrust and hostility in the United States toward communism. A second and much more potent Red Scare swept the country between the late 1940s and early 1960s. Many Americans came under suspicion, and serious breaches of civil liberties occurred in attempts to root out communist sympathizers.

Even though a massive military conflict between U.S. and Soviet forces never ultimately took place, an expensive arms race began in which both sides produced and stockpiled large amounts of weapons as a show of force and to deter a first strike by the enemy. In addition, both sides provided financial and military support to countries around the world in an attempt to influence the political leanings of those populations. Communist China joined the cold war during the 1950s and often partnered with the Soviet Union against U.S. interests.

Containment

U.S. political and military reaction to the threat posed by the Soviet Union was a policy called containment. According to the Bureau of International Information Programs, in *Outline of U.S. History*, this policy was championed by the U.S. diplomat George Kennan (1904–2005), who called for "firm and vigilant containment of Russian expansive tendencies." The gist of containment was explained by President Harry S. Truman (1884–1972; August 29, 2001, http://www.nato.int/docu/speech/1947/s470312a_e.htm) in a speech to Congress on March 12, 1947, and came to be known as the Truman Doctrine: "It must be the policy of the United States to support free peoples who are resisting attempted subjugation by armed minorities or by outside pressures." The Truman Doctrine marked an important change in U.S. foreign policy, which up to that time had mostly taken a hands-off approach to the internal affairs of other nations.

The United States left World War II in sound economic shape. All other major nations had suffered great losses during the war in their infrastructure, financial stability, and populations. Hoping to instill an atmosphere conducive to peace and the spread of capitalism, the United States invested heavily in the postwar economies of Western Europe and Japan. U.S. barriers to foreign trade were relaxed to build new markets for U.S. exports and to allow some war-ravaged nations to make money selling goods to U.S. consumers. Meanwhile, the United States enacted the Marshall Plan, which was designed to rebuild the allied nations of Europe and combat communism. Hundreds of millions of dollars in U.S. aid were transmitted to the governments of Greece and Turkey to help them stave off communist-led insurgencies (rebellions). Billions more went to the war-torn nations of Western Europe.

Nervousness in Western Europe about the closeness of Soviet military forces led to the creation in 1949 of the North Atlantic Treaty Organization (NATO)—a military coalition between the United States and eleven other nations. The NATO alliance provided added security for all the nations involved, because an attack against one was considered an attack against all.

In 1962 the United States and the Soviet Union came to the brink of nuclear war when U.S. intelligence agencies discovered the Soviets had installed nuclear missile facilities in Cuba. In response, President John F. Kennedy (1917–1963) imposed a blockade to prevent Soviet ships from bringing new supplies to Cuba. He demanded the nuclear facilities be removed and publicly warned the Soviets that any attack from Cuba on the United States would spur retaliation against the Soviet Union. After a suspenseful twelve-day standoff, the Soviets backed down and removed the missiles. The Cuban Missile Crisis was a turning point in the cold war. Negotiations began between the two superpowers on treaties to limit the testing and proliferation of nuclear weapons. These talks would proceed in fits and starts for decades.

Korea and Vietnam

In 1950 North Korean forces backed by the Soviet military invaded South Korea, setting off the Korean War. Caught off guard by the invasion, the United States rushed to defend South Korea from a communist takeover. Over the next three years U.S. and allied forces under the UN fought against North Korean and Chinese troops supported by the Soviet Union. The war ended in a stalemate, with both sides back where they had started—on either side of the thirty-eighth parallel (a line of latitude). In 1953 a cease-fire agreement ended the armed conflict in Korea. North Korea remained under communist control, whereas South Korea became a democracy protected by UN troops (primarily U.S. forces).

Also during the 1950s the U.S. military became involved in a conflict between communist North Vietnam and noncommunist South Vietnam. In an effort to bolster the defenses of the country, the United States sent thousands of military advisers to South Vietnam during the late 1950s and early 1960s. In 1964 the conflict escalated into full-scale civil war. Once again, the United States found itself in a remote Asian country trying to prevent the spread of communism.

The fight in Vietnam turned out to be a long and difficult one in which U.S. forces, assisted by a handful of other countries, were pitted against highly motivated forces equipped and backed by the Soviet Union and China. During the 1960s the United States was preoccupied with explosive social problems. Furthermore, there were widespread protests against the Vietnam War. By 1968 there were half a million U.S. troops in Vietnam. Nightly television coverage provided a bleak picture of the war's progress and helped turn public opinion against the war and President Lyndon B. Johnson (1908–1973). The United States was engaged in the war for more than a decade before withdrawing the last of its troops in 1975 and leaving South Vietnam to a communist takeover. According to the Bureau of International Information Programs, in *Outline of U.S. History*, the total cost of the Vietnam War exceeded $150 billion.

In both the Korean and Vietnam wars the United States chose to fight in a limited manner without using its arsenal of nuclear weapons or engaging Chinese or Soviet troops directly for fear of sparking another world war.

U.S. Defense Industry

Spending on national defense soared during World War II and then declined dramatically following the war's end. However, it quickly climbed again as the cold war heated up and remained high for nearly two decades. Full-scale mobilization of U.S. industries was not required for the Korean and Vietnam wars, as it had been during World War II. Instead, a defense industry developed during the cold war to supply the U.S. military on a continuous basis with the arms and goods it wanted. In a January 17, 1961, speech, President Dwight D. Eisenhower (1890–1969; July 1, 2000, http://mcadams.posc.mu.edu/ike.htm) described this arrangement to the American public: "We can no longer risk emergency improvisation of national defense; we have been compelled to create a permanent armaments industry of vast proportions. Added to this, three and a half million men and women are directly engaged in the defense establishment. We annually spend on military security more than the net income of all United States corporations."

The End of the Cold War

The presidency of Richard M. Nixon (1913–1994) brought a new approach to the cold war called détente—a French word meaning "to relax." During the early 1970s Nixon also moved to improve relations with the People's Republic of China (a communist government had assumed power in China following a revolution during the 1930s). However, U.S.-Soviet relations soured during the 1970s under pressure from President Jimmy Carter (1924–) about human rights issues in the Soviet Union. In 1979 the Soviet Union invaded Afghanistan, a move the United States strongly condemned. The Soviets were mired down in Afghanistan for nearly a decade and were unable to achieve military victory. In 1989 they finally withdrew all their troops.

Ronald Reagan (1911–2004) was president of the United States from 1981 through 1989. He took an aggressive stance against the Soviet Union, which he referred to as "the evil empire." The United States began a massive and expensive buildup in military strength, forcing the Soviet Union to do likewise. Reagan called the U.S. buildup the "peace through strength" approach. Soon, the Soviet Union faced serious economic problems, dissent (political opposition), and unrest in many of its territories. All these problems precipitated a breakup of the Soviet empire during the late 1980s and early 1990s into individually governed republics. The cold war was over, but its effects on U.S. national security and world politics would be long lasting.

AMERICAN TRAITORS

Throughout its history, the United States has faced threats from many foreign countries. Foreign agents secretly infiltrated the United States to obtain information (intelligence) about the nation's security mechanisms and to sabotage them. In some cases these efforts were aided by Americans who chose, for whatever reason, to act against U.S. interests and help its enemies. American traitors have existed since the nation was founded. One of the most notorious was Benedict Arnold (1741–1801), a Connecticut native who gained success as a military officer during the Revolutionary War. After being injured in battle and suffering a number of professional and personal setbacks, Arnold secretly accepted large sums of money from the British in exchange for his cooperation in their future military operations. However, before he could carry out these plans, one of his conspirators was captured by the colonists. Arnold fled to England, where he lived for the remainder of his life.

The most serious act of a traitor is defined as treason. Article three of the U.S. Constitution discusses treason as follows: "Treason against the United States, shall consist only in levying war against them, or in adhering to their enemies, giving them aid and comfort. No person shall be convicted of treason unless on the testimony of two witnesses to the same overt act, or on confession in open court." Since World War I the United States has passed a number of laws designed to thwart potential traitors from aiding and abetting U.S. enemies. James Willard Hurst explains in *The Law of Treason in the United States* (1971) that eleven cases of treason related to World War II were heard by the U.S. Supreme Court.

The cold war was an extremely active time for espionage (spying). The United States and the Soviet Union conducted massive intelligence and counterintelligence operations throughout this period. American spies played a key role in passing important information to Soviet agents. In *Espionage against the United States by American Citizens: 1947–2001* (July 2002, http://www.ncix.gov/archives/docs/espionageAgainstUSbyCitizens.pdf), Katherine L. Herbig and Martin F. Wiskoff provide an analysis of U.S. espionage cases. They note that the Defense Personnel Security Research Center's database includes information on 150 Americans who were convicted or strongly suspected of committing acts of espionage during this period. Figure 1.1 shows the number of known American spies active in each year between 1950 through 2001. Activity peaked during the mid-1980s and tapered off sharply after that time. The data in Figure 1.2 indicate that the Soviet bloc (the Soviet Union and affiliated nations in Eastern Europe) was the primary recipient of the information collected by American spies during the cold war.

In the latter part of the twentieth century there were several high-profile cases involving Americans within the

FIGURE 1.1

Known U.S. spies active by number and year, 1950–2001

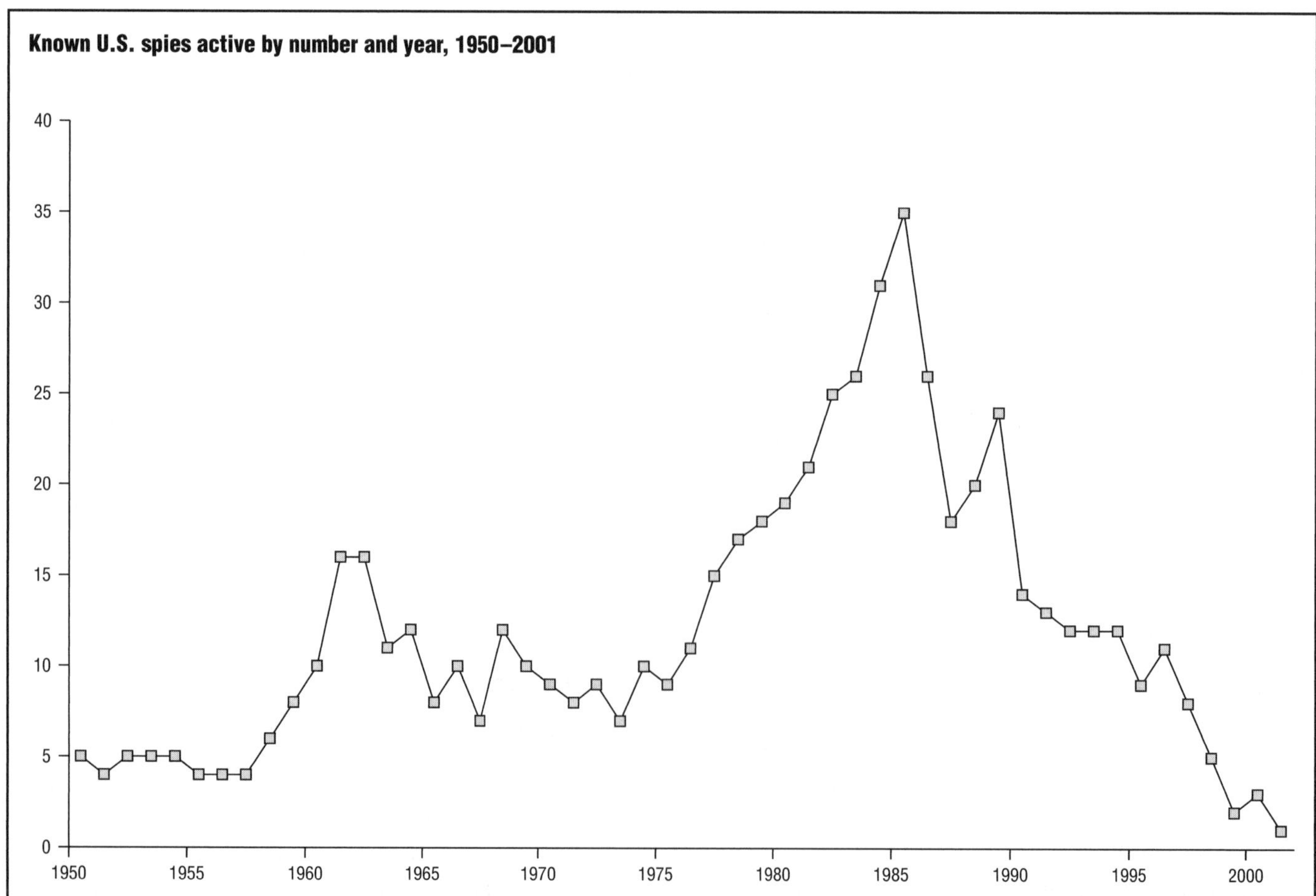

SOURCE: Adapted from Katherine L. Herbig and Martin F. Wiskoff, "Figure 2. Known Spies Active in Each Year, 1950 through 2001," in *Espionage against the United States by American Citizens: 1947–2001*, Defense Personnel Security Research Center, July 2002, http://www.ncix.gov/archives/docs/espionageAgainstUSbyCitizens.pdf (accessed August 11, 2008)

FIGURE 1.2

Recipients of espionage from U.S. spies, by region, number, and decade, 1950s–1990s

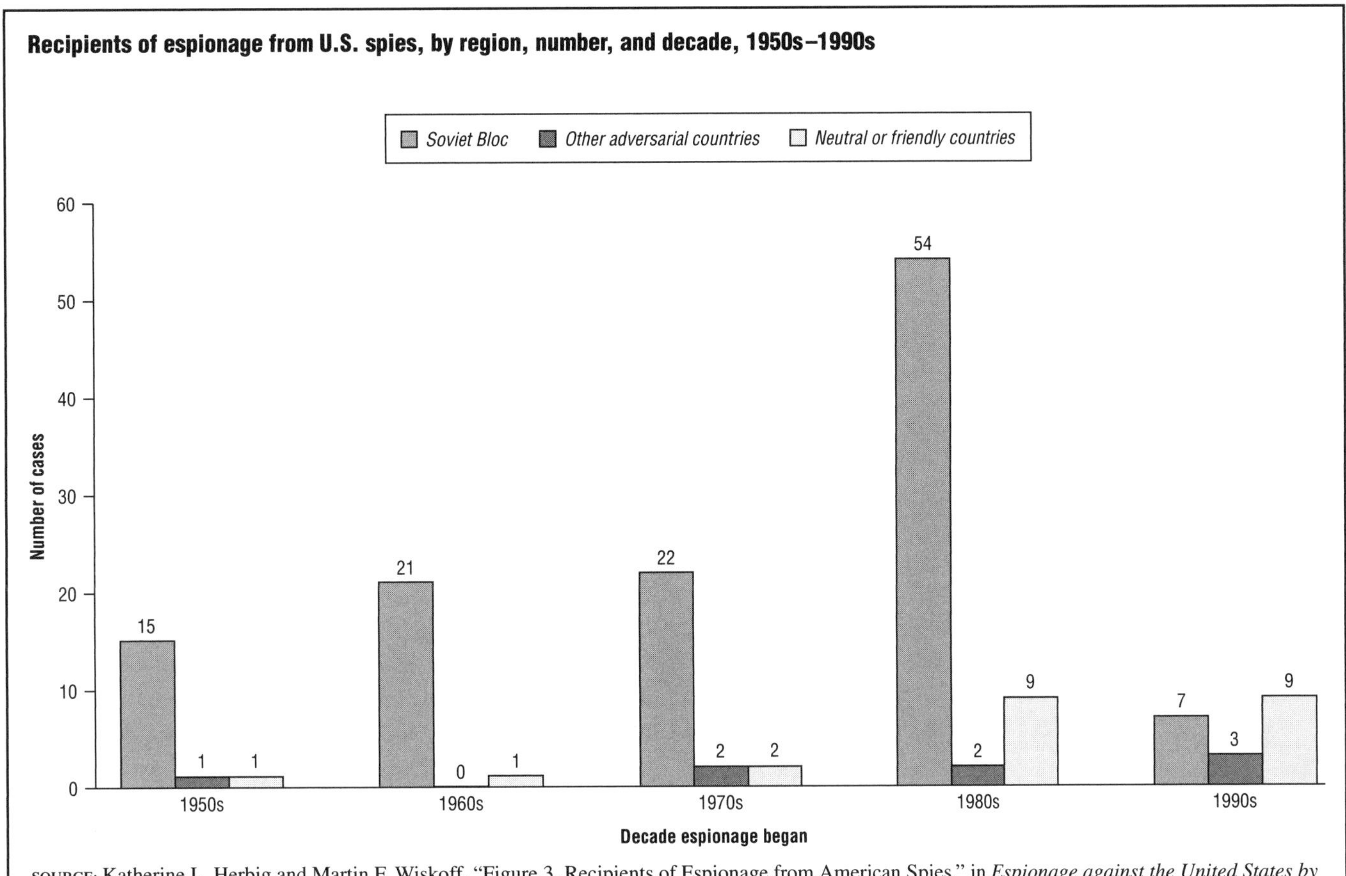

SOURCE: Katherine L. Herbig and Martin F. Wiskoff, "Figure 3. Recipients of Espionage from American Spies," in *Espionage against the United States by American Citizens: 1947–2001*, Defense Personnel Security Research Center, July 2002, http://www.ncix.gov/archives/docs/espionageAgainstUSbyCitizens.pdf (accessed August 11, 2008)

U.S. military or intelligence agencies caught spying for communist governments:

- Aldrich H. Ames (1941–) of the Central Intelligence Agency (CIA) spied for nine years for the Soviet Union.
- Ana Montes (1957–) was a Defense Intelligence Agency officer who spent fifteen years spying for Cuba.
- John A. Walker (1937–) of the U.S. Navy passed information to the Soviets for more than seventeen years.
- Clyde L. Conrad (1948–1998) of the U.S. Army was a Soviet spy for at least thirteen years.
- Robert Philip Hanssen (1944–) was an agent with the Federal Bureau of Investigation and spied for the Soviet Union for twenty-two years.

U.S. POST-VIETNAM MILITARY

The Vietnam War severely dampened the nation's willingness to commit U.S. troops to foreign conflicts. The long war had not saved South Vietnam from a communist takeover and had been costly in terms of money and human suffering. Over 8.7 million U.S. military personnel served during the Vietnam conflict. (See Table 1.1.) U.S. casualties included 58,220 killed and over 303,000 wounded. In addition, the war brought death and misery to millions of Vietnamese civilians. As a result, the American public and U.S. politicians were not keen to commit U.S. forces to future foreign conflicts.

During the 1980s the U.S. military had additional setbacks. An attempt to rescue hostages from the U.S. embassy in Iran in 1980 had to be aborted after a helicopter crash killed eight U.S. military personnel. (See Table 1.3.) U.S. Marines sent to Lebanon as part of a UN peacekeeping effort suffered a calamitous terrorist attack. More than two hundred of them were killed. U.S. troops did conduct successful operations in Grenada and Panama during the decade, but these were small and limited in scope. These incidents did not indicate to the American public or the world at large the full capabilities of the maturing U.S. military.

An influx of money during the 1970s and 1980s from the Carter and Reagan administrations financed the development of sophisticated weapons and computer technology. Training was also a priority, as was the reorganization of the military hierarchy at the top levels. As a result, U.S. forces performed extremely well in 1990 when a UN

TABLE 1.3

U.S. military deaths worldwide in selected military operations, selected years 1980–96

Military operation/incident	Casualty type	Total
Iranian Hostage Rescue Mission April 25, 1980	Nonhostile	8
Lebanon peacekeeping, August 25, 1982–February 26, 1984*	Hostile	256
	Nonhostile	9
	Total	265
Urgent Fury, Grenada, 1983	Hostile	18
	Nonhostile	1
	Total	19
Just Cause, Panama, 1989	Hostile	23
Persian Gulf War, 1990–1991		
Desert Shield	Nonhostile	84
Desert Storm	Hostile	148
	Nonhostile	151
	Total	299
Desert Shield/Storm	Total	383
Restore Hope/UNOSOM, Somalia, 1992–1994	Hostile	29
	Nonhostile	14
	Total	43
Uphold Democracy, Haiti, 1994–1996	Nonhostile	4

*Place of casualty, Lebanon

SOURCE: Adapted from "Table 13. Worldwide U.S. Active Duty Military Deaths, Selected Military Operations," in *Worldwide U.S. Active Duty Military Personnel Casualties: October 1979 through March 1998*, U.S. Department of Defense, March 1998, http://siadapp.dmdc.osd.mil/personnel/M07/mar98cas.pdf (accessed August 11, 2008)

coalition was formed to drive Iraqi troops from Kuwait during Operation Desert Storm. It was the first of several major conflicts that would take place in a new theater for U.S. military action: the Middle East.

THE MIDDLE EAST

Geographically, the Middle East is a region at the intersection of Asia, Africa, and Europe. There is no official designation of the countries that make up the Middle East. The term is largely a sociopolitical one used by those in the Western world to collectively describe a group of countries in and around the Arabian Peninsula. This group is often thought to extend from Iran in the east to the northwest coast of Africa. Some observers include other nearby countries, such as Turkey, Afghanistan, and Pakistan. In a historical context, the region now known as the Middle East once comprised the core of the Ottoman Empire, which was splintered into individual nations following World War I.

Peoples and Religions

In *The Modern Middle East: A Political History since the First World War* (2005), Mehran Kamrava of California State University, Northridge, notes that "there are vast differences between and within the histories, cultures, traditions, and politics" of the Middle Eastern countries. However, there are also powerful unifying characteristics within the region, primarily religion and historic ethnic commonalities.

Westerners tend to describe all Middle Eastern people as Arabs. The term *Arab* is actually an ethnic designation applied to certain tribes descended from Shem (or Sem), the oldest son of Noah in biblical history. The descendants of Shem are called Semites; they include the Babylonians and Phoenicians and the Hebrew tribes of ancient times. The Hebrews embraced the religion of Judaism and settled the kingdom of Israel. Arab tribes scattered throughout the region and were governed by various kings or tribal rulers. During the seventh century a new Arab leader emerged named Muhammad (c. 570–632), who would change the world by introducing a new religion called Islam.

The followers of Islam are called Muslims. They worship one God (whom they call Allah) and believe that Allah's messages were passed by the angel Gabriel to the prophet Muhammad in the land known today as Saudi Arabia. God's messages are called the Koran. This term is also used to refer to the messages in written form, which make up Islam's holy book. Most Muslims consider Islam much more than a religious practice; they believe it encompasses all areas of life, including social, economic, and political aspects.

By far, Islam is the most predominant religion in the Middle East. However, as with most religions, there are diverse belief sets within Islam. The two largest sects are called Sunni and Shia; their respective followers have historical disagreements about issues related to governance and theological interpretations. These disagreements sometimes lead to violent confrontations between fellow Muslims. Many other religions are practiced throughout the region but by small populations in most countries. The notable exception is Judaism, which is the predominant religion of Israel.

Ethnically, the modern Middle East is dominated by Arab peoples who reside mostly in Saudi Arabia, Jordan, Lebanon, Syria, Iraq, Egypt, and parts of northern Africa. There are substantial pockets of non-Arabs; for example, Persians descended from tribes in southwest Asia predominate in Iran, Turks in Turkey, Kurds in northern Iraq, and Jewish descendants of the ancient Hebrew tribes in Israel.

Thus, the Middle East is a complicated mosaic of societies in which some widely shared characteristics provide grounds for unity among much of the population. However, cultural, political, and religious differences within the region are a source of often violent confrontations between peoples. One such confrontation has grown to dominate the sociopolitical affairs of the Middle East and has become a source of great concern to U.S. national security interests: the Israeli-Palestinian conflict.

Israel and Palestine

Following World War I the League of Nations placed some territories of the former Ottoman Empire under the administration of Britain and France. Iraq and Palestine were administered by Great Britain, and Syria and Lebanon by France. This arrangement was called the Mandates System and was designed to be temporary, lasting only until the territories could mature into independent nations ruled by their own governments. The populations of the administered countries greatly resented foreign intervention in their affairs and viewed the arrangement as colonialism. As a result, there was much political and social unrest in these countries. Eventually, Iraq, Syria, and Lebanon did gain their independence.

Palestine was supposed to become a nation called the Palestinian Arab State. A variety of factors have prevented this from happening as described by the UN article "Question of Palestine" (February 1, 2008, http://www.un.org/Depts/dpa/ngo/history.html). The UN indicates that the Palestinian Mandate was in effect from 1922 through 1947. However, the British government had already promised Jewish leaders a "national home" for the Jewish people in Palestine. That promise had been made in a November 1917 letter from the British foreign secretary Arthur James Balfour (1848–1930) to Lord Lionel Walter Rothschild (1868–1937). The Balfour Declaration (August 2008, http://www.yale.edu/lawweb/avalon/mideast/balfour.htm) stated in part: "'His Majesty's Government view with favour the establishment in Palestine of a national home for the Jewish people, and will use their best endeavours to facilitate the achievement of this object, it being clearly understood that nothing shall be done which may prejudice the civil and religious rights of existing non-Jewish communities in Palestine, or the rights and political status enjoyed by Jews in any other country.'"

The Balfour Declaration pleased Zionists—Jews around the world seeking an independent Jewish state on the land inhabited in ancient times by the Hebrew tribes, that is, the Land of Israel. Most Jews had been driven from Palestine by the end of the second century. The land was subsequently ruled by the Byzantine Empire, the Persians, a series of Muslim rulers, and the Ottoman Empire. The many non-Jewish people (primarily Arab Muslims) inhabiting Palestine in the early twentieth century did not want to lose their own chance at statehood and give up land their ancestors had inhabited for centuries.

STATE OF ISRAEL. The Balfour Declaration spurred mass migrations of Jews from around the world to Palestine. The UN explains in "Question of Palestine" that migrations were particularly heavy during the 1930s from Nazi Germany and eastern Europe—areas where Jews were subject to harsh persecution and even extermination. Violence grew between the Arab Palestinians and the incoming Jewish peoples—both of whom claimed the land as their own. In 1947 the British government turned the problem over to the UN, which proposed splitting Palestine into two approximately even-sized states, one Jewish and one Arab. Jerusalem, a city considered sacred to both Jews and Muslims, was to be ruled under a Special International Regime. The partition plan did not please Arab rulers, and the violence in Palestine escalated.

In 1948 the Jewish population of Palestine declared itself a nation—the State of Israel—and found itself immediately at war with the armies of Palestine's neighbors and Arab supporters: Egypt, Transjordan (later Jordan), Iraq, Syria, and Lebanon. During the war Israeli forces captured more than three-fourths of the original territory of Palestine and most of Jerusalem. The remainder of the territory was held by the governments of Egypt and Jordan. These areas are called the Gaza Strip and the West Bank, respectively. (See Figure 1.3.) In the Six-Day War of 1967, Israel captured both of these areas and all of Jerusalem. In response, the UN issued Resolution 242, calling on Israel to withdraw from the areas it had just captured and for all states in the region to cease their "belligerency" and live in peaceful coexistence. This did not occur.

PALESTINIAN TERRITORIES. In 1964 the Palestine Liberation Organization (PLO) was appointed by a group of Arab nations to represent the political aspirations of Palestine. The PLO was an umbrella organization for a variety of Palestinian groups with varying views on the use of politics and violence to achieve their goals. The main group was al Fatah, which was led by Yasir Arafat (1929–2004). During its early years the PLO was often associated with acts of violence against Israeli civilians and soldiers. PLO splinter groups have been linked to many acts of terrorism around the world, including the killing of Israeli athletes at the 1972 Olympic Games in Munich, Germany. Meanwhile, Palestinian refugees fleeing wars and other violence spread throughout the Middle East and parts of Europe. They have played a substantial role in raising money and eliciting sympathy and support for the Palestinian cause around the world.

During the 1990s the PLO achieved a measure of legitimacy as the United States worked to obtain a peace agreement in the decades-old dispute over Palestine. In 1993 Arafat officially recognized the State of Israel as a legitimate government. In return, the Israeli government extended official recognition to the PLO as the legitimate representative of the Arab Palestinians. That same year the two sides reached an agreement called the Oslo Accords that laid out a plan for limited Palestinian control over some of its territories by a new government called the Palestinian National Authority (PNA). Full implementation of the plan has been thwarted by continued violence between the Palestinians and the Israelis. However, in 2005 Israel did withdraw its troops from the Gaza Strip.

FIGURE 1.3

Map of Israel, the West Bank, the Gaza Strip, and the Golan Heights, 2008

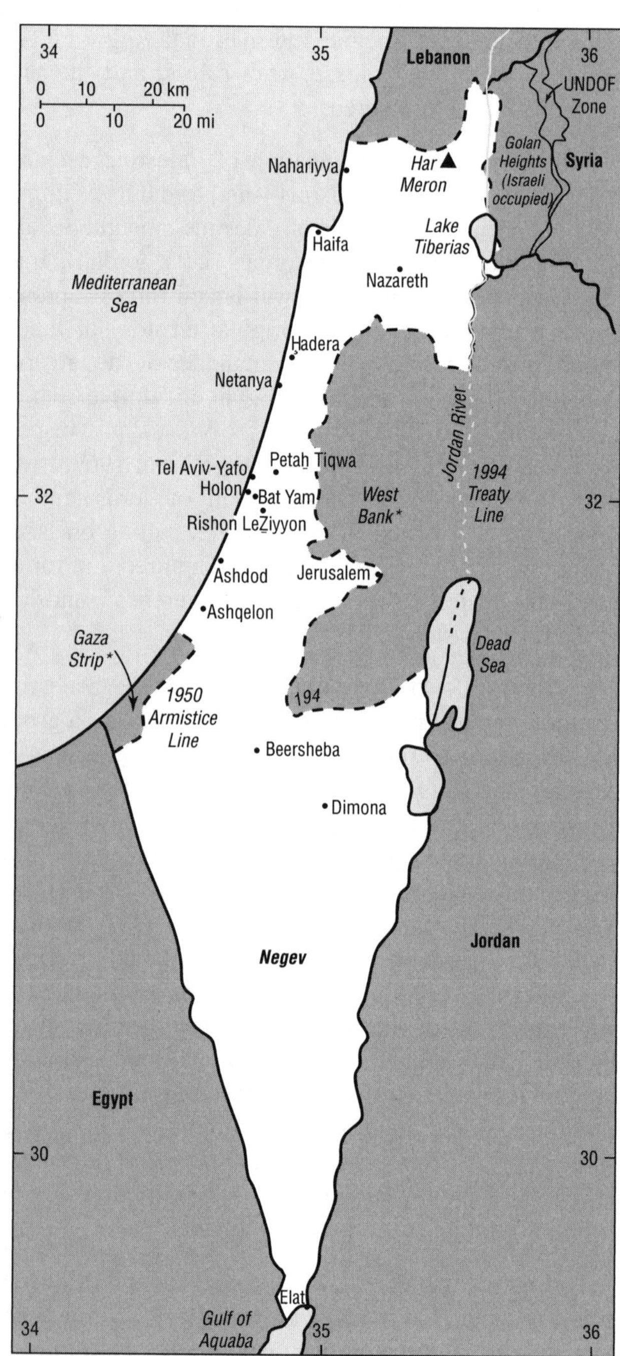

*Israeli-occupied with current status subject to the Israeli-Palestinian interim Agreement—permanent status to be determined through further negotiation.

SOURCE: "Map of Israel, the West Bank, the Gaza Strip, and the Golan Heights," in *Middle East Peace Process*, U.S. Department of State, May 27, 2003, http://www.state.gov/r/pa/ei/pix/b/nea/20958.htm (accessed August 11, 2008)

Arafat died in 2004 and was replaced by a close associate, Mahmoud Abbas (1935–), who was elected president of the PNA in 2005. In 2006 Palestinian voters gave members of the organization Hamas majority control of the PNA, relegating al Fatah to a minority position. The United States considers Hamas a foreign terrorist organization under U.S. law. The United States and al Fatah refused to recognize Hamas as the legitimate leading party in Palestine. The U.S. government forbade direct economic aid to Palestine in the wake of the Hamas elections. Abbas began an internal political battle with the elected Prime Minister Ismail Haniyeh (1962–), a member of Hamas. A near civil war erupted between Palestinian peoples allied with either side. In June 2007 Abbas declared a state of emergency and officially dissolved Haniyeh's government after Hamas forces routed al Fatah forces and seized military and political control of the Gaza Strip. Dozens of Palestinians were killed in the fighting. Abbas appointed a new prime minister, Salam Fayyad (1952–), but the appointment was largely ignored by Hamas leaders and supporters. The United States lifted its earlier sanctions to encourage development of the Abbas government. As of September 2008, Abbas and the al Fatah party controlled the West Bank and Hamas controlled the Gaza Strip.

The U.S. government considers Abbas a relatively moderate influence in Palestinian politics. Scott Wilson reports in "Abbas Dissolves Government as Hamas Takes Control of Gaza" (*Washington Post*, June 15, 2007) that "Abbas has called for peace talks with Israel, while the Hamas charter calls for the Jewish state's destruction." In September 2007 Abbas began meeting with the Israeli prime minister Ehud Olmert (1945–) in peace talks brokered by the United States. In June 2008 Israel did manage to achieve a shaky Egyptian-brokered truce with Hamas in the Gaza Strip. That area has been the source of frequent missile attacks on settlements in southern Israel. Israel agreed to cease military operations against militants in Gaza and to end an economic blockade. However, as of September 2008, negotiations had failed to yield an agreement acceptable to both sides.

U.S. Connection to the Middle East

Since World War I, U.S. political, economic, and military affairs have become greatly entangled with circumstances in the Middle East. As of September 2008, U.S. military forces occupied two nations in the region: Afghanistan and Iraq. Both invasions were driven by perceived threats to U.S. national security. In addition, there were ongoing issues related to the United States' alliance with Israel and U.S. dependence on petroleum from oil-rich nations of the Middle East.

The United States has been a staunch ally of Israel since that nation was founded. Support for Zionism within the United States was not extremely popular before World War II but grew tremendously when the horrors of the

FIGURE 1.4

Poll respondents' sympathies in the Israel-Palestine conflict, February 2008

IN THE MIDDLE EAST SITUATION, ARE YOUR SYMPATHIES MORE WITH THE ISRAELIS OR MORE WITH THE PALESTINIANS?

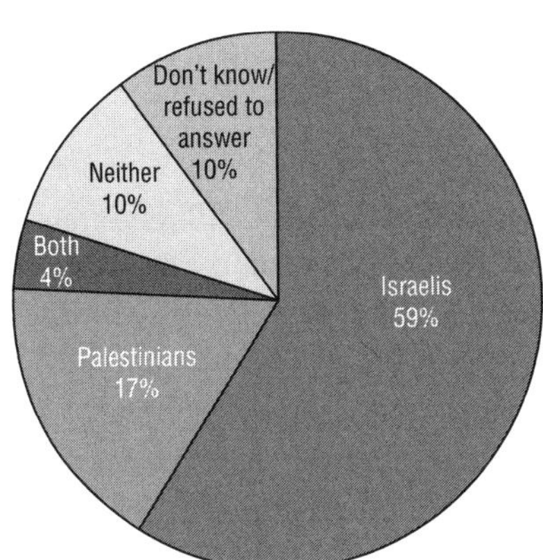

SOURCE: Adapted from "Question qn31. In the Middle East Situation, Are Your Sympathies More with the Israelis or More with the Palestinians?" in *Gallup Poll Social Series: World Affairs*, The Gallup Organization, February 2008, http://brain.gallup.com/documents/questionaire.aspx?STUDY=Po802010 (accessed August 8, 2008). Copyright © 2008 by The Gallup Organization. Reproduced by permission of The Gallup Organization.

FIGURE 1.5

Public opinion on whether the U.S. should pressure Israel or the Palestinians to resolve the Palestinian-Israeli conflict, February 2008

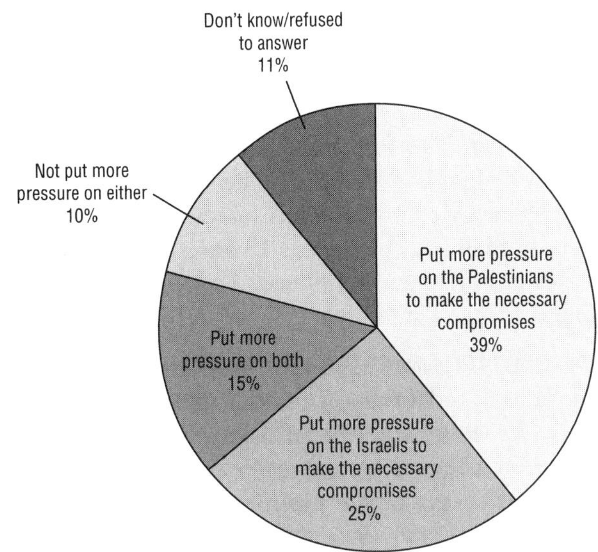

SOURCE: Adapted from "Question qn34. In Order to Resolve the Palestinian-Israeli Conflict, Do You Think the United States Should—Put More Pressure on the Palestinians to Make the Necessary Compromises, or Put More Pressure on the Israelis to Make the Necessary Compromises?" in *Gallup Poll Social Series: World Affairs*, The Gallup Organization, February 2008, http://brain.gallup.com/documents/questionnaire.aspx?STUDY=P0802010 (accessed August 8, 2008). Copyright © 2008 by The Gallup Organization. Reproduced by permission of The Gallup Organization.

Jewish holocaust in Europe came to light. President Truman was a strong advocate for a Jewish state in Palestine. In *Outline of U.S. History*, the Bureau of International Information Programs states that Truman officially recognized the new nation of Israel only fifteen minutes after it was formed.

U.S. political and financial support for Israel—one of the few true democracies in the region—has continued for decades and is a source of deep resentment among the predominantly Muslim peoples of the Middle East. Israel is considered a close ally of the United States and a major trading partner. Israel also enjoys popular support among the American people. Figure 1.4 shows the results of a poll conducted in February 2008 by the Gallup Organization on American sympathies in the Israeli-Palestinian conflict. Pollsters found that 59% of Americans expressed sympathy with Israel in the conflict. Only 17% of the respondents expressed sympathy for the Palestinians. In the same poll Gallup asked Americans which of the factions the U.S. government should pressure more to "make the necessary compromises" to resolve the conflict. More than a third (39%) of respondents said more pressure should be put on the Palestinians, whereas 25% advocated more pressure on the Israelis. (See Figure 1.5.) Another 15% thought both sides should receive more pressure from the U.S. government. Ten percent said neither side should be pressured more, and 11% did not provide an answer to the question.

Oil is another important connection between the United States and the Middle East. Interestingly, Israel is surrounded by oil-rich nations but has few natural petroleum reserves of its own. The United States and other industrialized nations consume much more oil than they produce and need a steady supply at low prices for their economies to function. Saudi Arabia, Iran, Iraq, and Kuwait, and other nations along the Persian Gulf are all rich in oil, and significant deposits are found elsewhere in the Middle East as well. In fact, in the late twentieth and early twenty-first centuries the Middle East was by far the world's top oil-producing region. This means that Middle Eastern oil producers can influence the United States and other nations by manipulating, or threatening to manipulate, the supply of oil. Furthermore, anything that endangers the flow of oil from the Middle East, such as war or political instability in the region, threatens U.S. national security and may motivate a response.

The United States faces a challenging problem in trying to maintain both its alliance with Israel and good relations with the oil-rich Middle Eastern countries, where Israel is unpopular at best. In 1973 Middle Eastern members of the Organization of Petroleum Exporting

Countries halted oil exports to the United States in retaliation for U.S. support of Israel. The oil embargo lasted five months. When shipments resumed, the price of oil had dramatically increased. Americans faced high prices, long lines, and shortages at the gas pumps.

In August 1990 President Saddam Hussein's (1937–2006) Iraqi military forces invaded Kuwait. President George H. W. Bush (1924–) acted to put together a coalition of international forces that successfully forced Iraq out of Kuwait. The Persian Gulf War, as it came to be known, was short lived and would be seen as a triumphant, if incomplete, victory by allied forces. Even though his military strength was weakened, Hussein was not removed from power in Iraq and continued to pose foreign relations problems for the United States for many years.

In 2003 President George W. Bush (1946–) conducted a U.S.-led invasion of Iraq that ousted Hussein from power. Following the invasion, U.S. and coalition military forces began a troubled occupation. As of September 2008, continuing violence by Iraqi insurgents (revolutionaries) and their sympathizers had prevented Iraqi authorities from establishing law and order and complete governmental control.

U.S. relations with Iran have also been troubled for decades. During the 1950s U.S. intelligence agencies helped install a pro-U.S. government in Iran with the help of that nation's leader (or shah). The shah's government was overthrown in 1979 during a revolution by conservative Muslims. President Carter allowed the shah to enter the United States for medical treatment, triggering an attack on the U.S. embassy in Tehran, Iran. Dozens of Americans were held hostage for more than a year, an event that brought a deep rift in U.S.-Iranian relations. In 2002 the United States learned that Iran had been secretly building nuclear facilities and conducting experiments that could lead to the development of nuclear weapons. Iran's nuclear capabilities and anti-American government are issues of great concern to U.S. national security.

INTERNATIONAL TERRORISM

Throughout most of U.S. history, national security concerns were centered on other nations. During the twentieth century, however, a new threat emerged: international terrorists. These are individuals with a common violent agenda who band together and attack the assets and people of nations with whom they have disagreements.

Worldwide terrorist attacks accelerated during the 1970s and 1980s, a time of heightened activity by militant Islamic groups opposed to Israel (and by association, the United States). U.S. diplomatic and military personnel stationed overseas were the primary targets of many of these attacks. Between 1979 and 1984 the U.S. embassies in Pakistan, Libya, Iran, Lebanon, and Kuwait were attacked. In 1998 the U.S. embassies in Kenya and Tanzania were destroyed by powerful car bombs. A dozen Americans died in the attacks, but hundreds of Africans were killed and thousands more injured. Off-duty U.S. military personnel have also been frequent targets of terrorist violence. During the 1980s more than two hundred of these personnel were killed by attacks in Lebanon, Germany, and other countries. In 1996 and 2000 terrorist acts in Saudi Arabia and Yemen, respectively, claimed the lives of three dozen U.S. troops and injured hundreds more.

Over the past two decades U.S. civilians abroad and at home have increasingly become targets for terrorist violence. The most horrific incidents have included the 1988 bombing of an airliner over Lockerbie, Scotland, that killed all 259 passengers and 11 more on the ground. In 1993 international terrorists visited U.S. soil. A car bomb planted in the underground garage at the World Trade Center in New York City killed six people and injured approximately one thousand.

These casualties paled in comparison to the tragedy produced by the September 11, 2001 (9/11), terrorist attacks. On that day four U.S. commercial airliners were commandeered by hijackers. Two of the planes were flown into the twin towers of the World Trade Center in New York City. A third plane was flown into the Pentagon in Washington, D.C. The fourth plane crashed in a field in Pennsylvania after passengers struggled with their hijackers. The attacks killed more than twenty-nine hundred people and stunned the world. Intelligence revealed that the hijackers were Middle Eastern terrorists associated with the group al Qaeda, led by Osama bin Laden (1957–). The U.S. government believed that bin Laden was being harbored by the Taliban government of Afghanistan and demanded that he be turned over to U.S. authorities. After the Taliban refused to do so, the U.S. military invaded Afghanistan. Even though the military operations were a success overall, the United States was not able to capture bin Laden and has found itself in a lingering guerrilla-type conflict with Taliban and al Qaeda fighters.

The 9/11 attacks dramatically altered the priorities of the U.S. government. President Bush launched a War on Terror and created a new U.S. Department of Homeland Security to strengthen national security. Furthermore, given that terrorism is a worldwide problem, the international community working through the UN had in place in 2008 thirteen agreements (called conventions or protocols) designed to enhance international cooperation in countering the terrorist threat. (See Table 1.4.)

WEAPONS OF MASS DESTRUCTION

Weapons of mass destruction (WMDs) are weapons that are capable of killing large numbers of people. For example, one atomic bomb has much more destructive power than many conventional weapons put together.

TABLE 1.4

International conventions and protocols regarding terrorism, 2008

1. **Convention on Offences and Certain Other Acts Committed On Board Aircraft**
   Signed in Tokyo on September 14, 1963.
   Convention entered into force on December 4, 1969.
   Status: 183 parties
2. **Convention for the Suppression of Unlawful Seizure of Aircraft**
   Signed in The Hague on December 16, 1970.
   Convention entered into force on October 14, 1971.
   Status: 182 parties
3. **Convention for the Suppression of Unlawful Acts Against the Safety of Civil Aviation**
   Signed in Montreal on September 23, 1971.
   Convention entered into force on January 26, 1973.
   Status: 185 parties
4. **Convention on the Prevention and Punishment of Crimes Against Internationally Protected Persons, including Diplomatic Agents**
   Adopted in New York on December 14, 1973.
   Convention entered into force on February 20, 1977.
   Status: 166 parties
5. **International Convention Against the Taking of Hostages**
   Adopted in New York on December 17, 1979.
   Convention entered into force on June 3, 1983.
   Status: 164 parties
6. **Convention on the Physical Protection of Nuclear Material**
   Signed in Vienna on October 26, 1979.
   Convention entered into force on February 8, 1987.
   Status: 130 parties
7. **Protocol for the Suppression of Unlawful Acts of Violence at Airports Serving International Civil Aviation, Supplementary to the Convention for the Suppression of Unlawful Acts against the Safety of Civil Aviation**
   Signed in Montreal on February 24, 1988.
   Protocol entered into force on August 6, 1989.
   Status: 161 parties
8. **Convention for the Suppression of Unlawful Acts Against the Safety of Maritime Navigation**
   Done in Rome on March 10, 1988.
   Convention entered into force on March 1, 1992.
   Status: 147 parties
9. **Protocol for the Suppression of Unlawful Acts Against the Safety of Fixed Platforms Located on the Continental Shelf**
   Done in Rome on March 10, 1988.
   Protocol entered into force on March 1, 1992.
   Status: 136 parties
10. **Convention on the Marking of Plastic Explosives for the Purpose of Detection**
    Done in Montreal on March 1, 1991.
    Convention entered into force on June 21, 1998.
    Status: 137 parties
11. **International Convention for the Suppression of Terrorist Bombings**
    Adopted in New York on December 15, 1997.
    Convention entered into force on May 23, 2001.
    Status: 153 parties
12. **International Convention for the Suppression of the Financing of Terrorism**
    Adopted in New York on December 9, 1999.
    Convention entered into force on April 10, 2002.
    Status: 160 parties
13. **International Convention for the Suppression of Acts of Nuclear Terrorism**
    Adopted in New York on April 13, 2005.
    Convention entered into force on July 7, 2007.
    Status: 115 parties
14. **2005 Amendment to the Convention on the Physical Protection of Nuclear Material**
    Not yet entered into force
    Status: 13 States have deposited instruments of ratification, acceptance or approval with the depositary.

TABLE 1.4

International conventions and protocols regarding terrorism, 2008
[CONTINUED]

15. **Protocol of 2005 to the Convention for the Suppression of Unlawful Acts Against the Safety of Maritime Navigation**
    Not yet entered into force
    Status: Two states have deposited instruments of ratification, acceptance or approval with the depositary.
16. **Protocol of 2005 to the Protocol for the Suppression of Unlawful Acts Against the Safety of Fixed Platforms Located on the Continental Shelf**
    Not yet entered into force
    Status: No states have deposited instruments of ratification, acceptance or approval with the depositary.

SOURCE: "International Conventions and Protocols," in *Country Reports on Terrorism, 2007*, U.S. Department of State, April 2008, http://www.state.gov/documents/organization/105904.pdf (accessed July 29, 2008)

The ferocity of the 9/11 attacks brought a new realization to the United States that terrorists would likely use WMDs if they could build or obtain them. At the same time, new national threats have arisen around the world, particularly from North Korea and Iran—countries that have developed or are thought to be pursuing a nuclear arsenal in defiance of the UN. The U.S. government has dubbed these defiant countries "rogue nations."

Thus, a new urgency has developed to safeguard existing WMDs around the world and to prevent new ones from being developed. The United States and the Soviet Union each began disarming and destroying nuclear weapons within their possession even before the cold war ended. However, there were still many such weapons in the Soviet Union when it disintegrated into separate republics in the early 1990s. This has been a source of lingering concern for U.S. policy makers. A variety of mechanisms have been put in place to ensure that old Soviet WMDs are not transferred to terrorist groups or rogue nations. This quest is made much more difficult by the addition of several new nations to the so-called nuclear club. The United States started the club with its development of atomic bombs during World War II. The Soviet Union (now Russia) joined several years later. Since that time, seven other nations are known or suspected to have tested nuclear weapons: the United Kingdom, France, China, India, Israel, Pakistan, and North Korea.

Besides the danger of nuclear weapons, the United States also faces a threat from chemical and biological WMDs. These are weapons that use chemical and/or biological agents as their killing force. The use of such weapons in warfare is not new; mustard gas was deployed by the Germans and the British during World War I and used by other nations after that time. UN treaties restrict the use of chemical and biological weapons in modern warfare. Therefore, the major danger is from terrorist groups and rogue nations that do not feel bound by international agreements or restraints.

U.S. FOREIGN POLICY GOALS

As he was inaugurated for his second term on January 20, 2005, President Bush (http://www.whitehouse.gov/news/releases/2005/01/20050120-1.html) stated:

> It is the policy of the United States to seek and support the growth of democratic movements and institutions in every nation and culture, with the ultimate goal of ending tyranny in our world. This is not primarily the task of arms, though we will defend ourselves and our friends by force of arms when necessary. Freedom, by its nature, must be chosen, and defended by citizens, and sustained by the rule of law and the protection of minorities. And when the soul of a nation finally speaks, the institutions that arise may reflect customs and traditions very different from our own. America will not impose our own style of government on the unwilling. Our goal instead is to help others find their own voice, attain their own freedom, and make their own way.

The United States is often described as "the world's policeman" because of its propensity to intervene and attempts to shape the outcome of foreign conflicts. Obviously, the nation has a vested interest in seeing a world free of tyranny and filled with democratically governed nations friendly to the United States. However, there is debate over the extent to which the United States should interfere in the internal matters of foreign countries. Even though the American people strongly support national defense and certain aspects of the policeman role, they are less certain about the United States' recent ventures into so-called nation building. The United States waged successful military campaigns against Afghanistan and Iraq that routed tyrannical leaders. However, the resulting power vacuums left it struggling to rebuild these war-torn and politically torn countries. The United States has essentially become the internal policeman of these two countries and responsible for their day-to-day operations in a manner unprecedented in U.S. history.

Figure 1.6 shows the results of a Gallup poll conducted in February 2008 that asked Americans about their level of support for various foreign policy goals. Ninety-seven percent of those asked said preventing future acts of international terrorism should be a "very important" or "somewhat important" goal. There was overwhelming

FIGURE 1.6

Public opinion poll on U.S. foreign policy goals, February 2008

I'M GOING TO READ A LIST OF POSSIBLE FOREIGN POLICY GOALS THAT THE UNITED STATES MIGHT HAVE. FOR EACH ONE PLEASE SAY WHETHER YOU THINK IT SHOULD BE A VERY IMPORTANT FOREIGN POLICY GOAL OF THE UNITED STATES, A SOMEWHAT IMPORTANT GOAL, NOT TOO IMPORTANT A GOAL, OR NOT AN IMPORTANT GOAL AT ALL. HOW ABOUT—

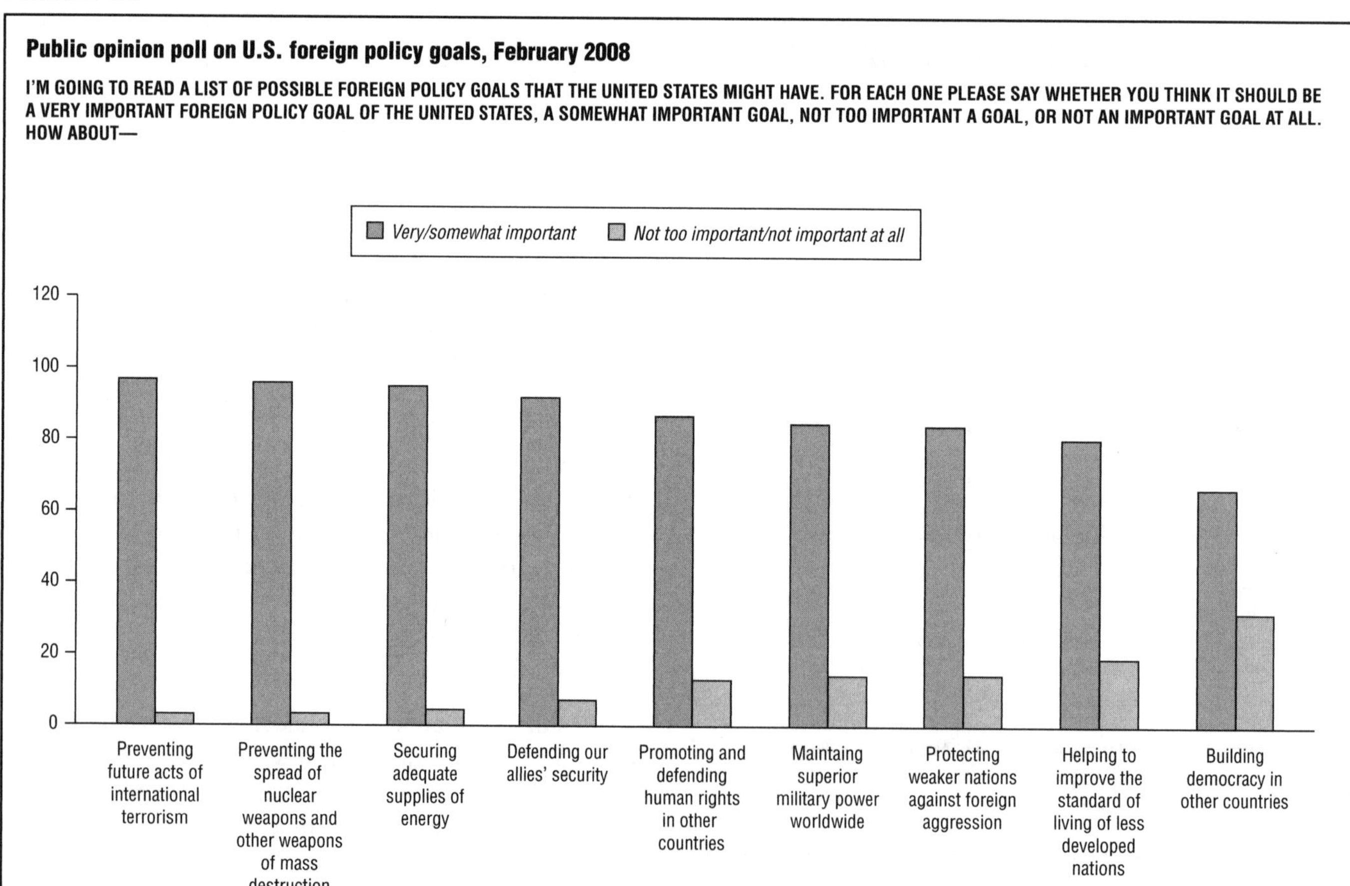

SOURCE: Adapted from "Question qn27. Next, I'm Going to Read a List of Possible Foreign Policy Goals That the United States Might Have. For Each One Please Say Whether You Think It should Be a Very Important Foreign Policy Goal of the United States, a Somewhat Important Goal, Not Too Important a Goal, or Not an Important Goal at All. How about—," in *Gallup Poll Social Series: World Affairs*, The Gallup Organization, February 2008, http://brain.gallup.com/documents.questionaire.aspx?Study=P0802010 (accessed July 9, 2008). Copyright © 2008 by The Gallup Organization. Reproduced by permission of The Gallup Organization.

support for preventing the spread of nuclear weapons and other weapons of mass destruction (95% support), securing adequate supplies of energy (95% support), and defending U.S. allies' security (90% support). More than 80% of respondents thought it was very or somewhat important to promote and defend human rights in other countries (87% support), maintain superior military power worldwide (85% support), protect weaker nations against foreign aggression (84% support), and help improve the standard of living of less developed nations (80% support). Only 66% of respondents expressed the same level of support for building democracy in other countries.

COST OF NATIONAL SECURITY

The United States spends a great deal of money to protect its national security. Tasks within this area fall to a number of federal agencies, primarily the U.S. Department of Defense (DOD), the U.S. Department of Homeland Security (DHS), and the CIA. Certain components and resources of other agencies, such as the U.S. Department of State and the Federal Bureau of Investigation, are also devoted to national security interests. From a cost standpoint, the largest expense, by far, is for national defense—U.S. military operations under the direction of the DOD.

National Defense

Military spending by the United States, particularly during wartime, has historically been extremely high. Table 1.5 shows the economic costs of every major U.S. war dating back to the Revolutionary War. The costs were estimated through June 2008 by CRS analysts. The costs are shown in current year and constant 2008 dollars. For example, the Revolutionary War is estimated to have cost $101 million at the time it was fought in the late 1770s. In 2008 dollars this would amount to $1.8 billion. World War II has been, by far, the most expensive war in U.S. history costing $4.1 trillion in 2008 dollars. The second-most expensive war has been the War on Terror waged since 9/11. The CRS estimates that as of June 2008 the expenses for the global War on Terror exceeded $859 billion.

A somewhat lower estimate has been provided by the U.S. Government Accountability Office (GAO). In *Global War on Terrorism: Reported Obligations for the Department of Defense* (June 13, 2008, http://www.gao.gov/new.items/d08853r.pdf), the GAO reports that the DOD had been appropriated a total of $635.9 billion by Congress through March 2008 to fight the global War on Terror. (See Figure 1.7.) The DOD had total financial obligations (payments made or due) of $562 billion as of March 2008. The GAO notes that it is required by law to submit quarterly updates to Congress on War on Terror costs and uses data provided monthly by the DOD to do so. However, the GAO complains that the DOD's monthly reports are of "questionable reliability," so the GAO values are considered approximations.

TABLE 1.5

Military costs of major U.S. Wars, as of June 2008

	Years of war spending	Peak year of war spending	
	Total military cost of war in millions/billions of dollars	War cost % GDP in peak year of war	Total defense % GDP in peak year of war
American Revolution	**1775–1783**		
Current year $	101 million		
Constant FY2008$	1,825 million	NA	NA
War of 1812	**1812–1815**	**1813**	
Current year $	90 million		
Constant FY2008$	1,177 million	2.2%	2.7%
Mexican War			
Current year $	**1846–1849**	**1847**	
Constant FY2008$	71 million		
	1,801 million	1.4%	1.9%
Civil War: Union	**1861–1865**	**1865**	
Current year $	3,183 million		
Constant FY2008$	45,199 million	11.3%	11.7%
Civil War: Confederacy	**1861–1865**		
Current year $	1,000 million		
Constant FY2008$	15,244 million	NA	NA
Spanish American War	**1898–1899**	**1899**	
Current year $	283 million		
Constant FY2008$	6,848 million	1.1%	1.5%
World War I	**1917–1921**	**1919**	
Current year $	20 billion		
Constant FY2008$	253 billion	13.6%	14.1%
World War II	**1941–1945**	**1945**	
Current year $	296 billion		
Constant FY2008$	4,114 billion	35.8%	37.5%
Korea	**1950–1953**	**1952**	
Current year $	30 billion		
Constant FY2008$	320 billion	4.2%	13.2%
Vietnam	**1965–1975**	**1968**	
Current year $	111 billion		
Constant FY2008$	686 billion	2.3%	9.5%
Persian Gulf War[a]	**1990–1991**	**1991**	
Current year $	61 billion		
Constant FY2008$	96 billion	0.3%	4.6%
Iraq[b]	**2003–present**	**2008**	
Current year $	616 billion		
Constant FY2008$	648 billion	1.0%	4.2%
Afghanistan/GWOT[b,c]	**2001–present**	**2007**	
Current year $	159 billion		
Constant FY2008$	171 billion	0.3%	4.0%
Post-9/11 domestic security (Operation Noble Eagle)[b]	**2001–present**	**2003**	
Current year $	28 billion		
Constant FY2008$	33 billion	0.1%	3.7%

The Office of Management and Budget (OMB) indicates in *Historical Tables, Budget of the United States Government, Fiscal Year 2009* (February 2008, http://www.gpoaccess.gov/usbudget/fy09/pdf/hist.pdf) that the United States was expected to spend $607.3 billion on national defense in 2008, up from $521.8 billion in 2006. (See Table 1.6.) The total federal budget for 2008 was estimated at $2.9 trillion. Thus, spending on national defense constituted 21% of the total budget. National defense has made up about 17% to 20% of total federal spending since the early 1990s. (See Figure 1.8.) Spending

TABLE 1.5

Military costs of major U.S. Wars, as of June 2008 [CONTINUED]

	Years of war spending	Peak year of war spending	
	Total military cost of war in millions/ billions of dollars	War cost % GDP in peak year of war	Total defense % GDP in peak year of war
Total post-9/11—Iraq, Afghanistan/GWOT, ONE[d]	2001–present	2008	
Current year $	809 billion		
Constant FY2008$	859 billion	1.2%	4.2%

Notes: [a]Most Persian Gulf War costs were offset by allied contributions or were absorbed by Department of Defense (DOD). Net costs to U.S. taxpayers totaled $4.7 billion in current year dollars.
[b]Totals for post-9/11 operations include all funds appropriated through the enactment of FY2008 supplemental appropriations and FY2009 "bridge fund" appropriations in P.L. 110–252, which the President signed into law on June 30, 2008. Totals are for military operations only and do not include costs of reconstruction assistance, diplomatic security, and other activities by other agencies. Figures for post-9/11 costs are for budget authority—all other figures are for outlays.
[c]Reflects funding for "Operation Enduring Freedom," the bulk of which is for operations in Afghanistan but which also includes amounts for operations in the Philippines, the Horn of Africa, and other areas.
[d]Based on data available from DOD, Congressional Research Service is not able to allocate $5.5 billion (in current year dollars) in FY2003 by mission. That amount included here in the total for all post-9/11 operations.
FY = Fiscal Year.

SOURCE: Stephen Daggett, "Military Costs of Major U.S. Wars," in *Costs of Major U.S. Wars*, Congressional Research Service, July 24, 2008, http://www.fas.org/sgp/crs/natsec/RS22926.pdf (accessed July 25, 2008)

on national defense spiked during World War II, reaching nearly 90% of the nation's total outlays. It dropped dramatically following the war and then rebounded during the early years of the cold war. Spending steadily decreased between about 1955 and 2000 before it began to slowly rise again beginning in about 2001.

One of the most expensive components of national defense over the long run is the cost for the development and testing of new highly sophisticated military equipment (such as aircraft, ships, submarines, and various types of weapons and bombs). In *Defense Acquisitions: Assessments of Selected Weapon Programs* (March 2008, http://www.gao.gov/new.items/d08467sp.pdf), the GAO lists the spending estimates between 2008 and 2012 for the future development of the DOD's ten most expensive equipment systems. (See Table 1.7.) The total cost of development for these ten systems alone will be $194.2 billion by 2012. The total cost for all major weapon systems will be $335.3 billion.

A Gallup poll conducted in March 2008 found Americans nearly evenly split on whether the nation's national defense is adequate or needs to be strengthened. Forty-seven percent of those asked said national defense was "not strong enough." (See Figure 1.9.) Another 41% said it was "about right." Only 10% felt that national defense was "stronger than needs to be." In the same poll, Gallup asked about spending on national defense. Less than a quarter (22%) of respondents said the U.S. spends "too little" on national defense and the military. (See Figure 1.10.) Thirty percent thought the spending was "about right," and 44% thought it was "too much."

FIGURE 1.7

Department of Defense (DOD) cumulative financial obligations and appropriations for the Global War on Terror (GWOT), fiscal years 2001–second quarter 2008

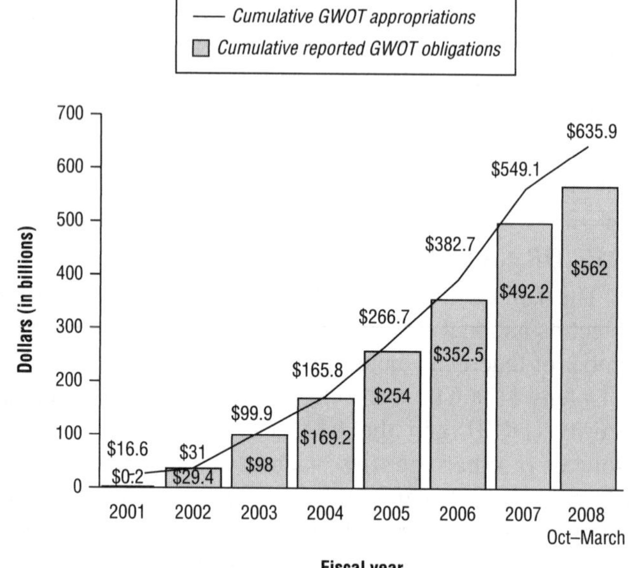

Notes: Reported GWOT obligations include Operation Noble Eagle, Operation Enduring Freedom, and Operation Iraqi Freedom, and generally reflect costs reported in DOD's cost-of-war reports.However, the fiscal year 2002 and 2003 figures include about $20.1 billion that according to DOD officials was war related but not reported in DOD's cost-of-war reports. GAO has assessed the reliability of DOD's obligation data and found significant problems, such that these data may not accurately reflect the true dollar value of GWOT obligations.

SOURCE: "Figure 1. DOD's Cumulative Reported GWOT Obligations and Cumulative GWOT Appropriations for Fiscal Years 2001 through 2007 and through the Second Quarter of Fiscal Year 2008 (October through March 2008)," in *Global War on Terrorism: Reported Obligations for the Department of Defense*, U.S. Government Accountability Office, June 13, 2008, http://www.gao.gov/new.items/d08853r.pdf (accessed July 24, 2008)

Other Spending

National security encompasses more than military operations. The DHS is responsible for preventing terrorists from striking inside the United States, fortifying U.S. defenses against an attack, and preparing the American people and emergency responders in case an attack does occur. In *Homeland Security Budget-in-Brief: Fiscal Year 2009* (February 2008, http://www.dhs.gov/xlibrary/assets/budget_bib-fy2009.pdf), the agency notes that it had a total budget authority of $42.9 billion in fiscal year 2007. It was expected to spend approximately $47 billion in 2008. The CIA is also devoted exclusively to national security pursuits. However, as explained further in Chapter 2, the agency's budget and spending are classified.

The OMB estimates in *Historical Tables, Budget of the United States Government, Fiscal Year 2009* that $34.8 billion in funds would be needed in 2008 to handle international affairs. This included operation of the nation's foreign

TABLE 1.6

Federal spending on national defense, 2006–13

[Millions of dollars]

Function and subfunction	2006	2007	2008 estimate	2009 estimate	2010 estimate	2011 estimate	2012 estimate	2013 estimate
National defense:								
Department of Defense—military:								
Military personnel	127,543	128,826	137,401	129,072	N/A	N/A	N/A	NA
Operation and maintenance	203,789	216,631	225,062	241,455	N/A	N/A	N/A	NA
Procurement	89 757	99 647	130 477	142 843	N/A	N/A	N/A	NA
Research, development, test, and evaluation	68,629	73,136	74,735	78,566	N/A	N/A	N/A	NA
Military construction	6,245	7,899	10,241	15,115	N/A	N/A	N/A	N/A
Family housing	3,717	3,473	4,290	3,358	N/A	N/A	N/A	NA
Other	−370	233	848	40,753	N/A	N/A	N/A	N/A
Subtotal, department of defense—military	499,310	529,845	583,054	651,162	566,662	537,737	540,942	549,278
Atomic energy defense activities	17,468	17,050	17,775	18,229	17,976	17,198	16,886	17,005
Defense-related activities	5,062	5,673	6,434	5,693	5,719	5,813	5,842	5,859
Total, national defense	**521,840**	**552,568**	**607,263**	**675,084**	**590,357**	**560,748**	**563,670**	**572,142**

N/A = Not available.

SOURCE: Adapted from "Table 3.2. Outlays by Function and Subfunction: 1962–2013," in *Historical Tables, Budget of the United States Government, Fiscal Year 2009*, Office of the President of the United States, Office of Management and Budget, February 2008, http://www.gpoaccess.gov/usbudget/fy09/pdf/hist.pdf (accessed July 29, 2008)

FIGURE 1.8

Total federal outlays devoted to national defense, 1940–2008

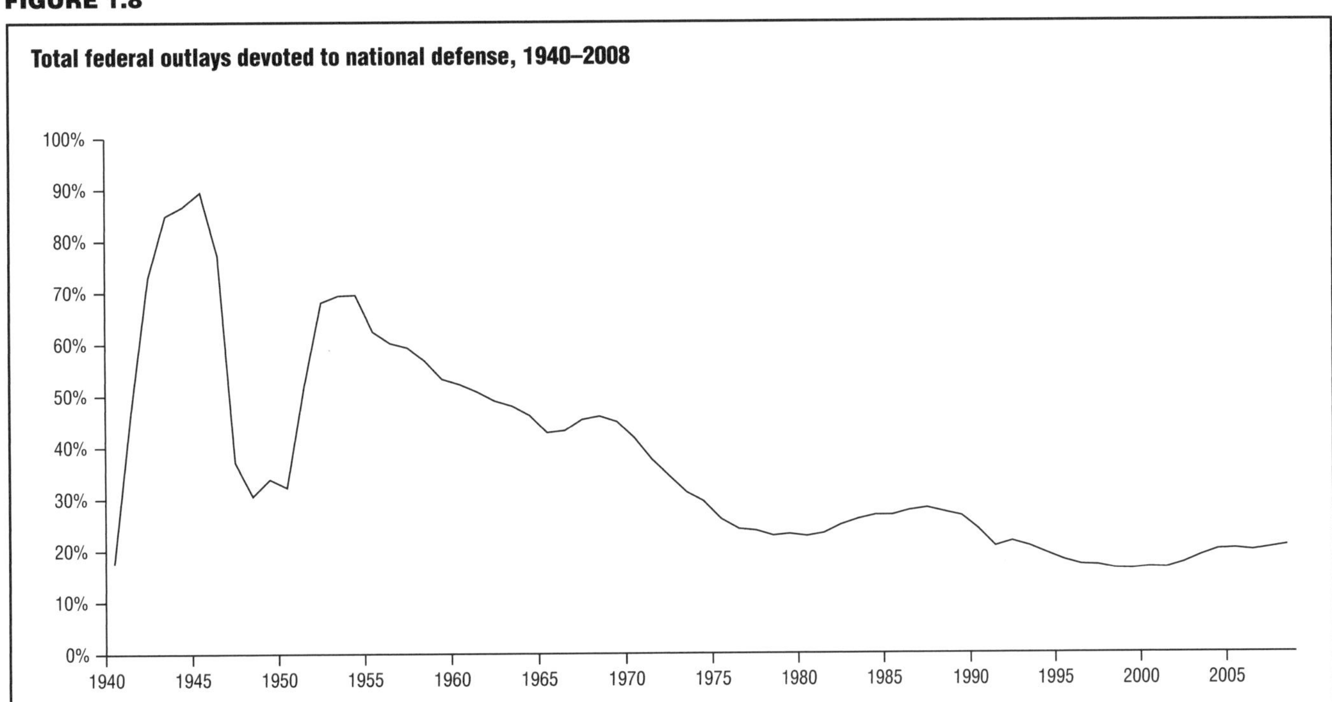

SOURCE: Adapted from "Table 3.1 Outlays by Superfunction and Function: 1940–2013," and "Table 1.1 Summary of Receipts, Outlays, and Surpluses or Deficits (−): 1789–2013," in *Historical Tables, Budget of the United States Government, Fiscal Year 2009*, Office of the President of the United States, Office of Management and Budget, February 2008, http://www.whitehouse.gov.omb/budget/fy2009/pdf/hist.pdf (accessed July 29, 2008)

affairs programs (e.g., embassies) and funds that would be provided to foreign nations for development, humanitarian causes, and security assistance. These tasks help ensure U.S. national security by developing and nurturing friendly relationships with other nations. Thus, it can be estimated that the United States planned to spend approximately $689 billion in 2008 to protect and enhance its national security interests. Note that this total does not include the amount spent by the CIA, because that agency's budget and spending are confidential.

TABLE 1.7

Planned funding for major defense programs, 2008–12

[Fiscal year 2008 dollars in billions]

Program	Fiscal year 2008	2009	2010	2011	2012	Total
Ballistic missile defense system	$8.9	$9.1	$9.1	$8.9	$8.8	$44.9
Joint strike fighter	6.7	6.9	8.1	8.4	11.3	$41.4
Virginia class submarine	2.9	3.7	3.9	3.8	4.7	$19.0
Future combat systems	3.6	3.2	3.2	3.2	3.7	$17.0
V-22 joint services advanced vertical lift aircraft	3.0	3.1	3.1	2.8	3.0	$15.0
DDG 1000 destroyer	3.5	2.8	2.9	2.7	2.6	$14.4
Future aircraft carrier CVN-21	3.1	4.6	1.7	0.6	3.4	$13.4
F-22A	4.4	4.3	0.5	0.4	0.5	$10.1
P-8A multi-mission maritime aircraft	0.9	1.2	2.9	2.7	2.5	$10.1
F/A-18 EF	2.1	1.7	1.9	1.6	1.5	$8.8
Funding for top 10 MDAP programs	39.1	40.6	37.3	35.2	42.0	$194.2
Funding for other 85 MDAP programs	33.2	31.5	26.9	25.4	24.1	$141.1
Total	$72.3	$72.1	$64.2	$60.6	$66.1	$335.3
Top 10 MDAP programs (percentage of total)	54	56	58	58	64	58

Notes: Numbers may not add due to rounding. The ballistic missile defense system is composed of several programs.
MDAP = Major Defense Acquisition Program.

SOURCE: "Table 3. Planned RDT&E and Procurement Funding for Major Defense Acquisition Programs, as of December 2006," in *Defense Acquisitions: Assessments of Selected Weapon Programs*, U.S. Government Accountability Office, March 2008, http://www.gao.gov/new.items/d08467sp.pdf (accessed August 8, 2008)

FIGURE 1.9

Public opinion poll on strength of the U.S. national defense, 1984–February 2008

DO YOU, YOURSELF, FEEL THAT OUR NATIONAL DEFENSE IS STRONGER NOW THAN IT NEEDS TO BE, NOT STRONG ENOUGH, OR ABOUT RIGHT AT THE PRESENT TIME?

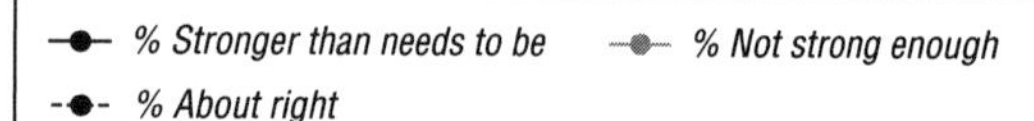

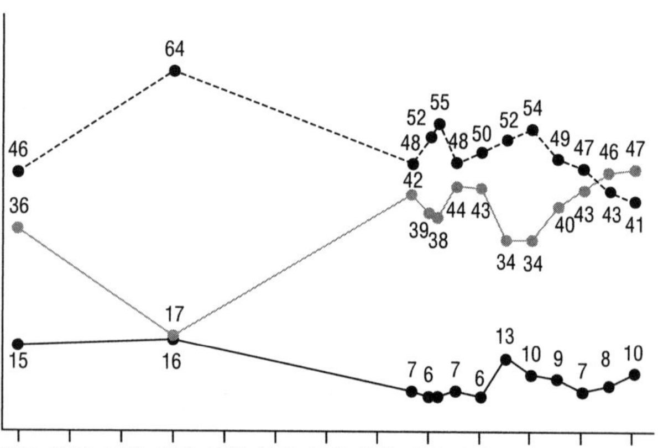

SOURCE: Frank Newport, "Do You, Yourself, Feel That Our National Defense Is Stronger Now Than It Needs to Be, Not Strong Enough, or about Right at the Present Time?" in *Almost Half of Americans Say Military Is Not Strong Enough*, The Gallup Organization, March 7, 2008, http://www.gallup.com/poll/104842/Almost-Half-Americans-Say-Military-Strong-Enough.aspx (accessed August 6, 2008). Copyright © 2008 by The Gallup Organization. Reproduced by permission of The Gallup Organization.

FIGURE 1.10

Public opinion poll on U.S. national defense and military spending, January 2001–February 2008

DO YOU THINK WE ARE SPENDING TOO LITTLE, ABOUT THE RIGHT AMOUNT, OR TOO MUCH ON NATIONAL DEFENSE AND THE MILITARY?

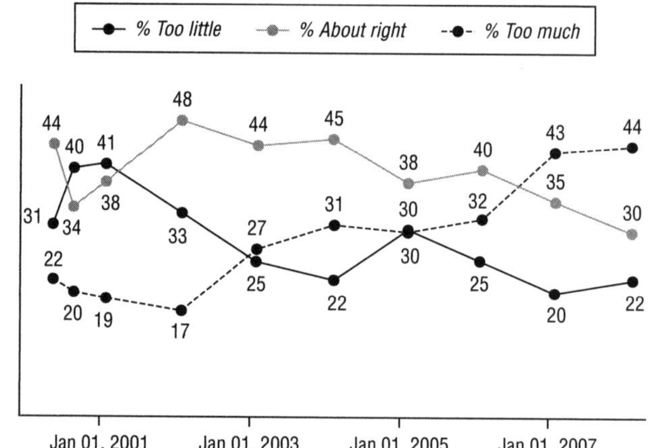

SOURCE: Frank Newport, "Do You Think We Are Spending too Little, about the Right Amount, or too Much on National Defense and the Military?" in *Almost Half of Americans Say Military Is Not Strong Enough*, The Gallup Organization, March 7, 2008, http://www.gallup.com/poll/104842/Almost-Half-Americans-Say-Military-Strong-Enough.aspx (accessed August 6, 2008). Copyright © 2008 by The Gallup Organization. Reproduced by permission of The Gallup Organization.

CHAPTER 2

THE ORGANIZATION OF NATIONAL SECURITY

The U.S. national security framework consists of government agencies and offices with responsibilities in various disciplines: policy making, military activities, intelligence gathering and analysis, diplomacy, criminal investigation, immigration control, and law enforcement. Interaction and cooperation between separate government entities and disciplines is crucial to ensure that U.S. goals are met for foreign policy and homeland security. Coordination of all functions is ultimately the responsibility of the president of the United States, who is the commander in chief of the nation's military forces and the chief decision maker for matters related to national security.

NATIONAL SECURITY COUNCIL

The National Security Council (NSC) is the top entity in the U.S. national security structure. It lies within the executive office of the president and includes decision makers at the highest levels of government. Table 2.1 lists the regular members and occasional attendees associated with the NSC. It was created following World War II (1939–1945) by the National Security Act of 1947, which was amended in 1949.

The NSC provides a forum for the president to discuss national security issues with his top advisers. The decisions and policies resulting from these meetings are implemented by the department heads within the government, chiefly the secretaries of the U.S. Departments of State (foreign affairs), Defense (military affairs), and the Treasury (economic affairs). The chairman of the Joint Chiefs of Staff is the highest ranking officer within the U.S. military and advises the president on military issues. The director of national intelligence heads a collection of agencies devoted to intelligence gathering and analysis. The assistant to the president for national security affairs is more commonly called the national security adviser. This person is not a member of a particular department or branch within the government but is chosen by the president to offer an independent viewpoint on national security matters.

U.S. DEPARTMENT OF DEFENSE

The U.S. Department of Defense (DOD) traces its history back to 1789, when it was created as the Department of War under the administration of President George Washington (1732–1799). Some of the nation's armed forces (U.S. Army, Navy, and Marine Corps) were already in operation, having been established in 1775 for the Revolutionary War (1775–1783). Following World War II Congress created a civilian (nonmilitary) agency within the government, led by a secretary of defense who had direct control over the armed forces including the newly created U.S. Air Force. This agency was eventually called the Department of Defense.

Figure 2.1 lists the main entities organized under the DOD. The Department of the Army evolved from the old Department of War. The Department of the Navy (which oversees the U.S. Marine Corps) was created in 1798. The Department of the Air Force was created following enactment of the National Security Act of 1947. The Office of the Inspector General is responsible for auditing the operations and finances of the DOD to ensure they are carried out in accordance with U.S. law and government policy.

The combatant commands are the operational arms of the U.S. combat forces. Some combatant commands have global responsibilities, whereas others are assigned specific geographic regions, for example, the European command covers most of Europe, parts of the Middle East, and most of Africa. Each combatant command includes forces from two or more military services (army, navy, marines, or air force).

The Joint Chiefs of Staff are planners and advisers on issues of national security. This office includes a chairman and a vice chairman and four chiefs of the military

TABLE 2.1

Membership of the National Security Council, 2008

Chair	President
Regular attendees	Vice President Secretary of State Secretary of the Treasury Secretary of Defense Assistant to the President for National Security Affairs
Military advisor	Chairman of the Joint Chiefs of Staff
Intelligence advisor	Director of National Intelligence
Invited to any meeting	The Chief of Staff to the President Counsel to the President Assistant to the President for Economic Policy
Attend meetings pertaining to their responsibilities	The Attorney General Director of the Office of Management and Budget
Attend meetings when appropriate	The heads of other executive departments and agencies, as well as other senior officials.

SOURCE: Adapted from "Membership of the National Security Council," in *National Security Council*, Office of the President of the United States, 2008, http://www.whitehouse.gov/nsc/ (accessed July 30, 2008)

services: the chief of staff of the army, the chief of naval operations, the chief of staff of the air force, and the commandant of the marine corps. The Joint Chiefs advise the president, the secretary of defense, and the NSC.

Reserve Components

Besides the regular forces of the U.S. military, there is an additional contingency force that makes up the reserve components. These include the Army, Navy, Air Force, and Marine Reserves and two National Guard components: the Army National Guard and Air National Guard. The personnel in the reserve components are part time, meaning that they are technically civilians but can be called to service when needed. The Army, Navy, Air Force, and Marine Reserves provide a backup source of trained personnel to their respective services. Many reservists were previously members of the regular armed forces.

The National Guard evolved from the colonial militias of early colonial America, which used trained civilian fight-

FIGURE 2.1

Department of Defense (DOD) organization chart, January 2008

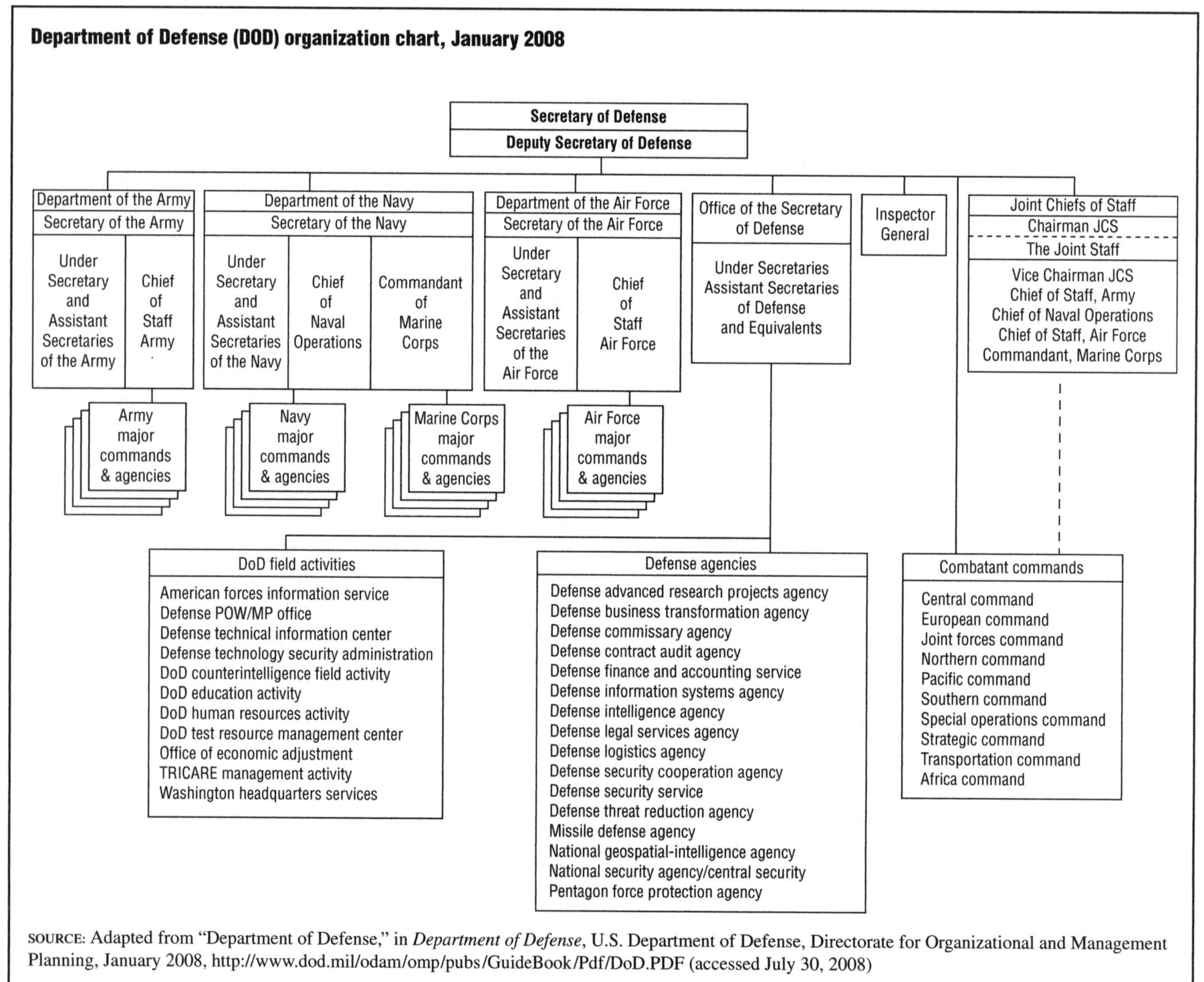

SOURCE: Adapted from "Department of Defense," in *Department of Defense*, U.S. Department of Defense, Directorate for Organizational and Management Planning, January 2008, http://www.dod.mil/odam/omp/pubs/GuideBook/Pdf/DoD.PDF (accessed July 30, 2008)

TABLE 2.2

Average troop strength for counter-terror operations, 2001–07

[In thousands]

	FY01	FY02	FY03	FY04	FY05	FY06	FY07
Average deployed by service	**51**	**77**	**220**	**216**	**245**	**247**	**256**
Army	8	17	110	143	156	156	156
Navy	29	30	42	25	29	32	40
Marine Corps	0	4	32	25	35	32	32
Air Force	14	26	35	24	25	27	27
Activated reserves state-side[a]	**NA[b]**	**51**	**92**	**87**	**66**	**50**	**46**
All OIF/OEF/ONE military personnel	**50**	**129**	**312**	**304**	**312**	**297**	**303**

Note: Average strength computed by the Defense Manpower Data Center by totaling the number of days deployed for each service member in a year and then dividing that figure by the 365 days in the year. Numbers may not add due to rounding.
[a]Activated reservists in the United States are training up for deployments, backfilling the positions of deployed active-duty personnel, or providing enhanced security at U.S. installations.
[b]Not available.
FY = Fiscal Year.
OIF = Operation Iraqi Freedom.
OEF = Operation Enduring Freedom.
ONE = Operation Noble Eagle.

SOURCE: Amy Belasco, "Table 7. Average Troop Strength for Iraq, Afghanistan, and Other Counter-Terror Operations, FY2001–FY2007," in *The Cost of Iraq, Afghanistan, and Other Global War on Terror Operations since 9/11*, Congressional Research Service, June 23, 2008, http://www.fas.org/sgp/crs/natsec/RL33110.pdf (accessed July 25, 2008)

ers who were under state control. It became a backup source for troops for the regular military services. The modern National Guard plays a dual federal-state role. State governments use the troops to provide security and protection services during natural disasters or other public emergencies. At the federal level the troops are trained, equipped, and deployed worldwide to support national security concerns. While deployed, these troops are integrated into the forces under the combatant commands.

Military Personnel

The DOD explains in "DOD 101: An Introductory Overview of the Department of Defense" (September 2008, http://www.defenselink.mil/pubs/dod101) that it has nearly 670,000 civilian employees and over 1.3 million personnel on active military duty. Another 1.1 million people serve in the National Guard and Reserves.

In *The Cost of Iraq, Afghanistan, and Other Global War on Terror Operations since 9/11* (June 23, 2008, http://www.fas.org/sgp/crs/natsec/RL33110.pdf), Amy Belasco of the Congressional Research Service (CRS) discusses the average number of service members deployed per year to Iraq, Afghanistan, and other counterterror operations. In fiscal year (FY) 2007 an average of 303,000 military personnel were deployed as part of the War on Terror. (See Table 2.2.) More than half (156,000) served in the U.S. Army.

JoAnne O'Bryant and Michael Waterhouse of the CRS state in *U.S. Forces in Iraq* (July 24, 2008, http://fas.org/sgp/crs/mideast/RS22449.pdf) that as of June 1, 2008, the United States had 99,600 regular U.S. Army personnel in Iraq and much smaller contingents of regular forces from the U.S. Marine Corps (20,200), the U.S. Navy (19,800), and the U.S. Air Force (10,800). (See Figure 2.2.) The reserve component included 18,300 members of the Army National Guard and 6,700 members of the Army Reserves. (See Figure 2.3.) Much smaller numbers of National Guard and Reserve personnel had been deployed for the other services.

FIGURE 2.2

Active military personnel in Iraq, by service, as of June 1, 2008

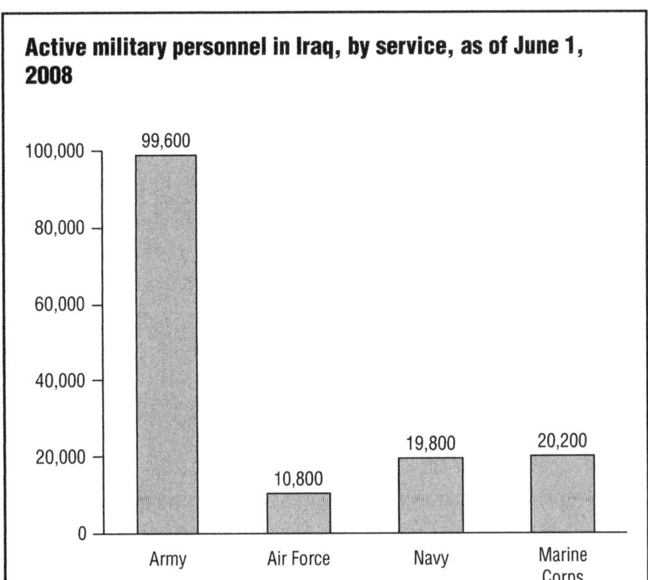

SOURCE: JoAnne O'Bryant and Michael Waterhouse, "Figure 1. Active Component Personnel in Iraq (as of June 1, 2008)," in *U.S. Forces in Iraq*, Congressional Research Service, July 24, 2008, http://fas.org/sgp/crs/mideast/RS22449.pdf (accessed August 8, 2008)

FIGURE 2.3

Reserve military personnel in Iraq, by service, as of June 1, 2008

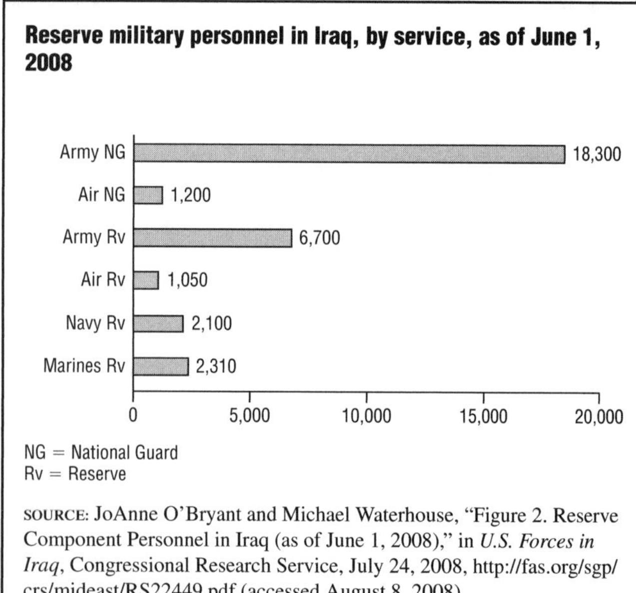

NG = National Guard
Rv = Reserve

SOURCE: JoAnne O'Bryant and Michael Waterhouse, "Figure 2. Reserve Component Personnel in Iraq (as of June 1, 2008)," in *U.S. Forces in Iraq*, Congressional Research Service, July 24, 2008, http://fas.org/sgp/crs/mideast/RS22449.pdf (accessed August 8, 2008)

TABLE 2.3

Components of U.S. intelligence community

Central Intelligence Agency (CIA)
Bureau of Intelligence and Research, Department of State (INR)
Defense Intelligence Agency (DIA)
National Security Agency (NSA)
National Reconnaissance Office (NRO)
National Geospatial-Intelligence Agency (NGA)
Federal Bureau of Investigation (FBI)
Army intelligence
Navy intelligence
Air Force intelligence
Marine Corps intelligence
Department of Homeland Security (DHS)
Coast Guard (CG)
Treasury department
Energy department
Drug Enforcement Agency (DEA)

Note: As defined at 50 U.S.C. 401a(4).

SOURCE: Adapted from Richard A. Best, Jr., "Intelligence Community," in *Intelligence Issues for Congress*, Congressional Research Service, May 30, 2008, http://www.fas.org/sgp/crs/intel/RL33539.pdf (accessed July 30, 2008)

THE INTELLIGENCE COMMUNITY

Intelligence is information, specifically information with strategic importance. Intelligence gathering means collecting information about individuals, groups, or nations that may pose a threat to U.S. national security. Reliable intelligence helps policy makers make sound decisions, plan effective strategies, and set reasonable priorities for the nation. Thus, intelligence is useful across many areas of national security, including military activities, foreign affairs, and law enforcement. Counterintelligence is a related field in which the goal is to thwart the intelligence gathering and hostile acts of one's enemies. For example, counterintelligence operations might include passing false information to known enemy spies. Both intelligence and counterintelligence are areas in which secretiveness and espionage (spying) play important roles.

The intelligence community (IC) consists of sixteen federal agencies and departments engaged in intelligence activities. (See Table 2.3.) The Central Intelligence Agency (CIA) is the primary agency concerned with U.S. intelligence and is self-contained. All other agencies are part of larger organizations devoted to other tasks within government. For example, eight of the agencies are part of the DOD. Their mission is primarily to support military operations. The U.S. Department of State (DOS) also maintains an intelligence agency, which is devoted mainly to furthering the diplomatic and foreign policy goals of the United States. The Federal Bureau of Investigation (FBI) focuses on internal threats posed by people and organizations physically located within the United States, whether foreign or domestic.

Even though the IC components have differing focal points, their roles are supposed to overlap with that of homeland security intelligence. (See Figure 2.4.) Cooperation and sharing of information between IC components is considered critical to protecting national security.

FIGURE 2.4

Dimensions of U.S. intelligence

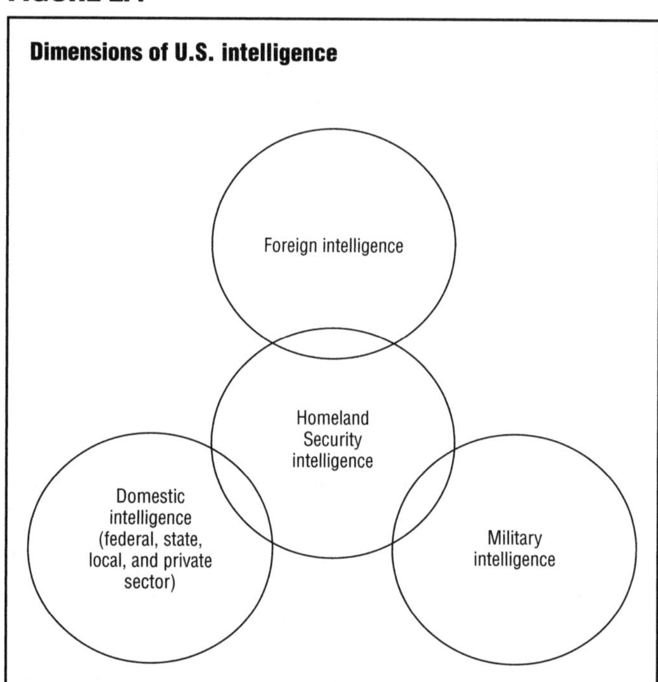

SOURCE: Todd Masse, "Figure 1. Dimensions of Intelligence," in *Homeland Security Intelligence: Perceptions, Statutory Definitions, and Approaches*, Congressional Research Service, August 18, 2006, http://www.fas.org/sgp/crs/intel/RL33616.pdf (accessed July 30, 2008)

DEFENSE INTELLIGENCE AGENCY

Military intelligence is information important to military decisions and activities. The conduct of military intelligence is coordinated by the Defense Intelligence

Agency (DIA). The DIA (2008, http://www.dia.mil/) states that its mission is to "provide timely, objective, and cogent [convincing or conclusive] military intelligence to warfighters, defense planners, and defense and national security policymakers." In 2008 it had over twelve thousand military and civilian employees. The agency is headquartered at the Pentagon in Washington, D.C. Other major facilities are located at the DIA Center at Bolling Air Force Base in Washington, D.C.; the Armed Forces Medical Intelligence Center at Fort Detrick in Frederick, Maryland; and the Missile and Space Intelligence Center at Redstone Arsenal in Huntsville, Alabama.

Evolution of Military Intelligence

Military intelligence has been practiced in the United States since the American Revolution. According to the CIA, in *Factbook on Intelligence* (2000, http://www.fas.org/irp/cia/product/facttell/index.html), President Washington asked and received permission from Congress to establish a "secret service fund" to pay for secret intelligence activities conducted by the new United States. This fund reportedly grew to more than 10% of the entire federal budget and was used to finance a number of undercover spy missions and paramilitary operations (military-type operations conducted with civilian participants) against foreign powers.

During the Civil War (1861–1865) the Union and Confederate sides used spies, sabotage, and propaganda to support their military efforts. Later in the nineteenth century, the first official permanent military intelligence agencies were formed in the U.S. Army and Navy. Both proved important during the Spanish-American War (1898). However, federal budget cuts and a lack of attention over the following decades left the agencies weakened, which hurt U.S. intelligence efforts during the United States' participation in World War I from 1917 through 1918.

Counterintelligence operations were much more successful and succeeded in stopping many enemy activities secretly undertaken in the United States by German intelligence agents. In the decades leading up to World War II, the U.S. Army and Navy intelligence agencies developed highly sophisticated cryptologic techniques. Cryptology is the science of secret codes. During World War II the Allies succeeded in breaking the extremely complex secret code used by the Germans to transmit military information internally. Code-breaking became a priority and a specialty of U.S. intelligence agencies, particularly during the cold war. Even before World War II ended the U.S. Army's Signal Intelligence Service began a small secret program to decode encrypted Soviet diplomatic communications. The program, later named Venona, would last for decades and reveal the identities of dozens of spies working for the Soviets in the United States. Near the end of the twentieth century international terrorism became a greater threat than the Soviet Union to U.S. national security. The military intelligence agencies were forced to change their organization and tactics to deal with new enemies not structured like traditional military hierarchies.

CENTRAL INTELLIGENCE AGENCY

The CIA is a civilian agency charged with collecting and analyzing intelligence and taking action to protect U.S. national security. The CIA headquarters are located in Langley, Virginia, at the George Bush Center for Intelligence. The number of employees is classified.

The CIA is the leading provider of U.S. intelligence and the primary support provider for the other IC agencies. Its analytical capabilities are supposed to be all-encompassing, and its reach is intended to be worldwide (outside the borders of the United States). In "Strategic Intent 2007–2011" (June 2, 2008, https://www.cia.gov/about-cia/strategic-intent-2007-2011.html), the CIA describes itself as follows:

> We are the nation's first line of defense. We accomplish what others cannot accomplish and go where others cannot go. We carry out our mission by:
>
> - Collecting information that reveals the plans, intentions and capabilities of our adversaries and provides the basis for decision and action.
> - Producing timely analysis that provides insight, warning and opportunity to the President and decisionmakers charged with protecting and advancing America's interests.
> - Conducting covert action at the direction of the President to preempt threats or achieve US policy objectives.

Figure 2.5 shows the organization chart for the major components of the CIA as of 2007.

History of the CIA

The CIA's roots lie in the Office of the Coordinator of Information—an office created in July 1941 by President Franklin D. Roosevelt (1882–1945). The surprise Japanese attack on Pearl Harbor, Hawaii, later that year was viewed as an immense intelligence failure and spurred the creation of a much more sophisticated and powerful agency called the Office of Strategic Services (OSS). The OSS began operating in June 1942. According to the CIA, in *Factbook on Intelligence*, OSS intelligence activities did not extend to Latin America (which was the responsibility of the FBI) and did not overlap with the ongoing work of DOD and DOS IC agencies. After World War II ended in 1945, the OSS was officially abolished, and its functions were transferred to the competing agencies.

In 1946 President Harry S. Truman (1884–1972) created a new civilian intelligence agency called the Central

FIGURE 2.5

Central Intelligence Agency (CIA) organization chart, 2007

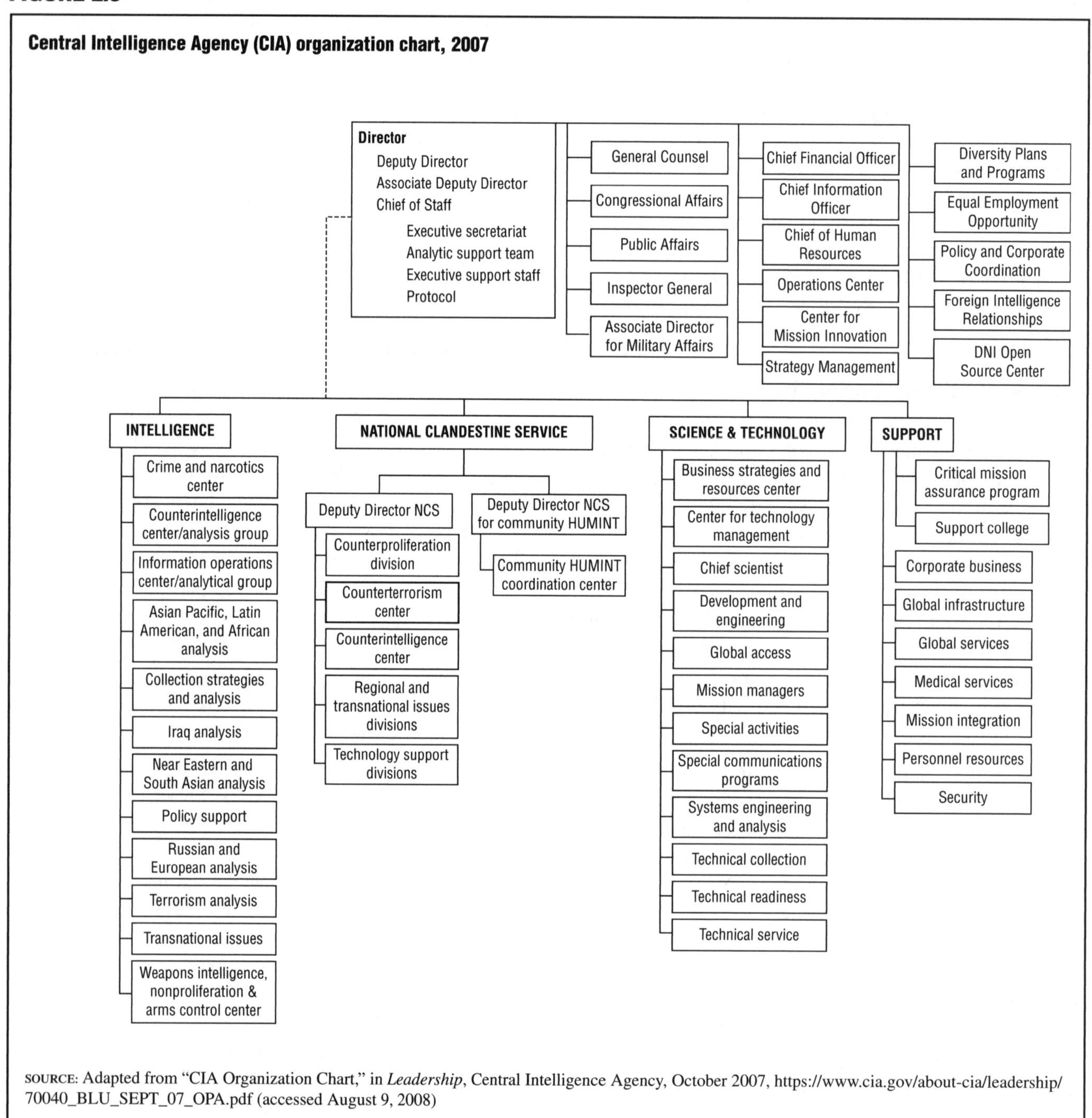

SOURCE: Adapted from "CIA Organization Chart," in *Leadership*, Central Intelligence Agency, October 2007, https://www.cia.gov/about-cia/leadership/70040_BLU_SEPT_07_OPA.pdf (accessed August 9, 2008)

Intelligence Group (CIG). The CIG was tasked with detecting strategic threats to the United States via the operation of clandestine (secret) activities around the world. It was designated an "all-source" component and granted access to all intelligence gathered by other IC agencies. The CIG was led by the first director of central intelligence (DCI), Rear Admiral Sidney W. Souers (1892–1973).

The National Security Act of 1947 created a new intelligence structure in which a Central Intelligence Agency operated under the direction of a National Security Council and the president. The act established the DCI as not only head of the CIA but also head of the entire IC and a key adviser to the president. However, the scope of the CIA was limited to matters outside of law enforcement and outside U.S. borders.

The passage of the Central Intelligence Agency Act in 1949 granted the CIA unprecedented financial freedom. In *Factbook on Intelligence*, the CIA notes that the act "exempted CIA from many of the usual limitations on the expenditure of federal funds. It provided that CIA funds could be included in the budgets of other departments and then transferred to the Agency without regard to the restrictions placed on the initial appropriation." The act also allowed the agency to use "confidential fiscal and administrative procedures." In other words, the CIA's budget and spending became state secrets.

In 2004 the Intelligence Reform and Terrorism Prevention Act amended the National Security Act to create a director of national intelligence who took over some of the tasks formerly performed by the DCI and established a separate position, the director of the CIA.

INTELLIGENCE REFORM

In the 1970s DOD and CIA intelligence operations came under fire when stories were published in the media about surveillance conducted against U.S. civilians. In 1970 the former army intelligence officer Christopher H. Pyle alleged his agency had collected massive amounts of intelligence on Americans engaged in protest activities, primarily against the Vietnam War (1955–1975). Pyle also claimed that plainclothes undercover army agents had been spying on protest groups since the 1960s. The allegations resulted in federal investigations led by Senator Sam J. Ervin (1896–1985; D-NC) and Senator Frank Forrester Church III (1924–1984; D-ID).

In 1974 Seymour M. Hersh stunned the nation when he alleged in "Huge C.I.A. Operation Reported in U. S. against Antiwar Forces, Other Dissidents in Nixon Years" (*New York Times*, December 22, 1974) that the CIA had engaged in a "massive, illegal domestic intelligence operation" against antiwar protestors and other groups. Hersh claimed that the CIA had intelligence files on at least ten thousand U.S. citizens and had engaged in illegal surveillance activities, such as wiretapping and mail interdiction since the 1950s. Spying on Americans was a direct violation of the CIA charter.

The U.S. Senate and U.S. House of Representatives investigations that followed uncovered more questionable activities by the CIA, including attempts to assassinate foreign leaders in Chile, the Congo, Cuba, the Dominican Republic, and Vietnam. In response, President Gerald R. Ford (1913–2006) issued an executive order banning the assassination of foreign officials. The Foreign Intelligence Surveillance Act (FISA) of 1978 established a Foreign Intelligence Surveillance Court (FISC) from which authorization must be obtained for the conduct of electronic surveillance or physical searches of people alleged to be acting on behalf of a foreign power to threaten U.S. national security. Originally, the FISC included seven district judges; in 2001 the U.S. Patriot Act amended FISA to require eleven judges on the FISC. More detailed information about FISA and the FISC is provided in Chapter 8.

INTELLIGENCE DISCIPLINES

According to the U.S. Intelligence Community (2008, http://www.intelligence.gov/2-business_cycle2.shtml), there are six major intelligence collection disciplines:

1. Human Intelligence (HUMINT)—the collection of intelligence from human sources. This includes both overt (open) activities by diplomats and military attachés and covert actions conducted by spies. HUMINT sources include documents, photographs, and people who live or work in foreign countries or travel to them. This intelligence discipline is widely used by the CIA, the DOS, the DOD, and the FBI.
2. Signals Intelligence (SIGINT)—the interception of electronic communications or other transmitted signals. The National Security Agency, which is headquartered at Fort Meade, Maryland, oversees SIGINT operations for the IC and is considered the nation's premier cryptologic organization.
3. Imagery Intelligence (IMINT)—the analysis of images obtained via photography, radar imaging, and other optical and electronic methods. The National Geospatial Intelligence Agency, which is headquartered in Bethesda, Maryland, manages all IMINT activities for the IC.
4. Measurement and Signature Intelligence (MASINT)—the derivation of intelligence data from sources other than IMINT and SIGINT. This discipline relies on techniques in a variety of scientific fields, including acoustics, optics, chemistry, and materials science. The DIA operates the central MASINT organization for the IC.
5. Geospatial Intelligence—the analysis and production of images of security-related facilities and activities around the world. This form of intelligence is conducted primarily by the National Geospatial Intelligence Agency.
6. Open-Source Intelligence—the collection and translation of publicly available information from non-U.S. media sources accessed through the Internet, television, newspapers, radio, and commercially produced databases. The major collectors of OSINT are the Foreign Broadcast Information Service and the DOD's National Air and Space Intelligence Center.

COUNTERINTELLIGENCE

The National Security Act of 1947 defines counterintelligence as "information gathered and activities conducted to protect against espionage, other intelligence activities, sabotage, or assassinations conducted by or on behalf of foreign governments or elements thereof, foreign organizations, or foreign persons, or international terrorist activities." The National Counterintelligence Policy Board explains in *National Counterintelligence*

Strategy of the United States (2007, http://www.ncix.gov/publications/policy/CIStrategy.pdf) that the IC conducts counterintelligence activities in both a defensive and offensive manner. The board lists four specific objectives for the nation's counterintelligence efforts:

- Secure the nation against foreign espionage and electronic penetration
- Protect the integrity of the U.S. intelligence system
- Support national policy and decisions
- Protect U.S. economic advantage, trade secrets, and know how

U.S. DEPARTMENT OF STATE

The DOS is the primary agency tasked with representing U.S. interests abroad through the use of diplomacy. Diplomacy is defined by *Merriam Webster's Collegiate Dictionary* (2003) as "the art and practice of conducting negotiations between nations" and "skill in handling affairs without arousing hostility." In a modern political sense, diplomacy can be defined as any foreign policy action short of armed aggression, for example, a trade embargo imposed on another nation to punish it for some transgression.

History

The DOS was created in 1789 from a previous agency known as the Department of Foreign Affairs. Historians consider Benjamin Franklin (1706–1790) to be the nation's first diplomat. In 1778 he was pivotal in securing two treaties with France: the Treaty of Amity and Commerce (which promoted trade) and the Treaty of Alliance (which formed a military alliance between the two nations). Franklin was called a plenipotentiary, a word derived from a Latin phrase meaning "full power." In other words, he had been granted full power to represent the U.S. government abroad.

The Treaty of Amity and Commerce was the first of many treaties the United States would forge with other nations regarding peaceful relations, commerce, travel, navigation, extradition of criminals, and other nonmilitary affairs. The Treaty of Alliance would be the only bilateral military agreement assumed by the United States for nearly two centuries.

Mission and Goals

In *Diplomacy: The U.S. Department of State at Work* (June 2008, http://www.state.gov/documents/organization/46839.pdf), the DOS states that it has four major goals:

- Protect the United States and Americans
- Advance democracy, human rights, and other global interests
- Promote international understanding of American values and policies
- Support U.S. diplomats, government officials, and all other personnel at home and abroad who make these goals a reality

The DOS explains that it has three contingents of employees. The Foreign Service includes more than eleven thousand Americans who work in foreign countries. Over thirty-seven thousand foreign nationals are employed by the DOS around the world. The Civil Service comprises more than nine thousand U.S. employees who work primarily in DOS offices in Washington, D.C.

At the highest level, DOS officials craft U.S. foreign policy in concert with the president and negotiate with the leaders and foreign ministers of other nations. The DOS is headed by the secretary of state, who is also a member of the president's cabinet and the NSC. Figure 2.6 shows the organization chart for the main components of the DOS as of January 2008.

U.S. Diplomatic Relations

According to the DOS, in the fact sheet "Independent States in the World" (August 19, 2008, http://www.state.gov/s/inr/rls/4250.htm), the United States recognized 194 independent states around the world in 2008. An independent state is defined by the DOS as "people politically organized into a sovereign state with a definite territory." The United States maintains embassies in most of these countries. An embassy is the central office of a diplomatic mission to another country and is typically located in that country's capital city. Officially, the ground occupied by a U.S. embassy is considered U.S. soil. (Likewise the ground occupied by any foreign embassy in the United States is considered the soil of that country.) Embassy branches, called consulates, may be located in other parts of the country. Each U.S. embassy is headed by an ambassador, who speaks for the U.S. government.

The DOS indicates that as of August 2008 the United States had official diplomatic relations with all but 4 of the 194 recognized independent states. Those four nations were:

- Bhutan
- Cuba
- Iran
- North Korea

Bhutan is a tiny mountainous country located between India and Tibet. For decades, Bhutan has chosen to remain isolated from the outside world to protect its deeply religious Buddhist society. The United States conducts informal relations with Bhutan through the U.S. embassy in India.

FIGURE 2.6

U.S. Department of State (DOS) organization chart, January 2008

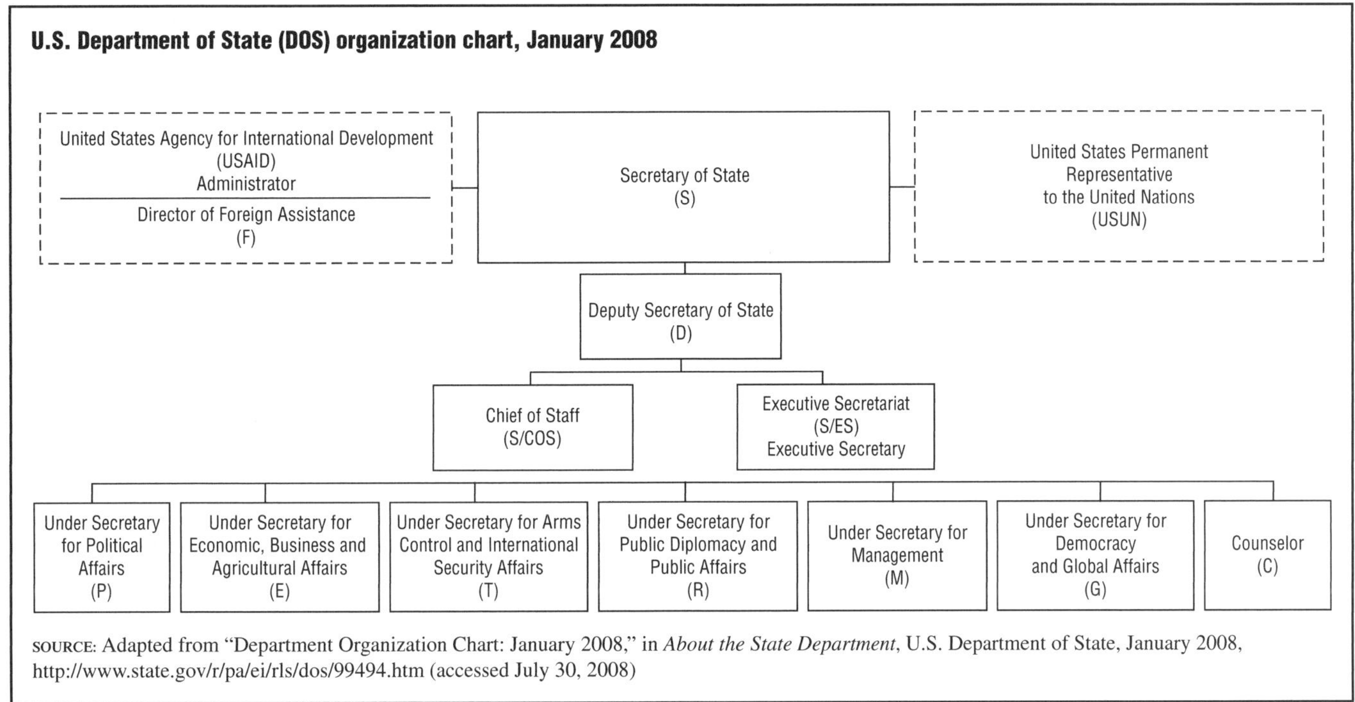

SOURCE: Adapted from "Department Organization Chart: January 2008," in *About the State Department*, U.S. Department of State, January 2008, http://www.state.gov/r/pa/ei/rls/dos/99494.htm (accessed July 30, 2008)

On January 3, 1961, the United States broke diplomatic ties with Cuba after it became obvious that Fidel Castro (1926–), the new Cuban leader, intended to form a communist government. In 1977 the United States opened an Interests Section office in Havana, Cuba. Even though it is staffed by U.S. Foreign Service personnel, the office is officially a part of the Swiss embassy. The U.S. Interests Section handles requests for visas and performs other diplomatic functions. Cuba maintains a similar office at the Swiss embassy in Washington, D.C.

On April 7, 1980, the United States broke diplomatic relations with Iran after the Iranian government refused to intervene on behalf of U.S. diplomats taken hostage by Iranian militants at the U.S. embassy. A U.S. Interests Section office was later opened at the Swiss embassy in Tehran, Iran. Likewise, Iran maintains an Interests Section office at the Pakistani embassy in Washington, D.C.

Following World War II the Korea Peninsula was split into two occupied territories: the north under Soviet control and the south under U.S. control. This was supposed to be a temporary arrangement until the two halves could be reunited as one nation. In 1948 South Korea adopted a constitution and became a sovereign nation. However, cold war politics and the Korean War (1950–1953) prevented reunification from occurring. The United States did not form diplomatic relations with the communist government that assumed power in North Korea.

In addition, the United States does not maintain an embassy in Taiwan, because that state is claimed by the People's Republic of China.

Language Shortfalls

As representatives of the U.S. government and people, DOS staff at foreign posts come into contact with many foreign nationals. Effective communication is one of the hallmarks of successful diplomacy. However, the U.S. Government Accountability Office (GAO) reports in *State Department: Staffing and Foreign Language Shortfalls Persist Despite Initiatives to Address Gaps* (August 1, 2007, http://www.gao.gov/new.items/d071154t.pdf) that in 2005 it found many foreign-language deficiencies in foreign-language skill requirements among DOS staff working in the more than three thousand positions. The GAO divided foreign languages into three broad categories based on the difficulty associated with learning the languages by native English speakers (see Figure 2.7):

- World languages—languages related to English, such as French, Italian, and Spanish. Just over half (55%) of the DOS positions analyzed required proficiency in world languages.
- Hard languages—languages with significant differences from English with particular linguistic difficulties. This category includes many languages, including Greek, Hebrew, Hindi, Persian, Russian, and Turkish. Twenty-nine percent of language-designated posts required skills in hard languages.
- Superhard languages—Arabic, Chinese, Japanese, and Korean. These languages are considered extremely difficult to learn. Sixteen percent of language-designated posts required skills in superhard languages.

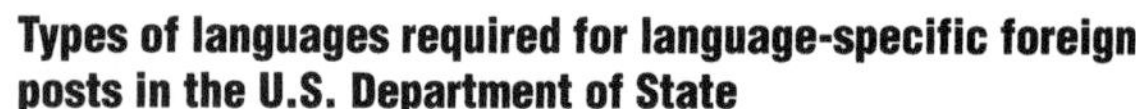

FIGURE 2.7

Types of languages required for language-specific foreign posts in the U.S. Department of State

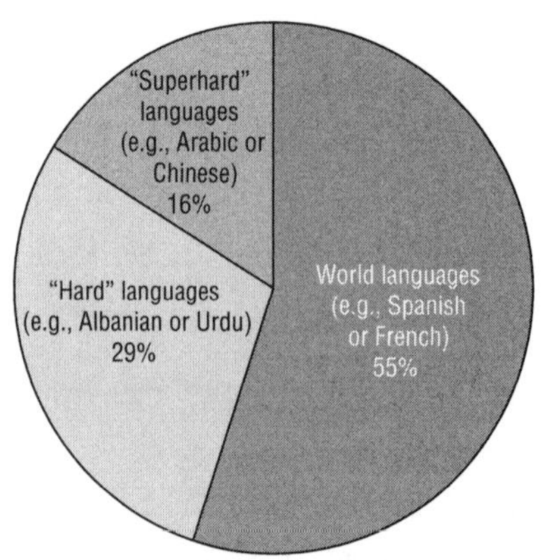

SOURCE: Adapted from "State's Foreign Language Requirements," in *State Department Staffing and Foreign Language Shortfalls Persist Despite Initiatives to Address Gaps*, U.S. Government Accountability Office, August 1, 2007, http://www.gao.gov/new.items/d071154t.pdf (accessed August 8, 2008)

In an earlier report on the same subject, *State Department: Staffing and Foreign Language Shortfalls Persist Despite Initiatives to Address Gaps* (August 2006, http://www.gao.gov/new.items/d06894.pdf), the GAO finds that in 2005, 75% of DOS personnel working in world-language posts were proficient in the required language. Proficiency was slightly worse (70%) among staff working in countries where hard languages are spoken. The largest deficiencies were found in DOS personnel required to be skilled in superhard languages. Less than two-thirds (62%) of these people met the language requirements of their posts. A breakdown by superhard language indicates 83% proficiency in Korean, 62% proficiency in Arabic, and 60% proficiency in Japanese and Chinese.

The gaps in language proficiency in Arabic and Korean among DOS staff are particularly troublesome because many of the U.S. national security issues are associated with the Middle East and North Korea.

Travel Documents: Passports and Visas

One of the functions performed by the DOS is the issuance of international travel documents: passports for U.S. citizens and visas for foreign citizens.

A passport is an official travel document that verifies a person's identity and nationality. The DOS issues passports to U.S. citizens. Most foreign governments require U.S. visitors to possess a passport and show it when entering and leaving their countries. Likewise, a passport is typically required for U.S. citizens to reenter the United States after traveling abroad.

A visa is a document that indicates permission has been given by a government for a person of foreign nationality to travel to that country. DOS offices at U.S. embassies and consulates can grant visas to foreign nationals to travel to the United States. A U.S.-granted visa indicates a person is eligible to enter the United States for a specific purpose. However, the determination on whether or not to grant entry is made by immigration officers at U.S. ports of entry (airports and land border crossings). In *Diplomacy*, the DOS notes that it reviews over eight million visa applications per year. There are two main types of visas: immigrant visas and nonimmigrant visas.

IMMIGRANT VISAS. Immigrant visas are required for foreign citizens who intend to live permanently in the United States. In general, these visas require the sponsorship of a relative or prospective employer in the United States. For example, immigrant visas are issued to foreign citizens who are related to U.S. citizens or U.S. Legal Permanent Residents by blood, adoption, or marriage. There is another category of immigrant visas for "special immigrants." These include Amerasians (Vietnam War–era children of U.S. soldiers and Vietnamese women) and the widows, widowers, and battered spouses or children of U.S. citizens.

The DOS also conducts an annual lottery to make available fifty thousand permanent resident visas to applicants from countries with low rates of immigration to the United States. The Diversity Immigrant Visa Program uses a computer-generated random drawing to select the foreign applicants. Residents of countries that have sent more than fifty thousand immigrants to the United States within the past five years are not eligible for the lottery. No one country participating in the lottery can receive more than 7% of the Diversity Immigrant Visas given out in any year.

According to the DOS (2008, http://www.travel.state.gov/pdf/FY07AnnualReportTableIII.pdf), 434,374 immigrant visas were issued during FY 2007. The vast majority (85%) went to applicants with immediate relatives or family sponsors in the United States. Asian applicants made up 44% of the total, accounting for the largest number of immigrant visas issued. (See Figure 2.8.) North American applicants made up 30% of the total and were the second-largest contingent. The DOS notes that the five nations whose citizens received the most U.S. immigrant visas during FY 2007 were:

- Mexico—53,327 visas
- The Philippines—44,193 visas
- China—34,153 visas
- India—30,930 visas
- Vietnam—21,739 visas

FIGURE 2.8

U.S. immigrant visas issued, by region of origin, fiscal year 2007

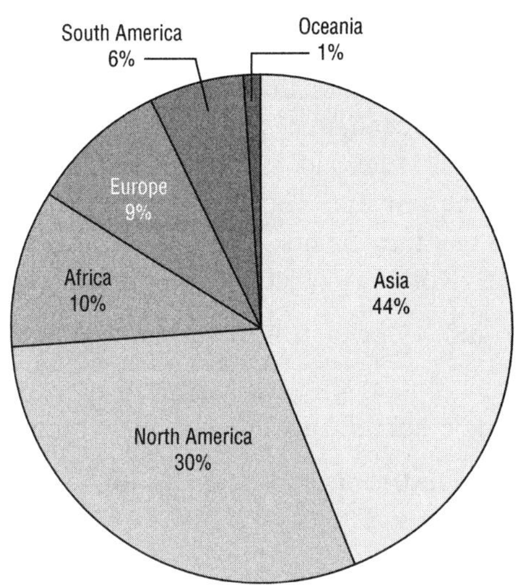

SOURCE: Adapted from "Table III. Immigrant Visas Issued (by Foreign State of Chargeability or Place of Birth), Fiscal Year 2007," in *Report of the Visa Office 2007*, U.S. Department of State, undated, http://www.travel.state.gov/pdf/FY07AnnualReportTableIII.pdf (accessed July 30, 2008)

FIGURE 2.9

U.S. nonimmigrant visas issued, by region of origin, fiscal year 2005

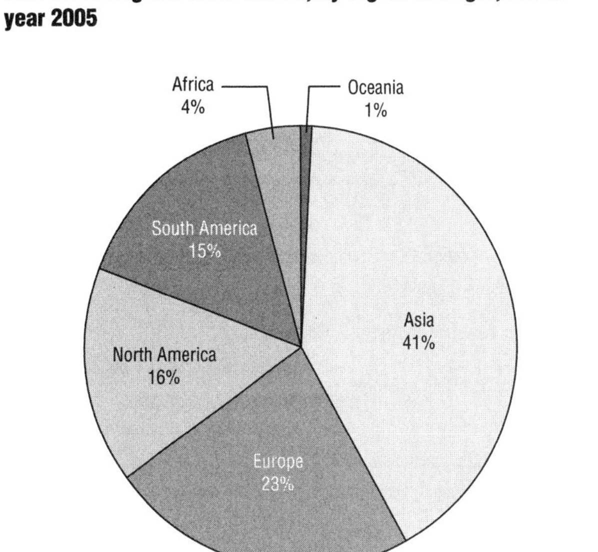

SOURCE: Adapted from "Table XVIII (Part II). Nonimmigrant Visas Issued by Nationality (Including Border Crossing Cards), Fiscal Years 1996–2005," in *Report of the Visa Office 2005*, U.S. Department of State, undated, http://travel.state.gov/visa/frvi/statistics/statistics_2787.html (accessed July 30, 2008)

Together, these countries accounted for 42% of all visas issued.

NONIMMIGRANT VISAS. Nonimmigrant visas are issued to people approved to visit the United States on a temporary basis, for example, to study, work, vacation, seek medical care, or conduct business.

The DOS (2008, http://www.travel.state.gov/pdf/FY07AnnualReportTableXVIII.pdf) states that 6.4 million nonimmigrant visas were issued during FY 2007. Furthermore, the DOS (2008, http://www.travel.state.gov/pdf/FY07AnnualReportTableXVIA.pdf) notes that 4.5 million (70%) of the visas were B-series documents issued to foreigners visiting the United States for business and/or pleasure reasons.

Asian applicants made up 41% of the total nonimmigrant visas, followed by European applicants with 23% of the total. (See Figure 2.9.) According to the DOS (2006, http://travel.state.gov/pdf/FY05tableXVIII.pdf), the five nations with the largest numbers of nonimmigrant visa recipients in FY 2005 were:

- Mexico—906,622 visas
- South Korea—386,524 visas
- India—378,039 visas
- China—325,955 visas
- Brazil—200,321 visas

FOREIGN AID

One of the historic diplomatic policies of the United States has been foreign aid (or foreign economic assistance as it is officially known). This includes humanitarian aid designed to generate goodwill for the United States. Since the terrorist attacks of September 11, 2001, foreign economic assistance has been increasingly viewed as a tool of national security.

The U.S. Agency for International Development (USAID) is the principal U.S. agency engaged in providing foreign economic assistance. Even though USAID is considered an independent agency, its administrator (the director of foreign assistance) reports to the secretary of state. USAID describes its mission and goals in *Strategic Plan: Fiscal Years 2007–2012* (May 7, 2007, http://www.state.gov/documents/organization/86291.pdf). According to the agency, its mission is to "advance freedom for the benefit of the American people and the international community by helping to build and sustain a more democratic, secure, and prosperous world composed of well-governed states that respond to the needs of their people, reduce widespread poverty, and act responsibly within the international system." Furthermore, it has seven strategic goals, which are defined in Table 2.4.

USAID tracks foreign aid amounts in *U.S. Overseas Loans and Grants, Obligations and Loan Authorizations Report*, which is commonly called the Greenbook. The

TABLE 2.4

U.S. Department of State and U.S. Agency for International Development strategic goal framework, May 2007

Strategic goal 1: Achieving peace and security

- Counterterrorism
- Weapons of mass destruction and destabilizing conventional weapons
- Security cooperation and security sector reform
- Conflict prevention, mitigation, and response
- Transnational crime
- Homeland security

Strategic goal 2: Governing justly and democratically

- Rule of law and human rights
- Good governance
- Political competition and consensus building
- Civil society

Strategic goal 3: Investing in people

- Health
- Education
- Social services and protection for especially vulnerable populations

Strategic goal 4: Promoting economic growth and prosperity

- Private markets
- Trade and investment
- Energy security
- Environment
- Agriculture

Strategic goal 5: Providing humanitarian assistance

- Protection, assistance, and solutions
- Disaster prevention and mitigation
- Orderly and humane means for migration management

Strategic goal 6: Promoting international understanding

- Offer a positive vision
- Marginalize extremism
- Nurture common interests and values

Strategic goal 7: Strengthening consular and management capabilities

- Consular services (visas, passports, American citizen services)
- Major management functions

SOURCE: "Department of State/USAID Joint Strategic Goal Framework," in *Strategic Plan: Fiscal Years 2007–2012*, U.S. Department of State, U.S. Agency for International Development, May 7, 2007, http://www.usaid.gov/policy/coordination/stratplan_fy07-12.pdf (accessed August 8, 2008)

online version of the Greenbook is available at http://qesdb.usaid.gov/gbk/. As of September 2008, the most recent year included in the Greenbook database was 2006. The United States provided nearly $40 billion in foreign economic assistance in that year.

Of the twenty countries that received U.S. economic assistance between 1997 and 2006, Iraq received the most: $22 billion. (See Table 2.5.) Other countries in the top five include Russia ($8.3 billion), Israel ($8 billion), Afghanistan ($6.7 billion), and Colombia ($5.7 billion). In 2006 alone, Iraq was the top recipient of U.S. economic assistance in 2006 with $4.4 billion. Afghanistan was second with $1.9 billion. The United States invaded Afghanistan and Iraq in 2001 and 2003, respectively, as part of its War on Terror and has invested billions of dollars in their rebuilding and stabilization.

In January 2006 Condoleezza Rice (1954–), the U.S. secretary of state, announced a new approach to the nation's foreign policy called transformational development. Larry Nowels and Connie Veillette of the CRS suggest in *Restructuring U.S. Foreign Aid: The Role of the Director of Foreign Assistance* (June 16, 2006, http://www.fas.org/sgp/crs/row/RL33491.pdf) that this approach is designed to "transform countries, through far-reaching, fundamental changes in institutions of governance, human capacity, and economic structure that enable a country to sustain further economic and social progress without depending on foreign aid." In other words, the goal is to help countries mature economically, politically, and socially so that they do not need U.S. assistance anymore. There are five primary objectives within the program:

- Peace and security from external and internal conflicts
- Just and democratic governance and strong rule of law
- People investments, such as health, education, and environment
- Economic growth, trade policy, and fiscal accountability
- Humanitarian assistance through emergency relief

Table 2.6 lists the foreign assistance program areas associated with each priority objective. Table 2.7 shows the framework for countries at various stages within their development. There are five stages of development:

- Rebuilding countries—these are postconflict countries lacking stability
- Developing countries—low-income and lower-middle-income countries that do not yet meet the U.S. Millennium Challenge Corporation's (MCC) performance criteria (the MCC is a government-owned corporation that oversees the Millennium Challenge Account—a foreign aid program for developing countries that meet certain performance criteria)
- Transforming countries—low-income and lower-middle-income countries that meet MCC performance criteria and political rights criterion
- Sustaining partnership countries—higher income countries that have economic, trade, and security relationships with the United States
- Restrictive countries—these are states of concern because of significant governance issues

In addition, Table 2.7 notes that some foreign assistance activities are applied at a regional or global level.

As of September 2008, the MCC (http://www.mca.gov/countries/index.php) listed forty countries that were eligible for MCC assistance.

PUBLIC DIPLOMACY

Public diplomacy is diplomacy directed toward the foreign public at large, rather than just toward foreign governments. In *U.S. Public Diplomacy: State Department*

TABLE 2.5

Top twenty countries receiving U.S. economic assistance, 1997–2006

[In millions, historical $US]

Country name	1997	1998	1999	2000	2001	2002	2003	2004	2005	2006	Total
Iraq	8	0.1	0.1	0.1	0.2	38.8	3,802.20	7,674.30	6,277.70	4,423.70	**22,225**
Russia	318.5	389.1	1,601.60	709.7	603	521.4	779.2	950.7	1,262.10	1,207.60	**8,343**
Israel	1,250.00	1,200.00	1,080.00	949.1	847.4	730.7	597.4	556.8	481.9	336.6	**8,030**
Afghanistan	30.1	2.8	32.5	42.9	102.1	507.2	723.7	1,543.00	1,775.80	1,932.80	**6,693**
Colombia	79.2	87.7	278.7	1,156.60	256.4	536.2	659.8	657.7	722.6	1,257.80	**5,693**
Jordan	156.1	89.2	221.9	275.3	195.4	238	1,055.70	429.6	375.5	351.3	**3,388**
Ethiopia	92.8	126.4	147	277.4	210.6	175.9	597.9	433	685.9	319.4	**3,066**
Pakistan	43.1	27.7	83.4	19.3	187.2	787.8	332.8	355.8	453.8	643	**2,934**
Sudan	27.8	65.9	92.8	50.9	95.9	122.1	187.8	477.3	885.2	758.4	**2,764**
Peru	156	187.4	225.4	203.7	215.9	285.4	228.9	272.6	190.6	338.4	**2,304**
Indonesia	35.3	100.7	256.2	242.3	194	204.2	201.1	160.1	585.8	265.4	**2,245**
Serbia and Montenegro	1.6	10.8	141.2	320.8	377.4	262.1	253.3	251.3	226.1	5.8	**1,850**
India	127.6	130.6	186	184.5	220.8	225.9	177.2	189.6	200.8	172.8	**1,816**
Bolivia	136.7	113.4	137.7	239.4	201.5	187	206.5	178.3	161.8	223.6	**1,786**
Ukraine	97.5	272.8	281.5	194.9	65.3	99.5	78.8	149.4	163.1	158	**1,561**
Kenya	29.5	66.9	78.2	89.7	158.2	93.5	123.7	177.8	242.4	390.5	**1,450**
Uganda	65.6	85.8	75.1	76.1	95	100.7	178.5	216	267.5	279.2	**1,440**
Haiti	113.1	118.7	106.8	83.9	94.3	62.4	83.5	162.5	223.7	241.6	**1,291**
Bosnia & Herzegovina	186.5	302	210.9	117.9	148.1	63	79.5	63.6	46.6	62.2	**1,280**
Philippines	40.4	71.3	74.5	77.4	139.9	156.8	170.5	185.8	135.2	179.9	**1,232**

SOURCE: Adapted from "Economic Assistance, Total," in *U.S. Overseas Loans and Grants (Greenbook)*, U.S. Department of State, U.S. Agency for International Development, September 2006, http://qesdb.usaid.gov/cgi-bin/broker.exe?_program=gbkprogs.program_list.sas&_service=default&unit=N (accessed August 2, 2008)

TABLE 2.6

U.S. foreign assistance objectives and program areas

Goal	"To help build and sustain democratic, well-governed states that respond to the needs of their people, reduce widespread poverty and conduct themselves responsibly in the international system."				
Objectives	Peace and security	Governing justly and democratically	Investing in people	Economic growth	Humanitarian assistance
			Other USG agency contributions		
Foreign assistance program areas	• Counter terrorism • Combating WMD • Stabilization operations and defense reform • Counternarcotics • Transnational Crime • Conflict mitigation and response	• Rule of law and human rights • Good governance • Political competition and consensus-building • Civil society	• Health • Education • Social services and protection for vulnerable populations	• Macroeconomic foundation for growth • Trade and investment • Financial sector • Infrastructure • Agriculture • Private sector competitiveness • Economic opportunity • Environment	• Protection, assistance and solutions • Disaster readiness • Migration management

USG = United States Government.
WMD = Weapons of Mass Destruction.

SOURCE: Adapted from "Appendix I: Foreign Assistance Framework," in *Strategic Plan: Fiscal Years 2007–2012*, U.S. Department of State, U.S. Agency for International Development, May 7, 2007, http://www.usaid.gov/policy/coordination/stratplan_fy07-12.pdf (accessed August 8, 2008)

Efforts to Engage Muslim Audiences Lack Certain Communication Elements and Face Significant Challenges (May 2006, http://www.gao.gov/new.items/d06535.pdf), the GAO mentions that the purpose of public diplomacy is "to understand, inform, engage, and influence the attitudes and behavior of global audiences in ways that support the United States' strategic interests."

Public diplomacy projects are conducted by various entities within the U.S. government, including the DOS, the DOD, USAID, and the Broadcasting Board of Governors. The projects are designed in accordance with guidance provided by the White House and the NSC (specifically the deputy national security adviser for strategic communications and global outreach).

Broadcasting Board of Governors

The Broadcasting Board of Governors oversees government and government-sponsored international broadcasting

TABLE 2.7

U.S. foreign assistance framework

	Category definition	End goal of U.S. foreign assistance	Graduation trajectory
Rebuilding countries	States in or emerging from and rebuilding after internal or external conflict.	Stable environment for good governance, increased availability of essential social services, and initial progress to create policies and institutions upon which future progress will rest.	Advance to the developing or transforming category.
Developing countries	States with low or lower-middle income, not yet meeting MCC* performance criteria, and the criterion related to political rights.	Continued progress in expanding and deepening democracy, strengthening public and private institutions, and supporting policies that promote economic growth and poverty reduction.	Advance to the transforming category.
Transforming countries	States with low or lower-middle income, meeting MCC performance criteria, and the criterion related to political rights.	Government, civil society and private sector institutions capable of sustaining development progress.	Advance to the sustaining partnership category or graduate from foreign assistance.
Sustaining partnership countries	States with upper-middle income or greater for which U.S. support is provided to sustain partnerships, progress, and peace.	Continued partnership as strategically appropriate where U.S. support is necessary to maintain progress and peace.	Continue partnership or graduate from foreign assistance.
Restrictive countries	States of concern where there are significant governance issues.	Civil society empowered to demand more effective democracies and states respectful of human dignity, accountable to their citizens, and responsible towards their neighbors.	Advance to other relevant foreign assistance category.
Global or regional	Activities that advance the five objectives, transcend a single country's borders, and are addressed outside a country strategy.	Achievement of foreign assistance goal and objectives.	Determined based on criteria specific to the global or regional objective.

*Millennium Challenge Corporation.

SOURCE: Adapted from "Appendix I: Foreign Assistance Framework," in *Strategic Plan: Fiscal Years 2007–2012*, U.S. Department of State, U.S. Agency for International Development, May 7, 2007, http://www.usaid.gov/policy/coordination/stratplan_fy07-12.pdf (accessed August 8, 2008)

services, including both radio and television. Even though these services have a variety of different audiences, they have the common goal of delivering information about U.S. actions, goals, culture, and opinions to people who might otherwise not have access to them. The Board of Governors (2008, http://www.bbg.gov/about/index.html) states that broadcasting services reach approximately 175 million people per week. The International Broadcasting Bureau (IBB; March 12, 2008, http://www.ibb.gov/ibb_broadcasters.html) performs the administrative and marketing activities of the Board of Governors and provides transmission services for the broadcasters. In 2008 there were seven broadcasters:

- Voice of America—this service began operating on the radio in 1942 and has grown to include programs in fifty-three languages. It airs more than one thousand hours per week of news, information, and educational and cultural shows. Its worldwide audience is estimated at ninety-four million people.
- Alhurra—Alhurra means "the free one" in Arabic. It is a commercial-free network that provides Arabic-language news and feature stories throughout the Middle East. Alhurra is operated by the Middle Eastern Television Network, a nonprofit organization funded by Congress.
- Radio Sawa—this Arabic-language radio service began broadcasting in 2002 throughout the Middle East and features pop music, news, sports, and other features. It is transmitted via various radio frequencies, including AM, FM, short wave, and the Internet. For example, Radio Sawa is found on FM station 100.4 in Baghdad, Iraq. Internet users in Egypt, the Persian Gulf, Iraq, Morocco, Sudan, and the Levant (countries along the eastern Mediterranean Sea) can also listen to live broadcasts.
- Radio Farda—Farda means "tomorrow" in Farsi (or Persian), one of the primary languages of Iran. Radio Farda, a collaboration of Voice of America and Radio Free Europe/Radio Liberty, airs news and music programming via AM and shortwave radio, digital audio satellite, and the Internet.
- Radio and TV Martí—these two services are operated by the Office of Cuba Broadcasting. They include programs on a variety of topics.
- Radio Free Europe/Radio Liberty—this service can be heard across eastern Europe and Central and Southwestern Asia. The broadcasts are in thirty-two languages and are available over the radio and Internet.
- Radio Free Asia—this service broadcasts approximately two hundred hours per week by radio in ten languages to Burma, Cambodia, China, Laos, North Korea, Tibet, and Vietnam and provides audio streams over the Internet.

LAW ENFORCEMENT AGENCIES

U.S. law enforcement agencies play an important part in defending national security through counterterrorism and counterintelligence operations. They attempt to

TABLE 2.8

U.S. law enforcement agencies engaged in counterterrorism, 2008

Department of the Treasury
- Office of Foreign Assets Control
- Office of Terrorist and Financial Intelligence

Department of Justice
- Counterterrorism training and resources for law enforcement
- Federal Bureau of Investigation—Counterterrorism
- FBI—Most Wanted Terrorists

Department of Homeland Security
- Coast Guard
- Customs and Border Protection (CBP)
- Directorate for Preparedness
- Immigration and Customs Enforcement
- Policy Directorate
- Research and Technology — Centers of Excellence
- Transportation Security Agency (TSA)
- U.S. Secret Service

SOURCE: Adapted from "U.S. Counterterrorism Team," in *U.S. Counterterrorism Team*, U.S. Department of State, 2006, http://www.state.gov/s/ct/team/(accessed August 11, 2008)

detect potential terrorists or other foreign agents and prevent them from carrying out harmful actions. If spying or a terrorist attack does occur, they investigate the incident and help capture those responsible. Table 2.8 provides a list of the main agencies that, along with the White House, the DOS, USAID, the DOD, and the IC, are considered part of the U.S. counterterrorism team.

Patriot Act

After the September 11, 2001, terrorist attacks, lawmakers quickly put together a new law designed to help the United States fight the terrorist threat. The Uniting and Strengthening America by Providing Appropriate Tools Required to Intercept and Obstruct Terrorism (USA PATRIOT) Act of 2001 is known simply as the Patriot Act. The act consists of ten titles:

- Title I—Enhancing Domestic Security against Terrorism
- Title II—Enhanced Surveillance Procedures
- Title III—International Money Laundering Abatement and Antiterrorist Financing Act of 2001
- Title IV—Protecting the Border
- Title V—Removing Obstacles to Investigating Terrorism
- Title VI—Providing for Victims of Terrorism, Public Safety Officers, and Their Families
- Title VII—Increased Information Sharing for Critical Infrastructure Protection
- Title VIII—Strengthening the Criminal Laws against Terrorism
- Title IX—Improved Intelligence
- Title X—Miscellaneous

One of the purposes of the act is to facilitate better cooperation and information sharing between government agencies, particularly between the IC and law enforcement agencies.

Law Enforcement Agencies

The law enforcement agencies making up the U.S. counterterrorism team fall under the U.S. Departments of the Treasury, Justice, and Homeland Security. (See Table 2.8.)

U.S. DEPARTMENT OF THE TREASURY. The U.S. Department of the Treasury contains two offices related to counterterrorism and counterintelligence. The Office of Foreign Assets Control (OFAC) oversees and enforces economic and trade sanctions that the United States places on foreign entities (countries, terrorists, criminals, and other individuals and organizations). In certain situations, this office can also freeze foreign assets held in the United States and wield control over foreign financial transactions taking place in the United States. As of August 2008, the OFAC had sanctions in place with thirteen countries. (See Table 2.9.)

The Office of Terrorism and Financial Intelligence combines intelligence and enforcement functions to protect the U.S. financial system against foreign threats, including rogue nations, narcotics traffickers, and terrorist financiers and money launderers.

U.S. DEPARTMENT OF JUSTICE. The primary agency of the U.S. Department of Justice (DOJ) devoted to counterterrorism and counterintelligence is the FBI. As mentioned earlier, the FBI focuses on threats posed by people and organizations physically located within the United States. John F. Fox explains in "The Birth of the Federal Bureau of Investigation: Office of Public/Congressional Affairs" (July 2003, http://www.fbi.gov/libref/historic/history/artspies/artspies.htm) that the FBI

TABLE 2.9

Sanction programs, August 2008

	Program last updated:
Balkans sanctions	03/04/2008
Belarus sanctions	05/20/2008
Burma sanctions	07/29/2008
Cote d'Ivoire (Ivory Coast) sanctions	09/19/2006
Cuba sanctions	08/01/2008
Democratic Republic of the Congo sanctions	03/30/2007
Iran sanctions	11/20/2007
Iraq sanctions	07/08/2008
Former Liberian Regime of Charles Taylor sanctions	05/23/2007
North Korea sanctions	06/26/2008
Sudan sanctions	07/31/2008
Syria sanctions	07/10/2008
Zimbabwe sanctions	07/25/2008

SOURCE: "OFAC Country Sanctions Programs," in *OFAC Country Sanctions Program*, U.S. Department of the Treasury, Office of Foreign Assets Control, August 2008, http://www.treas.gov/offices/enforcement/ofac/programs/ (accessed August 8, 2008)

was created in 1908 during the administration of President Theodore Roosevelt (1858–1919). Its primary focus was the investigation of a handful of federal crimes, such as land fraud. During World War I (1914–1918) the FBI acquired new responsibilities in counterintelligence, particularly the prevention of espionage and sabotage. One of the DOJ agents involved in this work was a young man named J. Edgar Hoover (1895–1972). In 1924 Hoover was appointed head of the FBI. It was a position he held until his death in 1972.

During the 1920s and 1930s the agency was preoccupied with gangsters and bank robbers. At the onset of World War II, the FBI once again took a key role in combating foreign spies. It was also granted power by President Franklin D. Roosevelt to investigate subversives (people who attempt to undermine or overthrow the government). Throughout the cold war the FBI considered Communist Party members and sympathizers within the United States a serious threat to national security. During the late 1960s a new element arose within American society that concerned the FBI. It was called "the new left" and included violent anti–Vietnam War, antiestablishment protestors and activists. Hoover established a massive surveillance program called the Counter Intelligence Program that would later arouse claims that the agency had violated the civil liberties of law-abiding Americans engaged in peaceful antiwar protests. During the 1970s new limits were placed on the FBI's abilities to conduct counterintelligence and domestic security investigations.

International terrorism became a priority for the nation as the cold war fizzled out. In 1986 Congress gave the FBI jurisdiction over terrorist acts committed against American citizens outside U.S. borders. The agency played a crucial role in investigating the bombings at the Khobar Towers in Saudi Arabia in 1996, the bombings at two U.S. embassies in East Africa in 1998, and a terrorist attack against the *USS Cole* in Yemen in 2000. The FBI also played a crucial role in investigating the terrorism bombing of the World Trade Center in 1993 and the terrorist attacks of September 11, 2001. The Patriot Act greatly expanded the FBI's role in counterterrorism by allowing broader use of surveillance techniques by intelligence agents.

U.S. DEPARTMENT OF HOMELAND SECURITY. The U.S. Department of Homeland Security was established by President George W. Bush (1946–) in 2002 and began operations in 2003. Major counterterrorist and counterintelligence agencies within this department are the Transportation Security Agency, the U.S. Coast Guard, the U.S. Customs and Border Protection, the U.S. Immigration and Customs Enforcement, and the U.S. Secret Service. (See Table 2.8.) The roles of these agencies are discussed at length in Chapter 5.

CHAPTER 3
INTERNATIONAL TERRORISM

In the late twentieth century international terrorism replaced the cold war as the United States' greatest national security concern. Terrorism is not new. It has plagued the world for centuries. What is different is the scope and reach of terrorist acts. In the past the vast majority of terrorist acts were committed by people with domestic or regional grievances. The terrorists had narrow agendas and limited resources for achieving them. This is no longer true. The goals and means of some terrorist groups have broadened considerably. The technological advancements that have made international travel and communication possible have made it easier for terrorists to extend their reach to all parts of the world. Likewise, their weapons and methods are much more sophisticated and deadly. The combination of all these factors has made the U.S. homeland a viable and attractive target for international terrorism.

WHAT IS TERRORISM?

Terrorism is not easily or universally defined. Within U.S. law and government agencies there are differing definitions of terrorism. In the U.S. Code, Title 22 (January 3, 2007, http://www4.law.cornell.edu/uscode/html/uscode22/usc_sup_01_22.html) focuses on foreign relations. Chapter 38, section 2656f(d) of that code provides the following definitions:

- Terrorism—"politically motivated violence perpetrated against noncombatant targets by subnational groups or clandestine agents"
- International terrorism—"terrorism involving citizens or the territory of more than 1 country."

One of the key components defining terrorism is its political nature. This excludes violence committed solely for financial gain, personal reasons, or other nonpolitical purposes. A second major component of terrorism is that noncombatants (civilians) are targeted. This distinguishes international terrorism from traditional war making in which official military forces are pitted against one another. Subnational means less than (or lower than) national. Clandestine means secret. By this definition, international terrorism is not perpetrated openly (as war would be) by the governments of nations. Instead, it is associated with lesser groups or with secret national agents.

FOREIGN TERRORIST ORGANIZATIONS

The Office of the Coordinator for Counterterrorism in the U.S. Department of State (DOS) identifies groups for designation as Foreign Terrorist Organizations (FTOs). This is a legal process, and any group deemed an FTO can challenge the designation in the U.S. Court of Appeals for the District of Columbia Circuit up to thirty days after the designation is published in the *Federal Register*. To be designated as an FTO, an organization must meet the following criteria:

- Be a foreign organization
- Engage in terrorist activity or terrorism as defined by federal law or retain the capability and intent to engage in terrorist activity or terrorism
- The terrorist activity of the organization threatens the security of Americans or the national defense, foreign relations, or economic interests of the United States

The most recent list of FTOs was compiled in April 2008 and listed forty-four organizations. (See Table 3.1.) It is illegal for any person who is in the United States or subject to U.S. jurisdiction to knowingly provide "material support or resources" to a designated FTO. U.S. financial institutions are required to take control over any funds in their possession that were deposited by an FTO or one of its agents and report the funds to the U.S. Department of the Treasury. Finally, alien members or

TABLE 3.1

Foreign Terrorist Organizations (FTOs) designated by the U.S. government, 2007

Name	Acronym or alias	Primary location	Note
Abu Nidal Organization	ANO	Iraq & Lebanon	Largely inactive
Abu Sayyaf Group		Philippines	Seeks Islamic state
Al-Aqsa Martyrs Brigade		Palestine	Seeks Palestinian state
Al-Qa'eda in Iraq	QJBR	Iraq	Seeks Islamic state
Al-Qa'eda in the Islamic Maghreb	AQIM		Seeks Islamic state
Ansar al-Sunnah		Iraq	Seeks Islamic state
Armed Islamic Group	GIA	Algeria	Seeks Islamic state
Asbat Al-Ansar		Lebanon	Seeks Islamic state
Aum Shinrikyo		Japan	Religious cult
Basque Fatherland and Liberty	ETA	Spain	Seeks Marxist state
Communist Party of the Philippines/New People's Army	CPP/NPA	Philippines	Seeks Communist state
Continuity Irish Republican Army		Ireland	Anti-British rule
Gama'a al-Islamiyya	Islamic Group	Egypt	Seeks Islamic state
HAMAS	Islamic Resistance Movement	Palestine	Seeks Islamic Palestinian state
Harakat ul-Mujahidin	HUM	Pakistan & Kashmir	Anti-Indian rule of Kashmir
Hezbollah	Party of God	Lebanon	Shia Islamic organization
Islamic Jihad Group		Central Asia	Seeks Islamic state
Islamic Movement of Uzbekistan	IMU	South Asia	Seeks Islamic state
Jaish-e-Mohammed	JEM or Army of Mohammed	Pakistan & Kashmir	Seeks to unite Kashmir & Pakistan
Jemaah Islamiya organization	JI	Indonesia	Seeks Islamic caliphate
al-Jihad		Egypt	Seeks Islamic state
Kahane Chai	Kach	Israel	Radical Jewish group
Kongra-Gel		Turkey & Iraq	Seeks Kurdish state
Lashkar-e Tayyiba	LT or Army of the Righteous	Pakistan & Kashmir	Anti-Indian rule of Kashmir
Lashkar i Jhangvi	LJ	Pakistan	Islamic militants
Liberation Tigers of Tamil Eelam	LTTE	Sri Lanka	Seeks Tamil state
Libyan Islamic Fighting Group	LIFG	Libya	Opposes Qadhafi regime
Moroccan Islamic Combatant Group	GICM	Morocco	Seeks Islamic state
Mujahedin-e Khalq Organization	MEK	Iran	Opposes Iranian regime
National Liberation Army	ELN	Colombia	Seeks Marxist state
Palestine Liberation Front	PLF	Lebanon	Seeks Palestinian state
Palestinian Islamic Jihad	PIJ	Palestine	Seeks Palestinian state
Popular Front for the Liberation of Palestine	PFLP	Syria & Lebanon	Seeks Palestinian state
PFLP-General Command	PFLP-GC	Syria	Seeks Palestinian state
al-Qa'eda		Middle East	Seeks worldwide Islamic caliphate
Real IRA	RIRA	Ireland	Anti-British rule
Revolutionary Armed Forces of Colombia	FARC	Colombia	Anti-Colombian government
Revolutionary Nuclei	RN, formerly ELA	Greece	Largely inactive
Revolutionary Organization 17 November	17N	Greece	Radical leftist group
Revolutionary People's Liberation Party/Front	DHKP/C	Turkey	Seeks Marxist state
Shining Path	SL or Sendero Luminoso	Peru	Seeks Communist state
United Self-Defense Forces of Colombia	AUC	Colombia	Largely inactive

SOURCE: Adapted from "Terrorist Organizations," in *Country Reports on Terrorism, 2007*, U.S. Department of State, April 2008, http://www.state.gov/documents/organization/105904.pdf (accessed July 29, 2008)

representatives of an FTO are not allowed to enter the United States and, in some cases, can be deported.

STRUCTURE OF A TERRORIST ORGANIZATION

There are five major components of a terrorist organization (see Figure 3.1):

- Underlying conditions—these are social, economic, religious, and political factors that provide the base for terrorist tendencies to take root and grow. Examples include poverty, government corruption and oppression, and ethnic and religious conflicts.
- International environment—the world has become a more accessible place. Widespread modes of transportation and communication allow terrorists to travel, plan, and coordinate attacks with greater sophistication. There has been a general trend toward more open national borders, particularly in Europe. Poorer countries lack the resources (and sometimes the political will) to completely guard their borders. All these factors facilitate the ease of movement for terrorists.
- States—some countries provide physical safe havens for terrorist organizations, allowing them to live and train within their territories. Terrorists also benefit from nations that facilitate or ignore organization activities, such as fund-raising or buying weapons. In "State Sponsors of Terrorism" (February 4, 2005, http://www.state.gov/s/ct/c14151.htm), the DOS lists five countries—Cuba, Iran, North Korea, Sudan, and Syria—that the United States considers to be terrorist sponsors. (See Table 3.2.) The United States claims these countries "have repeatedly provided support for acts of international terrorism," as defined under the Export Administration Act, the Arms Export Control Act, and the Foreign Assistance Act.

FIGURE 3.1

Structure of terrorism

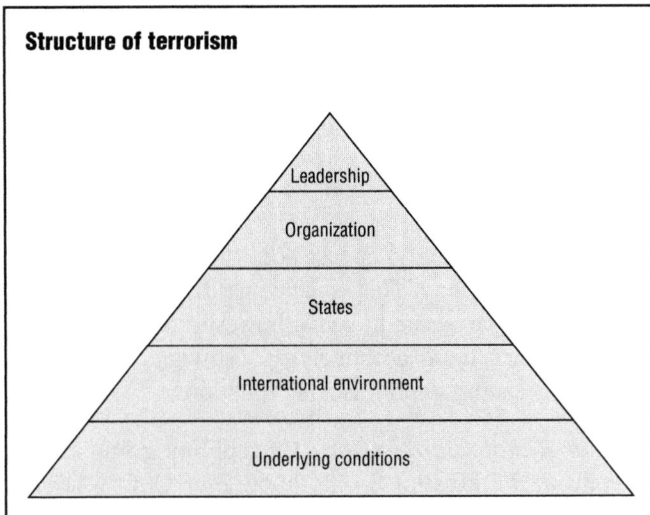

SOURCE: "Figure 1. The Structure of Terror," in *National Strategy for Combating Terrorism*, U.S. Department of State, February 2003, http://www.state.gov/documents/organization/60172.pdf (accessed August 11, 2008)

TABLE 3.2

Countries identified by U.S. government as state sponsors of terrorism, by date of designation

Country	Designation date
Cuba	March 1,1982
Iran	January 19, 1984
North Korea	January 20, 1988
Sudan	August 12, 1993
Syria	December 29, 1979

SOURCE: *State Sponsors of Terrorism*, U.S. Department of State, February 4, 2005, http://www.state.gov/s/ct/c14151.htm (accessed August 9, 2008)

- Organization—the three previously mentioned structural elements provide a foundation that allows terrorist groups to recruit, plan, organize, train, raise money, hide from justice, arm themselves, and launch attacks.
- Leadership—the leaders of a terrorist organization develop strategies and provide directions that link all the supporting factors together. Some organizations are based on a strong military-style hierarchy, where the loss of leadership can seriously damage or even destroy the organization's capabilities. Other groups use a looser structure based on a network of cells that may have some individual power to make decisions and launch attacks. For these organizations, the loss of top leaders may not be as devastating to the overall structure.

ROOTS OF MODERN TERRORISM

Throughout U.S. history there have been incidents of politically motivated violence directed against civilians. During the late 1800s and early 1900s there were a number of such incidents. One of the most famous attacks occurred on September 16, 1920, when a bomb exploded in a horse-drawn wagon in the financial district of New York City, killing dozens of people. The crime was never solved. Like similar acts of the era, this one was blamed on radical political activists with left-wing ideologies, such as socialism, communism, or anarchism. (Anarchy is a belief that governments should not exist.)

Terrorism in the early twentieth century was much more common in Europe because of political conflicts within and between the countries there. World War I (1914–1918) was triggered when Franz Ferdinand (1863–1914), the Archduke of Austria, was assassinated by Serbian nationalists while visiting the city of Sarajevo, which was then a part of Serbia in the Balkans.

MOTIVATIONS OF TERRORISM

Nationalism has been a frequent inspiration for terrorism and is driven by people desiring to remove their government or drive out an occupying power. The Palestinian cause has become a rallying point for many militant radicals in the Middle East. Disillusioned Palestinians and their supporters have used terrorism against Israel and the world at large to push their agenda for statehood. As of 2007, there were six FTOs devoted specifically to the Palestinian cause. (See Table 3.1.)

As defined under U.S. law, terrorism is "politically motivated violence." As such, religion is not considered a major motivator driving terrorist acts. However, most FTOs support causes or peoples associated with one faith: Islam. (See Table 3.1.) Examples include struggles for statehood and opposition to prevailing governments in Palestine and various countries in the Middle East and South Asia, particularly the Philippines, Iraq, Algeria, Lebanon, Egypt, Indonesia, Pakistan, and Morocco.

Exceptions include FTOs pursuing nationalist causes in Spain, the Philippines, Ireland, Sri Lanka, Colombia, Greece, Turkey, and Peru. Many of these terrorist organizations have agendas grounded in socialism, Marxism, and communism. Some nationalist struggles have religious dimensions. For example, the Irish FTOs are linked to a struggle between political factions divided over Northern Ireland's inclusion in the United Kingdom. These factions are also split along religious lines, with one side predominantly Catholic and the other predominantly Protestant. In addition, there are religion-based FTOs in Japan and Israel.

Islamic Connection

The notes in Table 3.1 indicate that many FTOs seek an Islamic state or caliphate. A caliphate is a geopolitical area spanning the territory of many countries, all under the rule of an Islamic leader called a caliph. The Muslim

Student Association explains in "The Rightly-Guided Caliphs" (2008, http://www.usc.edu/dept/MSA/politics/firstfourcaliphs.html) that there have been four "rightly-guided" caliphs—Abu Bakr (c. 573–634), Umar (c. 586–644), Uthman (c. 574–656), and Ali (c. 600–661)—all of whom lived during the seventh century. Some Muslim leaders since that time have called themselves caliphs, most recently the sultans of the Ottoman Empire, which was broken up after World War I. At the height of its geopolitical power in the thirteenth century, the Islamic world encompassed a broad swath of land from Southeast Asia, across the Middle East and North Africa, and into westernmost Europe (modern-day Spain). However, this area was fractured politically and under the rule of various Muslim factions that were not unified under a single caliph.

There are two main branches within Islam: Shia and Sunni. In *A Country Study: Iraq* (November 8, 2005, http://lcweb2.loc.gov/frd/cs/iqtoc.html), the U.S. Library of Congress indicates that the primary difference between the two divisions concerns the leadership of the caliph. Shiites believe that Ali and his descendants are the only rightful heirs to lead the caliphate. Sunnis support a broader interpretation of who can be the caliph. In addition, there are other theological differences between the two branches. All these differences have contributed to historical civil wars and to modern conflicts between the two factions.

SALAFISM. Within the Sunni branch of Islam there is a belief system called Salafism that has been closely associated with some of the most violent FTOs. Salafism is variously described as a fundamentalist, traditionalist, or orthodox approach to Islam. The growth of this religious movement during the twentieth century is detailed in the Canadian Broadcasting Company documentary *War without Borders* (December 1, 2004, http://www.cbc.ca/fifth/warwithoutborders/salafist.html). It should be noted that the media often use the term *wahhabi* to refer to the Salafist branch of Islam. This word is derived from the name of an eighteenth-century Arab named Muhammad ibn Abd-al-Wahhab (1703–1792), who was a well-known Salafist scholar.

According to *War without Borders*, the Salafist movement seeks to practice Islam as it was practiced by its earliest followers during the eighth century. Salafists believe that Islam has been misinterpreted and misapplied since that time. There is a minority within this faction that champions a revolutionary style of Salafism in which violence is considered justifiable to re-create the Islamic caliphates of ages past.

Revolutionary Salafism has its roots in an organization called the Muslim Brotherhood that began in Egypt in 1928. Originally dedicated to education and social reform, it evolved into a political organization that embraced terrorism during the 1940s. Over the following decades the Muslim Brotherhood adopted as its spiritual leader the Egyptian intellectual Sayyid Qutb (1906–1966). Qutb became a major proponent of Islamism (a belief that governments should operate in strict accordance with Islamic law). He had briefly attended college in the United States during the 1940s and was highly critical of the "debauchery" in American society. Qutb advocated the use of violence, particularly against non-Muslims, in the quest for an Islamist society. This violence has been called a jihad (holy war) by the Western media; however, the Arabic term *jihad* translates more accurately as "struggle" and has a variety of meanings within Islamic tradition.

War without Borders notes that splinter groups broke away from the Muslim Brotherhood after Qutb was executed in 1966 by the Egyptian government. These groups have embraced the concepts of revolutionary Salafism and the use of violent jihad, even against fellow Muslims deemed to be less than true believers. The most well known of these groups are Takfir wal-Hijra, which was largely wiped out during the 1970s; the Egyptian Islamic Jihad; and al Qaeda. During the late 1980s the latter two groups merged under the leadership of Osama bin Laden (1957–), a wealthy man from a prominent Saudi family. The ultimate goal of al Qaeda is to destroy the "near enemy" (governments of the region considered non-Islamist) and the "far enemy" (the West, particularly the United States) to re-create the caliphate. Figure 3.2 shows the area the U.S. government believes that bin Laden wishes to include in an Islamic caliphate.

FIGURE 3.2

Map of area U.S. officials believe that Osama bin Laden wishes to make into pan-Islamic caliphate

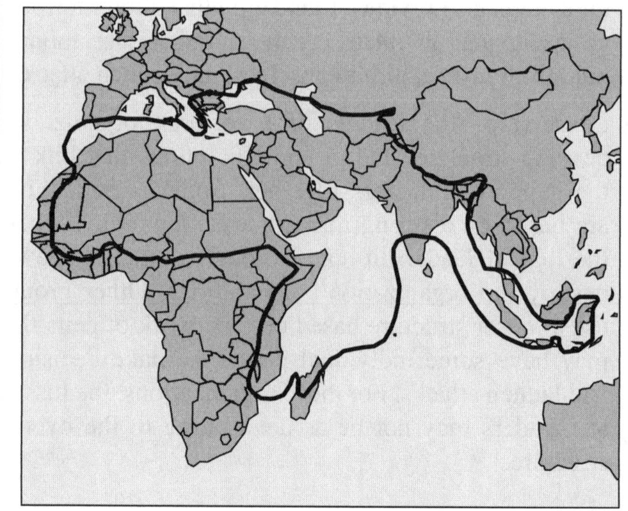

SOURCE: "Bin Ladin's 'Pan-Islamic Caliphate'," in *Counterterrorism Calendar, 2008*, National Counterterrorism Center, 2008, http://www.nctc.gov/docs/ct_calendar_2008.pdf (accessed August 2, 2008)

MAJOR TERRORIST ORGANIZATIONS

Some of the FTOs listed in Table 3.1 have ceased to be major participants in terrorist attacks. In some cases this is because of cease-fires or other political agreements that have dampened violent opposition. For example, the FTOs operating in Ireland have been relatively inactive since the late 1990s because of peace agreements accepted by most parties involved in the conflict. Extremely hierarchal FTOs have diminished in power following the deaths of their leaders. This occurred within the Abu Nidal organization after the 2002 death of its leader in Iraq.

As of September 2008, the FTOs of most interest to the United States were those that had a major influence on political events in the Middle East and/or posed the greatest threat to U.S. interests. The three most prominent groups that are described in this chapter are based on information from the Office of the Coordinator for Counterterrorism's *Country Reports on Terrorism 2007* (April 2008, http://www.state.gov/s/ct/rls/crt/2007/).

Hamas

Hamas is an acronym for Harakat al-Muqawama al-Islamiya, meaning "Islamic Resistance Movement." Its primary area of operation is in Palestine, where it seeks to install an Islamic state. Hamas evolved from the Muslim Brotherhood and has used both political and terrorist methods to pursue its goals. These two functions are carried out by different divisions within the organization. Terrorist activities are associated with the Izz al-Din al-Qassam Brigades of paramilitary fighters.

According to the Office of the Coordinator for Counterterrorism, the Hamas brigades have conducted many terrorist attacks, including suicide bombings, against civilian and military targets in Israel but have not directly attacked U.S. interests. The overall policy for the FTO is determined by decision makers based in Damascus, Syria.

Hamas is believed to have tens of thousands of supporters and sympathizers. Its activities are chiefly funded through donations collected from Palestinians living around the world and from wealthy private individuals in Saudi Arabia and other Arab countries. The FTO's popularity in Palestine is attributed in large part to its social and charitable works, including schools, medical clinics, and youth camps. As mentioned in Chapter 1, Hamas members were elected in sufficient numbers during the January 2006 elections to take over majority control of the Palestinian National Authority (PNA)—the existing governing body in Palestine. Hamas attacks against Israel dramatically decreased following the election, until June 2006, when Hamas forces attacked a group of Israeli soldiers, killing two and kidnapping another. In response, Israel imposed strict travel and economic sanctions against Palestinians in the Gaza Strip. In 2007 a military-type coup by Hamas forces routed PNA from the Gaza Strip. Hamas unofficially seized control of the area and continued to wage bomb and rocket attacks against Israeli targets. In mid-2008 a cease-fire agreement was reached with Israel in exchange for lifting the economic and travel restrictions in the Gaza Strip.

Hezbollah

In English Hezbollah means "Party of God." Hezbollah is a powerful organization based in Lebanon and consists of Shiites (adherents to Shia Islam). It also calls itself Islamic Jihad or Islamic Jihad for the Liberation of Palestine. Hezbollah emerged in Lebanon following Israel's invasion of that nation in 1982. The organization has strong ties to Iran because of the latter's predominantly Shiite population. Lebanon also contains a majority Shiite population. Until early 2006 Hezbollah was also closely associated with Syria. That relationship cooled after Syrian agents were implicated in the assassination of the Lebanese prime minister Rafiq Hariri (1944–2005) in 2005.

Hezbollah is blamed for a number of terrorist attacks against Israeli and U.S. interests, including some of the most notorious incidents of the 1980s and 1990s. Specifically, U.S. officials believe Hezbollah agents bombed U.S. embassy buildings and U.S. Marine facilities in Lebanon in 1983 and 1984, killing over 300 Americans; hijacked TWA Flight 847 in 1985 and killed a U.S. Navy diver aboard the plane; and participated in the 1996 bombing of the Khobar Towers (a housing facility for U.S. military personnel) in Saudi Arabia, during which 19 Americans were killed and 515 injured.

Lebanon bounds Israel to the north. During the middle of the first decade of the 2000s the Lebanese government allowed Hezbollah militias to essentially take control of southern Lebanon, ostensibly to guard against an Israeli attack. There were many skirmishes between the militias and Israeli military forces. In July 2006 Hezbollah agents crossed the border and kidnapped two Israeli soldiers. In response, Israel conducted air strikes and fired missiles against a variety of targets in Lebanon, before launching a ground invasion. Likewise, Hezbollah fired hundreds of rockets into Israel. Following approximately a month of fighting, a cease-fire was brokered by the United Nations (UN). It called for the withdrawal of Israeli troops from Lebanon and the disarming of Hezbollah fighters. According to the Office of the Coordinator for Counterterrorism, Hezbollah did reduce its military presence in southern Lebanon in 2007. However, it is believed to maintain caches of weapons in the area.

Al Qaeda

The FTO called al Qaeda, meaning "the foundation" or "the base," gained prominence during the 1990s as a sophisticated and well-funded organization capable of conducting terrorist attacks around the world, including on U.S. soil. Its members are predominantly Sunni and include some devoted adherents of Salafism. The FTO's original name was the International Front for Fighting Jews and Crusaders.

Al Qaeda was founded in 1988 by bin Laden. He followed the precepts of the Muslim Brotherhood and believed that violence was a necessary tool for ridding Muslim lands of unbelievers. During the 1980s he had fought against Soviet forces occupying Afghanistan. Following the Soviet withdrawal, he united and trained his fighters to wage war against regional regimes he considered non-Islamist and against Israel and the United States. The rise to power of bin Laden and al Qaeda are described at length by the National Commission on Terrorist Attacks upon the United States in *The 9/11 Commission Report* (2004, http://www.9-11commission.gov/report/911Report.pdf).

In 1991 bin Laden left Saudi Arabia and set up his organization in Sudan in northern Africa. From there he moved to Afghanistan in 1996. Throughout the 1990s bin Laden issued statements urging Muslims around the world to kill Americans and their allies. In 1998 he and his cohorts published a fatwa in an Arabic-language newspaper in London. (A fatwa is an interpretation of Islamic law usually written by a scholar or religious authority.) Al Qaeda's fatwa declared war on the United States. According to *Frontline* (May 1998, http://www.pbs.org/wgbh/pages/frontline/shows/binladen/who/interview.html), bin Laden said during an interview with an ABC reporter: "We believe that the worst thieves in the world today and the worst terrorists are the Americans.... We do not have to differentiate between military or civilian. As far as we are concerned, they are all targets."

By 1998 bin Laden had consolidated his power within al Qaeda and raised sufficient funds to launch carefully planned and directed attacks against U.S. interests. The organization was not strictly hierarchal in structure but featured a network of semi-independent cells of followers. Between 1998 and 2001 al Qaeda agents conducted a series of stunning terrorist attacks: in 1998 bombings at two U.S. embassies in Africa killed more than two hundred people and injured another five thousand; in 2000 the bombing of the USS *Cole* in Yemen killed seventeen Americans and wounded thirty-nine others; and in 2001 more than twenty-nine hundred people were killed when hijackers crashed three airplanes into both towers of the World Trade Center in New York City and the Pentagon in Washington, D.C., and a fourth airplane crashed in Pennsylvania.

Following the September 11, 2001 (9/11), terrorist attacks, the U.S. military invaded Afghanistan and killed, captured, or chased into hiding many of al Qaeda's leaders. Bin Laden eluded detection, and as of September 2008 remained at large. Even though al Qaeda's organization and capabilities were initially disrupted by the U.S. invasion, the FTO regained much of its strength with help from friendly tribal leaders across the border in western Pakistan. The U.S. Office of the Coordinator for Counterterrorism notes in *Country Reports on Terrorism 2007* that al Qaeda has regained much of its operational capabilities, has replaced its captured or killed operatives, and has restored some centralized control over the organization. It is believed that al Qaeda's planning and operational leadership has been taken over by Ayman al-Zawahiri (1951–), a former physician from Egypt. Bin Laden is called the group's ideological figurehead.

Following the 2003 invasion of Iraq, a terrorist group led by the Jordanian Abu Musab al-Zarqawi (1966–2006) renamed itself al Qaeda in Iraq and launched a massive campaign of violence against allied troops, foreign workers and journalists, and Iraqi civilians. The group conducted many kidnappings, beheadings, and suicide bombings as part of the insurgency (resistance) movement. The killing of al-Zarqawi in a U.S. bombing raid in 2006 helped dampen the power and capabilities of the FTO. It was further weakened throughout 2007 and early 2008 by U.S. military operations conducted in Iraq with help from that nation's military forces, tribal leaders, and civilians.

In 2006 and 2007 two North African terrorist groups merged with al Qaeda: the Algerian Salafist Group for Preaching and Combat, which renamed itself al Qaeda in the Islamic Maghreb (AQIM), and the Libyan Islamic Fight Group. Maghreb is a geographical region that encompasses much of North Africa and generally includes Morocco, Algeria, and Tunisia. AQIM has been blamed for numerous suicide bombing attacks against Algerian government workers and civilians and a December 2007 attack against the UN headquarters in Algeria. Even though al Qaeda's influence grows in northern Africa, FTO operations in the eastern African nation of Somalia have been crippled by the military forces of the African Union (AU). The AU is an organization of African nations dedicated to strengthening Africa's economic and political role in the world.

WHY DID THE UNITED STATES BECOME A TARGET?

The United States has become a target of international terrorism for a variety of reasons. Many FTOs blame U.S. foreign policy for the continuing Palestinian problem and resent long-standing U.S. support for Israel. In addition, there has been the United States' historical support for governments in the Middle East considered corrupt and oppressive. Finally, the U.S. invasion and occupation of Afghanistan and Iraq (both predominantly Muslim countries) have fueled terrorist responses. These are the factors most often named by FTOs that target U.S. interests around the world.

Israel-Palestine Conflict

The United States has always had a special bond with Israel. These ties were forged soon after Israel was founded in 1948. The cold war was just beginning, and the United States found itself with few allies outside of Western Europe. A democratic pro-U.S. government was seen as a huge asset amid the unfriendly regimes dominating the Middle East. Carol Migdalovitz of the Congressional Research Service describes in *Israel: Background and Relations with the United States* (June 6, 2008, http://www.fas.org/sgp/crs/mideast/RL33476.pdf) the U.S.-Israeli relationship as "a close friendship based on common democratic values, religious affinities, and security interests."

Migdalovitz notes that Israel was the largest recipient of U.S. foreign aid for more than two decades, from the late 1970s to the late 1990s. U.S. administrations have worked for decades to push negotiations between Israel and its enemies to resolve the Palestinian problem and other issues. President Jimmy Carter (1924–) mediated a 1979 peace treaty between Israel and Egypt. During the 1990s Israel and Palestine negotiated on many occasions at the urging of President Bill Clinton (1946–). These meetings culminated in an offer in 2000 from Israel for an independent Palestinian state composed of most of the West Bank and all the Gaza Strip. The Palestinian leadership rejected the offer.

In February 2008 the Gallup Organization conducted a poll in which it asked participants if they believed that Israel and Palestine will one day be able to live in peace. A majority (59%) of those asked thought that such a scenario is not possible. (See Figure 3.3.) Another 39% of respondents indicated optimism for peace between the two factions that have been unofficially at war for more than fifty years.

FIGURE 3.3

Public opinion on whether Israel and the Arab nations will ever achieve peace, February 2008

DO YOU THINK THERE WILL OR WILL NOT COME A TIME WHEN ISRAEL AND THE ARAB NATIONS WILL BE ABLE TO SETTLE THEIR DIFFERENCES AND LIVE IN PEACE?

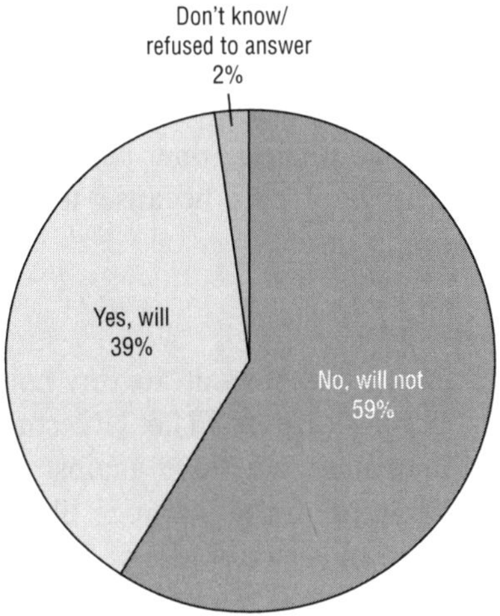

SOURCE: Adapted from "Question qn32. Do You Think There Will or Will Not Come a Time When Israel and the Arab Nations Will Be Able to Settle Their Differences and Live in Peace?" in *Gallup Poll Social Series: World Affairs*, The Gallup Organization, February 2008, http://brain.gallup.com/documents/questionnaire.aspx?STUDY=P0802010 (accessed August 8, 2008). Copyright © 2008 by The Gallup Organization. Reproduced by permission of The Gallup Organization.

Cold War Politics and Their Legacy

During the cold war, the U.S. government's premier foreign policy goal was to stop the spread of communism from the Soviet Union. The United States sometimes supported oppressive, nondemocratic governments in other countries when it believed the alternative was for them to become dominated by communists or otherwise ally themselves with the Soviet Union. Such support was often criticized as betraying American ideals and could lead to resentment of the United States among the oppressed population of these countries.

THE SHAH OF IRAN. U.S. support for the Iranian shah Mohammad Reza Pahlavi (1919–1980) until his ouster in 1979 was strongly resented by most of the Iranian population. James Risen reports in "Secrets of History: The C.I.A. in Iran" (*New York Times*, April 16, 2000) that the Central Intelligence Agency (CIA) helped initiate a military coup in Iran in 1953 that put a pro-U.S. government into power. Even though widely suspected in Iran, U.S. involvement in Iran was kept secret from the American people for nearly half a century.

According to Risen, the CIA cooperated with British intelligence agents and the shah and his supporters to oust the elected Prime Minister Mohammad Mosaddeq (1882–1967; who served under the shah, but wielded great power) and install a new prime minister with pro-British and pro-U.S. leanings. The plot was driven by economic and political factors. Mosaddeq tried to nationalize Iran's oil supplies, which had been under the control of the British since World War II (1939–1945). U.S. involvement was based on fears of the powerful Communist Party within Iran and Mosaddeq's alleged socialist sympathies. The coup proceeded poorly, but was ultimately successful at installing a puppet prime minister and consolidating the shah's power.

Western interference in Iran's government became a rallying cry for radicals who accused the shah of oppressing his people and stealing oil profits. Risen notes that U.S. involvement in the 1953 coup resulted in "a generation of anti-American hatred in one of the Middle East's most powerful countries." In 1979 the shah was overthrown during a revolution that put the conservative

Islamic cleric Ayatollah Ruhollah Khomeini (1900–1989) into power. The United States was caught off guard by the revolution and did not evacuate the U.S. embassy in Iran. Shortly thereafter, dozens of Americans were captured by Iranian militants and held hostage for more than a year—an incident that further damaged U.S.-Iranian relations. Diplomatic relations between the two nations were severed, and both governments have vilified (spread negative information about) one another ever since. During the 1980s the United States provided support to another dictatorship, that of Saddam Hussein (1937–2006) in Iraq, in part because it saw Iraq as a useful ally against Iran.

U.S. Wars with Iraq

In 1990 Iraq invaded Kuwait, its tiny neighbor to the south, over a border dispute. The UN condemned the action and implemented sanctions against Iraq. In 1991 a U.S.-led coalition of military forces liberated Kuwait from Iraqi forces in only six weeks of fighting.

Saudi Arabia was a member of the coalition that opposed Iraq and worked closely with the United States during the war. This relationship was to have many consequences. Saudi Arabia is the birthplace of Muhammad (c. 570–632) and contains many sites considered sacred by Muslims. The Saudi rulers allowed U.S. troops to set up bases within the kingdom during the war, greatly angering some Muslims. The U.S.-Saudi collaboration became an issue of contention for Islamic radicals and Islamists. In his 1998 fatwa against the United States, bin Laden pointed to the collaboration as proof that the Saudi regime was non-Islamic and illegitimate. The United States maintained military bases in Saudi Arabia for more than a decade after the war ended.

In 2003 the United States invaded Iraq again as part of its War on Terror. The U.S. intelligence community claimed that Iraq had collaborated with al Qaeda and was amassing weapons of mass destruction, but these claims would later prove false. The U.S. military operation in Iraq enjoyed initial successes, with Hussein ousted from power and a more democratic government installed. A strong insurgency manifested, however, driven by Hussein supporters and militant elements opposed to the occupation, and eventually the violence grew into a deadly civil struggle between Iraqi factions divided by religious and political differences. (See Chapter 4.) The United States' involvement in Iraq deepened anti-American sentiments.

NOTABLE TERRORIST ACTS AND ATTEMPTS

Palestinian resistance groups have been responsible for many acts of terrorism since the founding of Israel in 1948. Until the 1960s these acts were largely restricted to areas within Israel and the Palestinian territories. The emergence of the Palestine Liberation Organization and various splinter groups changed the dynamics of terrorism, giving it a more international reach. Airline hijackings became a vexing problem throughout the region. Palestinian militants also ventured frequently into Western Europe to carry out terrorist acts.

Except for diplomatic personnel, Americans were not usually the target of terrorist attacks before the 1980s. This changed dramatically after the 1982 invasion of Lebanon by Israel. Israeli forces withdrew in 1983 and were replaced by international forces that included U.S. troops. This precipitated a number of deadly attacks against Americans in Lebanon and other nations. Kidnappings of U.S. citizens in Lebanon also became common; however, most victims were eventually released unharmed. By the end of the decade airline hijackings around the world had largely been eliminated because of heightened airport security.

During the early 1990s international terrorists began striking on U.S. soil. In 1993 there were two such attacks: an ambush at CIA headquarters in Virginia by a lone gunman and a bombing at the World Trade Center in New York City. Within the next few years the al Qaeda terrorist network under bin Laden became a major force in international terrorism and began specifically targeting U.S. interests worldwide. On 9/11 members of this network hijacked and commandeered four American airliners. Three of the airplanes were purposely flown into buildings: the Pentagon in Washington, D.C., and both towers of the World Trade Center in New York City. The fourth plane crashed in Pennsylvania, after a struggle between the hijackers and the passengers. In total, nearly three thousand people were killed in the one-day attacks.

The United States responded by declaring a War on Terror. U.S. military forces subsequently invaded Afghanistan and Iraq. This precipitated many acts of terrorism against natives and U.S. civilians in these countries by militants. A hallmark of twenty-first-century terrorism has been suicide bombings, which were relatively uncommon before this time.

The Most Serious Terrorist Incidents

Various media sources, private organizations, and government agencies maintain lists of some of the thousands of terrorist acts that have occurred around the world over the past few decades. The DOS features a listing in "Significant Terrorist Incidents, 1961–2003: A Brief Chronology" (March 2004, http://www.state.gov/r/pa/ho/pubs/fs/5902.htm). The following are only a few of the events mentioned by the DOS that have had major effects in terms of U.S. casualties or influence on U.S. foreign policy and public opinion:

- Olympic Games, Munich, Germany (1972)—Palestinian terrorists seized eleven Israeli athletes, nine of which were subsequently killed. West German authorities launched a bungled rescue attempt as the terrorists attempted to leave the country with their hostages. The Black September group was blamed for this terrorist incident.

- Air France Airliner, Entebbe, Uganda (1976)—terrorists hijacked a plane containing 258 passengers and forced it to land in Entebbe. Israeli commandos infiltrated Uganda and rescued the hostages. The terrorists were members of the German right-wing organization Baader-Meinfhof and the Popular Front for the Liberation of Palestine.
- U.S. embassy, Tehran, Iran (1979–81)—sixty-six American diplomatic personnel were held hostage in the embassy by militant Iranian students supported by the conservative Islamic government of Ayatollah Khomeini. All hostages were eventually released unharmed.
- U.S. embassy, Beirut, Lebanon (1983)—the Islamic Jihad claimed responsibility for bombing the embassy. The attack killed 63 people and injured 120.
- U.S. Marine Barracks, Beirut, Lebanon (1983)—Islamic Jihad claimed responsibility for a bombing that killed 242 Americans. Fifty-eight French troops were killed in a similar attack on a French military compound.
- Restaurant, Torrejon, Spain (1984)—Hezbollah claimed responsibility for a bomb that killed eighteen U.S. servicemen and injured eighty-three.
- TWA Airliner (1985)—Lebanese Hezbollah terrorists hijacked the flight and held it for seventeen days, forcing it to fly to and from various airports around the Middle East. The terrorists killed an American hostage, a sailor in the U.S. Navy.
- *Achille Lauro* Cruise Liner (1985)—terrorists with the Palestine Liberation Front seized the cruise liner on the Mediterranean Sea with more than seven hundred hostages aboard. An American passenger in a wheelchair was thrown overboard.
- Discotheque, Berlin, Germany (1986)—Libyan terrorists bombed a nightclub popular with U.S. soldiers. Two solders were killed and seventy-nine were injured.
- Pan Am Flight 103 (1988)—Libyan terrorists placed a bomb on the plane that exploded in flight over Lockerbie, Scotland. All 259 passengers and a number of people on the ground were killed.
- World Trade Center (1993)—a car bomb explosion in the underground garage killed six people and injured approximately one thousand. U.S. authorities blamed the followers of an Egyptian cleric living in the United States: Omar Abdel-Rahman (1938–).
- Khobar Towers, Dhahran, Saudi Arabia (1996)—several terrorist groups claimed responsibility for bombing a housing facility for U.S. troops. Nineteen U.S. military personnel were killed and 515 were wounded.
- U.S. embassies, Nairobi, Kenya, and Dar es Salaam, Tanzania (1998)—bombs exploded nearly simultaneously at the embassies, killing 301 people and injuring thousands. The terrorist group al Qaeda, led by bin Laden, was blamed for the attacks.
- USS *Cole*, Aden, Yemen (2000)—a small explosives-laden boat rammed the U.S. destroyer and killed seventeen American personnel and wounded thirty-nine. Members of al Qaeda were blamed for the incident.
- World Trade Center, New York City, and Pentagon, Washington, D.C. (2001)—three hijacked planes piloted by terrorists were flown into these buildings, killing nearly three thousand people, primarily Americans. A fourth plane crashed before reaching its target, and all aboard were killed. Members of al Qaeda were blamed for the attacks.
- Nightclubs in Bali, Indonesia (2002)—an FTO linked to al Qaeda conducted bombings that killed 202 people, mostly foreign tourists.

Two more recent terrorist events are also notable:

- Trains in Madrid, Spain (2004)—the Moroccan Islamic Combatant Group, an FTO linked to al Qaeda, bombed several commuter trains during morning rush hour. Nearly two hundred people were killed and hundreds more injured.
- Subway and bus in London, England (2005)—suicide bombers struck the mass transit system in different locations during morning rush hour. More than fifty people were killed and hundreds injured. According to *Report of the Official Account of the Bombings in London on 7th July 2005* (May 11, 2006, http://www.official-documents.co.uk/document/hc0506/hc10/1087/1087.pdf) by the British government, the bombings were carried out by four young Muslim men with extremist views. The primary motivation was believed to be "perceived injustices carried out by the West against Muslims."

THWARTED ATTEMPTS. Besides the completed terrorist acts described here, there have been several notable unsuccessful attempts since the 1990s in which the terrorists were thwarted by law enforcement or otherwise failed to complete their missions. In "Convicted Bomb Conspirator Linked to Plots" (September 20, 2001, http://archives.cnn.com/2001/US/09/18/inv.yousef.background/index.html), Phil Hirschkorn reports that in 1994 a terrorist cell in the Philippines led by the Pakistani Ramsi Yousef (1968–) was preparing to bomb nearly a dozen airliners bound from Asia to the United States and to assassinate the pope. The plan was discovered when the bomb makers accidentally set their apartment on fire and fled the building. Police recovered a laptop computer containing important evidence at the scene and captured one of Yousef's companions. Yousef was the mastermind behind the 1993 bombing of the World Trade Center and the nephew of Khalid Sheikh Mohammed (1964–)—a top al Qaeda figure believed to have overseen the 9/11 terrorist attacks. Both men were eventually captured by law enforcement.

According to the article "Ahmed Ressam: The Would-Be Millennium Bomber" (CBC News, July 27, 2005), in December 1999 Ahmed Ressam (1967–) was caught trying to enter Port Angeles, Washington, near a Canadian border crossing, with a car full of explosives. Authorities believe the man was acting under al Qaeda orders to bomb targets during New Year's Eve celebrations.

In December 2001 a Briton named Richard Reid (1973–) was on a commercial airliner flying from Paris to Miami when he tried to set off explosives hidden in his shoes. He was thwarted and overpowered by people aboard the plane and turned over to authorities. Reid was dubbed by the media as the "shoe bomber."

In "Sorting through the Terror Plot" (*Newsday*, August 13, 2006), Les Payne reports that in August 2006 British police captured two dozen suspects in England accused of planning to blow up as many as ten planes bound from Europe to the United States. The plot centered on the use of liquid explosives hidden in carry-on items, such as sports drinks.

9/11 Terrorist Attacks

For many Americans and people around the globe, the events of 9/11 were the most stunning terrorist attacks. In one day nineteen individuals managed to kill more than twenty-nine hundred people and completely destroy the World Trade Center—a center of international commerce and symbol of U.S. economic power. In 2002 Congress and President George W. Bush (1946–) created the National Commission on Terrorist Attacks on the United States to investigate all the circumstances relating to the terrorist attacks. For nearly two years the commission reviewed relevant documents and interviewed more than one thousand people as part of its investigation. In 2004 its findings were published in the *9/11 Commission Report*.

The report uses data and information collected from a variety of sources to re-create the events leading up to and occurring on and after 9/11. On the morning of the attacks the nineteen terrorists boarded four separate commercial airliners bound from the East Coast to the West Coast. Less than an hour after takeoff of each plane, the hijackers overpowered the cockpit crews and assumed piloting control. Figure 3.4, Figure 3.5, Figure 3.6, and Figure 3.7 show the flight paths of each commandeered plane. American Airlines Flight 11 and United Airlines Flight 175 crashed into the twin towers of the World Trade Center in New York City. American Airlines

FIGURE 3.4

Path of American Airlines Flight 11 on September 11, 2001

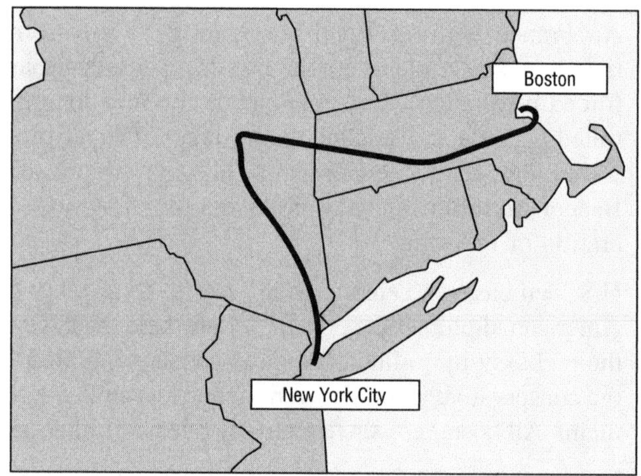

SOURCE: Adapted from "American Airlines Flight 11," in *The 9/11 Commission Report*, National Commission on Terrorist Attacks upon the United States, July 22, 2004, http://www.9-11commission.gov/report/911Report.pdf (accessed August 10, 2008)

FIGURE 3.5

Path of United Airlines Flight 175 on September 11, 2001

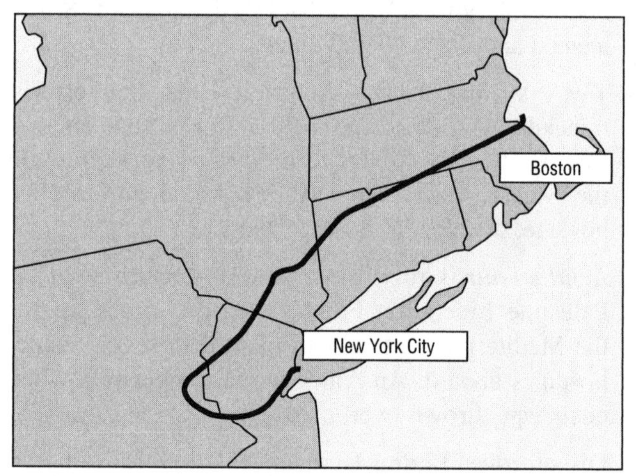

SOURCE: Adapted from "United Airlines Flight 175," in *The 9/11 Commission Report*, National Commission on Terrorist Attacks upon the United States, July 22, 2004, http://www.9-11commission.gov/report/911Report.pdf (accessed August 10, 2008)

Flight 77 was flown into the Pentagon in Washington, D.C. United Airlines Flight 93 crashed into a field near Shanksville, Pennsylvania, after passengers stormed the cockpit. The hijackers' target for that plane is believed to have been the U.S. Capitol in Washington, D.C.

The *9/11 Commission Report* traces the plotting, execution, and aftermath of the attacks. Extensive interviews were conducted with intelligence and law enforcement

FIGURE 3.6

Path of American Airlines Flight 77 on September 11, 2001

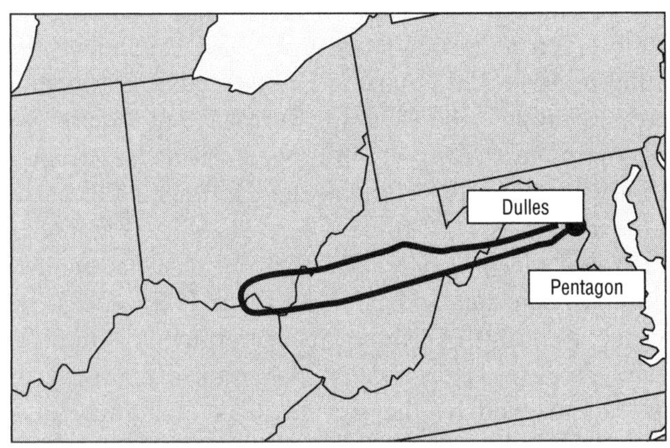

SOURCE: Adapted from "American Airlines Flight 77," in *The 9/11 Commission Report*, National Commission on Terrorist Attacks upon the United States, July 22, 2004, http://www.9-11commission.gov/report/911Report.pdf (accessed August 10, 2008)

FIGURE 3.7

Path of United Airlines Flight 93 on September 11, 2001

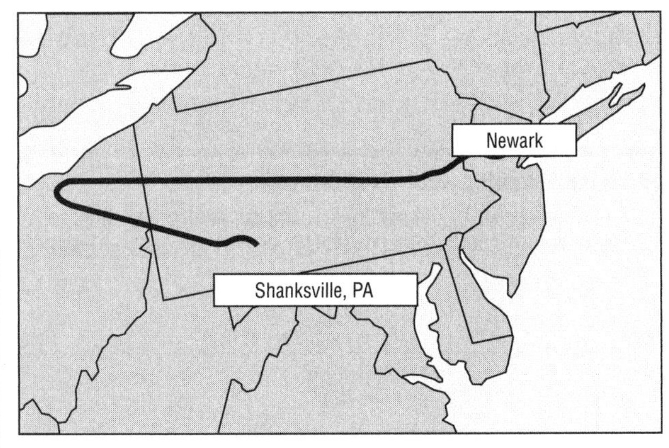

SOURCE: Adapted from "United Airlines Flight 93," in *The 9/11 Commission Report*, National Commission on Terrorist Attacks upon the United States, July 22, 2004, http://www.9-11commission.gov/report/911Report.pdf (accessed August 10, 2008)

agencies to determine background information on the hijackers and their operation. Much of that information came from captured top al Qaeda figures, such as Khalid Sheikh Mohammed. All the hijackers were from the Middle East; sixteen of them were Saudi nationals. According to the report, six of the men were "lead operatives" who represented the most intelligent and best trained of the team. Four of these men piloted the hijacked planes after having studied for months at American flight schools. The lead operatives lived in the United States for up to a year before the day of the attacks. Thirteen of the men were so-called muscle hijackers, who were selected to assist in overpowering the flight crew and passengers. They arrived in the United States only months before the attacks after undergoing extensive training at al Qaeda terrorist camps in Afghanistan.

All the terrorists were selected for the operation because of their willingness to martyr themselves for the Islamist cause espoused by bin Laden. However, the commission found that only a handful of people within al Qaeda knew the details and scope of the hijack plan before it was carried out.

Country Reports on Terrorism 2007

In April 2008 the Office of the Coordinator for Counterterrorism published *Country Reports on Terrorism 2007*. The report includes statistics gathered by U.S. agencies on the number, location, and type of terrorist incidents committed around the world each year and the number of people killed, injured, or kidnapped during these incidents. Additional information includes detailed data on Americans affected by terrorist incidents.

According to the report, 14,499 terrorist attacks were reported in 2007, resulting in 22,685 deaths and injury to 44,310 people. Table 3.3 shows the fatalities by country for the fourteen countries that experienced the most deaths due to terrorism. Nearly 43% of all terrorist attacks—6,212 attacks—occurred in Iraq and caused 13,600 fatalities. More than 1,120 terrorist attacks were reported in Afghanistan, a 16% increase compared to 2006. Terrorist attacks in Africa were up 96% compared to 2006 and were associated with political and social turmoil in and around Somalia, Niger, and Kenya.

More than half of all terrorism victims in 2007 were Muslims. Over twenty-four hundred children were injured or killed by acts of terrorism. In nearly two-thirds

TABLE 3.3

Deaths due to terrorism, by country, 2007

Country	Fatalities
Iraq	13,606
Afghanistan	1,966
Pakistan	1,335
India	1,093
Thailand	859
Somalia	767
Sudan	403
Chad	368
Colombia	364
Sri Lanka	241
Philippines	209
Algeria	192
Democratic Republic of the Congo	178
Russia	150

SOURCE: "Chart 6. Deaths by Country in 2007," in *2007 Report on Terrorism*, National Counterterrorism Center, April 30, 2008, http://wits.nctc.gov/reports/crot2007nctcannexfinal.pdf (accessed August 2, 2008)

(63%) of all terrorist attacks, the perpetrator was not identified. The remaining 36% of attacks were blamed on up to 130 FTOs. Suicide attacks, in which the perpetrator blew up him- or herself during the attack, increased by 50% in 2007 compared to 2006.

According to the report, only nineteen American civilians were killed as a result of terrorist incidents during 2007: seventeen in Iraq and two in Afghanistan.

U.S. PUBLIC OPINION ON TERRORISM

Since 9/11 the possibility of new terrorist attacks on U.S. soil has been a source of concern for many Americans. The Gallup Organization conducts polls on a variety of topics related to national security. During several polls performed since early 2002, Gallup pollsters have asked Americans how much they personally worry about the possibility of future terrorist attacks in the United States. When this question was first asked in March 2002, nearly half (48.9%) of the people asked expressed "a great deal" of worry, whereas 26.4% expressed "a fair amount" of worry. (See Table 3.4.) Thus, a total of 75.3% of respondents were worried a fair amount or a great deal about the possibility of a future terrorist attack in the United States. Following the U.S.-led invasion of Iraq in March 2003, this total increased to 78.9% (48.6% worried "a great deal" and 30.3% worried "a fair amount"). By March 2008 the total had decreased slightly to 73.1%, including 39.8% that worried "a great deal" and 33.3% that worried "a fair amount" about future terrorist attacks within the country.

Gallup polls reveal that Americans hold an increasingly pessimistic view about which side is "winning" the War on Terror. Around two-thirds of respondents told Gallup in early 2002 that the United States and its allies were "winning" the War on Terror. (See Figure 3.8.) This optimistic viewpoint followed the successful U.S. military invasion of Afghanistan. Optimism faded over the next year as U.S. forces were unable to capture bin Laden and faced stiff resistance from terrorist elements within Afghanistan. In March 2003 the U.S. successfully invaded Iraq and overthrew its government. Americans became hopeful again about U.S. progress against terrorism, as indicated by the second peak in Figure 3.8. In April 2003 Gallup found that nearly 65% of respondents thought the United States and its allies were "winning" the war. Since that time optimism has faded dramatically. Iraq became embroiled in civil war in the years following the invasion, and Iraqi insurgents (resistance fighters) inflicted demoralizing damage to U.S. and allied forces. Polls conducted from mid-2004 through mid-2007 indicated that more Americans thought that neither side was winning. In June 2007 a majority (51%) of those asked said that neither side was winning. Another 29% thought the United States and its allies were winning, and 20% said the terrorists were winning the war. (See Figure 3.9.)

TABLE 3.4

Public opinion on the likelihood of a terrorist attack occurring in the United States, selected dates, 2002–08

QUESTION: NEXT, I'M GOING TO READ A LIST OF PROBLEMS FACING THE COUNTRY. FOR EACH ONE, PLEASE TELL ME IF YOU PERSONALLY WORRY ABOUT THIS PROBLEM A GREAT DEAL, A FAIR AMOUNT, ONLY A LITTLE, OR NOT AT ALL? FIRST, HOW MUCH DO YOU PERSONALLY WORRY ABOUT—THE POSSIBILITY OF FUTURE TERRORIST ATTACKS IN THE U.S.?

Date	A great deal	A fair amount	Only a little	Not at all	Don't know	Refused
3/9/2008	39.840	33.300	19.570	7.170	0	0.110
3/14/2007	41.110	32.280	19.060	7.440	0	0.120
3/16/2006	44.870	30.790	17.780	6.350	0.160	0.060
3/10/2005	41.280	26.900	24.680	6.830	0.120	0.200
3/11/2004	38.210	29.350	24.080	8.260	0.100	0
3/25/2003	48.610	30.310	16.440	4.500	0.140	0
3/7/2002	48.900	26.430	19.950	4.540	0.180	0

SOURCE: "Next, I'm Going to Read a List of Problems Facing the Country. For Each One, Please Tell Me If You Personally Worry about This Problem a Great Deal, a Fair Amount, Only a Little, or Not at All? First, How Much Do You Personally Worry about—the Possibility of Future Terrorist Attacks in the U.S.?" in *Create a Trend*, 2008, The Gallup Organization, http://brain.gallup.com/documents/trendQuestion.aspx?QUESTION=164259&Advanced=0&Search ConType =1&SearchTypeAll=terrorist (accessed August 2, 2008). Copyright © 2008 by The Gallup Organization. Reproduced by permission of The Gallup Organization.

FIGURE 3.8

Public opinion on whether the U.S. and its allies or the terrorists are winning the war against terrorism, selected dates, 2001–07

The U.S. and its allies — Neither side — The terrorists

70
60
50
40
30
20
10
0

10/14/2001 4/14/2002 10/14/2002 4/14/2003 10/14/2003 4/14/2004 10/14/2004 4/14/2005 10/14/2005 4/14/2006 10/14/2006 4/14/2007

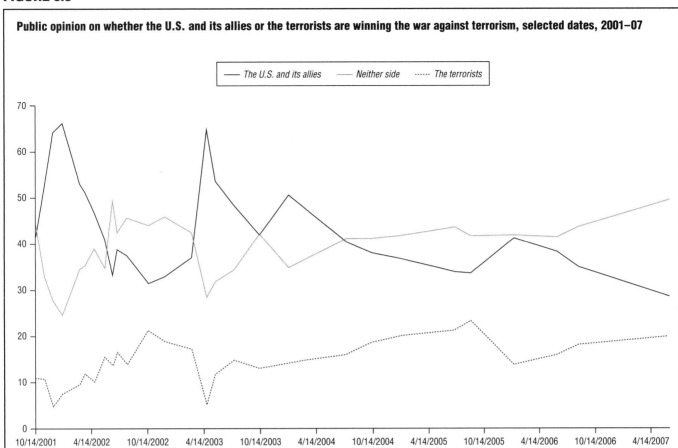

SOURCE: Adapted from "Who Do You Think Is Currently Winning the War against Terrorism—the U.S. and Its Allies, Neither Side, or the Terrorists?" in *Create a Trend*, The Gallup Organization, June 2007, http://brain.gallup.com/documents/trendQuestion.aspx?QUESTION=160441&Advanced=0&SearchConType=1&SearchTypeAll=Who%20do%20you%20think%20is%20currently%20winning%20the%20war%20against%20terrorism (accessed August 6, 2008). Copyright © 2007 by The Gallup Organization, Reproduced by permission of The Gallup Organization.

FIGURE 3.9

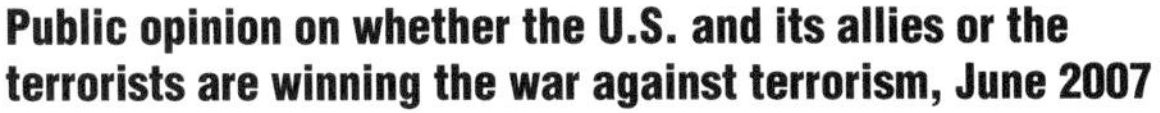
Public opinion on whether the U.S. and its allies or the terrorists are winning the war against terrorism, June 2007

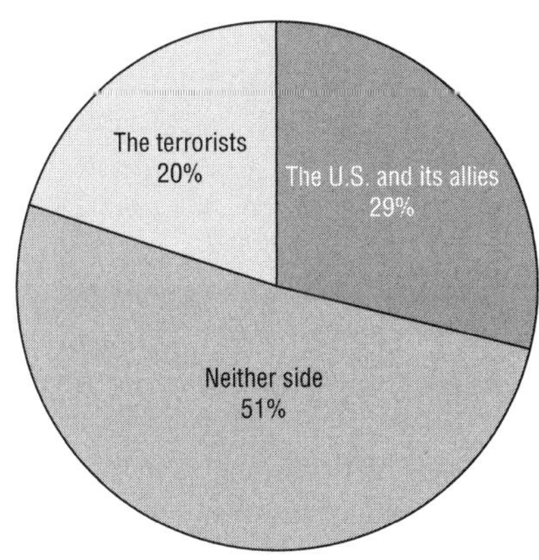

SOURCE: Adapted from "Question qn33. Who Do You Think Is Currently Winning the War against Terrorism—the U.S. and Its Allies, Neither Side, or the Terrorists?" in *June Wave 2*, Gallup, June 2007, http://brain.gallup.com/documents/trendQuestion.aspx?QUESTION=160441&Advanced=0&SearchConType=1&SearchTypeAll=terrorist (accessed August 6, 2008). Copyright © 2007 by The Gallup Organization. Reproduced by permission of The Gallup Organization.

CHAPTER 4

THE WAR ON TERROR: AFGHANISTAN AND IRAQ

The United States' immediate response to the terrorist attacks of September 11, 2001 (9/11), was to invade Afghanistan. The goal was twofold: capture or kill Osama bin Laden (1957–; the mastermind of the attacks) and the other members of the al Qaeda terrorist organization and drive the Taliban government from power for harboring and supporting al Qaeda. The invasion was a resounding military success. The repressive Taliban was defeated and replaced by a more liberal, U.S.-friendly regime. Major terrorist training camps were destroyed and many members of al Qaeda were captured or forced to flee. The victory was not complete, however, because bin Laden was neither captured nor killed. Instead, he escaped and, as of September 2008, continued to motivate terrorist violence against the United States. Furthermore, the Taliban and its supporters have remained in Afghanistan and wage a surprisingly strong insurgency (resistance) against the occupying forces.

In 2003 the United States opened a new front in the War on Terror by invading Iraq. The invasion was driven by claims from the U.S. intelligence community that Iraq had collaborated with al Qaeda and was amassing weapons of mass destruction (WMDs). These claims would later prove to be false. The U.S. military operation in Iraq was at first successful. The longtime Iraqi dictator Saddam Hussein (1937–2006) was ousted from power, and a new, more democratic government was slowly installed. However, a fierce insurgency erupted, driven by Hussein supporters and militant elements opposed to the occupation. Over time, the violence widened into a bitter and deadly civil struggle between Iraqi factions divided by religious and political differences.

As of September 2008, U.S. troops still occupied Afghanistan and Iraq. With the increasing number of U.S. casualties, particularly in Iraq, the American public has become more dissatisfied about the course of the War on Terror.

AFGHANISTAN

Afghanistan is a landlocked country in south central Asia. Its largest neighbors are Pakistan to the east and south and Iran to the west. (See Figure 4.1.) Turkmenistan, Uzbekistan, and Tajikistan border Afghanistan to the north. Its capital is Kabul in the east central portion of the country. The Central Intelligence Agency (CIA) indicates in *The World Factbook: Afghanistan* (September 4, 2008, https://www.cia.gov/library/publications/the-world-factbook/geos/af.html) that Afghanistan covers 647,500 square kilometers (250,000 square miles) and is slightly smaller than the state of Texas. The population was estimated at 32.7 million as of July 2008.

A Legacy of War

The history of Afghanistan revolves around an ancient group of people called the Pashtun. As described by the article "Peoples: Pashtun" (*National Geographic*, July 2005), the Pashtun have lived in this region for centuries and survived conquest by many invaders, including the Persians, Macedonians, Turks, and Mongols. They have earned a reputation as being fierce fighters. However, the Pashtun are also known for in-fighting and waging blood feuds among themselves. They are a group of tribes that together make up the largest surviving tribal society in the world. They adhere to an ancient strict code of conduct called *pakhtunwalimale* that specifies rules for all areas of society and everyday life. The Pashtun were known by the Persian term *Afghan* long before their land was called Afghanistan.

Afghanistan's Islamic history dates back to the seventh century and is described by the Library of Congress (LOC) in *A Country Study: Afghanistan* (November 7, 2005, http://lcweb2.loc.gov/frd/cs/aftoc.html). In 637 Muslims from the Arab empire invaded the region and maintained power for several centuries. The LOC notes that "from the seventh

FIGURE 4.1

Map of Afghanistan, 2008

SOURCE: "Afghanistan," in *The World Factbook*, Central Intelligence Agency, 2008, https://www.cia.gov/library/publications/the-world-factbook/geos/af.html (accessed August 9, 2008)

through the ninth centuries, most inhabitants of what is present-day Afghanistan, Pakistan, southern parts of the former Soviet Union, and areas of northern India were converted to Sunni Islam."

In *World Factbook*, the CIA reports that the founding of modern Afghanistan occurred in 1747, when warring Pashtun tribes were united under one leader. At that time the British Empire ruled the land to the east (India and modern-day Pakistan) and the Russians controlled the "stans" to the north. British and Afghan rulers warred over control of Afghanistan until 1919, when the country won its independence. What followed was a series of monarchies culminating in a 1978 coup that installed a highly unpopular communist government. In 1979 the Soviet Union invaded Afghanistan to prevent a brewing revolution and preserve communist rule. The Soviets waged a decade-long war but were driven out by well-armed rebels who called themselves the mujahideen (holy warriors).

Mujahideen and bin Laden

The mujahideen were young Muslims who came from around the world to fight against the Soviet forces as part of a jihad (holy war). In 1980 a wealthy young man named Osama bin Laden traveled from his homeland in Saudi Arabia to help the mujahideen. His role is described at length by the National Commission on Terrorist Attacks upon the United States in *The 9/11 Commission Report* (2004, http://www.9-11commission.gov/report/911Report.pdf). Bin Laden's specialty was raising money and recruiting volunteers, who came to be known as the Arab Afghans. He excelled at organizing fundraising networks that included charities and wealthy donors throughout the world. These funds were used to buy arms and provide training for the Arab Afghans.

The United States, anxious to see its communist enemy defeated in Afghanistan, supported the mujahideen in its efforts. The *9/11 Commission Report* notes that the United States and Saudi Arabia secretly supplied billions of dollars worth of weapons and equipment to the mujahideen through Pakistani military intelligence. However, there is no record of U.S. involvement with bin Laden or the Arab Afghans, who had their own funding sources. In 1988 the Soviets decided to withdraw from Afghanistan in the face of unrelenting resistance from the mujahideen. Bin Laden and his compatriots were reluctant to dismantle their well-funded and highly trained organization, so they decided to maintain it for future jihads. They began calling it al Qaeda, which means "the base" or "the foundation." In 1989 many of al Qaeda's operations were moved to Sudan at the invitation of that country's leader. However, some training camps were maintained in Afghanistan and neighboring Pakistan to train young militant Muslims as jihadists.

The Taliban and bin Laden

The demise of the communist government in Afghanistan left a power vacuum. Rival mujahideen factions began fighting for control. In *A Country Study: Afghanistan*, the LOC describes these events and notes that during the Soviet occupation the mujahideen were often described in the Western press as "'freedom fighters'—as if their goal were to establish a representative democracy in Afghanistan—in reality these groups each had agendas of their own that were often far from democratic." Civil war racked the country until the mid-1990s, when a new political-military force—the Taliban—achieved power. The LOC points out that most members of the Taliban were Pashtun who attended or had recently graduated from religious schools called madrassas in southern Afghanistan and Pakistan.

According to the *9/11 Commission Report*, madrassas are privately funded religious schools that teach strict fundamentalist forms of Islam. The schools abounded in southern Pakistan, because the government could not afford to educate the many Afghan refugees who had fled there to escape the violence in their own country. The report notes that "these schools produced large numbers of half-educated young men with no marketable skills but with deeply held Islamic views." Eventually, Pakistan became concerned about the presence of so many militant young men within its borders, so it encouraged them to return to Afghanistan and restore order there.

By 1996 the Taliban had seized control over most of Afghanistan. In May of that year bin Laden moved the bulk of his al Qaeda organization from Sudan back to Afghanistan. By this time he had enlarged his focus from regional Islamic causes to what the *9/11 Commission Report* calls "hatred of the United States." This development traces back to the 1990 Iraqi invasion of Kuwait. At that time bin Laden reportedly approached Saudi rulers and offered to organize a mujahideen force to drive out the Iraqis, but he was turned down. Saudi Arabia allied with the United States during the subsequent Persian Gulf War and allowed U.S. troops to deploy from Saudi soil. This decision infuriated Islamic fundamentalists, because they oppose the presence of nonbelievers in Saudi Arabia, the birthplace of Muhammad (c. 570–632). After criticizing Saudi leaders, bin Laden had his passport taken away. However, he managed to leave the country in 1991 and eventually turned up in Afghanistan, where he developed a close relationship with the Taliban leader Mohammed Omar (1958–).

Throughout the remainder of the decade bin Laden expanded his al Qaeda network with the blessing of the Afghan Taliban regime. In 1998 he publicly announced his intention to wage a jihad against the United States by issuing a fatwa (a religious declaration) that was published in an Arabic-language newspaper in England. As described in Chapter 3, al Qaeda operatives then carried out a series of attacks against U.S. interests, including the 1998 bombings at two U.S. embassies in Africa, the 2000 bombing of the USS *Cole* in Yemen, and 9/11.

U.S. WAR IN AFGHANISTAN

According to the *9/11 Commission Report*, on the evening of the 9/11 attacks President George W. Bush (1946–) addressed the nation about the tragedy and warned, "We will make no distinction between the terrorists who committed these acts and those who harbor them." The United States quickly identified the 9/11 hijackers as al Qaeda operatives under the control of bin Laden and knew that it was Afghanistan that had harbored them.

U.S. View of the Taliban

Peter L. Bergen claims in *Holy War, Inc.: Inside the Secret World of Osama bin Laden* (2001) that the U.S. government was optimistic about the Taliban when it first seized power in Afghanistan. Bergen writes, "The State Department, which relied heavily on the Pakistanis for information on Afghanistan, was willing to embrace any group that looked as if it might bring some degree of stability to the country." Besides security concerns, the U.S. government had other priorities in Afghanistan, including a planned oil pipeline by a U.S. energy company and curbing Afghanistan's enormous illegal drug trade. There was hope that the new Afghan regime could help in these areas. However, U.S. leaders quickly became disillusioned with the Taliban.

As Bergen notes, the Taliban imposed laws blending "ultrapurist" Islam with traditional Pashtun customs. The result was a society in which men were forbidden to shave or trim their beards. All forms of entertainment, such as listening to the radio or flying a kite, were outlawed. Women were forced to cover themselves with thick head-to-toe cloaks called burkas and were not allowed in public unless accompanied by a male relative. The vast majority of women were forbidden to work or obtain an education. Taliban laws were enforced by religious police who roamed the streets beating violators with sticks. Bergen includes a 1997 quote from the U.S. secretary of state Madeleine Albright (1937–) in which she said, "We are opposed to the Taliban because of their despicable treatment of women and children, and their general lack of respect for human dignity." By this time the Afghan people had suffered from decades of war that had destroyed most of the country's infrastructure; their economy was in shambles and food was in short supply.

As 2001 began the United States was well aware that the Taliban was harboring terrorists. In 1999 and 2000 the United Nations (UN) Security Council imposed economic sanctions on Afghanistan as punishment for its actions. In December 2000 the UN demanded that bin Laden be surrendered and that all terrorist training camps be closed within a month. The article "Taliban Reacts to Sanctions with Boycott of American, Russian Goods" (CNN.com, December 20, 2000) notes that the demands were spurred by the United States and Russia, who claimed that Afghanistan was a "haven of lawlessness." The Taliban angrily refused to comply, insisting that there was no evidence against bin Laden and that the sanctions were motivated by anti-Islamic sentiment.

United States Invades Afghanistan

Within days after 9/11 the United States had decided to target Afghanistan. In an address to Congress on September 20, 2001, President Bush publicly blamed al Qaeda and bin Laden for the attacks and demanded that the Taliban hand over bin Laden and his top lieutenants or the United States would strike. According to the *9/11 Commission Report*, the demands had already been privately passed to the Taliban through the Pakistani government, which the United States had warned "would be at risk" unless it helped the United States against Afghanistan. Bush's speech also noted, "Every nation, in every region, now has a decision to make: either you are with us, or you are with the terrorists." As expected, Afghanistan refused to comply with U.S. demands.

By October 2001 a U.S. war plan had been compiled that was originally called Infinite Justice, but fears about offending religious sensibilities prompted a quick name change to Operation Enduring Freedom when U.S. officials learned that Muslims associate the term *infinite justice* with God's power. The *9/11 Commission Report* states that Operation Enduring Freedom had four phases:

- Phase One—deploy U.S. forces to Afghanistan's neighbors in readiness for an invasion. This step was begun almost immediately and entailed the cooperation of Pakistan and Uzbekistan.
- Phase Two—conduct air strikes on Afghan targets and pair U.S. Special Operations teams with Taliban opposition groups to conduct damaging raids on al Qaeda strongholds. Even before this time, the CIA had been collaborating with opposition groups in northern Afghanistan known collectively as the Northern Alliance. Phase two began on October 7, 2001, and proceeded quickly. By the end of the month the United States had achieved most of its objectives.
- Phase Three—launch a ground invasion of Afghanistan to "topple the Taliban regime and eliminate al Qaeda's sanctuary." By early December 2001 the coalition of U.S. and Northern Alliance forces had captured all major Afghan cities. However, bin Laden and Omar escaped.
- Phase Four—the United States called this phase "security and stability operations." It began on December 22, 2001, when a new leader—Hamid Karzai (1957–; an Afghani Pashtun)—was installed as the head of the nation's interim government. However, bringing security and stability to Afghanistan proved to be a daunting task.

A COALITION OF THE WILLING

In December 2001 Afghan opposition leaders met with UN officials at the Bonn Conference in Bonn, Germany, to work out a plan for establishing a new permanent government for Afghanistan. The Bonn Agreement established three priorities: security, reconstruction, and political stability. The UN called for a multinational military force to secure the area in and around Kabul (Afghanistan's capital). The result was the International Security Assistance Force (ISAF). The North Atlantic Treaty Organization (NATO) points out in "ISAF History" (September 2, 2008, http://www.nato.int/isaf/topics/history/index.html) that the "ISAF is not a UN force, but is a coalition of the willing deployed under the authority of the UN Security Council." The countries contributing troops to the ISAF fund its operations.

In 2003 NATO assumed control of the ISAF and began expanding its area of responsibility beyond Kabul to the remainder of Afghanistan. ISAF expansion has included the formation of provincial reconstruction teams (PRTs). These are small teams including both military and civilian personnel who are stationed around the country to protect and support international aid agencies and reconstruction workers. In "Provincial Reconstruction Teams Reconnecting Afghanistan" (March 14, 2008, http://www.america.gov/st/peacesec-english/2008/March/20080313173952idybeekcm0.581402.html), the U.S. Department of State indicates that in March 2008 twenty-six PRTs were operating throughout Afghanistan, fourteen of them led by the United States. The PRTs assist the Afghan people through infrastructure, education, and economic development projects, such as building roads, hospitals, and schools and supplying agricultural supplies and aid.

In 2006 the ISAF relieved U.S. and allied troops and expanded its command to include the entire country. According to NATO, in "ISAF Regional Commands & PRT Locations" (http://www.nato.int/ISAF/docu/epub/pdf/isaf_placemat.pdf), as of September 1, 2008, approximately 47,600 troops from forty nations were in the ISAF. Over 37% (17,790) of the troops were American. The countries with the next largest contingents were the United Kingdom (8,380), Germany (3,332), France (2,660), and Canada (2,500). Approximately 34,600 of the ISAF troops were in the southern and eastern regions of Afghanistan bordering Pakistan.

Kenneth Katzman of the Congressional Research Service (CRS) explains in *Afghanistan: Post-war Governance, Security, and U.S. Policy* (September 2, 2008, http://www.fas.org/sgp/crs/row/RL30588.pdf) that in September 2008 there were approximately 33,600 U.S. forces in Afghanistan including those in the ISAF and those conducting antiterrorism missions under Operation Enduring Freedom. Katzman notes that the United States has given more than $25 billion in aid to Afghanistan since the Taliban fell in late 2001.

The Taliban Resurges

In 2006 there was an upswing in militant violence in Afghanistan, particularly in the southern part of the country. In "Who Are the Militants in Afghanistan?" (BBC News, August 18, 2006), Pam O'Toole reports that the insurgents represent a multitude of factions, including former Taliban leaders, warlords, people engaged in the lucrative drug trade, new graduates of Pakistani madrassas, and an assortment of radical Islamic militants. O'Toole states that the situation is complicated by a "complex web of shifting allegiances, tribal, ethnic and local rivalries and feuds within Afghan society."

According to the LOC, in *Country Profile: Afghanistan* (August 2008, http://lcweb2.loc.gov/frd/cs/profiles/Afghanistan.pdf), in 2008 Taliban fighters were crossing in and out of neighboring Pakistan to elude ISAF and U.S. forces. Figure 4.2 shows the western region of Pakistan known as the Federally Administered Tribal Areas (FATA). The

FIGURE 4.2

Map of the Federally Administered Tribal Areas (FATA) of Pakistan

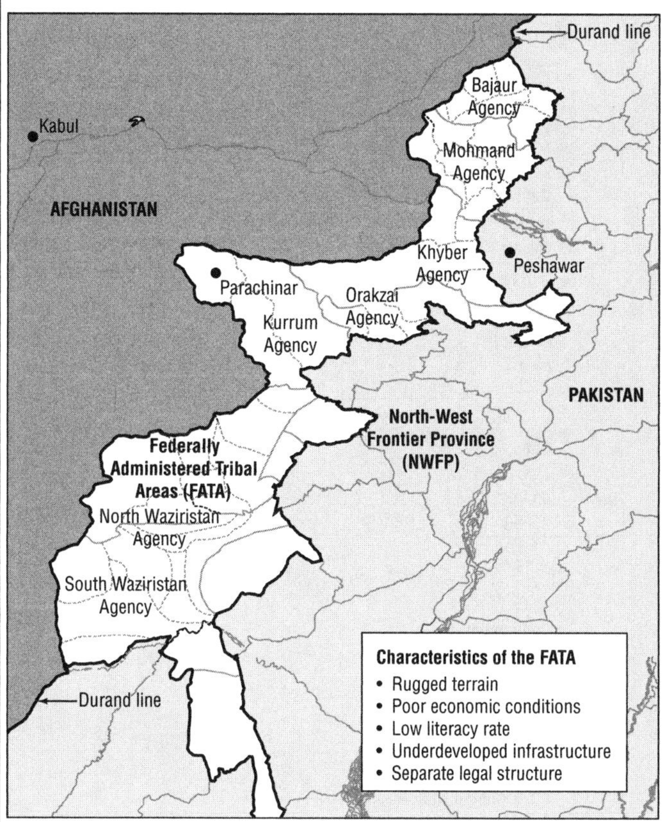

The boundaries and names used on this map do not imply official endorsement or acceptance by the U.S. government.

SOURCE: "Figure 1. Map of the Federally Administered Tribal Areas, Pakistan," in *Combating Terrorism: U.S. Efforts to Address the Terrorist Threat in Pakistan's Federally Administered Tribal Areas Require a Comprehensive Plan and Continued Oversight*, U.S. Government Accountability Office, May 20, 2008, http://www.gao.gov/new.items/d08820t.pdf (accessed July 24, 2008)

FATA is one of the poorest and most rugged regions of the country and has a separate legal structure that makes it difficult to control by the central Pakistani government. As a result, the FATA is believed to provide safe haven for Afghan Taliban fighters. The LOC estimates that in early 2008 the Taliban controlled an estimated 10% of Afghanistan, and the Afghan government controlled 30%. The remainder was controlled by various local tribes.

AFGHANISTAN: POLITICAL AND SOCIAL CONDITION

Following the U.S. invasion, Afghanistan began a series of democratic reforms. In "Karzai Wins Afghan Election" (Associated Press, November 4, 2004), Stephen Graham reports that in 2004 national presidential elections were held in which Karzai won 55% of the vote. His closest competitor captured just 16% of the vote. Even though the election itself was relatively violence-free, the country has struggled with internal problems, including battling warlords and drug traffickers. Karzai will serve a five-year term and has pledged to double the country's income by 2009.

According to the LOC, in *Country Profile: Afghanistan*, Afghanistan has tried to rebuild its educational system with the help of international aid. Approximately ninety-five hundred schools were open around the country in 2008. However, Taliban forces frequently attack and destroy public schools. In 2007, 35% of public schools in the southern provinces had to be closed due to Taliban activity. The Taliban has reportedly opened its own Islamic fundamentalist schools in the territory it controls. In 2002 Kabul University reopened with approximately twenty-four thousand students enrolled, including females. By 2007 seven additional universities had opened. However, the total university enrollment dropped to 22,700 students.

Illiteracy among adults is a tremendous problem. The LOC estimates that in 2006 approximately 57% of men and 87% of women were illiterate. Decades of war have left the population impoverished with little access to health care and high rates of malnutrition. The LOC estimates that a quarter of the population has no access to health care at all. The mortality rates for Afghan infants, children, and women in childbirth are among the world's highest. Lack of clean drinking water and poor sanitation have allowed parasitic and infectious diseases to flourish. An estimated eight hundred thousand Afghans are disabled. Approximately one million Afghans were believed to be drug addicts in 2005. Health authorities worry that high rates of intravenous drug use combined with poor overall health and sanitation conditions make Afghans extremely susceptible to infection with the human immunodeficiency virus, the virus that causes the acquired immunodeficiency syndrome. Thousands of people are believed to be infected with the disease.

The LOC notes that despite the influx of billions of dollars of aid since 2001, the Afghan government provides little welfare to its people. Wealth has become concentrated in a small elite portion of the population, and government corruption is a problem. The vast majority of people subside on less than $2 per day and are dependent on nongovernmental foreign aid organizations. The LOC warns that "widespread economic hardship" increasingly weakens support for the government among the Afghan people.

Drug Trade

Since the fall of the Taliban in 2001, Afghanistan has become a major producer of opium poppies, the source of heroin. The UN Office on Drugs and Crime (UNODC) indicates in *2008 Opium Winter Rapid Assessment Survey in Afghanistan* (February 2008, http://www.unodc.org/documents/crop-monitoring/Afghan-winter-survey-Feb08-short.pdf) that the nation produces more than 90% of the world's illegal opium. Approximately 193,000 hectares (477,000 acres) of opium poppies were grown in Afghanistan in 2007, nearly two-thirds of it in the southern provinces. This is the area most troubled by insurgent and Taliban activity. The UNODC reports that Afghan opium poppy farmers earn as much $5,000 per hectare (just over $2,000 per acre). Most pay an *usher* (tax) of 10% on their earnings to nongovernmental elements, such as Taliban fighters, who provide security for the farmers. Opium poppy farming is believed to be a source of major financial support for the Taliban.

In "Afghanistan's Soaring Drug Trade Hits Home" (*Christian Science Monitor*, March 13, 2008), Anand Gopal states that Afghanistan produces approximately $4 billion worth of opium poppies per year, accounting for just over half of the nation's total economic production. Aid agencies in the country report that drug abuse by Afghans is "the fastest-growing social problem in the country."

AFGHANISTAN: THE AMERICAN TOLL AND PUBLIC OPINION

Between October 7, 2001, and August 2, 2008, 561 U.S. military personnel died during Operation Enduring Freedom. (See Table 4.1.) Nearly two-thirds (354) of the deaths were because of hostilities (i.e., active combat). The remaining 207 deaths were classified as nonhostile. Most of the nonhostile deaths were because of accidents. (See Table 4.2.) Furthermore, 2,309 U.S. military personnel were wounded in battle during this period. An additional 1,845 suffered nonhostile injuries, and 5,192 came down with diseases or other medical conditions serious enough to require medical air transport.

Table 4.3 was compiled in June 2008 by the CRS. The table lists the money appropriated to Operation Enduring Freedom from fiscal year (FY) 2001 to FY 2009. Note that the U.S. Department of Defense (DOD) and other federal agencies are appropriated money by Congress in two ways: through the regular annual budget process and through occasional supplemental appropriations known as bridge funds. According to the CRS, appropriations for the war in Afghanistan totaled $172.6 billion as of June 2008. This amount included all regular and supplemental appropriations that had been enacted and those that were pending, but expected to be approved. The vast majority of the money ($159.8 billion) was appropriated to the DOD. Another $12.4 billion went for related foreign aid and diplomatic operations. The U.S. Department of Veterans Affairs had received approximately $400 million for its medical operations.

In September 2006 and July 2008 the Gallup Organization conducted polls to determine American attitudes about U.S. military operations in Afghanistan. (See Table 4.4.) The pollsters asked: "In general, how would you say things are going for the U.S. in Afghanistan—very well, moderately well, moderately badly, or very badly?" The results indicate a nearly even split. In the 2008 poll 46% of those asked believed things were going well in Afghanistan (5% very well and 41% moderately well). Fifty-one percent of respondents thought things were going badly (33% moderately badly and 18% very badly). These percentages are similar to those recorded in the 2006 poll.

Despite the relative pessimism about how the war is proceeding, a majority of Americans believed sending military troops to Afghanistan is not a mistake. Figure 4.3 shows the results of Gallup polls on this issue dating back to late 2001. At that time and during January 2002 the vast majority of respondents (89% and 93%, respectively) said the United States had not made a mistake in sending

TABLE 4.1

U.S. military deaths in Operation Enduring Freedom (OEF), by demographic characteristics, October 7, 2001–August 2, 2008

	Totals
Casualty type	
Hostile	354
Nonhostile	207
Total	**561**
Gender	
Male	547
Female	14
Total	**561**
Officer/enlisted	
Officer	85
E5–E9	250
E1–E4	226
Total	**561**
Age	
<22	108
22–24	108
25–30	153
31–35	80
>35	112
Total	**561**
Component	
Active	454
Reserve	30
National Guard	77
Total	**561**
Race/ethnicity	
American Indian or Alaska Native	8
Asian	6
Black or African American	46
Hispanic or Latino	48
Multiple races, pending, or unknown	2
Native Hawaiian or Pacific Islander	8
White	443
Total	**561**

Note: Casualty areas include in/around Afghanistan, Republic of the Philippines, Southwest Asia and other locations.

SOURCE: Adapted from "Operation Enduring Freedom Military Deaths, October 7, 2001 through August 2, 2008," in *DoD Personnel and Military Casualty Statistics: Military Casualty Information*, U.S. Department of Defense, August 2, 2008, http://siadapp.dmdc.osd.mil/personnel/CASUALTY/OEFDEATHS.pdf (accessed August 8, 2008)

TABLE 4.2

U.S. military casualties in Operation Enduring Freedom (OEF), by demographic characteristics, October 7, 2001–August 2, 2008

Casualty type	Total
Killed in action	286
Died of wounds[a]	68
Died while missing in action	*
Died while captured	*
Total hostile deaths	**354**
Accident	152
Illness	17
Homicide	1
Self-inflicted	23
Undetermined	7
Pending[b]	7
Total non-hostile deaths	**207**
Total deaths	**561**
Total—wounded in action (WIA)	**2,309**
Wounded—no medical air transport required	1,075
Wounded—medical air transport required[c]	1,234
Total—Non-hostile-related medical air transports	**7,037**
Non-hostile injuries—medical air transport required[c]	1,845
Diseases/other medical—medical air transport required[c]	5,192
Total—medical air transports (hostile and non-hostile)	**8,271**

*None reported
[a]Includes died of wounds where wounding occurred in theater and death occurred elsewhere.
[b]Pending means final category to be determined at a later date.
[c]Reported by Force Health Protection and Readiness.

SOURCE: Adapted from "Global War on Terrorism—Operation Enduring Freedom by Casualty Category within Service, October 7, 2001 through August 2, 2008," in *DoD Personnel and Military Casualty Statistics: Military Casualty Information*, U.S. Department of Defense, August 2, 2008, http://siadapp.dmdc.osd.mil/personnel/CASUALTY/WOTSUM.pdf (accessed August 8, 2008)

military forces to Afghanistan. The question was asked again in mid-2004, mid-2007, and mid-2008. During these polls slightly lower percentages (72%, 70%, and 68%, respectively) agreed that sending troops to Afghanistan had not been a mistake.

In addition, Gallup finds that a majority of Americans favor sending more U.S. troops to Afghanistan. (See Figure 4.4.) In July 2008, 59% of respondents favored sending additional U.S. troops to Afghanistan to fight al Qaeda and Taliban terrorists, whereas 38% opposed this measure. The percentages are close to those recorded by Gallup in a poll conducted in August 2007.

IRAQ

Iraq is bordered on the east by Iran, on the north by Turkey, on the west by Syria and Jordan, and on the south by Saudi Arabia. (See Figure 4.5.) The tiny nation of Kuwait also lies to the south and abuts Iraq's small stretch of coastline on the Persian Gulf. The capital of Iraq is Baghdad. According to the CIA, in *The World Factbook: Iraq* (September 4, 2008, https://www.cia.gov/library/publications/the-world-factbook/geos/iz.html), Iraq covers 437,072 square kilometers (168,754 square miles) and is slightly larger than twice the size of the state of Idaho. Iraq is crossed by two large rivers—the Tigris and Euphrates—whose waters provide a broad fertile plain in the center of the country. The remainder of the landscape is primarily desert. The population of Iraq was estimated at just over 28.2 million as of July 2008. Most of the population is Arab (75% to 80%) but includes a Kurdish sector (15% to 20%) and other ethnic minorities. Nearly all Iraqis are Muslim (97%), with approximately two-thirds Shiite and one-third Sunni.

The history of Iraq is described at length by the LOC in *Country Profile: Iraq* (August 2006, http://lcweb2.loc.gov/frd/cs/profiles/Iraq.pdf). In ancient times this land was called Mesopotamia (land between the rivers) and attracted many great civilizations. Over the centuries it was ruled by the Sumerians, Amorites, Babylonians, Hittites, Assyrians, Chaldeans, Persians, Macedonians, Parthians, and Sassanians. From the eighth century through the thirteenth century the Arab empire had Baghdad as its capital. This is the time period when most of the population adopted Islam. However, disagreements between followers of the Shiite and Sunni sects plagued the empire throughout its history. The Arab dynasty was conquered by the Mongols, which then fell to the Ottoman Empire in the 1500s. During World War I (1914–1918) the Ottomans lost control to the British, who occupied Iraq until it became independent in 1932.

The LOC reports that ethnic, tribal, and religious differences made political stability impossible to maintain after the country achieved its independence. Iraq was ruled by a variety of leaders who seized power via coups and revolts. During the mid-1950s a secular (nonreligious) movement arose called the Baath Party that had the support of the nation's intellectuals and military. By 1970 the Baathist Saddam Hussein had consolidated his political power and became Iraq's new dictator. He began a campaign of extermination against his internal enemies. In 1980 Hussein decided to invade neighboring Iran, a country that had recently undergone a revolution that put Islamic clerics in power. Both countries had long-standing border disputes with each other. The LOC estimates that the eight-year war killed between five hundred thousand and one million people.

U.S. Relations with Iraq: 1960s to 1990s

In 1967 Iraq fought with other Arab countries against Israel in the Six-Day War. In protest of U.S. support for Israel during the war, Iraq severed diplomatic ties with the United States. Ties were restored in 1984 because the United States and Iraq shared a common enemy at that time: Iran. Iranian militants had seized the U.S. embassy in Iran in late 1979 and held American personnel hostage for 444 days before releasing them. As a result, the United States had a vested interest

TABLE 4.3

Budget authority for Operation Enduring Freedom, 2001–09

[CRS estimates in billions of budget authority]

By operation and funding source	FY01 & FY02[a]	FY03	FY04	FY05	FY06	FY07	FY08[b]	Cum. enacted thru FY08 consol. approp.	Pending FY08 req.[a]	Pdg. FY09 req.[c]	Cum: FY01-FY09 bridge in house-passed H. R. 2642, 6–19–08[c]
Operation Enduring Freedom (OEF)/Afghanistan and GWOT											
Department of Defense	20.0	14.0	12.4	17.2	17.9	34.9	**13.0**	**129.2**	**21.3**	**14.0**	**159.8**
Foreign aid and diplomatic ops[d]	0.8	0.7	2.2	2.8	1.1	1.9	**1.1**	**10.6**	**0.9**	**1.1**	**12.4**
VA medical[e]	0	0	0	0	0.0	0.1	**0.2**	**0.3**	**0.0**	**0.0**	**0.4**
Total: OEF	**20.8**	**14.7**	**14.5**	**20.0**	**19.0**	**36.9**	**14.3**	**140.2**	**22.2**	**15.1**	**172.6**

Notes: Because DOD has not provided a breakdown by operation for all appropriations received, CRS estimates unobligated budget authority using past trends as shown in DOD's Defense Finance Accounting Service (DFAS) reports, *Supplemental & Cost of War Execution Reports* and other budget justification materials.
CRS budget authority (BA) totals are higher than DOD figures because CRS includes all funding provided in supplementals, bridge funds or baseline appropriations for Iraq and the Global war on Terror as well as transfers from DOD's baseline funds for GWOT requirements, and enhanced security. CRS also splits the $25 billion provided in the FY2005 Title IX bridge between the $1.8 billion obligated in FY2004 and the remainder available for FY2005; all those funds are scored as FY2004 because they were available upon enactment in August 2005. Figures include funds provided in P.L. 107–38, the first emergency supplemental after 9/11, and funds allocated in P.L. 107–117. Numbers may not add due to rounding.
CRS = Congressional Research Service. GWOT = Global War on Terror.
[a]CRS combined funds for FY2001 and FY2002 because most were obligated in FY2002 after the 9/11 attacks at the end of FY2001. In FY2008, CRS includes funds for enhanced security in DOD's regular budget, and excludes as non-war related DOD request for funds to cover higher fuel prices for its regular program and accelerate the replacement of Walter Reed for a more consistent definition of war costs.
[b]Includes funds provided in the First Continuing Resolution (H.J.Res 52/P.L. 110–92), FY2008 DOD Appropriations Act (H.R. 3222/P.L. 110–116) and the FY2008 Consolidated Appropriations Act (H.R 2764/P.L. 110–161).
[c]Reflects H.R. 2642 as passed by the House on June 19, 2008 excluding funding not related to Iraq and Afghanistan and $4.9 billion in DOD funds notrelatedto war; excludes $1.4 billion in the regular FY2009 State/USAID request for Iraq and Afghanistan.
[d]Foreign operations figures include monies for reconstruction, development and humanitarian aid, embassy operations, counter narcotics, initial training of the Afghan and Iraqi army, foreign military sales credits, and Economic Support Funds. For FY2007, figures reflect State Department figures; for FY2008, figures reflect Joint Explanatory Statement for Division J, FY2008 Consolidated Appropriations Act (P.L. 110–161) in December 17, 2007 Congressional Record; may be revised by State Department at a later date.
[e]Medical estimates reflect figures in VA's FY2008 budget justifications, and CRS estimate of OIF/OEF shares of $3.6 billion added by Congress to VA Medical in FY2008 Consolidated Appropriations Act (P.L. 110–161).

SOURCE: Adapted from Amy Belasco, "Table 4. Budget Authority for Iraq, Afghanistan, and Other Global War on Terror (GWOT) Operations: FY2001–FY2009 Bridge Request," in *The Cost of Iraq, Afghanistan, and Other Global War on Terror Operations since 9/11*, Congressional Research Service, June 23, 2008, http://www.fas.org/sgp/crs/natsec/RL33110.pdf (accessed July 25, 2008)

TABLE 4.4

Public opinion on how the Afghanistan war is going, July 2008

IN GENERAL, HOW WOULD YOU SAY THINGS ARE GOING FOR THE U.S. IN AFGHANISTAN—VERY WELL, MODERATELY WELL, MODERATELY BADLY, (OR) VERY BADLY?

	Very well	Moderately well	Moderately badly	Very badly	No opinion	Total well	Total badly
2008 Jul 25–27	5	41	33	18	3	46	51
2006 Sep 15–17	6	43	30	16	5	49	46

SOURCE: Frank Newport, "In General, How Would You Say Things Are Going for the U.S. in Afghanistan—Very Well, Moderately Well, Moderately Badly, (or) Very Badly?" in *Afghan War Edges out Iraq As Most Important for U.S.*, The Gallup Organization, July 30, 2008, http://www.gallup.com/poll/109150/Afghan-War-Edges-Iraq-Most-Important-US.aspx?version=print (accessed August 9, 2008).

in seeing Iraq succeed in its war against Iran. However, *Shaking Hands with Saddam Hussein: The U.S. Tilts toward Iraq, 1980–1984* (February 25, 2003, http://www.gwu.edu/~nsarchiv/NSAEBB/NSAEBB82/) notes that the U.S.-Iraqi relationship cooled after U.S. officials publicly condemned Iraq for using chemical weapons during the war.

The article "On This Day: 1990" (BBC News, 2006) notes that in August 1990 Iraqi military forces invaded nearby Kuwait after Hussein accused the Kuwaitis of taking oil from an oil field near the border between the two countries. The international community almost universally condemned Iraq's actions. Other Arab countries and the UN Security Council demanded that Iraq leave Kuwait, but to no avail. The UN imposed strict economic sanctions that would remain in place for many years. President George H. W. Bush (1924–) put together a U.S.-led coalition of international military forces for Operation Desert Storm, which began in January 1991 with the bombing of strategic

FIGURE 4.3

Public opinion on whether the U.S. made a mistake in sending military forces to Afghanistan, June 2008

DO YOU THINK THE UNITED STATES MADE A MISTAKE IN SENDING MILITARY FORCES TO AFGHANISTAN, OR NOT?

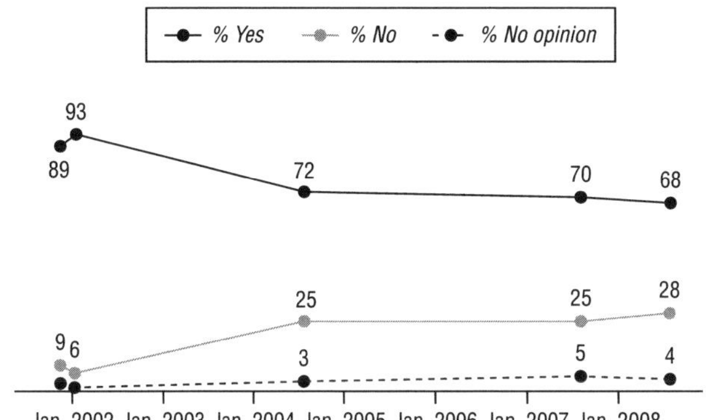

SOURCE: Frank Newport, "Do You Think the United States Made a Mistake in Sending Military Forces to Afghanistan, or Not?" in *Afghan War Edges out Iraq As Most Important for U.S.*, The Gallup Organization, July 30, 2008, http://www.gallup.com/poll/109150/Afghan-War-Edges-Iraq-Most-Important-US.aspx?version=print (accessed August 8, 2008). Copyright © 2008 by The Gallup Organization. Reproduced by permission of The Gallup Organization.

FIGURE 4.4

Public opinion on whether additional U.S. troops should be sent to Afghanistan, August 2007 and July 2008

WOULD YOU FAVOR OR OPPOSE SENDING ADDITIONAL U.S. TROOPS TO AFGHANISTAN TO FIGHT AL QAEDA AND TALIBAN TERRORIST OPERATIONS IN THAT COUNTRY?

Asked of half sample

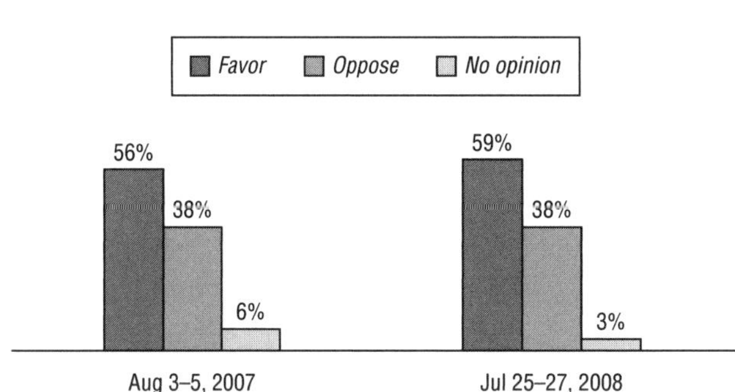

SOURCE: Frank Newport, "Would You Favor or Oppose Sending Additional U.S. Troops to Afghanistan to Fight Al Qaeda and Taliban Terrorist Operations in That Country?" in *Afghan War Edges out Iraq As Most Important for U.S.*, The Gallup Organization, July 30, 2008, http://www.gallup.com/poll/109150/Afghan-War-Edges-Iraq-Most-Important-US.aspx?version=print (accessed August 9, 2008). Copyright © 2008 by The Gallup Organization. Reproduced by permission of The Gallup Organization.

FIGURE 4.5

Map of Iraq, 2007

SOURCE: "Iraq," in *Country Analysis Briefs: Iraq*, U.S. Department of Energy, Energy Information Administration, August 2007, http://www.eia.doe.gov/emeu/cabs/Iraq/pdf.pdf (accessed August 9, 2008)

targets within Iraq. By the end of February the coalition had liberated Kuwait and seriously damaged Iraq's infrastructure and military capabilities. The DOD states in *DoD Personnel and Military Casualty Statistics: Military Casualty Information* (May 2008, http://siadapp.dmdc.osd.mil/personnel/CASUALTY/WCPRINCIPAL.pdf) that the United States lost 382 troops in the Persian Gulf War. More than 2.2 million U.S. military personnel served in that war.

In April 1991 the UN Security Council passed Resolution 687 (http://www.iaea.org/OurWork/SV/Invo/resolutions/res687.pdf), which set forth the terms of the cease-fire between Iraq and Kuwait. It also called on Iraq to "agree not to acquire or develop nuclear weapons" or any related technology and to declare the "locations, amounts, and types" of all existing nuclear weapons and usable materials within Iraq and turn them over to the International Atomic Energy Agency (IAEA) for destruction. For the remainder of the decade Iraq followed a pattern of denial and deception with IAEA inspections and refused to abide by Resolution 687 and subsequent Resolutions 707, 715, 1051, 1284, and 1441. In 1998 a defiant Hussein had the inspectors kicked out of the country. (For a timeline of events, see the IAEA's "In Focus: IAEA and Iraq" [2003, http://www.iaea.org/NewsCenter/Focus/IaeaIraq/index.shtml].)

The Kurds

The Kurds are an ethnic group found mostly in the mountainous regions of northern Iraq. Their history is described by Lokman I. Meho in "The Kurds and Kurdistan: A General Background" (Lokman I. Meho and Kelly L. Maglaughlin, comp., *Kurdish Culture and Society: An Annotated Bibliography*, 1997). The area inhabited by the Kurds was once called Kurdistan. The land was divided in the 1500s between the Persian and Ottoman empires. After World War I, predominantly Kurdish territory was split between the modern states of Turkey, Iraq, Iran, and Syria. However, the Kurds see themselves as a distinct group and have long pursued their own independent nation.

The struggle of the Iraqi Kurds against Hussein and the Iraqi government is reviewed by Frank Viviano in "The Kurds in Control" (*National Geographic*, January 2006). During the 1980s and early 1990s Hussein's government killed an estimated 100,000 to 180,000 Kurds and destroyed thousands of their villages. Much of the killing occurred near the end of the Iran-Iraq War as punishment for Kurdish support of Iran. The genocide included the use of chemical weapons against the Kurds during the so-called Anfal Campaign. (For more information about this campaign, see the Human Rights Watch report *Genocide in Iraq: The Anfal Campaign against the Kurds* [July 1993, http://www.hrw.org/reports/1993/iraqanfal/].)

According to Viviano, the United States chose at first to ignore the genocide so as not to antagonize Hussein, a would-be American ally during the late 1980s. This attitude changed following Iraq's invasion of Kuwait in 1991. Immediately after the war, U.S., British, and French military forces began enforcing a no-fly zone over the Kurdish territories in northern Iraq to prevent Hussein from attacking the Kurds with aircraft or bombs. International protection allowed the Kurdish population to flourish; by the end of the decade they had developed their own semi-independent government and a highly trained militia called the Peshmerga, which means "those who face death."

U.S. Relations with Iraq: Post 9/11

By the time of 9/11, the United States had experienced an entire decade of problems with Iraq. A no-fly zone had been put in place over southern Iraq to protect the largely Shiite population from a crackdown by Hussein's government (which was predominantly Sunni Muslim). Iraq had quickly denounced the no-fly zones as illegal and often fired at U.S. and British warplanes enforcing them. As reported in "Western Warplanes Bomb Iraq No-Fly Zone, U.S. Says" (CNN.com, October 23, 2000), the result was that the Iraqi ground-based air defense system was bombed many times. Hussein's continuing defiance of UN resolutions was worrying to U.S. officials, who feared that Iraq was hiding a program to build WMDs.

According to the *9/11 Commission Report*, President George W. Bush "wondered immediately after the [9/11] attack whether Saddam Hussein's regime might have had a hand in it." The U.S. intelligence community investigated possible connections and found no compelling case of Iraqi involvement. Nevertheless, some members of the Bush administration, particularly the U.S. deputy secretary of defense Paul D. Wolfowitz (1943–), thought the United States should strike Iraq as part of the ensuing War on Terror. The DOD recommended action be taken against three priority targets: al Qaeda, the Taliban in Afghanistan, and Iraq for posing a "strategic threat to the United States." Reportedly, Iraq was included on the list for its "long-standing involvement in terrorism" and "its interest in weapons of mass destruction." The United States opened the War on Terror by invading Afghanistan; however, Iraq remained a high-priority concern. On January 29, 2002, during his annual State of the Union speech (http://www.whitehouse.gov/news/releases/2002/01/20020129-11.html), President Bush described Iraq as a member of an "axis of evil" in the world.

Throughout the remainder of the year the Bush administration worked to garner UN approval for a military strike against Iraq. These efforts were driven by reports from the U.S. intelligence community that Iraq was amassing WMDs. In October intelligence officials presented Bush with "National Intelligence Estimate: Iraq's Continuing Programs for Weapons of Mass Destruction" (June 10, 2008, http://homepage.ntlworld.com/jksonc/docs/nie-iraq-wmd.html). This document declared that Iraq had restarted its nuclear weapons program and would likely have a nuclear weapon within a decade. Iraq was also thought to have new chemical and biological weapons. The evolution of this report was later examined in *Report to the President of the United States* (March 31, 2005, http://www.wmd.gov/report/wmd_report.pdf) by the Commission on the Intelligence Capabilities of the United States Regarding Weapons of Mass Destruction.

According to the commission, one of the major pieces of evidence against the Iraqis was their alleged purchase of nuclear material (uranium yellowcake) from Niger. The president mentioned this purchase in his State of the Union speech in January 2003. In February 2003 the U.S. secretary of state Colin Powell (1937–) addressed the UN and presented the U.S. case for military action against Iraq. The UN had already passed Resolution 1441 in late 2002 condemning Iraq for its continuing defiance of previous UN resolutions and for refusing to allow IAEA inspectors back into the country. However, the United States was unable to convince the UN that a military response was necessary. Only Britain pledged to fully support the U.S. plan for war.

According to the White House, in the press release "President Says Saddam Hussein Must Leave Iraq within 48 Hours" (http://www.whitehouse.gov/news/releases/2003/03/20030317-7.html), on the evening of March 17, 2003, President Bush addressed the nation and presented his case for war against Iraq. He warned about the dangers of Iraqi

WMDs, particularly in the hands of terrorists. He mentioned the UN resolutions that had been passed and Iraq's failure to abide by weapons inspections. He noted that the intelligence gathered "leaves no doubt that the Iraq regime continues to possess and conceal some of the most lethal weapons ever devised." Bush gave Hussein and his sons forty-eight hours to leave Iraq or face military action. He told the Iraqi people, "We will tear down the apparatus of terror and we will help you to build a new Iraq that is prosperous and free."

The coalition gathered by the United States for the impending war was smaller than the one garnered against Iraq in 1990. In 2003 only Great Britain pledged troops; many other nations, though, contributed small military forces, money, or equipment (most notably Spain, Australia, and Israel). France, Russia, and China, in particular, were opposed to military action against Iraq.

WAR IN IRAQ

In the early morning hours of March 20, 2003, Operation Iraqi Freedom began with a massive bombardment of Iraqi targets. That evening, U.S. troops surged across the Kuwaiti border to begin the ground campaign. Coalition forces quickly overcame Iraqi resistance. By early April U.S. troops were in Baghdad, and British troops had captured cities in southern Iraq. Initially, there was jubilation by some Baghdad citizens at the toppling of Hussein's regime. However, the environment quickly deteriorated as mass looting and lawlessness broke out and many buildings were burned. U.S. troops were unsuccessful at restoring civil order.

By mid-April the Kurdish Peshmerga (with U.S. help) had captured the northern cities of Kirkuk (Karkūk) and Mosul. As described by *NewsHour*, in "U.S. Strengthens Grip on N. Iraq in Bid to Calm Turkey" (April 12, 2003, http://www.pbs.org/newshour/updates/niraq_04-12-04.html), this development greatly upset Turkish officials, who feared that the Kurds would try to assert their ancient claim to Kurdistan and establish an independent state in northern Iraq. Turkey had even threatened to invade Iraq from the north if the United States allowed Kurds to hold major Iraqi cities. *NewsHour* notes that the Peshmerga retreated and U.S. forces took control of Kirkuk and Mosul. Once again, looting and mayhem became a problem in occupied areas.

By the end of April the invasion was complete. In the press release "President Bush Announces Major Combat Operations in Iraq Have Ended" (http://www.whitehouse.gov/news/releases/2003/05/20030501-15.html), the White House notes that on May 1, 2003, President Bush announced that the major combat operations in Iraq had ended. He said, "The United States and our allies have prevailed.... And now our coalition is engaged in securing and reconstructing that country."

According to the Department of State, in *Patterns of Global Terrorism 2003* (April 2004, http://www.state.gov/documents/organization/31912.pdf), by the end of 2003 coalition forces had killed or captured forty-two of the fifty-five most-wanted members of Iraq's former regime, including Hussein, who was captured in December 2003. In October 2005 Hussein went on trial in Iraq for war crimes committed against his people during his rule. He was found guilty and, in December 2006, hanged for his crimes.

INSURGENCY AND SECTARIAN VIOLENCE

After the defeat of the Iraqi army, the United States was faced with a campaign of violence that threatened to destabilize Iraqi society and government and that took the lives of many Iraqis, Americans, and other foreigners within Iraq. These attacks were carried out by a wide variety of individuals and groups that are often referred to collectively as insurgents.

During 2006 sectarian violence escalated between Iraqi Sunnis and Shiites. As noted earlier, the Iraqi population is approximately two-thirds Shiite and one-third Sunni. Shiites primarily inhabit the southern part of the country and were repressed under Hussein's Sunni-dominated regime. In February 2006 a bombing that nearly destroyed the al-Askariya Shia Mosque in Samarra triggered violence that killed more than four hundred people over the following week.

In *Measuring Stability and Security in Iraq* (August 2006, http://www.defenselink.mil/pubs/pdfs/Security-Stabilty-ReportAug29r1.pdf), the DOD states that the number of sectarian incidents in Iraq rose between May 2005 and July 2006. During May 2005 nearly one hundred sectarian incidents were recorded. This number changed little on a monthly basis through January 2006. In February 2006 the number soared to nearly three hundred incidents per month. It decreased slightly during April and was then around five hundred incidents per month from May through July 2006. The DOD also tracks daily coalition and Iraqi casualties between April 2004 and August 2006. At the beginning of this period just over twenty casualties per day were reported for both groups. By August 2006 the number of average daily casualties among coalition forces had dropped to less than 20 per day, whereas the rate among Iraqis had soared to nearly 120 per day.

By January 2007 the internal situation in Iraq was dire. In *Prospects for Iraq's Stability: A Challenging Road Ahead* (January 2007, http://www.dni.gov/press_releases/20070202_release.pdf), the Office of the Director of National Intelligence states "the term 'civil war' does not adequately capture the complexity of the conflict in Iraq, which includes extensive Shia-on-Shia violence, al-Qa'ida and Sunni insurgent attacks on Coalition forces, and widespread criminally motivated violence." The office notes that Iraqi Shiites, in particular, were deeply mistrustful of U.S. efforts to forge a new government in the country.

Iraq's New Government

From May 2003 to June 2004 Iraq was governed by the Coalition Provisional Authority (CPA), which was a temporary civil government body installed by the United States and the United Kingdom. The CPA was replaced by an Iraqi transitional government that developed a new constitution. In 2005 the constitution was upheld by a national referendum (vote), and Iraq held its first national elections to elect members of the Iraq Council of Representatives.

In March 2006 the first session of the Iraq Council of Representatives was held. The delegates had difficulty choosing a prime minister who was acceptable to the three main factions within Iraq: Shiites, Sunni, and Kurds. After more than a month of negotiation, an acceptable compromise was reached in Nouri al-Maliki (1950–), a Shiite. Throughout the summer of 2006 Prime Minister al-Maliki worked to choose a cabinet of ministers to administer Iraq's government programs.

In *Securing, Stabilizing, and Rebuilding Iraq—Progress Report: Some Gains Made, Updated Strategy Needed* (July 23, 2008, http://www.gao.gov/new.items/d081021t.pdf), the U.S. Government Accountability Office (GAO) notes that between 2003 and 2008 the United States had appropriated approximately $48 billion to U.S. agencies for the rebuilding of Iraq. Specifically, this money was used to bolster the Iraqi government and rebuild Iraq's security forces and infrastructure and utilities (e.g., electricity and water supplies). The GAO complains that the Iraqi government had spent little of the money it had available for such projects. The Iraqi government spent only 28% of the amount budgeted for the total government in 2007. (See Figure 4.6.) Only 11% of the amount budgeted was spent on central ministries (which are responsible for security and other public essentials), 41% on water resources, 0.06% on electricity, and 0.03% on oil resources.

One of the primary goals of the new government (and the United States and the United Kingdom) has been to build the Iraqi Security Forces (ISF—both army and police) to a level and strength capable of taking over security control in the country. This has proven to be extremely difficult. Figure 4.7 shows the number of trained ISF as of March 2005, January 2007, April 2008, and projected for 2010. By January 2007 the ISF numbered 323,000 personnel. However, a National Security Council states in *Highlights of the Iraq Strategy Review* (January 2007, http://www.whitehouse.gov/nsc/iraq/2007/iraq-strategy011007.pdf) that "substantially fewer numbers are present for duty on a given day." Likewise, in *Securing, Stabilizing, and Rebuilding Iraq—Progress Report: Some Gains Made, Updated Strategy Needed* (June 2008, http://www.gao.gov/new.items/d08837.pdf), the

FIGURE 4.6

Iraqi budget utilization ratios for total government and selected ministries, 2005–07

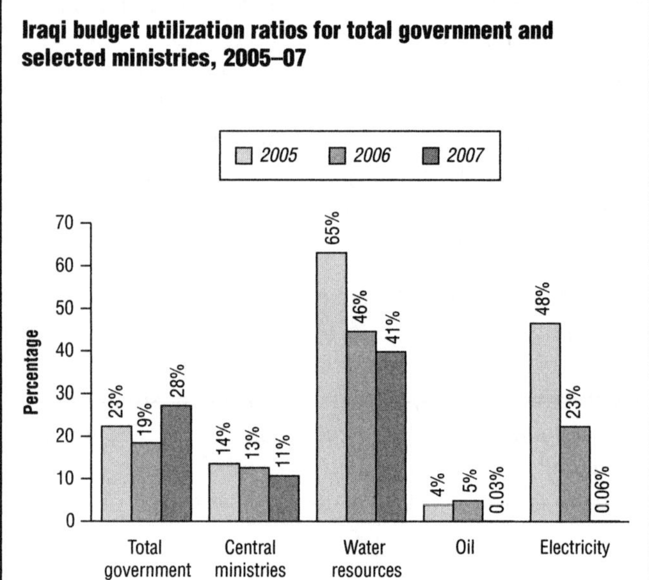

SOURCE: "Figure 3. Iraqi Budget Execution Ratios for Total Government and Selected Ministries, 2005 to 2007," in *Securing, Stabilizing, and Rebuilding Iraq: Progress Report: Some Gains Made, Updated Strategy Needed*, U.S. Government Accountability Office, July 23, 2008, http://www.gao.gov/new.items/d081021t.pdf (accessed July 24, 2008)

FIGURE 4.7

Number of trained Iraqi security forces, March 2005, January 2007, and April 2008 and projected for 2010

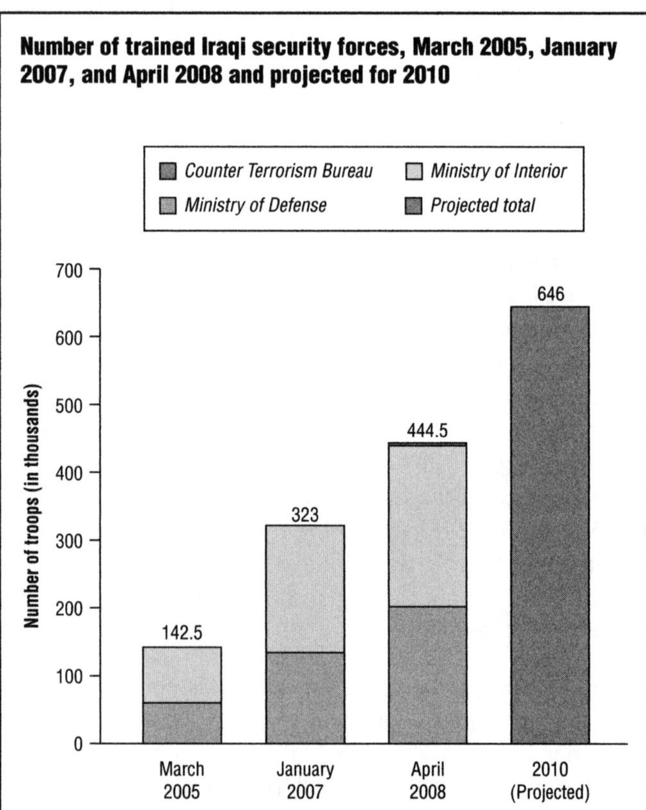

SOURCE: "Figure 6. Number of Trained Iraqi Security Forces, March 2005 through 2010," in *Securing, Stabilizing, and Rebuilding Iraq: Progress Report: Some Gains Made, Updated Strategy Needed*, U.S. Government Accountability Office, June 2008, http://www.gao.gov/new.items/d08837.pdf (accessed August 8, 2008)

GAO notes that the DOD count of "trained" ISF personnel included Iraqis who had died or were absent without leave. Approximately 24,500 Iraqi soldiers were believed to have deserted in 2007, casting serious doubts about the actual number of ISF personnel that are available for duty.

The Surge and the New Way Forward

By January 2007 the violence in Iraq was at an all-time high. The American public was increasingly displeased with the course of the war, and some lawmakers demanded that U.S. troops leave Iraq as soon as possible. President Bush proposed in a January 10, 2007, radio address a different strategy dubbed the "The New Way Forward" (http://www.whitehouse.gov/news/releases/2007/01/20070110-3.html). Rather than troop withdrawals, the new strategy called for additional U.S. troops to be sent to Iraq in an attempt to curb the violence. Figure 4.8 shows the number of U.S. forces in Iraq between March 2003 and July 2008. U.S. troop strength increased by approximately forty thousand people during the troop surge. The result was a dramatic decrease in violence in Iraq. Figure 4.9 shows the average number of daily attacks reported per month in Iraq from May 2003 through June 2008 based on Defense Intelligence Agency data. Daily attacks peaked in late 2006 and early 2007 and then plummeted through early 2008.

On September 13, 2007, Bush addressed the nation and announced that the surge had achieved many of its goals. As a result, he pledged to reduce troop levels in Iraq by a substantial number over the next ten months. Officially, "The New Way Forward" ended in July 2008. President Bush set a goal in "The New Way Forward" that the Iraqi government would assume responsibility for security in all of Iraq's eighteen provinces by November 2007. This goal was not met. Only nine provinces had made the transition as of May 2008. (See Figure 4.10.)

U.S. INTELLIGENCE—"DEAD WRONG"

During and after the invasion of Iraq, U.S. forces searched the country for WMDs, but found none. An outcry in the American media spurred President Bush to establish an investigatory commission to find out why U.S. prewar intelligence about Iraq had been wrong.

On March 31, 2005, the Commission on the Intelligence Capabilities of the United States Regarding Weapons of Mass Destruction issued its final report, *Report to*

FIGURE 4.8

Number of U.S. forces in Iraq, March 2003–July 2008

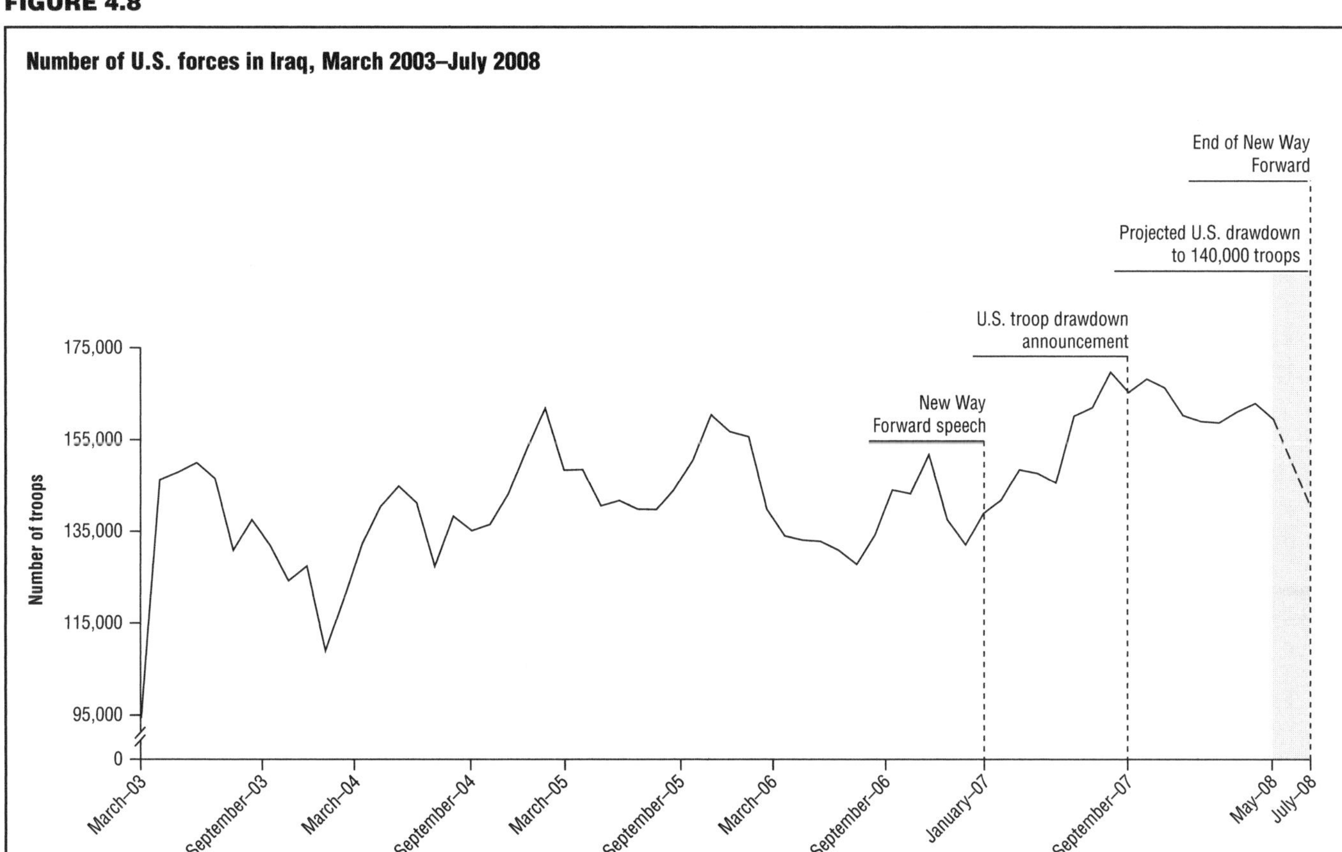

Note: For all months prior to February 2008, the Department of Defense (DOD) provided the Government Accountability Office (GAO) with end-of-month data for the number of U.S. troops in Iraq. In February 2008, DOD began to provide GAO with data from the beginning of the month.

SOURCE: "Figure 4. U.S. Forces in Iraq, March 2003 to July 2008," in *Securing, Stabilizing, and Rebuilding Iraq: Progress Report: Some Gains Made, Updated Strategy Needed*, U.S. Government Accountability Office, June 2008, http://www.gao.gov/new.items/d08837.pdf (accessed August 8, 2008)

FIGURE 4.9

Average number of daily insurgent attacks in Iraq, May 2003—July 2008

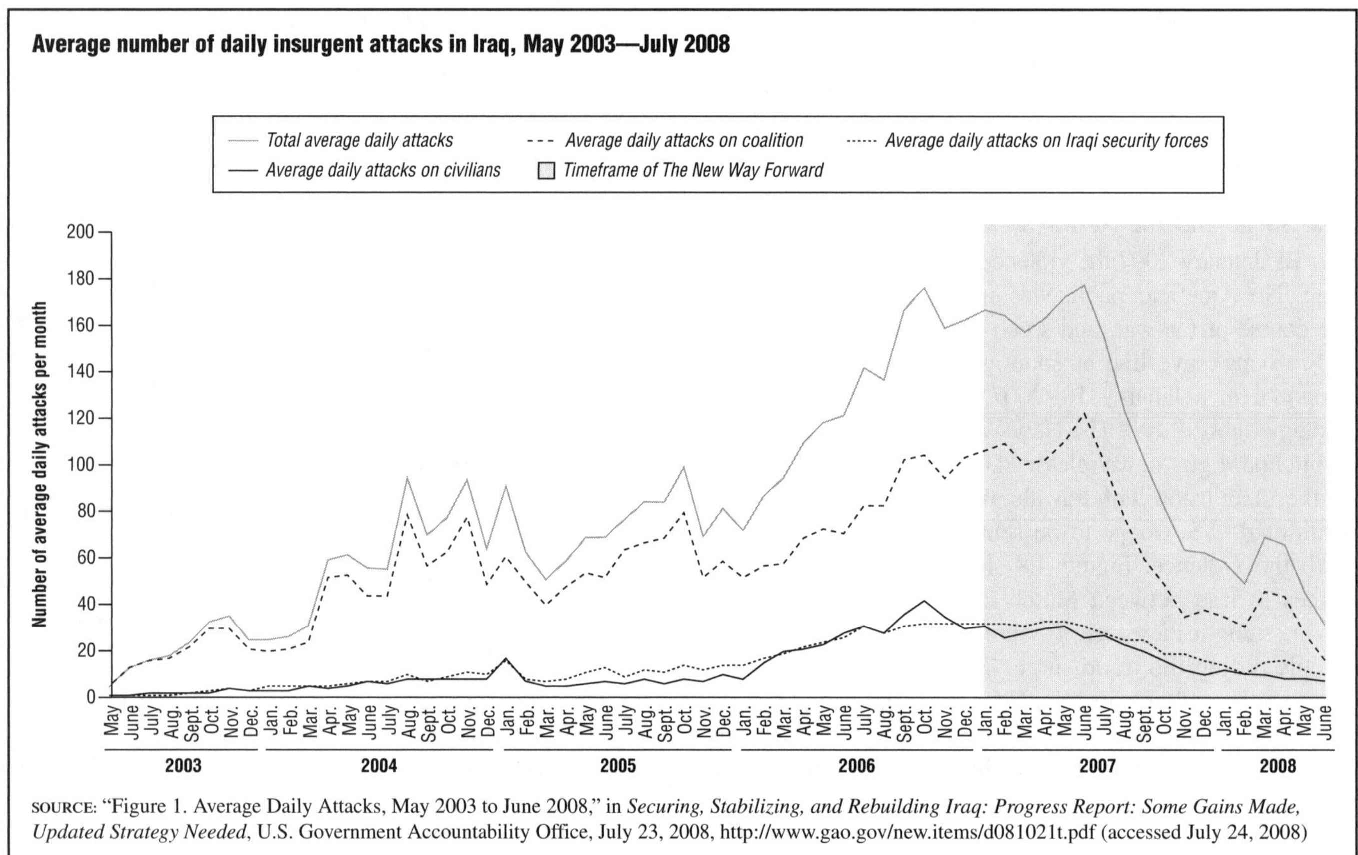

SOURCE: "Figure 1. Average Daily Attacks, May 2003 to June 2008," in *Securing, Stabilizing, and Rebuilding Iraq: Progress Report: Some Gains Made, Updated Strategy Needed*, U.S. Government Accountability Office, July 23, 2008, http://www.gao.gov/new.items/d081021t.pdf (accessed July 24, 2008)

the President of the United States (http://www.wmd.gov/report/wmd_report.pdf). Its assessment was extremely critical, noting, "We conclude that the Intelligence Community was dead wrong in almost all of its pre-war judgments about Iraq's weapons of mass destruction." The commission found that U.S. intelligence agents had been shocked following the 1991 Persian Gulf War to learn that Iraq's nuclear weapons program had advanced much more than they had suspected and that Hussein had previously unknown stockpiles of chemical weapons. Their suspicions had deepened throughout the 1990s because of Hussein's dogged defiance of IAEA inspections. The commission acknowledged that "Saddam acted to the very end like a man with much to hide. And the dangers of underestimating our enemies were deeply underscored by the attacks of September 11, 2001."

The commission learned that U.S. intelligence agents had obtained much false information from unreliable informants and poor data sources. For example, the evidence that Iraq had purchased yellowcake from Niger turned out to be based on documents that were forgeries. Intelligence officials had ignored information that did not support their preconceived notion about Iraq's guilt. Some analysts had reported that there were no conclusive links between Iraq and al Qaeda and believed that Hussein (a secular leader) and bin Laden (a religious fundamentalist) did not trust or like each other, making cooperation extremely unlikely.

The commission found that Iraq did have an active and productive nuclear weapons program through 1991. However, much of the infrastructure had been destroyed by coalition bombing during the Persian Gulf War, and the Iraqi scientists involved in the program had been reassigned to other tasks. Thus, there had been no active program within Iraq to develop or acquire WMDs for quite some time. The commission noted, "The harm done to American credibility by our all too public intelligence failings in Iraq will take years to undo." The commission's findings were embarrassing to the Bush administration, which had pressed the international community for the invasion.

IRAQ: THE AMERICAN TOLL AND PUBLIC OPINION

Between March 19, 2003, and August 2, 2008, 4,122 U.S. military personnel died during Operation Iraqi Freedom. (See Table 4.5.) Of the total deaths, 2,586 occurred during active combat. (See Table 4.6.) The remaining 768 deaths were classified as nonhostile. In addition, 30,490 personnel were wounded, 8,840 suffered nonhostile injuries, and 24,689 suffered diseases serious enough that they required medical air transport.

FIGURE 4.10

Political status of Iraqi provinces, May 2008

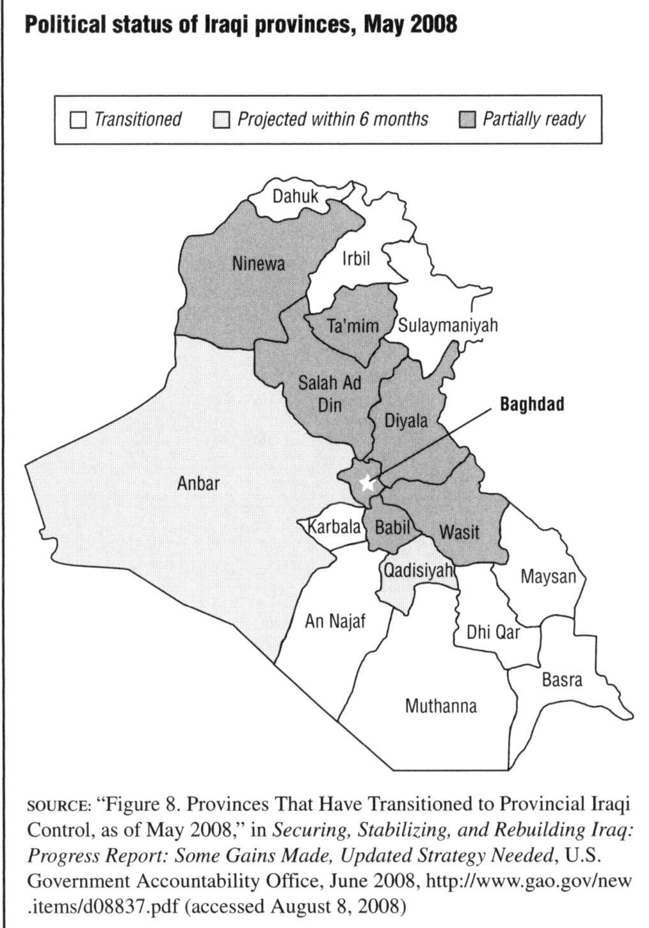

SOURCE: "Figure 8. Provinces That Have Transitioned to Provincial Iraqi Control, as of May 2008," in *Securing, Stabilizing, and Rebuilding Iraq: Progress Report: Some Gains Made, Updated Strategy Needed*, U.S. Government Accountability Office, June 2008, http://www.gao.gov/new.items/d08837.pdf (accessed August 8, 2008)

TABLE 4.5

U.S. military deaths in Operation Iraqi Freedom (OIF), by demographic characteristics, March 19, 2001–August 2, 2008

	Totals
Casualty type	
Hostile	3,354
Nonhostile	768
Total	**4,122**
Gender	
Male	4,023
Female	99
Total	**4,122**
Officer/enlisted	
Officer	386
E5–E9	1,350
E1–E4	2,386
Total	**4,122**
Age	
<22	1,217
22–24	1,000
25–30	1,045
31–35	406
>35	454
Total	**4,122**
Component	
Active	3,366
Reserve	299
National Guard	457
Total	**4,122**
Race/ethnicity	
American Indian or Alaska Native	40
Asian	77
Black or African American	391
Hispanic or Latino	441
Multiple races, pending, or unknown	43
Native Hawaiian or Pacific Islander	48
White	3,082
Total	**4,122**

Note: Data subject to change.

SOURCE: Adapted from "Operation Iraqi Freedom Military Deaths, March 19, 2001 through August 2, 2008," in *DoD Personnel and Military Casualty Statistics: Military Casualty Information*, U.S. Department of Defense, August 2, 2008, http://siadapp.dmdc.osd.mil/personnel/CASUALTY/oif-deaths-total.pdf (accessed August 8, 2008)

Table 4.7 was compiled in June 2008 by the CRS. The table lists the money appropriated to Operation Iraqi Freedom from FY 2001 to FY 2009, including bridge funds and pending amounts. As of June 2008, appropriations for the war in Iraq totaled \$656.1 billion. The vast majority of the money (\$619.5 billion) was appropriated to the DOD. Another \$34 billion went for related foreign aid and diplomatic operations. The Department of Veterans Affairs had received approximately \$2.5 billion for its medical operations.

The U.S.-led invasion of Iraq has endured much international criticism. When the war began, the American public was torn, but generally favorable, about the idea. This support faded dramatically in the face of continuing insurgency and the rising U.S. death toll in Iraq. Since 2003 the Gallup Organization has conducted many polls on American attitudes about the war in Iraq. Figure 4.11 shows the results obtained by Gallup when it asked Americans whether or not the United States "made a mistake" in sending troops to Iraq. In March 2003 approximately 75% of respondents said it had not been a mistake to send U.S. troops to Iraq. Over the following five years, support for the war dropped dramatically. By July 2008 only 40% of respondents thought the United States had not erred by sending troops to Iraq. By contrast, the percentage of respondents who thought the war had been a mistake increased from 23% in March 2003 to 56% in July 2008.

Gallup also finds that most Americans favor setting a timetable for removing U.S. troops from Iraq. Since June 2005 all but one poll have indicated that more than 50% of respondents favored setting such a timetable. (See Table 4.8.) In February 2008, 60% of respondents favored a timetable, whereas 35% thought the United States should keep troops in Iraq "until the situation gets better."

In July 2008 Americans believed by a small margin (44%) that the war in Afghanistan is "more important" for the United States than the war in Iraq (38%). (See Figure 4.12.) As a result, a majority of poll respondents

TABLE 4.6

U.S. military casualties in Operation Iraqi Freedom (OIF), by category, October 7, 2001–August 2, 2008

Casualty type	Total
Killed in action	2,586
Died of wounds[a]	756
Died while missing in action	7
Died while captured	5
Total hostile deaths	**3,354**
Accident	492
Illness	78
Homicide	22
Self-inflicted	156
Undetermined	10
Pending[b]	10
Total non-hostile deaths	**768**
Total deaths	**4,122**
Total wounded (WIA)	**30,490**
Wounded—no medical air transport required	21,211
Wounded—medical air transport required[c]	9,279
Total—non-hostile-related medical air transports	**33,529**
Non-hostile injuries—medical air transport required[c]	8,840
Diseases/other medical—medical air transport required[c]	24,689
Total—medical air transports (hostile and non-hostile)	**42,808**

[a]Includes died of wounds where wounding occurred in theater and death occurred elsewhere.
[b]Pending means final category to be determined at a later date.
[c]Reported by Force Health Protection and Readiness.

SOURCE: Adapted from "Global War on Terrorism—Operation Iraqi Freedom by Casualty Category within Service, March 19, 2003 through August 2, 2008," in *DoD Personnel and Military Casualty Statistics: Military Casualty Information*, U.S. Department of Defense, August 2, 2008, http://siadapp.dmdc.osd.mil/personnel/CASUALTY/OIF-Total.pdf (accessed August 8, 2008)

supported moving U.S. troops from Iraq to Afghanistan to fight al Qaeda and Taliban terrorists. In July 2008, 57% of respondents favored such a move, whereas 36% were opposed to it. (See Figure 4.13.) The percentage favoring moving U.S. troops from Iraq to Afghanistan was up slightly from 52% support reported in August 2007.

TABLE 4.7

Budget authority for Operation Iraqi Freedom, 2001–09

[CRS estimates in billions of budget authority]

By operation and funding source	FY01 & FY02[a]	FY03	FY04	FY05	FY06	FY07	FY08[b]	Cum.enacted thru FY08 consol. approp.	Pending FY08 req.[a]	Pdg. FY09 req.[c]	Cum: FY01-FY09 bridge in house-Passed H.R. 2642, 6–19–08[c]
Operation Iraqi Freedom (OIF)[d]											
Department of Defense	0	50.0	56.4	83.4	98.1	129.6	**73.8**	**491.3**	**80.0**	**52.0**	**619.5**
Foreign aid and diplomatic ops[e]	0	3.0	19.5	2.0	3.2	3.2	**0.9**	**31.7**	**2.5**	**1.4**	**34.0**
VA medical[f]	0	0	0	0.2	0.4	0.9	**0.7**	**2.2**	**0.0**	**0.0**	**2.5**
Total: Iraq	**0.0**	**53.0**	**75.9**	**85.5**	**101.7**	**133.6**	**75.5**	**525.2**	**82.5**	**53.4**	**656.1**

Notes: Because DOD has not provided a breakdown by operation for all appropriations received, CRS estimates unobligated budget authority using past trends as shown in DOD's Defense Finance Accounting Service (DFAS) reports, *Supplemental & Cost of War Execution Reports* and other budget justification materials. CRS budget authority (BA) totals are higher than DOD figures because CRS includes all funding provided in supplementals, bridge funds or baseline appropriations for Iraq and the Global war on Terror as well as transfers from DOD's baseline funds for GWOT requirements, and enhanced security. CRS also splits the $25 billion provided in the FY2005 Title IX bridge between the $1.8 billion obligated in FY2004 and the remainder available for FY2005; all those funds are scored as FY2004 because they were available upon enactment in August 2005. Figures include funds provided in P.L. 107–38, the first emergency supplemental after 9/11, and funds allocated in P.L. 107–117. Numbers may not add due to rounding. CRS = Congressional Research Service. GWOT = Global War on Terror.

[a]CRS combined funds for FY2001 and FY2002 because most were obligated in FY2002 after the 9/11 attacks at the end of FY2001. In FY2008, CRS includes funds for enhanced security in DOD's regular budget, and excludes as non-war related DOD request for funds to cover higher fuel prices for its regular program and accelerate the replacement of Walter Reed for a more consistent definition of war costs.

[b]Includes funds provided in the First Continuing Resolution (H.J.Res 52/P.L. 110–92), FY2008 DOD Appropriations Act (H.R. 3222/P.L. 110–116) and the FY2008 Consolidated Appropriations Act (H.R. 2764/P.L. 110–161).

[c]Reflects H.R. 2642 as passed by the House on June 19, 2008 excluding funding not related to Iraq and Afghanistan and $4.9 billion in DOD funds not related to war; excludes $1.4 billion in the regular FY2009 State/USAID request for Iraq and Afghanistan.

[d]DOD's new estimate in FY2007 for Iraq shows BA from FY2003 as $48 billion, $2 billion higher than reported by DFAS without identifying a source for these funds.

[e]Foreign operations figures include monies for reconstruction, development and humanitarian aid, embassy operations, counter narcotics, initial training of the Afghan and Iraqi army, foreign military sales credits, and Economic Support Funds. For FY2007, figures reflect State Department figures; for FY2008, figures reflect Joint Explanatory Statement for Division J, FY2008 Consolidated Appropriations Act (P.L. 110–161) in December 17, 2007 Congressional Record; may be revised by State Department at a later date.

[f]Medical estimates reflect figures in VA's FY2008 budget justifications, and CRS estimate of OIF/OEF shares of $3.6 billion added by Congress to VA Medical in FY2008 Consolidated Appropriations Act (P.L. 110–161).

SOURCE: Adapted from Amy Belasco, "Table 4. Budget Authority for Iraq, Afghanistan, and Other Global War on Terror (GWOT) Operations: FY2001–FY2009 Bridge Request," in *The Cost of Iraq, Afghanistan, and Other Global War on Terror Operations since 9/11*, Congressional Research Service, June 23, 2008, http://www.fas.org/sgp/crs/natsec/RL33110.pdf (accessed July 25, 2008)

FIGURE 4.11

Public opinion on whether the U.S. made a mistake in sending military forces to Iraq, selected dates, 2003–08

IN VIEW OF THE DEVELOPMENTS SINCE WE FIRST SENT OUR TROOPS TO IRAQ, DO YOU THINK THE UNITED STATES MADE A MISTAKE IN SENDING TROOPS TO IRAQ, OR NOT?

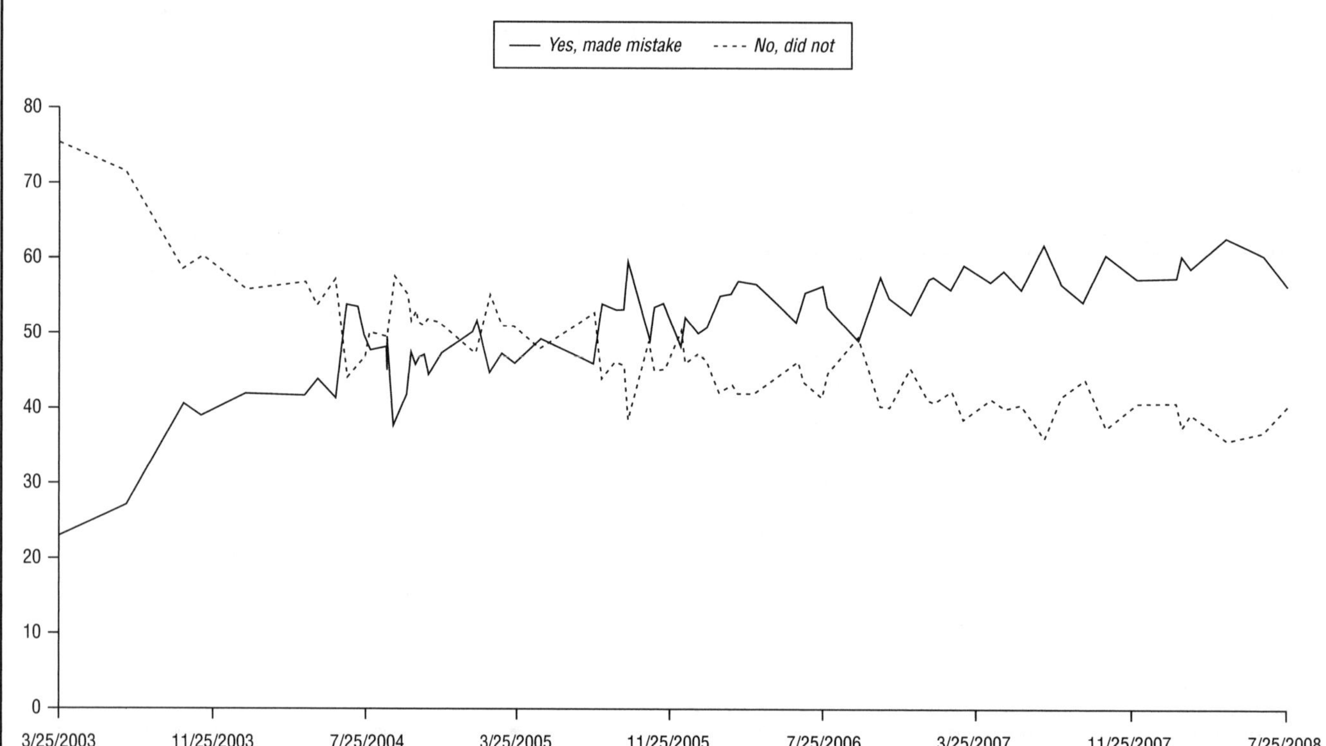

SOURCE: Adapted from "In View of the Developments since We First Sent Our Troops to Iraq, Do You Think the United States Made a Mistake in Sending Troops to Iraq, or Not?" in *Create a Trend*, The Gallup Organization, 2008, http://brain.gallup.com/documents/trendQuestion.aspx?QUESTION=165532&Advanced=0&SearchConType=In%20view%20of%20the%20develoments%20since%20we%20first%20sent%20our%20troops%20to%20Iraq,%20do%20you%think%20the%20United%20States%20made%20a%20mistake%20sending %20troops%20to%20Iraq,%20ro%20not? (accessed August 6, 2008). Copyright © 2008 by The Gallup Organization. Reporduced by permission of The Gallup Organization.

TABLE 4.8

Public opinion on whether a timetable should be set for removing troops from Iraq, July 2008

IF YOU HAD TO CHOOSE, WHICH DO YOU THINK IS BETTER FOR THE U.S.: TO KEEP A SIGNIFICANT NUMBER OF TROOPS IN IRAQ UNTIL THE SITUATION THERE GETS BETTER, EVEN IF THAT TAKES MANY YEARS, OR TO SET A TIMETABLE FOR REMOVING TROOPS FROM IRAQ AND TO STICK TO THAT TIMETABLE REGARDLESS OF WHAT IS GOING ON IN IRAQ AT THE TIME?

	Keep troops in Iraq until the situation gets better	Set timetable for removing troops from Iraq	No opinion
	%	%	%
2008 Feb 21–24	35	60	5
2008 Feb 8–10	39	56	5
2007 Nov 30–Dec 2	38	59	3
2007 Sep 14–16	38	59	4
2007 Sep 7–8	35	60	5
2007 May 4–6	36	59	5
2007 Apr 13–15	38	57	4
2005 Jun 29–30	48	49	3
2005 Jun 24–26	44	51	5

SOURCE: Frank Newport, "If You Had to Choose, Which Do You Think Is Better for the U.S.: To Keep a Significant Number of Troops in Iraq until the Situation There Gets Better, Even If That Takes Many Years, or to Set a Timetable for Removing Troops from Iraq and to Stick to That Timetable Regardless of What Is Going on in Iraq at the Time?" in *Exploring the Iraq Timetable Issue*, The Gallup Organization, August 5, 2008, http://www.gallup.com/poll/109294/Exploring-Iraq-Timetable-Issue.aspx?version=print (accessed August 9, 2008). Copyright © 2008 by The Gallup Organization. Reproduced by permission of The Gallup Organization.

FIGURE 4.13

Public opinion on whether U.S. troops should be moved from Iraq to Afghanistan, August 2007 and July 2008

WOULD YOU FAVOR OR OPPOSE MOVING U.S. TROOPS FROM IRAQ TO AFGHANISTAN IN ORDER TO FIGHT AL QAEDA AND TALIBAN TERRORIST OPERATIONS IN AFGHANISTAN?

Asked of half sample

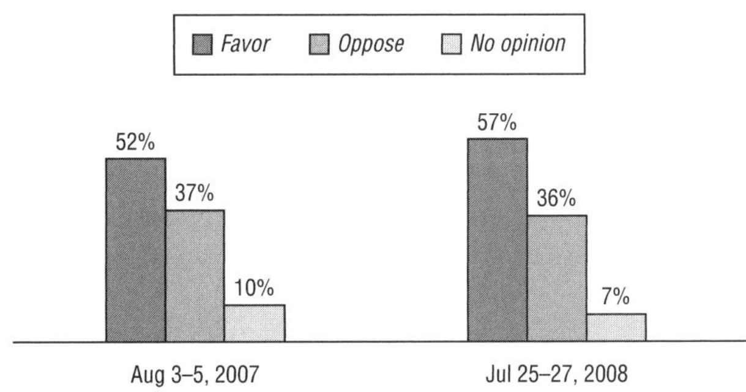

SOURCE: Frank Newport, "Would You Favor or Oppose Moving U.S. Troops from Iraq to Afghanistan in Order to Fight al Qaeda and Taliban Terrorist Operations in Afghanistan?" in *Afghan War Edges out Iraq As Most Important for U.S.*, The Gallup Organization, July 30, 2008, http://www.gallup.com/poll/109150/Afghan-War-Edges-Iraq-Most-Important-US.aspx?version=print (accessed August 9, 2008). Copyright © 2008 by The Gallup Organization. Reproduced by permission of The Gallup Organization.

FIGURE 4.12

Public opinion on whether the Iraq war or the Afghanistan war is more important for the United States, July 2008

IF YOU HAD TO CHOOSE, WHICH IS THE MORE IMPORTANT WAR FOR THE UNITED STATES: THE WAR IS IRAQ OR THE WAR IS AFGHANISTAN?

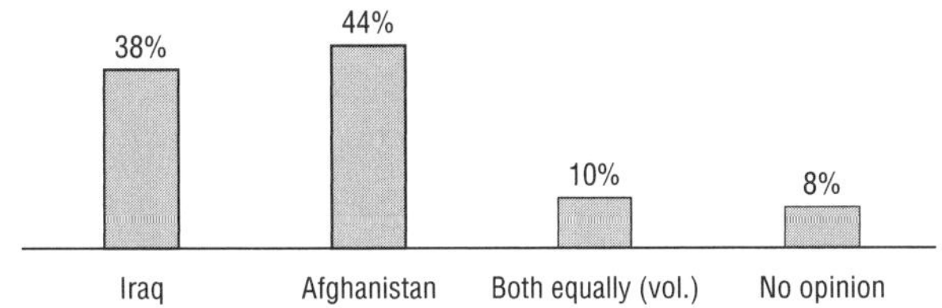

(vol.) = Volunteered Response.

SOURCE: Frank Newport, "If You Had to Choose, Which Is the More Important War for the United States: The War in Iraq or the War in Afghanistan?" in *Afghan War Edges out Iraq As Most Important for U.S.*, The Gallup Organization, July 30, 2008, http://www.gallup.com/poll/109150/Afghan-War-Edges-Iraq-Most-Important-US.aspx?version=print (accessed August 9, 2008). Copyright © 2008 by The Gallup Organization. Reproduced by permission of The Gallup Organization.

CHAPTER 5
THE WAR ON TERROR: HOMELAND SECURITY

Protecting the U.S. homeland from terrorist attacks is a formidable and challenging task. The scope is enormous. According to the Central Intelligence Agency, in *The World Factbook: United States* (August 21, 2008, https://www.cia.gov/library/publications/the-world-factbook/geos/us.html#People), the United States encompasses over 3.5 million square miles of territory and, as of July 2008, it had a population of 303.8 million. U.S. borders span more than one hundred thousand miles and are difficult to protect against illegal entry. There are hundreds of land border crossings, seaports, and international airports that must be secured. The United States has vast air and rail transportation systems and many highly concentrated metropolitan areas, all of which are attractive targets for terrorists. American society is relatively open with little restriction on movement or access to public places, and foreign visitors are welcomed. The American people are diverse, encompassing a variety of races, ethnic groups, and religions. This makes it easier for foreign terrorists to hide within the population and wait for an opportunity to strike—as happened on September 11, 2001 (9/11).

To counter the vulnerabilities inherent to American society, the U.S. government has developed a homeland security infrastructure that coordinates the efforts of many agencies at the federal, state, and local levels. The overall goal is threefold: to prevent terrorists from striking in the United States, to fortify U.S. defenses against an attack, and to prepare the American people and emergency responders in case an attack does occur.

U.S. DEPARTMENT OF HOMELAND SECURITY

The U.S. Department of Homeland Security (DHS) was established by President George W. Bush (1946–) in 2002 and began operating in 2003. It has been given three primary responsibilities: prevent terrorist attacks from occurring within the United States, reduce the nation's vulnerability to terrorist attacks and the damage caused by them, and facilitate quick and effective recovery in the event of an attack. The DHS works in concert with other federal entities devoted to national security, particularly the intelligence community (IC), the U.S. military, and the Federal Bureau of Investigation (FBI). Besides this horizontal cooperation, the DHS is also supposed to coordinate homeland security efforts in a vertical manner—across federal, state, and local government levels. State and local officials are particularly important to the task of emergency response, because they represent the first wave of government assistance in the event of a terrorist attack.

The DHS brought together dozens of agencies and offices that had previously operated as separate entities. Some had been independent; others had been part of larger organizations, such as the U.S. Departments of Justice (DOJ), Treasury, Transportation, Energy, and Agriculture, the FBI, and the U.S. General Services Administration.

Figure 5.1 shows an organization chart for the DHS as of March 2008. The major components of the agency are described in Table 5.1.

NATIONAL STRATEGY FOR HOMELAND SECURITY

The terrorist attacks of 9/11 made evident to U.S. leaders that the country lacked a coordinated strategy for protecting the U.S. homeland from terrorism. In October 2007 President Bush issued *National Strategy for Homeland Security* (http://www.whitehouse.gov/infocus/homeland/nshs/NSHS.pdf). The strategy lists three primary goals of homeland security (see Table 5.2):

- Prevent and disrupt terrorist attacks
- Protect the American people, critical infrastructure, and key resources
- Respond to and recover from incidents

FIGURE 5.1

Department of Homeland Security (DHS) organization chart, March 2008

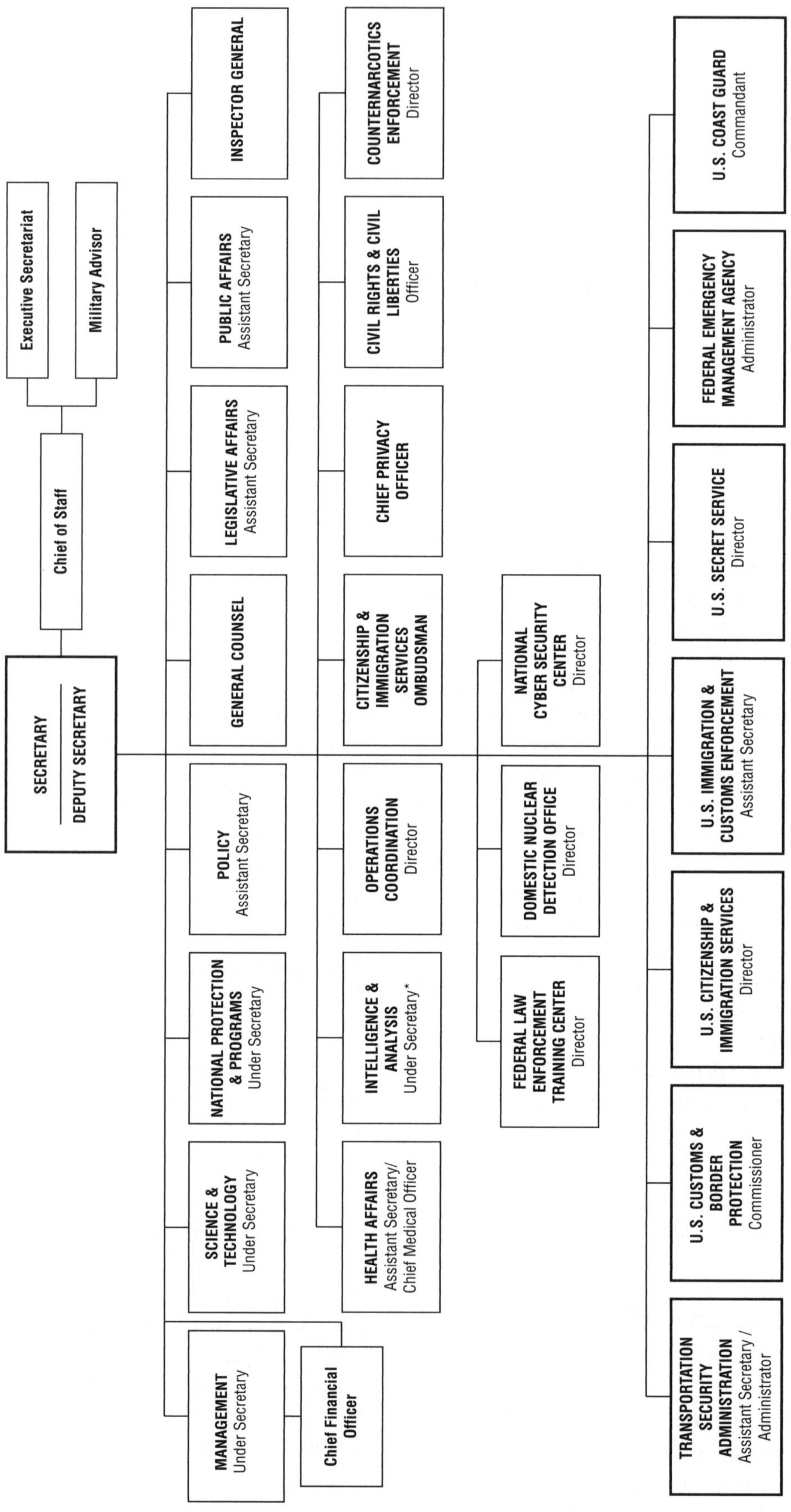

SECRETARY
DEPUTY SECRETARY

Chief of Staff
Executive Secretariat
Military Advisor

MANAGEMENT
Under Secretary

Chief Financial Officer

SCIENCE & TECHNOLOGY
Under Secretary

NATIONAL PROTECTION & PROGRAMS
Under Secretary

POLICY
Assistant Secretary

GENERAL COUNSEL

LEGISLATIVE AFFAIRS
Assistant Secretary

PUBLIC AFFAIRS
Assistant Secretary

INSPECTOR GENERAL

HEALTH AFFAIRS
Assistant Secretary/
Chief Medical Officer

INTELLIGENCE & ANALYSIS
Under Secretary*

OPERATIONS COORDINATION
Director

CITIZENSHIP & IMMIGRATION SERVICES OMBUDSMAN

CHIEF PRIVACY OFFICER

CIVIL RIGHTS & CIVIL LIBERTIES
Officer

COUNTERNARCOTICS ENFORCEMENT
Director

FEDERAL LAW ENFORCEMENT TRAINING CENTER
Director

DOMESTIC NUCLEAR DETECTION OFFICE
Director

NATIONAL CYBER SECURITY CENTER
Director

TRANSPORTATION SECURITY ADMINISTRATION
Assistant Secretary /
Administrator

U.S. CUSTOMS & BORDER PROTECTION
Commissioner

U.S. CITIZENSHIP & IMMIGRATION SERVICES
Director

U.S. IMMIGRATION & CUSTOMS ENFORCEMENT
Assistant Secretary

U.S. SECRET SERVICE
Director

FEDERAL EMERGENCY MANAGEMENT AGENCY
Administrator

U.S. COAST GUARD
Commandant

*Under Secretary for Intelligence & Analysis title created by Public Law 110-53, Aug. 3rd, 2007

SOURCE: "U.S. Deparment of Homeland Security," in *About the Department: Organizational Chart*, U.S Department of Homeland Security, March 30, 2008, http://www.dhs.gov/xlibrary/assets/DHS_OrgChart.pdf (accessed August 8, 2008)

TABLE 5.1

Department of Homeland Security (DHS) agencies, 2008

DHS agency	Acronym	Purpose
Transportation Security Administration	TSA	Protects the transportation system and ensures the freedom of movement for people and commerce.
U.S. Customs & Border Protection	CBP	Protects the sovereign borders of the United States at and between official ports of entry. Also protects economic security by regulating and facilitating the lawful movement of goods and persons across U.S. borders.
U.S. Citizenship & Immigration Services	USCIS	Grants immigration and citizenship benefits, promotes an awareness and understanding of citizenship, and ensures the integrity of the immigration system.
U.S. Immigration and Customs Enforcement	ICE	Investigates the illegal introduction of goods, terrorists and other criminals seeking to cross our nation's borders.
U.S. Secret Service	USSS	Protects the President, Vice President, and other dignitaries and designated individuals; enforces laws relating to obligations and securities of the United States; investigates financial and electronic crimes; and protects the White House and other buildings within the Washington, D.C. area.
Federal Emergency Management Agency	FEMA	Leads the federal government's role in preparing for, preventing, mitigating the effects of, responding to, and recovering from domestic disasters and emergencies, whether natural or man-made, including acts of terror.
U.S. Coast Guard	USCG	Principal federal agency responsible for maritime safety, security and stewardship.
Federal Law Enforcement Training Center	FLETC	Federal government's principal provider of world-class, interagency training of federal law enforcement personnel.
Domestic Nuclear Detection Office	DNDO	Improve the nation's capability to detect and report unauthorized attempts to import, possess, store, develop, or transport radiological or nuclear material for use against the nation, and to further enhance this capability over time.
Office of Health Affairs	OHA	Department of Homeland Security's principal agent for all medical and health preparedness.
Office of Intelligence & Analysis	I&A	Responsible for the department's intelligence and information gathering and sharing capabilities for and among all components of DHS.
Science & Technology Directorate	S&T	Provides federal, state, local, tribal and territorial officials with state-of-the-art technology and other resources.
Office of Operations Coordination	OPS	Integrates DHS and interagency operations and planning to prevent, protect, respond to and recover from terrorist threats attacks or threats from other man-made/natural disasters.

SOURCE: Adapted from "Summary Information by Organization," in *Homeland Security Budget-in-Brief: Fiscal Year 2009*, U.S. Department of Homeland Security, February 2008, http://www.dhs.gov/xlibrary/assets/budget_bib-fy2009.pdf (accessed August 8, 2008)

TABLE 5.2

Major components of National Strategy for Homeland Security

Prevent and disrupt terrorist attacks

- Deny terrorists, their weapons, and other terror-related materials entry to the homeland
- Disrupt terrorists and their capacity to operate in the United States
- Prevent violent Islamic extremist radicalization in the United States

Protect the American people, critical infrastructure, and key resources

- Deter the terrorist threat
- Mitigate vulnerabilities
- Minimize consequences

Respond to and recover from incidents

- Strengthen the foundation for an effective national response
- Asses situation and take initial action
- Expand operational capabilities, as needed
- Commence short-term recovery actions to stabilize the affected area and demobilize assets
- Ensure an effective transition to long-term rebuilding and revitalization efforts

SOURCE: Adapted from *National Strategy for Homeland Security*, Office of the President of the United States, U.S. Department of Homeland Security, October 5, 2007, http://www.whitehouse.gov/infocus/homeland/nshs/NSHS.pdf (accessed August 8, 2008)

The report explains "the last goal entails creating and transforming our homeland security principles, systems, structures, and institutions. This includes applying a comprehensive approach to risk management, building a culture of preparedness, developing a comprehensive Homeland Security Management System, improving incident management, better utilizing science and technology, and leveraging all instruments of national power and influence." Figure 5.2 shows the four-step management system that DHS uses to carry out its three goals.

PREVENT AND DISRUPT TERRORIST ATTACKS

The goal to prevent and disrupt terrorist attacks focuses primarily on gathering and sharing intelligence, securing the nation's borders and transportation systems, and conducting law enforcement counterterrorism activities.

Role of Intelligence

As described in Chapter 2, intelligence is information about one's enemies. The *National Strategy for Homeland Security* calls for a highly coordinated and integrated framework for intelligence gathering and analysis. One of the roles of the IC is tactical threat analysis. This is the collection and analysis of reliable information about terrorist plots and plans. This task is led by the director of central intelligence (the head of the IC) and by FBI and DHS intelligence agents. Intelligence achieved from this task allows the development of effective preventive action—that is, the disruption of planned terrorist plots and the capture of the terrorists. Preventive activities are spearheaded by the FBI through a collection of law enforcement entities called joint terrorism task forces (JTTFs). The FBI operates a national JTTF out of its headquarters in Washington, D.C.

A second important intelligence task is strategic analysis of the enemy. This is a deep and comprehensive delving into the history, motivations, workings, and structures of terrorist organizations to identify their members and means of financial support. The goal is to determine their vulnerabilities, intentions, and capabilities. This task is led by the director of central intelligence, the FBI, and the DHS.

FIGURE 5.2

Homeland security management system, 2007

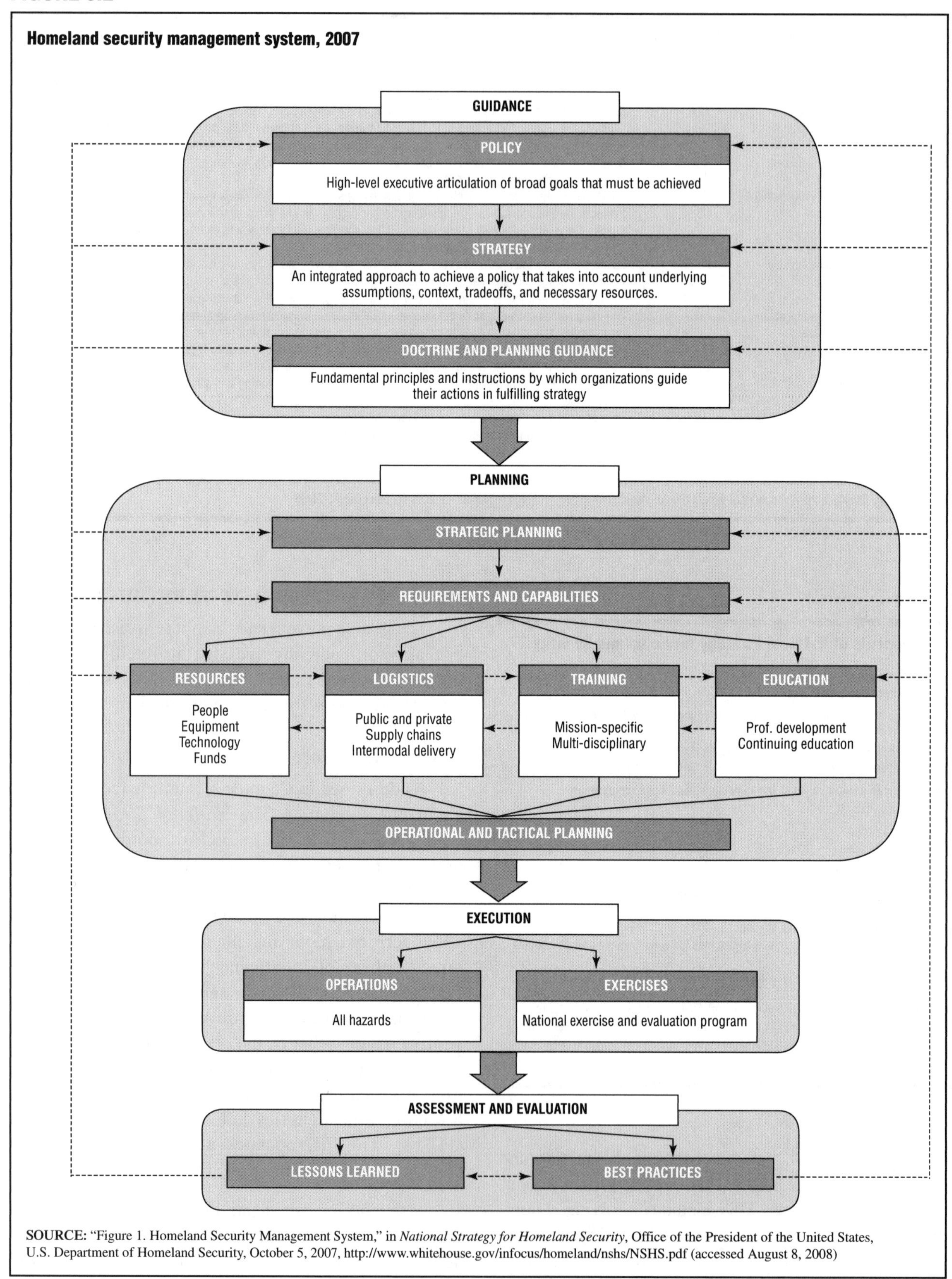

SOURCE: "Figure 1. Homeland Security Management System," in *National Strategy for Homeland Security*, Office of the President of the United States, U.S. Department of Homeland Security, October 5, 2007, http://www.whitehouse.gov/infocus/homeland/nshs/NSHS.pdf (accessed August 8, 2008)

Border Security

The U.S. Customs and Border Protection (CBP) is responsible for protecting U.S. borders from the illegal entry of people and goods. At the same time, it must ensure that legal visitors and cargo have relatively easy passage into and out of the United States. Since becom-

TABLE 5.3

DHS programs for screening cargo entering the United States

Screening cargo

- The Container Security Initiative (CSI) creates a security regime to prescreen and evaluate maritime containers— before they are shipped from foreign ports—through automated targeting tools, ensuring that high-risk cargo is examined or scanned.
- The Customs-Trade Partnership Against Terrorism (C-TPAT) is a voluntary U.S. Customs and Border Protection program whereby participating businesses undergo a review of security procedures and adopt enhanced security measures in order to expedite shipping.
- The Megaports Initiative is a Department of Energy program in which the United States collaborates with foreign trade partners to enhance their ability to scan cargo for nuclear and other radiological materials at major international seaports.
- The Secure Freight Initiative is a comprehensive model for securing the global supply chain that seeks to enhance security while keeping legitimate trade flowing. It leverages shipper information, host country government partnerships, and trade partnerships to scan cargo containers bound for the United States.

SOURCE: "Screening Cargo," in *National Strategy for Homeland Security*, Office of the President of the United States, U.S. Department of Homeland Security, October 5, 2007, http://www.whitehouse.gov/infocus/homeland/nshs/NSHS.pdf (accessed August 8, 2008)

ing a part of the DHS in 2003, the CBP has been given an important priority: detect terrorists and their weapons and prevent them from entering the United States. This is besides the CBP's many other responsibilities, including screening all traffic (people, vehicles, and cargo) into and out of the country for illegal activities or contraband. The task is enormous, because U.S. borders are long, cross-border traffic is voluminous, and the country's economy is dependent on international trade. According to the CBP, in "Securing America's Borders—CBP 2007 Fiscal Year in Review" (November 6, 2007, http://www.cbp.gov/xp/cgov/about/accomplish/07_year_review.xml), the CBP staffed 326 ports of entry and inspected 411 million travelers and 120 million land, air, and sea vehicles in fiscal year 2007. Table 5.3 lists some of the major programs operated by federal agencies, including the CBP and the U.S. Department of Energy to screen foreign cargo that enters the United States.

Transportation Security

The issue of transportation security is of particular importance to the United States. The vulnerability of the nation's transportation system became painfully clear on 9/11. On that day nineteen terrorists were able to board commercial airliners as passengers, seize the cockpits during flight, and pilot the planes on missions of violent destruction. Three of the airliners were crashed into buildings—the twin towers of the World Trade Center in New York City and the U.S. Pentagon in Washington, D.C. The fourth plane crashed in Pennsylvania after a revolt by the passengers. Its probable destination was the U.S. Capitol in Washington, D.C. The combined attacks left nearly three thousand dead. Americans were stunned by the ease with which the terrorists were able to commandeer the planes. A variety of shortcomings and oversights in U.S. aviation security procedures had been exploited with disastrous results.

The events that transpired during the hijackings have been pieced together by investigators based largely on cell phone calls from crew members and passengers on the planes. A detailed chronology and description of these calls is included in *The 9/11 Commission Report* (2004, http://www.9-11commission.gov/report/911Report.pdf). The report was compiled by the National Commission on Terrorist Attacks upon the United States, an organization created by President Bush and Congress to investigate all the circumstances relating to the 9/11 terrorist attacks.

The commission believes the terrorists used small sharp items (e.g., box cutters) as weapons to attack and subdue crewmembers and passengers as the hijackings began. The terrorists were either allowed entry or forced their way into the cockpits, where they overcame and may have killed the cockpit crews. Before and during 9/11 it had been standard policy for decades on commercial airliners for crewmembers to offer no resistance to armed hijackers. This policy evolved after a spate of hijackings in the United States during the late 1960s and early 1970s. In most of those events the hijackers demanded to be flown to a specific destination (often Cuba), and once there, they released the passengers and crew unharmed. The implementation of tougher security measures and x-ray screening at U.S. airports virtually eliminated hijacking aboard domestic U.S. flights. Thus, it had not been viewed as a serious threat to U.S. commercial aviation for some time. As a result, U.S. planes did not have fortified cockpit doors in 2001.

AIR PASSENGERS AND BAGGAGE. In 1988 Pan Am Flight 103 was en route from London to New York City when a bomb in the luggage compartment exploded, tearing apart the plane. It crashed near the small village of Lockerbie, Scotland, killing all 259 passengers and crewmembers and 11 people on the ground. It was later determined that terrorists had managed to hide a bomb inside a radio that was somehow tagged for placement aboard the plane, even though it did not belong to a passenger. Following this incident, the United States implemented stricter regulations and inspection of passenger baggage.

According to the *9/11 Commission Report*, it was standard procedure in 2001 to hold a high-risk passenger's luggage until that person had boarded the plane. This was to prevent a terrorist from checking baggage containing explosives and then not boarding the plane. It was assumed that if both passenger and luggage were aboard, then there was no danger posed by the luggage. Mohamed Atta (1968–2001) is believed to have been the ringleader of the 9/11 hijackers. He piloted American Airlines Flight 11 into the first tower at the World Trade Center. Before boarding his flight in Boston, Atta had been picked by a computerized prescreening system for heightened security measures. As a result, his checked baggage was not loaded onto the plane until it had been confirmed that he was aboard the aircraft.

The 9/11 terrorist attacks changed many assumptions and conventions that had guided aviation security for decades. First, it became obvious that terrorists were willing to die as part of their missions. Thus, it was not inconceivable that a terrorist could both check in luggage containing explosives and board the plane. Second, the use by the terrorists of small, sharp, but seemingly innocuous objects that had passed through passenger screening precipitated dramatic changes in screening procedures. Tweezers, nail files and clippers, pocket knives, box cutters, and other small sharp objects were confiscated from people and their carry-on bags during screening. Eventually, these restrictions were relaxed for some items; however, the prohibition on box cutters was still in effect as of September 2008.

In November 2001 Congress passed the Aviation and Transportation Security Act. It created the Transportation Security Administration within the U.S. Department of Transportation (TSA). In 2003 the TSA was made a part of the newly created DHS. The TSA is responsible for protecting the United States' transportation systems.

Regarding air travel, the agency conducts preflight screening of passengers and baggage at airports and provides air marshals on selected flights. The air marshal program was begun in 1970 in response to a rash of hijackings. At that time the program was overseen by the Customs Service (now the CBP). More than one thousand agents were trained to thwart attempted hijackings. They flew undercover (dressed as passengers) on various flights and were armed. The program was discontinued in 1974. During the mid-1980s the program was restarted, but only for international flights of U.S. airlines. In "Our Mission" (August 12, 2007, http://www.tsa.gov/lawenforcement/mission/index.shtm), the TSA notes that there were less than fifty armed air marshals in the program when the 9/11 terrorist attacks occurred. President Bush greatly expanded the program and placed it under the TSA. Several thousand new agents have been trained as "sky marshals." Besides flying undercover on domestic and international flights, these agents also staff positions in the National Counterterrorism Center and the FBI's JTTFs. Another program operated under the TSA allows certain airline crew members to fly armed. Federal Flight Deck Officers are trained in firearm usage and other skills needed to thwart a hijacker.

In December 2001 a terrorist aboard a commercial airliner flying from Paris to Miami tried to set off explosives hidden in his shoes. The so-called shoe bomber was overpowered by passengers aboard the plane and turned over to authorities. The incident prompted airport screeners to have passengers remove their footwear for closer inspection. Following the August 2006 discovery of a plot by British terrorists to use liquid explosives hidden in carry-on items, such as sports drinks, the TSA immediately banned the carrying on of all liquid and gel items. In "Security Screening" (August 12, 2007, http://www.tsa.gov/what_we_do/screening/index.shtm), the TSA reports that it performs explosives screening on every piece of luggage that goes onto commercial airliners in the United States.

PROGRAMS FOR SCREENING PEOPLE. Table 5.4 lists some of the major programs currently used or in development to screen people for national security purposes. One of the most controversial is the REAL ID program. The *9/11 Commission Report* recommended that the federal government "set standards for the issuance of birth certificates and sources of identification, such as drivers licenses." In response, Congress passed the Intelligence Reform and Terrorism Prevention Act of 2004, later superseded by the REAL ID Act of 2005. It called for all state-issued drivers licenses or other state-issued IDs to meet specific standards for security and integrity by May 2008. The act and the controversy surrounding it are described in detail by Todd B. Tatelman of the Congressional Research Service in *The REAL ID Act of 2005: Legal, Regulatory, and Implementation Issues* (April 1, 2008, http://www.fas.org/sgp/crs/misc/RL34430.pdf). Tatelman notes that many questions have been raised

TABLE 5.4

DHS programs for screening people entering the United States

Screening cargo

- The REAL ID Act establishes federal standards for state-issued driver's licenses and non-driver's identification cards.
- Secure Flight will require airlines to submit passenger information to DHS for flights that operate to, from, and within the United States, as well as those that fly over the continental United States.
- The Student and Exchange Visitor Information System (SEVIS) is an internet-based system that is improving America's ability to track and monitor foreign students and exchange visitors.
- The United States Visitor and Immigrant Status Indicator Technology (US-VISIT) program, when fully implemented, will create an entry and exit system that matches foreign travelers' arrival and departure records using biometrics to screen applicants for admission to the United States.
- The Western Hemisphere Travel Initiative (WHTI) reduces the number of identification and citizenship documents that may be used by persons entering or re-entering the United States, from more than 8,000 documents, to a few dozen secure documents. This expedites document review at ports of entry while combating fraudulent documents.
- The Visa Waiver Program (VWP) enables nationals of over two dozen countries to travel to the United States for tourism or business for stays of 90 days or less without obtaining a visa.

SOURCE: "Screening People," in *National Strategy for Homeland Security*, Office of the President of the United States, U.S. Department of Homeland Security, October 5, 2007, http://www.whitehouse.gov/infocus/homeland/nshs/NSHS.pdf (accessed August 8, 2008)

about the constitutionality of the act. In addition, state legislators have complained about the costs and difficulties of implementing the act.

The DHS did not release final regulations for the REAL ID program until January 2008. At that time the National Council of State Legislators complained in "State Groups Acknowledge Final REAL ID Regulations" (January, 11, 2008, http://www.ncsl.org/programs/press/2008/pr011108RealID.htm) that implementing the program was going to cost the states an estimated $3.9 billion, but Congress had appropriated less than 3% of that amount. In April 2008 the federal government granted all the states an extension until December 31, 2009, to meet the requirement of the act. REAL ID–compliant drivers licenses will be required by most Americans by 2014 to board federally regulated aircraft or enter federal government facilities.

Domestic Counterterrorism

Domestic counterterrorism involves the efforts of law enforcement agencies to investigate, prevent, and interdict (hamper or stop) terrorist activity inside the United States.

One of the major initiatives of this mission has been the creation of new JTTFs at FBI offices around the country. JTTFs are investigational units that consist of agents from multiple federal, state, and local law enforcement organizations. The FBI has also established a terrorism watch list that contains information about people under investigation for terrorist links. Officials of federal, state, local, or foreign governments can contact the FBI's Terrorist Screening Center (TSC) if they believe they have encountered an individual on the terrorism watch list. Between December 1, 2003, and April 30, 2007, 96,711 reports of suspected watch list encounters were referred to the TSC call center. (See Table 5.5.) Sixty percent of the calls came from CBP agents. As of April 2007, the terrorist watch list contained approximately 724,000 records. (See Figure 5.3.) The DOJ notes that the number of records in the database is not equivalent to the number of known or suspected terrorists in the system, because a single individual can have multiple records.

TABLE 5.5

Number of encounters with suspected terrorists reported by government agencies to the Terrorist Screening Center, December 1, 2003 to April 30, 2007

Referring agency	Number of referrals	Percent of referrals
DHS–CBP	58,266	60
Other federal	19,965	21
State and local	17,967	19
Foreign government	513	<1
Total	**96,711**	**100%**

DHS = Department of Homeland Security.
CBP = Customs and Border Protection.

SOURCE: "Exhibit 1-2. Watchlist Encounters Referred to the TSC Call Center by Organization," in *Follow-up Audit of the Terrorist Screening Center*, U.S. Department of Justice, September 2007, http://www.usdoj.gov/oig/reports/FBI/a0741/final.pdf (accessed August 8, 2008)

FIGURE 5.3

Number of terrorist watch list records maintained by the Terrorist Screening Center

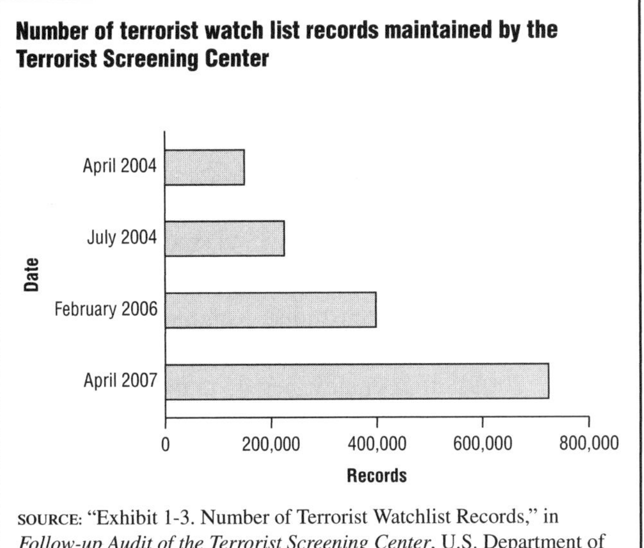

SOURCE: "Exhibit 1-3. Number of Terrorist Watchlist Records," in *Follow-up Audit of the Terrorist Screening Center*, U.S. Department of Justice, September 2007, http://www.usdoj.gov/oig/reports/FBI/a0741/final.pdf (accessed August 8, 2008)

In 2005 President Bush directed the FBI to combine all of its intelligence and counterterrorism elements (that had been operating separately) into one organization under the direction of a high-ranking FBI official. The FBI's National Security Branch (October 4, 2005, http://www.fbi.gov/hq/nsb/nsb_mission.htm) was the result. Its stated mission is "to protect the U.S. against weapons of mass destruction, terrorist attacks, foreign intelligence operations, and espionage."

DOMESTIC TERRORIST CASES. Domestic counterterrorism investigations by the FBI have produced a number of arrests and convictions. The following are a few of the major cases:

- 1993 World Trade Center Bombers—the FBI investigation of the 1993 bombing of the World Trade Center underground garage resulted in the convictions of six terrorists, including the ringleader, Ramsi Yousef (1968–), a Kuwaiti national of Pakistani descent. In 1998 Yousef was sentenced to life in prison plus 240 years for his role in the bombing. Yousef had also put a bomb aboard a Filipino airliner in 1994 that killed one man and masterminded a foiled plot that same year to blow up nearly a dozen airliners bound from Asia to the United States. He is the nephew of Khalid Sheikh Mohammed (1964–), a top al Qaeda figure believed to have overseen the 9/11 terrorist attacks.

- Zacarias Moussaoui (1968–)—in August 2001 the FBI arrested Moussaoui for an immigration violation. He had been attending flight school in Minnesota and had aroused suspicions by his odd behavior. After 9/11 the FBI held Moussaoui as a material witness, believing that he was supposed to be the so-called twentieth hijacker. He was charged with conspiring to commit terrorist acts. According to the article "Timeline: Moussaoui Case" (FOXNews.com, May 3, 2003), in January 2002 a long trial began in which Moussaoui represented himself and was often chastised by the judge for outbursts in the courtroom. In April 2005, after many legal maneuvers by his defense team, Moussaoui pleaded guilty to all counts and faced the death penalty. The judge allowed survivors and family members of victims of the 9/11 attacks to testify during the sentencing phase. Some of them testified on Moussaoui's behalf, believing him innocent of the charges and suffering from delusions. In May 2006 he was sentenced to life in prison.
- Lackawanna Six—this group of American citizens of Yemeni descent is accused of going to Afghanistan in early 2001 to support the Taliban and take terrorist training at al Qaeda camps. In 2002 they were arrested by the FBI in Lackawanna, New York (a small town near Buffalo), and subsequently tried and convicted of supporting a foreign terrorist organization. Each received a sentence of between seven and ten years in prison. A seventh conspirator was indicted, but was out of the country. As of September 2008, that man (Jaber A. Elbaneh [1966–]) was on the FBI's list of Most Wanted Terrorists (http://www.fbi.gov/wanted/terrorists/fugitives.htm).
- Portland Seven—this cell operated out of Portland, Oregon, and included seven people (six men and one woman) accused of conspiring against U.S. troops in Afghanistan. Mark Larabee notes in "Filing Details 'Portland 7' Plot" (*Oregonian*, November 20, 2003) that all the men had tried to enter Afghanistan in 2001, but only one was successful. He was subsequently killed by Pakistani troops at an al Qaeda training camp. The remaining six were arrested in the United States in 2002 and received varying sentences. Most of the cell members were American citizens.
- Iyman Faris (1969–)—Faris is a naturalized American citizen born in Kashmir. In 2003 he was arrested and charged with conspiring with the al Qaeda leader Osama bin Laden (1957–) to commit terrorism in the United States. Faris worked as a truck driver in Ohio and is believed to have been scoping out potential targets for terrorist attacks. According to the DOJ, in the press release "Iyman Faris Sentenced for Providing Material Support to al Qaeda" (October 28, 2003, http://www.usdoj.gov/opa/pr/2003/October/03_crm_589.htm), one of these targets was the Brooklyn Bridge in New York City. Faris pleaded guilty and was sentenced to twenty years in prison.
- Northern Virginia Jihad—this network included eleven men of varying nationalities who were accused of operating a terrorist network in northern Virginia that supported the Taliban and Lashkar-e-Taiba (a foreign terrorist organization) and conspired to wage war against the United States. In the press release "Randall Todd Royer and Ibrahim Ahmed Al-Hamdi Sentenced for Participation in Virginia Jihad Network" (April 9, 2004, http://www.usdoj.gov/opa/pr/2004/April/04_crm_225.htm), the DOJ states that most of the men had attended terrorist training camp in Pakistan. A series of trials in 2004 resulted in convictions and sentences of various lengths for nine of the men. Two of the accused were acquitted.
- Lodi network—soon after 9/11 the FBI began investigating a mosque in Lodi, California, for alleged links between two Pakistani imams (spiritual leaders) and their followers with al Qaeda. The two imams were detained on immigration violations and ultimately left the country under threat of deportation. In early 2006 two members of the Lodi community, a father and son, were tried for terrorism charges. The father pleaded guilty to a lesser immigration charge. The son was convicted for attending a terrorist training camp in Pakistan and lying about it to the FBI. The FBI's handling of the Lodi case has been criticized by some observers as overzealous. This charge is examined in detail in the *Frontline* documentary *The Enemy Within* (October 10, 2006, http://www.pbs.org/wgbh/pages/frontline/enemywithin/). *Frontline* outlines the events that led up to the trials and presents the viewpoint of a retired FBI agent that the case was handled poorly and lacked sufficient evidence of wrongdoing. The documentary also examines the negative effects the case has had on the Pakistani population and on Muslim relations in Lodi.
- The Fort Dix Conspirators—in May 2007 six Muslim men from New Jersey and Philadelphia were arrested and charged with planning a terrorist attack against Fort Dix, a U.S. Army base in New Jersey. The FBI explains in the press release "Attack Foiled: Undercover Probe Busts Terror Plot" (May 8, 2007, http://www.fbi.gov/page2/may07/ftdix050807.htm) that the men had collected an arsenal of weapons and hoped to kill as many soldiers as possible during the attack. As of September 2008, their cases had not proceeded to trial.
- The JFK Terror Plot—in June 2007 four men were arrested for conspiring to blow up fuel supply lines and tanks at the John F. Kennedy International Airport in New York City. In the press release "Four Individuals Charged in Plot to Bomb John F. Kennedy Interna-

tional Airport" (June 2, 2007, http://newyork.fbi.gov/dojpressrel/pressrel07/plot060207.pdf), the FBI states that one of the men, an American citizen from Guyana, formerly worked at the airport. His conspirators were from Guyana and Trinidad. All four were allegedly part of a Muslim extremist network. As of September 2008, their cases had not gone to trial.

PROTECT THE AMERICAN PEOPLE, CRITICAL INFRASTRUCTURE, AND KEY RESOURCES

Warning of Attacks

One of the tasks of the DHS is to operate a national warning system that keeps the public apprised about the nation's relative risk at any time to a terrorist attack. The Homeland Security Advisory System (HSAS) uses a color-coded risk scheme of green, blue, yellow, orange, and red. The green level coincides with a low risk. The risk gradually increases as the colors proceed through blue (guarded risk), yellow (elevated risk), orange (high risk), and red (severe risk). At each risk level there are a number of suggested measures for the public to take in preparation for a terrorism attack. These are basically commonsense recommendations regarding useful precautions or actions that should be taken in the event of any emergency.

When the HSAS was introduced in March 2002, the risk level was set at yellow. It has been raised several times since then from yellow to orange in response to intelligence information that a terrorist attack might be pending. At times the threat level has been raised only for certain sectors, such as the mass transit systems or commercial airlines. A recent such occurrence was on August 10, 2006, when a red threat level was issued for commercial air flights from the United Kingdom to the United States. The threat level was raised from yellow to orange for all other commercial flights in or out of the United States. These changes were in response to news that British authorities had foiled a plot in which terrorists had planned to set off liquid explosives aboard U.S.-bound flights. The red alert was in effect for only three days before being lowered to orange.

Critical Infrastructure and Key Assets

Protecting critical infrastructure and key assets is a key component of the *National Strategy for Homeland Security*. The National Infrastructure Protection Plan (NIPP; 2006, http://www.dhs.gov/xlibrary/assets/NIPP_Plan.pdf) defines critical infrastructure as the "assets, systems, and networks, whether physical or virtual, so vital to the United States that the incapacity or destruction of such assets, systems, or networks would have a debilitating impact on security, national economic security, public health or safety, or any combination of those matters." Likewise, the NIPP defines key assets as "publicly or privately controlled resources essential to the minimal operations of the economy and government."

Examples of critical infrastructure include sectors that are essential to survival (e.g., agriculture, food, and water) and those with economic, political, or social importance (e.g., the banking and chemical industries and the postal service). Infrastructure includes both distinct structures, such as buildings and dams, and the networks and components that make up the nation's telecommunications and cyber (Internet) systems. Key assets include "individual targets" that are not essential or vital, but have national importance. The Statue of Liberty is a prime example. The government also includes high-profile events, such as the Super Bowl.

The protection of infrastructure and assets is addressed in more detail in two additional U.S. government reports: *National Strategy to Secure Cyberspace* (February 2003, http://www.whitehouse.gov/pcipb/cyberspace_strategy.pdf) and *National Strategy for the Physical Protection of Critical Infrastructures and Key Assets* (February 2003, http://www.whitehouse.gov/pcipb/physical_strategy.pdf).

According to the latter report, there are more than two million farms and commercial and government buildings and facilities in the United States. In addition, there are thousands of water reservoirs and treatment plants, hospitals, emergency service providing facilities, dams, and energy producing plants. The nation's transportation system is enormous, including five thousand public airports alone. Finally, there are fifty-eight hundred historic buildings, national monuments, and icons. The responsibility among federal agencies for protecting all these resources has been divided up as shown in Table 5.6. This list is based on Homeland Security Presidential Directive 7 (December 17, 2003, http://www.whitehouse.gov/news/releases/2003/12/20031217-5.html).

Catastrophic Threats

Catastrophic threats are those posed by weapons of mass destruction (WMDs). WMDs are unconventional weapons that use nontraditional means to cause destruction and death, primarily nuclear technology or the release of chemical or biological agents. The primary goals under this mission are to develop more effective detection and data-sharing techniques, preventive agents (such as vaccines), and antidotes and treatments to counter the risks posed by WMD attacks.

The Centers for Disease Control and Prevention (CDC) is a federal agency within the U.S. Department of Health and Human Services. Since its founding in 1946, the CDC has been responsible for protecting national public health, including the prevention and control of infectious diseases and other hazards. Following the terrorist attacks of 9/11 and the anthrax letter attacks that began later that month, the CDC has been tasked with preparing the United States for the health threats posed by WMDs.

TABLE 5.6

Agencies responsible for critical infrastructure and key resources, 2006

Sector-specific agency	Critical infrastructure/ key resources sector
Department of Agriculture[a]	
Department of Health and Human Services[b]	Agriculture and food
Department of Defense[c]	Defense industrial base
Department of Energy	Energy[d]
Department of Health and Human Services	Public health and healthcare
Department of the Interior	National monuments and icons
Department of the Treasury	Banking and finance
Environmental Protection Agency	Drinking water and water treatment systems
Department of Homeland Security	
Office of Infrastructure Protection	Chemical
	Commercial facilities
	Dams
	Emergency services
	Commercial nuclear reactors, materials, and waste
Office of Cyber Security and Telecommunications	Information Technology Telecommunications
Transportation Security Administration	Postal and shipping
Transportation Security Administration, United States Coast Guard[e]	Transportation system[f]
Immigration and Customs Enforcement, Federal Protective Service	Government facilities

[a]The Department of Agriculture is responsible for agriculture and food (meat, poultry, and egg products).
[b]The Department of Health and Human Services is responsible for food other than meat, poultry, and egg products.
[c]Nothing in this plan impairs or otherwise affects the authority of the Secretary of Defense over the Department of Defense (DOD), including the chain of command for military forces from the President as Commander in Chief, to the Secretary of Defense, to the commander of military forces, or military command and control procedures.
[d]The Energy sector includes the production, refining, storage, and distribution of oil, gas, and electric power, except for commercial nuclear power facilities.
[e]The U.S. Coast Guard is the SSA for the maritime transportation mode.
[f]The Department of Transportation and the Department of Homeland Security will collaborate on all matters relating to transportation security and transportation infrastructure protection.

SOURCE: "Table S-1. Sector-Specific Agencies and HSPD-7 Assigned CI/KR Sectors," in *National Infrastructure Protection Plan, 2006*, Office of the President of the United States, U.S. Department of Homeland Security, 2006, http://www.dhs.gov/xlibrary/assets/NIPP_Plan.pdf (accessed August 5, 2008)

RESPOND TO AND RECOVER FROM INCIDENTS

Emergency Preparedness

The DHS office of National Protection and Programs has programs and activities designed for emergency response professionals and the general public. At the professional level, the DHS offers training programs and grants for emergency planning.

For the general public, the DHS (2008, http://www.ready.gov/) provides information on how Americans should prepare for emergencies, including natural disasters and terrorist attacks. The Ready Campaign calls on every American to do three activities:

- Put together an emergency supply kit (see Table 5.7 for the suggested list of items)
- Prepare a family emergency plan that includes detailed instructions about how family members will communicate their whereabouts to each other if they become separated
- Stay informed about local conditions, the potential for emergency situations to develop, and the appropriate responses to take for particular emergencies

TABLE 5.7

Items recommended by the U.S. Department of Homeland Security for a basic emergency supply kit

Water, one gallon of water per person per day for at least three days, for drinking and sanitation
Food, at least a three-day supply of non-perishable food
Battery-powered or hand crank radio and a NOAA weather radio with tone alert and extra batteries for both
Flashlight and extra batteries
First aid kit
Whistle to signal for help
Dust mask, to help filter contaminated air, and plastic sheeting and duct tape to shelter-in-place
Moist towelettes, garbage bags and plastic ties for personal sanitation
Wrench or pliers to turn off utilities
Can opener for food (if kit contains canned food)
Local maps

SOURCE: "Recommended Items to Include in a Basic Emergency Supply Kit," in *Ready America: Get a Kit Checklist*, Office of the President of the United States, U.S. Department of Homeland Security, undated, http://www.ready.gov/america/_downloads/checklist.pdf (accessed August 11, 2008)

Emergency Response

In any emergency, including a terrorist attack, the initial response is by local and state officials. These so-called first responders include police officers, firefighters, emergency medical technicians, hazardous materials response teams, rescue squads, bomb squads, officials with local and state emergency management agencies, and similar personnel.

FEDERAL ROLE. At the federal level the primary role of emergency preparedness and response is assumed by the Federal Emergency Management Agency (FEMA). FEMA became part of the DHS in 2003. FEMA personnel are dispatched following disasters (e.g., hurricanes and earthquakes) to provide large-scale services for displaced people. For example, after Hurricane Katrina hit the Gulf Coast in 2005, FEMA operated shelters and provided funds to victims left homeless by the devastation. The agency also offers training programs for first responders and helps local and state emergency management agencies prepare disaster and response plans.

Other DHS programs related to emergency preparedness and response are:

- National Disaster Medical System—this is a public/private system of hundreds of volunteer medical teams around the country. The system is overseen by FEMA and is designed to support local hospitals and emergency medical services in the event of a catastrophic disaster.

- Strategic National Stockpile—formerly called the National Pharmaceutical Stockpile, this is a national repository maintained by the CDC that includes large supplies of antibiotics, antidotes, and other medications, as well as medical and surgical supplies. According to the CDC (June 30, 2008, http://www.bt.cdc.gov/Stockpile/), one of the goals of the repository is to provide rapid delivery of Push Packages to disaster areas. Push Packages are packages containing a broad selection of medicines and medical supplies that can be delivered quickly and cover an array of medical emergencies likely to be encountered by first responders in the field.
- Citizen Corps—this is a national system of volunteers trained to respond at the local level to terrorism events. A National Citizen Corps Council is overseen by the DHS and includes members representing various emergency response organizations and groups from the public and private sectors. A listing of all Citizen Corps around the country is available at http://www.citizencorps.gov/citizenCorps/allCouncilList.do.

PERFORMANCE OF THE DHS

In *Department Celebrates Five Years* (August 6, 2008, http://www.dhs.gov/xabout/history/gc_1206633633513.shtm), the DHS provides a list of its accomplishments during its first five years in operation. (See Table 5.8.) The DHS states that it has accomplished a number of tasks that have helped secure the homeland and assist Americans affected by natural disasters. However, the agency is not without its critics. In early 2007 the Democratic members of the U.S. House of Representatives Committee on Homeland Security issued a report card assessing DHS performance in seventeen areas. (See Table 5.9.) The agency received no A grades and only four B or B− grades; most of the remaining grades were C or C− grades. The DHS received an F for employee morale. In addition, there were three grades of incomplete, meaning that the agency had not completed implementing planned programs in these specific areas. It should be noted that the report card was prepared by only the Democratic members of the House committee and was not endorsed by the Republican members.

A much more independent analysis of the DHS has been provided by the U.S. Government Accountability Office (GAO). In *Department of Homeland Security: Progress Report on Implementation of Mission and Management Functions* (September 6, 2007, http://www.gao.gov/new.items/d071081t.pdf), the GAO assesses fourteen of the agency's missions and/or management areas. Within each of these areas the GAO identifies a specific number of performance expectations (goals) and measures the progress made by the agency in achieving these goals. Progress is measured in terms of actions taken by the DHS to "generally achieve" a certain percentage of the goals. The following is a summarization of the results:

- Acquisition management—25% to 50% of goals
- Aviation security—50% to 75% of goals
- Border security—25% to 50% of goals

TABLE 5.8

Major accomplishments of Department of Homeland Security as of March 1, 2008

- **Securing the border**—Built more than 302 miles of fencing and increased number of agents from 10,500 to more than 17,500 by the end of 2008
- **Screening travelers**—Screened 2 million travelers per day, required secure travel documents, checked more than 113 million foreign visitors' fingerprints and performed 20 layers of screening
- **Screening ports and cargos**—Screened more than 97% of inbound cargo for radiation at our seaports
- **Protecting infrastructure**—Established national standards for chemical facility security and chemicals in transit and issued over 200 actionable cyber alerts
- **Enforcing immigration laws**—Removed over 275,000 illegal aliens, interdicted more than 86,000 illegal migrants at sea, and secured fines and judgments of more than $30 million against violating employers
- **Responding to disasters**—Responded to over 400 major disasters and assisted more than 3.78 million individuals
- **Naturalized**—More than 2 million citizens between 2003 and 2006
- **Countering drugs**—Seized more than 7 million pounds of drugs and made 8,920 arrests at land and sea

SOURCE: "Highlights from the First Five Years," in *Department Celebrates Five Years*, U.S. Department of Homeland Security, August 6, 2008, http://www.dhs.gov/xabout/history/gc_1206633633513.shtm(accessed August 8, 2008)

TABLE 5.9

Congressional report card on performance of Department of Homeland Security, 2007

Border security	Incomplete
Emergency preparedness/FEMA	C−
Emergency communications	C
Aviation security	C
Port security	C−/D+
Surface transportation security	C
Critical infrastructure	Incomplete
Information sharing	C
Science & technology	C
Biosecurity	B−
Chemical plant security	B−
Domestic nuclear detection office	B
Management and organization	Incomplete
Employee morale	F
Procurement	C−
Civil liberties and civil rights	C
Chief Privacy Officer	B−

SOURCE: "2007 Annual Report Card," in *The State of Homeland Security 2007*, Majority Staff of the Committee on Homeland Security, March 2007, http://homeland.house.gov/SiteDocuments/20070413143439-12273.pdf (accessed July 1, 2008)

- Critical infrastructure protection—50% to 75% of goals
- Emergency preparedness and response—0% to 25% of goals
- Financial management—25% to 50% of goals
- Human capital management—0% to 25% of goals
- Immigration enforcement—50% to 75% of goals
- Immigration services—25% to 50% of goals
- Information technology management—0% to 25% of goals
- Maritime security—75% to 100% of goals
- Real property management—50% to 75% of goals
- Science and technology—0% to 25% of goals
- Surface transportation security—50% to 75% of goals

Overall, the GAO believes the DHS has made the most progress in the area of maritime security (i.e., seaport and sea vessel security, maritime intelligence, and maritime supply chain security). The GAO reports little achievement of goals in four areas: emergency preparedness and response, human capital management (i.e., managing and paying its employees), information technology management, and science and technology (i.e., identifying and developing countermeasures to chemical, biological, radiological, nuclear, and other terrorist threats).

COSTS OF HOMELAND SECURITY

Table 5.10 shows the federal government funding enacted and requested for the DHS according to the agency's fiscal year 2009 federal budget request. For accounting purposes, the federal government operates on a fiscal year (FY) that begins in October and runs through the end of September. Thus, FY 2009 covers the time period of October 1, 2008, through September 30, 2009. Each year by the first Monday in February the president must present a proposed budget to the U.S. House of Representatives. The budget must be approved by the House and the U.S. Senate.

For FY 2009 President Bush requested $50.5 billion for the DHS. The three DHS agencies with the largest requests were the CBP ($10.9 billion), the U.S. Coast Guard ($9.3 billion), and the TSA ($7.1 billion). In FY 2007 the DHS had regular budget authority for nearly $43 billion and received approximately $7.3 billion in supplemental or emergency funding. In FY 2008 the agency had just over $47 billion in regular budget authority and received more than $5.6 billion in supplemental and emergency funding.

TABLE 5.10

Department of Homeland Security (DHS) budget authority, by agency, February 2008

	FY 2007 revised enacted[a]	FY 2008 enacted[b]	FY 2009 president's budget[c]
	$000	$000	$000
Departmental operations[c]	$603,525	$571,791	$752,593
Analysis and operations	299,663	306,000	333,521
Office of the Inspector General	98,685	108,711	101,023
U.S. Customs & Border Protection	7,746,259	9,306,725	10,941,231
U.S. Immigration & Customs Enforcement	4,696,641	5,054,317	5,676,085
Transportation Security Administration	6,329,291	6,819,859	7,101,828
U.S. Coast Guard	8,554,067	8,741,053	9,346,022
U.S. Secret Service	1,485,617	1,595,496	1,639,346
National Protection and Programs Directorate	942,436	902,076	1,286,100
Office of Health Affairs	9,917	116,500	161,339
Federal Emergency Management Agency	4,571,716	5,522,178	6,566,794
FEMA: Grants[d]	4,048,500	4,117,800	2,200,000
U.S. Citizenship & Immigration Services	2,216,240	2,539,845	2,689,726
Federal Law Enforcement Training Center	253,279	267,666	274,126
S&T Directorate	968,131	830,335	868,837
Domestic Nuclear Detection Office	480,968	484,750	563,800
Total:	**$43,304,935**	**$47,285,102**	**$50,502,371**
Less rescission of prior year carryover funds:[e]	**(313,005)**	**(262,249)**	—
Adjusted total budget authority:	**$42,991,930**	**$47,022,853**	**$50,502,371**
Emergency funding/supplemental:[f]	**$7,290,193**	**$5,630,000**	**$ —**

[a]FY 2007 revised enacted reflects a transfer from DOD to USCG ($90 million) pursuant to P.L. 109–289, the transfer of FEMA Public Health ($33.885 million) to the Department of Health and Human Services, and the transfer from FEMA Disaster Relief ($13.5 million) to Office of the Inspector General pursuant to P.L. 109–295; and technical adjustments to reflect FEMA NFIF mandatory fund ($2.631 billion), USSS Retirement Fund ($200 million), USCG Trust Funds ($244.202 million), CBP Customs Unclaimed Goods ($5.897 million), and revised fee estimates for CBP ($36.347 million), TSA Transportation Threat Assessment and Credentialing fees (−$45.101 million) and Aviation Security offset, CBP Small Airport estimates ($.950 million) and FEMA Radiological Emergency Preparedness Program (−$6 million) to reflect net of collections based on the FY 2008 request.
[b]FY 2008 enacted reflects a transfer from DOD to USCG ($110 million) pursuant to P.L. 110–161 and the transfer from FEMA Disaster Relief ($16 million) to Office of the Inspector General pursuant to P.L. 110–161; revised fee estimates for FEMA NFIF mandatory fund ($2.833 billion), USSS Retirement Fund ($210 million), USCG Trust Funds ($280.273 million), CBP Customs Unclaimed Goods ($5.897 million), and CBP fees ($24.324 million).
[c]Departmental Operations is comprised of the Office of the Secretary & Executive Management, the Office of the Federal Coordinator for Gulf Coast Rebuilding, the Office of the Undersecretary for Management, the Office of the Chief Financial Officer, an
[d]Includes the following FEMA appropriations: State and Local Programs & Emergency Management Perf. Grants, and Assistance to Firefighters Grants.
[e]Reflects scorekeeping adjustment for rescission of prior year unobligated balances: FY 2007 enacted rescission of prior year unobligated balances from USCG (−$102.793 million), TSA (−$66.712 million), S&T (−$125 million), USSS (−$2.5 million), Counterterrorism Fund (−$16 million); FY 2008 enacted rescission of prior year unobligated balances from FEMA (−$37.176 million); CBP (−$27.625 million); USCG (−$146.847 million); OSEM (−$16.295 million); USM (−$.444 million); CFO (−$.380 million); CIO (−$.493 million); A&O (−$8.7 million); TSA (−$4.5 million); Counter-Terrorism Fund (−$8.480 million); S&T (−$.217 million); NPPD (−$1.994 million): OHA (−$.045 million); DNDO (−$.368 million); ICE (−$5.137 million); OIG (−$.032 million); USCIS (−$.672 million); WCF (−$2.506 million); FLETC (−$.334 million).
[f]In order to obtain comparable figures, Total Budget Authority excludes: FY 2007 emergency funding pursuant to P.L. 109–295 for the Global War on Terror (1.829 billion: $22 million - FLETC, $175.8 million - USCG, $30 million - ICE, $1.601 billion - CBP); FY 2007 Supplemental Funding pursuant to P.L. 110–28 (OSEM - $.900 million; A&O - $8 million; OIG - $4 million; CBP - $150 million; ICE - $6 million; TSA - $395 million; USCG- $150.293 million; NPPD - $24 million; FEMA - $4.567 billion; CIS - $8 million; S&T - $5 million; DNDO - $135 million); FY 2008 Emergency Funding pursuant to P.L. 110–161 (CBP - $1.531 billion; ICE - $526.900 million; USCG $166.100 million; NPPD $275 million; FEMA - $3.030 billion; CIS - $80 million; FLETC - $21 million)

SOURCE: Adapted from "Total Budget Authority by Organization," in *Homeland Security Budget-in-Brief: Fiscal Year 2009*, U.S. Department of Homeland Security, February 2008, http://www.dhs.gov/xlibrary/assets/budget_bib-fy2009.pdf (accessed August 8, 2008)

CHAPTER 6
COUNTRIES OF CONCERN

For much of its history, U.S. national security concerns were focused primarily on other nations, and international terrorism was at most a secondary issue. During the cold war the Soviet Union and China amassed huge military forces and thousands of nuclear weapons. For decades the United States fought the spread of communism with diplomatic and economic means and through long military engagements in Korea and Vietnam. The United States, however, never engaged in direct military conflict with the Soviet Union or China for fear of starting a nuclear war. Since the end of the cold war the threats posed by other nations to the United States have greatly diminished, but they have not disappeared.

Communist China has become strong politically and militarily and strives to wield more diplomatic and economic power in the world. Even though the United States views this transformation uneasily, relatively good relations between the two countries have been maintained. The same was true for the U.S.-Russian relationship until conflict broke out in August 2008 between Russia and neighboring Georgia, a former republic of the Soviet Union. The Georgian region of South Ossetia borders Russia and has historically been politically and culturally aligned with Russia. In 1991 South Ossetia declared itself a separate republic, but Georgia refused to acknowledge the separation. Russian and Georgian troops maintained an uneasy peace along the border until Georgia accused Russia of launching a missile into Georgian territory. Days later Russian troops swept into South Ossetia claiming that Georgian troops had attacked them and Russian citizens living in the breakaway region. The Russians seized control of South Ossetia and launched air raids against certain parts of Georgia. Russia's actions evoked strong criticism from world leaders, including President George W. Bush (1946–). As of September 2008, Russian troops remained in South Ossetia. This situation and continued Russian support for two other breakaway territories in the region—Abkhazia (officially a part of Georgia) and Trans-Dniester (officially a part of Moldova)—have created a tense political climate that is reminiscent of the cold war and threatens future relations between Russia and the United States.

The situation in the Middle East is also troublesome. Many nondemocratic regimes in the region flourish on oil revenues but repress their populations, who are now restless and militant-minded. U.S. support of these repressive governments and for Israel during its long-standing conflict with the Palestinians has aggravated anti-American sentiments. Some countries are considered a threat because U.S. policy makers worry their governments might provide international terrorists with weapons or other support, which happened in Afghanistan before the September 11, 2001, terrorist attacks. Meanwhile, the lure of the ultimate weapon has tempted a handful of nations to defy international conventions and develop nuclear weapons programs. Some of these countries are U.S. allies, but others are openly hostile toward the United States. The members of this latter group are of great concern to U.S. national security.

THE UNITED STATES' GREATEST ENEMIES

On January 29, 2002, just a few months after the September 11, 2001, terrorist attacks, President Bush described in his annual State of the Union speech (http://www.whitehouse.gov/news/releases/2002/01/20020129-11.html) an "axis of evil" in the world consisting of Iraq, Iran, and North Korea. These three nations were singled out for allegedly sponsoring terrorist acts and trying to build or obtain weapons of mass destruction (WMDs). In 2003 the United States invaded Iraq to remove it as a threat to national security. As described in Chapter 4, the result has been a long and difficult struggle for U.S. forces against

TABLE 6.1

Public opinion on which country is the United States' greatest enemy, February 2008

WHAT ONE COUNTRY ANYWHERE IN THE WORLD DO YOU CONSIDER TO BE THE UNITED STATES' GREATEST ENEMY TODAY?

	Feb. 11–14, 2008
	%
Iran	25
Iraq	22
China	14
North Korea/Korea	9
United States itself	3
Afghanistan	3
Pakistan	2
Russia	2
Saudi Arabia	1
Venezuela	1
Other	6
None (vol.)	2
No opinion	3

(vol.) = Volunteered response.

SOURCE: Lydia Saad, "What One Country Anywhere in the World Do You Consider to Be the United States' Greatest Enemy Today?" in *North Korea Drops out of Top Three U.S. "Enemies,"* The Gallup Organization, March 28, 2008, http://www.gallup.com/poll/105835/North-Korea-Drops-Top-Three-US-Enemies.aspx?version=print (accessed August 4, 2008).

TABLE 6.2

Public opinion on which country is the greatest threat to world stability, December 2007

WHAT SINGLE COUNTRY DO YOU CONSIDER TO BE THE GREATEST THREAT TO STABILITY IN THE WORLD?

Scale	%	N
Other	5.12	51
Don't know	4.24	43
Refused	0.53	5
None	0.42	4
Any/all	0.00	0
Afghanistan	2.39	24
China	19.56	196
Iran	30.64	307
Iraq	8.61	86
Israel	0.64	6
Korea/North Korea	9.91	99
Pakistan	2.19	22
Russia	4.23	42
Saudi Arabia	0.66	7
USA	10.86	109

N = Population.

SOURCE: "Question qn4. What Single Country Do You Consider to Be the Greatest Threat to Stability in the World?" in *December Panel Survey*, The Gallup Organization, December 2007, http://brain.gallup.com/documents/question.aspx?question=163068&advanced=0&searchcontype=1&searchtypeall=threat+to+stability (accessed August 9, 2008).

determined and deadly militants opposed to the occupation. However, the toppling of the Iraqi leader Saddam Hussein (1937–2006) did effectively eliminate Iraq from membership in the axis of evil.

In *North Korea Drops out of Top Three U.S. "Enemies"* (March 28, 2008, http://www.gallup.com/poll/105835/North-Korea-Drops-Top-Three-US-Enemies.aspx), Lydia Saad of the Gallup Organization reports on a February 2008 poll that asked Americans to name the one country in the world they considered to be "America's greatest enemy." Iran garnered the most mentions (25%). (See Table 6.1.) Other nominees included Iraq (22%), China (14%), and North Korea/Korea (9%). Together, these four countries were named by 70% of poll participants. Three percent of respondents identified Afghanistan, and interestingly, the United States itself, as the United States' greatest enemy. Pakistan and Russia each garnered 2% of the vote. Saudi Arabia and Venezuela were each named by 1% of the poll participants. According to Saad, Iran was also named the United States' greatest enemy in 2006 and 2007 Gallup polls.

In December 2007 the Gallup Organization asked Americans to name the country they considered "to be the greatest threat to stability in the world." Iran received the most mentions (31%), compared to China (20%), the United States (11%), Korea/North Korea (10%), and Iraq (9%). (See Table 6.2.)

IRAN

Iran lies in a section of Asia known as the Middle East. (See Figure 6.1.) The nation's capital is Tehran. Iran's largest neighbors include Turkmenistan to the north, Afghanistan and Pakistan to the east, and Turkey and Iraq to the West. The Persian Gulf lies to the south of Iran and separates it from Kuwait, Saudi Arabia, Qatar, and Bahrain. The Strait of Hormuz, a narrow passage, separates Iran from the United Arab Emirates and Oman. The Strait of Hormuz is the only connection between the Persian Gulf and the open ocean.

For centuries Iran was part of a series of empires and was called Persia by the outside world. In 1935 its name was officially changed to Iran. Beginning in 1941 the country was led by Shah Mohammad Reza Pahlavi (1919–1980). In 1979 the shah was overthrown by his people and forced to leave the country during a revolution that swept the Islamic cleric Ayatollah Ruhollah Khomeini (1900–1989) into power. The country adopted a constitution and changed its name to the Islamic Republic of Iran. Khomeini initiated a cultural revolution that sought to remove influences of Western culture and instill conservative Islamic morals and customs. He served as Iran's supreme leader until his death in 1989, when he was replaced by Sayyid Ali Khamenei (1939–).

The supreme leader is considered Iran's spiritual leader and chief of state for life. Every four years the

FIGURE 6.1

Map of Iran, 2007

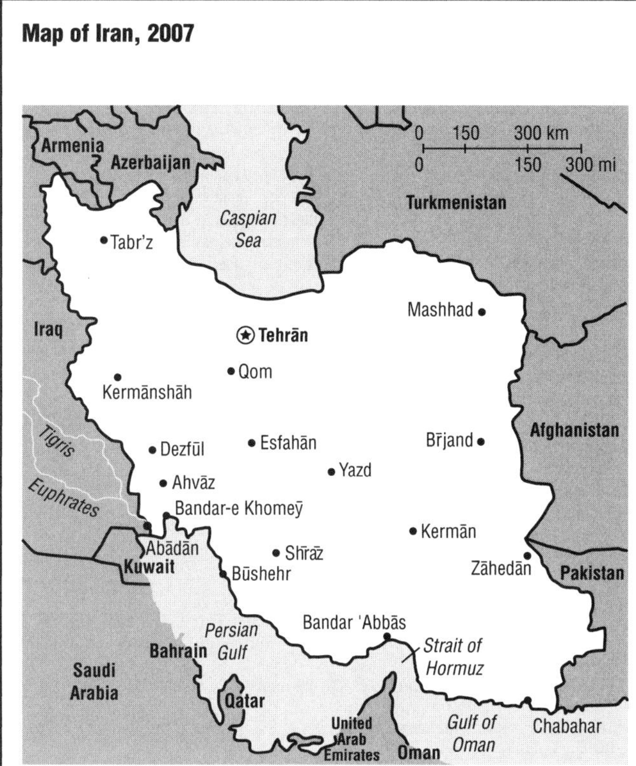

SOURCE: "Iran," in *Country Analysis Briefs: Iran*, U.S. Department of Energy, Energy Information Administration, October 2007, http://www.eia.doe.gov/emeu/cabs/Iran/Background.html (accessed August 11, 2008)

country elects government officials, including a president and members of the 290-seat Majlis (the Iranian parliament). The most recent parliamentary elections were held in 2008. In *The World Factbook: Iran* (August 21, 2008, https://www.cia.gov/library/publications/the-world-factbook/geos/ir.html), the Central Intelligence Agency (CIA) notes that 170 of the seats were won by Islamic conservatives and Islamists—Muslims who advocate absolute integration of Islam into matters of government. In 2005 the conservative Mahmoud Ahmadinejad (1956–) was elected president of Iran by a wide majority. Presidential elections are held every four years.

Iran has substantial petroleum resources. The CIA estimates that in 2006 Iran produced nearly 4.2 million barrels per day, most of which was exported. Oil accounts for 85% of the government's revenue.

Foreign Relations

In 1979 President Jimmy Carter (1924–) allowed the ousted shah of Iran to enter the United States for medical treatment. The United States had supported the shah throughout his reign, even though his regime was considered brutal and corrupt by the Iranian people. The U.S. action incited radical elements within Iran who feared that the United States planned to reinstall the shah to power. Angry groups of students protested in the streets and then seized the U.S. embassy in Tehran. Dozens of American hostages were held at the embassy for 444 days until their release in 1981.

Despite repeated demands from the U.S. government, Khomeini refused to intervene in the hostage crisis. During and after the Iranian Revolution Khomeini often criticized the United States, referring to it as "the great Satan." Carter tried a variety of diplomatic and military options to release the hostages during their long ordeal. Diplomatic relations with Iran were terminated and Iranian assets in U.S. banks were frozen. A rescue attempt by U.S. troops in 1980 ended in disaster when some of the helicopters accidentally crashed after secretly entering Iran. Eight U.S. servicemen were killed. The hostage release was ultimately achieved via diplomatic means. The hostage crisis severely damaged U.S. relations with Iran, and as of September 2008 the two countries had not restored diplomatic relations with each other.

Hussein launched an invasion of Iran by Iraqi forces in 1980. The resulting war lasted until 1988. In *A Country Study: Iraq* (November 8, 2005, http://lcweb2.loc.gov/frd/cs/iqtoc.html#iq0024), the Library of Congress (LOC) explains that the war was motivated by a variety of political, religious, and ethnic factors. Hussein's largely secular government feared the spread of Islamic conservatism from Iran to Iraq. In addition, Iraqis are predominantly of Arab descent, whereas Iranians are mostly of Persian ethnicity. Both countries are primarily Muslim with the Shia version of Islam practiced by a majority of their populations. However, Iraq's ruling party at the time was made up of Sunni Muslims. There are centuries-old disputes between the two factions of Islam. The LOC notes that Hussein and Khomeini had deep personal differences and that Hussein saw the war as a chance to enhance Iraq's power in the Middle East. However, eight years of bloody fighting produced no clear winner, so a cease-fire was finally negotiated.

In 1984 the U.S. Department of State (DOS) designated Iran as a state sponsor of terrorism because of Iranian support for organizations such as Hamas, Hezbollah, and the Palestinian Islamic Jihad. As of September 2008, Iran retained this designation, making it subject to a variety of sanctions and legal penalties imposed by the United States.

During the mid-1990s executive orders issued by President Bill Clinton (1946–) and passage of the Iran-Libya Sanctions Act of 1996 put restrictions on U.S. and international investments in Iran. Table 6.3 lists the U.S. sanction laws targeting Iran as of December 2007. Note that in 2006 the Iran-Libya Sanctions Act was renamed the Iran Sanctions Act because of improving relations between the United States and Libya.

TABLE 6.3

U.S. sanctions laws targeting Iran, December 2007

U.S. law	Sanctionable activities	Use of sanctions
Iran, North Korea, and Syria Nonproliferation Act[a]	Transfer to Iran of goods, services, or technology listed in various multilateral export control arrangements or that contribute to weapons of mass destruction or missile programs.	Sanctions imposed 111 times since 2000 in Iran-related cases, including: • 52 instances against Chinese parties, • 9 instances against North Korean parties, • 8 instances against Syrian parties, and • 7 instances against Russian parties.
Iran-Iraq Arms Nonproliferation Act of 1992[b]	Transfer to Iran of controlled goods or technology so as to contribute "knowingly and materially" to Iran's efforts to acquire destabilizing numbers and types of advanced conventional weapons.	Sanctions imposed 12 times in 2002 and 2003.
Iran Sanctions Act[c]	Investment of $20 million or more within a 12-month period that directly and significantly contributed to the enhancement of Iran's ability to develop its petroleum resources. Exports, transfers, or other provision to Iran of any goods, services, technology or other items knowing that the provision of such items would contribute materially to Iran's ability to acquire or develop chemical, biological, or nuclear weapons or related technologies; or destabilizing numbers and types of advanced conventional weapons.	Sanctions never imposed, though state officials note that the law has been used as a tool in diplomatic efforts.

[a]This law was enacted as the Iran Nonproliferation Act of 2000; Restriction on Extraordinary Payments in Connection with the International Space Station, Pub. L. No. 106–178, 114 Stat. 38; Syria was added to the act in 2005 by the Iran Nonproliferation Amendments Act of 2005, Pub. L. No. 109–112, §4, 119 Stat. 2366, 2369; and North Korea was added in 2006 by the North Korea Nonproliferation Act of 2006, Pub. L. No. 109–2353, 120 Stat. 2015.

[b]Enacted by the National Defense Authorization Act for fiscal year 1993, Pub. L. No. 102–484, Title XVI, 106 Stat. 2315, 2571–75 (1992). We are unable to distinguish between Iran and Iraq sanction cases, as this information is classified.

[c]This act was originally enacted as the Iran-Libya Sanctions Act of 1996, Pub. L. No. 104–172, 110 Stat. 1541; Libya was removed from the law in 2006 by the Iran Freedom Support Act, Pub. L. No. 109–293, 120 Stat. 1344. Proliferation-related sanctionable activities were added to the law in 2006.

SOURCE: Adapted from "Table 1. U.S. Sanction Laws Targeting Iran," in *Iran Sanctions: Impact in Furthering U.S. Objectives Is Unclear and Should Be Reviewed*, U.S. Government Accountability Office, December 2007, http://www.gao.gov/new.items/d0858.pdf (accessed August 5, 2008)

Late in the 1990s Iranian voters elected moderate reform-minded candidates to the presidency and the Majlis, and many observers became optimistic about improved U.S.-Iranian relations. These expectations were dashed when conservatives reasserted their authority in the Iranian government, and Iran's nuclear ambitions were exposed. Iran's alleged support of violent anti-American insurgents in Iraq has further strained U.S.-Iranian relations.

Iran's Nuclear Program

The Treaty on the Non-proliferation of Nuclear Weapons (NPT; 2000, http://www.un.org/events/npt2005/npttreaty.html) originally went into force in 1970 after being negotiated by the United Nations (UN). The United States and the Soviet Union were among the original signers of the treaty. It forbids countries with nuclear weapons from transferring nuclear weapons or related explosive devices "to any recipient whatsoever." No assistance can be offered to a nonnuclear weapon nation to manufacture or acquire the weapons. The parties to the treaty also agree to "preventing diversion of nuclear energy from peaceful uses to nuclear weapons" and to take measures leading toward nuclear disarmament. The International Atomic Energy Agency (IAEA), founded in 1957, verifies that parties comply with the NPT.

According to Sharon Squassoni of the Congressional Research Service (CRS), in *Iran's Nuclear Program: Recent Developments* (September 6, 2006, http://www.fas.org/sgp/crs/nuke/RS21592.pdf), the National Council of Resistance of Iran (NCR) alerted the world in 2002 about Iran's nuclear activities. The NCR is a coalition of Iranian dissident groups based outside the country. The NCR reported that Iran had nuclear facilities at Natanz (which is approximately 100 miles [161 km] north of Esfahan) and near Arak (a small town southwest of Qom). (See Figure 6.1.)

IAEA investigators discovered that "significant" nuclear activities had been taking place that were not reported to the IAEA, which was a violation of the NPT that Iran ratified in 1970. Iranian officials admitted they had been conducting a number of undeclared activities, and that in the late 1980s they received a so-called nuclear cookbook with instructions for producing nuclear weapon parts. The cookbook was allegedly created by the Pakistani scientist Abdul Qadeer Khan (1935–), who has been linked to many illicit transfers of nuclear technology to nonnuclear nations. Squassoni notes that IAEA inspectors found two uranium enrichment facilities at Natanz—a pilot-scale plant in operation and a commercial-scale plant under construction. Iran had been conducting experiments with heavy-water reactors at the Arak site.

In late 2003 Iran ceased some of its uranium enrichment activities and began negotiations with IAEA officials and diplomats from three European Union countries: Germany, France, and the United Kingdom. However, negotiations broke down in August 2005, and Iran resumed operations and construction at its nuclear facilities. The IAEA reported Iran to the UN Security Council for violating the NPT.

UN RESOLUTIONS. Between July 2006 and March 2008 the UN Security Council passed four resolutions calling on Iran to suspend its nuclear activities and begin cooperating fully with IAEA investigators. In *Iran: U.S. Concerns and Policy Responses* (May 6, 2008, http://assets.opencrs.com/rpts/RL32048_20080506.pdf), Kenneth Katzman of the CRS describes Resolutions 1696, 1737, 1747, and 1803. According to Katzman, the requirements of the latter three resolutions can be summed up as follows:

- Iran must suspend its uranium enrichment programs
- The transfer to Iran of nuclear, missile, and similar materials is prohibited unless the materials are intended for use in light-water nuclear reactors
- Iran is forbidden to export arms or technology that could be used to produce WMDs
- The assets of dozens of Iranian individuals and companies are to be frozen in other countries
- Travel bans or restrictions are to be placed against dozens of Iranian individuals

In addition, the resolutions call on other nations to refuse to export arms to Iran or conduct new business with Iran and to monitor Iranian bank activities within their borders and air and sea shipments bound for Iran.

Katzman notes that Iran has steadfastly refused to cease its uranium enrichment activities as demanded by the UN resolutions.

INCENTIVES AND THREATS. Katzman reports that European Union nations and the United States have repeatedly offered Iran incentives, including cessation of some U.S. sanctions, in return for Iran's compliance with the UN resolutions. Several Western nations have also threatened new sanctions if Iran does not comply. Strict measures are routinely opposed by China and Russia, who have historically been trading partners of Iran. Predominantly Muslim countries have also been reluctant to support UN actions against Iran.

The rhetoric expressed by U.S. and Iranian leaders has escalated dramatically in recent years. In a September 2006 speech, President Bush (September 5, 2006, http://www.whitehouse.gov/news/releases/2006/09/20060905-4.html) quoted President Ahmadinejad as saying that Western nations that wish to have good relations with Iran should "bow down before the greatness of the Iranian nation and surrender" and if they do not that Iran will force them to surrender. Bush responded, "America will not bow down to tyrants," and reiterated his vow that "the world's free nations will not allow Iran to develop a nuclear weapon."

IS IRAN DEVELOPING NUCLEAR WEAPONS? In late 2007 U.S. fears about Iran's possible nuclear weapons program were cooled somewhat by the release of *Iran: Nuclear Intentions and Capabilities* (November 2007, http://www.dni.gov/press_releases/20071203_release.pdf). In this report the Office of the Director of National Intelligence (ODNI) expresses the following opinions:

- "Moderate confidence" that as of mid-2007 Iran had not restarted its nuclear weapons program.
- "Moderate-to-high confidence" that in mid-2007 Iran did not have a nuclear weapon.
- "Moderate-to-high confidence" that Iran "at a minimum is keeping open the option to develop nuclear weapons."
- "Moderate confidence" that Iran probably will be technically capable of producing enough highly enriched uranium to produce a nuclear weapon sometime between 2010 and 2015.

The ODNI concludes that Iran's decision to halt its nuclear weapons program in 2003 was probably driven by "international pressure," giving hope to current and future U.S. and UN efforts in this regard.

Iran's Role in Iraq

Besides the United States' long-standing concerns about Iran's links to international terrorism and possible nuclear weapons program, the United States is deeply troubled by Iranian support of insurgents in Iraq. This issue is explored at length by Katzman, in *Iran's Activities and Influence in Iraq* (August 22, 2008, http://www.fas.org/sgp/crs/mideast/RS22323.pdf). As noted earlier, the Muslim populations of both Iran and Iraq are predominantly Shiite. According to Katzman, "Iran's strategy in Iraq has been to perpetuate domination of Iraq's government by pro-Iranian Shiite Islamists, while also developing leverage over the United States by aiding Shiite militias that are willing to combat U.S. forces." Iran reportedly saw the ousting of Hussein by U.S. forces in 2003 as an opportunity for pro-Iranian Shiites to assume power in Iraq. Iranian involvement in Iraq through 2005 is believed to have been mostly political. The situation changed dramatically in 2006 with a sudden escalation of sectarian violence between Shiites and Sunnis in Iraq.

Moqtada Al Sadr (1973?–) is an Iraqi Shiite cleric with religious and political ties to Iran. He has many followers including tens of thousands of militiamen called the Jaysh al-Mahdi (JAM; Mahdi Army). Katzman notes that in 2005 Iran began shipping arms to JAM and encouraging attacks against Sunnis and occupying U.S. forces. JAM is believed to have received logistical aid from Iranian Qods agents. The Qods (or Jerusalem Force) is a politically conservative military organization in Iran that aids pro-Iranian militants in other countries. The U.S. military has reportedly captured more than a dozen Qods agents inside Iraq.

Throughout 2007 and early 2008 U.S. military leaders accused Iran of supplying JAM with money, support, and arms, including armor-piercing explosives that have killed hundreds of U.S. troops. Another Iran-linked faction in Iraq is called the Badr Organization. Badr militiamen have reportedly infiltrated the Iraqi Security Forces (army and police) and instigated violence against Iraqi Sunnis. However, in 2007 JAM and Badr forces began fighting against one another for control of Shiite-majority cities in Iraq. Shiite civilians were often the casualties in these skirmishes. Lessening civilian and political support for the militants and a U.S. troop surge between 2007 and 2008 have combined to weaken JAM and Badr power. In May 2007 U.S. and Iranian diplomats met in Iraq to begin discussions about stabilizing Iraq. It is believed that Iran dramatically reduced arms shipments to Iraq around that time. Katzman concludes that Iranian influence remains "extensive" in Iraq, but is projected to fade as Iraqi nationhood becomes stronger.

The Future of U.S.-Iranian Relations

In *The National Security Strategy of the United States of America* (March 2006, http://www.whitehouse.gov/nsc/nss/2006/nss2006.pdf), President Bush notes that "we may face no greater challenge from a single country than from Iran." He also states, "The Iranian regime sponsors terrorism; threatens Israel; seeks to thwart Middle East peace; disrupts democracy in Iraq; and denies the aspirations of its people for freedom. The nuclear issue and our other concerns can ultimately be resolved only if the Iranian regime makes the strategic decision to change these policies, open up its political system, and afford freedom to its people. This is the ultimate goal of U.S. policy. In the interim, we will continue to take all necessary measures to protect our national and economic security against the adverse effects of their bad conduct."

The Bush administration has continuously denied that the United States is planning military action against Iran. Nevertheless, there were widespread media reports in the spring of 2008 that the U.S. military was developing plans for a military strike against Iran. According to the article "El Baradei Warns against Strike on Iran" (CNN, June 22, 2008), Mohamed El Baradei (1942–), the head the IAEA, told an Arab television interviewer that the Middle East would become "a ball of fire" if Iran was attacked. The remarks came soon after Israel waged a practice aerial military exercise widely believed to be a warning to Iran about its nuclear program. Israeli officials have publicly threatened a military strike against Iran's nuclear reactors. The two countries are bitter enemies. In 2005 Ahmadinejad, who was the newly elected conservative president of Iran, reportedly said that Israel should be "wiped off the map."

TABLE 6.4

Public opinion on whether the true purpose of Iran's nuclear program is to produce nuclear power or to produce nuclear weapons, December 2007

FROM WHAT YOU HAVE HEARD OR READ, DO YOU THINK THE TRUE PURPOSE OF IRAN'S NUCLEAR PROGRAM IS—TO PRODUCE NUCLEAR POWER OR TO PRODUCE NUCLEAR WEAPONS?

	Total N: 1004	
Mean: N/A	%	N
To produce nuclear power	27.23	273
To produce nuclear weapons	66.71	669
Don't know	4.63	46
Refused	1.43	14

N = Population.

SOURCE: Question qn11. From What You Have Heard or Read, Do You Think the True Purpose of Iran's Nuclear Program Is—to Produce Nuclear Power or to Produce Nuclear Weapons?" in *December Panel Survey*, The Gallup Organization, December 2007, http://brain.gallup.com/documents/questionnaire.aspx?STUDY=P0712010(accessed August 4, 2008). Copyright © 2007 by The Gallup Organization. Reproduced by permission of The Gallup Organization.

U.S. Public Opinion about Iran

In December 2007 the Gallup Organization polled Americans on their opinions about Iran's nuclear program. Over two-thirds (67%) of the respondents said the "true purpose" of Iran's nuclear program is to produce nuclear weapons. (See Table 6.4.) Only 27% thought the program's "true purpose" is to produce nuclear power. Thirty-three percent of respondents said Iran's nuclear program poses a "very serious" threat. (See Table 6.5.) Twenty-eight percent thought it poses a "somewhat serious" threat, and 37% said it does not pose a threat.

NORTH KOREA

North Korea is a small country that sits on a peninsula jutting out of the coastline of East Asia. (See Figure 6.2.) The nation's capital is Pyongyang. North Korea is bordered on the north by China and Russia and to the south by South Korea. Japan lies a few hundred miles to the southeast, across the Sea of Japan. North and South Korea were once a single nation. Japan invaded Korea in 1905 and occupied it through World War II (1939–1945). Following the war, the Allied powers split the Korea Peninsula into two countries, with the northern part falling under Soviet control and the southern part under U.S. control. In

TABLE 6.5

Public opinion on whether Iran's nuclear program poses a serious threat to the United States, December 2007

DO YOU THINK IRAN'S NUCLEAR PROGRAM POSES A SERIOUS THREAT TO THE UNITED STATES, OR NOT? [IF YES, ASK:] IS THAT A VERY SERIOUS THREAT OR A SOMEWHAT SERIOUS THREAT?

	Total N: 1004	
Mean: N/A	**%**	**N**
Yes, very serious threat	32.88	330
Yes, somewhat serious threat	28.36	285
No, does not pose a threat	37.42	376
Don't know	1.22	12
Refused	0.12	1

N = Population.

SOURCE: "Question qn10. Do You Think Iran's Nuclear Program Poses a Serious Threat to the United States, or Not? [IF YES, ASK:] Is That a Very Serious Threat or a Somewhat Serious Threat?" in *December Panel Survey*, The Gallup Organization, December 2007, http://brain.gallup.com/documents/questionnaire.aspx?STUDY=P0712010(accessed August 4, 2008). Copyright © 2007 by The Gallup Organization. Reproduced by permission of The Gallup Organization.

FIGURE 6.2

Map of North Korea, 2006

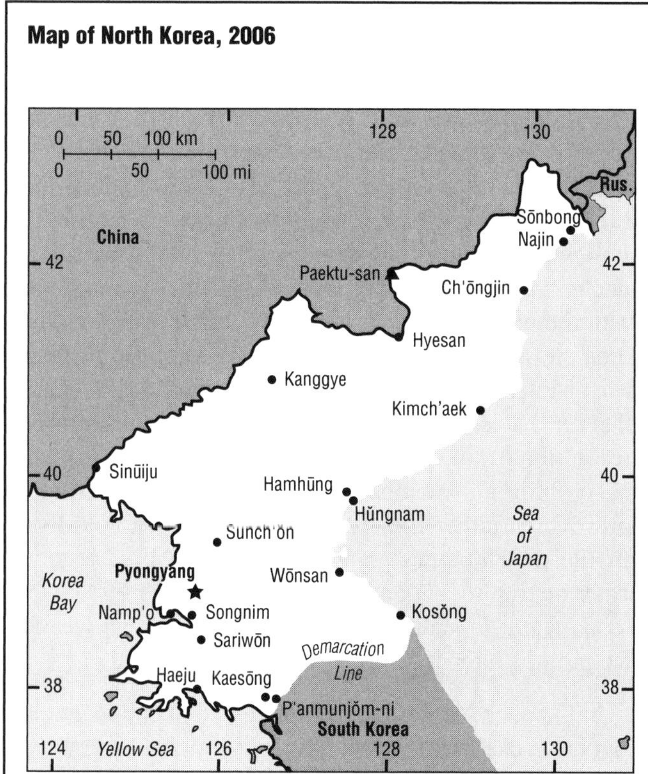

SOURCE: "North Korea," in *Country Analysis Briefs: North Korea*, U.S. Department of Energy, Energy Information Administration, February 2006, http://www.eia.doe.gov/emeu/cabs/North_Korea/pdf.pdf (accessed August 11, 2008)

1948 South Korea became an independent nation called the Republic of Korea. North Korea calls itself the Democratic People's Republic of Korea. It was ruled by Kim Il Sung (1912–1994) from 1948 until his death in 1994, when his son Kim Jong-Il (1942–) assumed power.

In *The World Factbook: North Korea* (September 4, 2008, https://www.cia.gov/library/publications/the-world-factbook/geos/kn.html), the CIA describes North Korea as a "communist state one-man dictatorship." All of its political parties are controlled by the major party: the Korean Workers' Party. Even though elections were held in 2003, Kim Jong-Il was the only person nominated for chief of state and ran unopposed. The country has a 687-seat Supreme People's Assembly; however, candidates are appointed by the nation's rulers and run unopposed in elections. The CIA reports that decades of poor governance and economic mismanagement have rendered North Korea unable to feed many of its people. The population is highly dependent on international food aid and is believed to suffer from widespread malnutrition and poor living conditions. Most of the nation's resources are used to maintain its large military establishment, which is estimated to number around one million troops. North Korea's total population was estimated at nearly 23.5 million in July 2008.

Foreign Relations

In 1950 North Korean forces backed by the Soviet military invaded South Korea, setting off the Korean War. The United States was caught off guard by the invasion but rushed to defend South Korea from a communist takeover. Over the next three years U.S. and allied forces under the UN fought against North Korean and Chinese troops supported by the Soviet Union. The war ended in a stalemate with both sides back where they had started: on either side of the thirty-eighth parallel (a line of latitude). In 1953 a cease-fire agreement ended the armed conflict in Korea. North Korea remained under communist control, whereas South Korea became a democracy protected by UN troops (primarily U.S. forces).

During the war the United States imposed economic sanctions against North Korea that would last for more than four decades. North Korea became highly dependent on its communist allies, particularly the Soviet Union and China, for foreign trade. The breakup of the Soviet Union in the early 1990s eliminated a major political ally and trading partner for North Korea; however, its close relationship with China has continued.

North Korea's Nuclear Program

Larry A. Niksch of the CRS notes in *North Korea's Nuclear Weapons Program* (May 25, 2006, http://fpc.state.gov/documents/organization/67840.pdf) that in 1985 North Korea signed the NPT. In 1987 it began operating an atomic reactor near Pyongyang, ostensibly to produce electrical power. U.S. intelligence agencies discovered in 1989 that the reactor had been shut down for more than two months. It is suspected that the used fuel rods in the reactor were removed and reprocessed for their plutonium content. (High-grade plutonium can be used to produce a nuclear weapon.) Similar reactor shutdowns occurred in successive years. During a May 1994 shutdown approximately eight thousand used fuel rods were removed. Scientists estimate these rods likely contained enough plutonium to produce four to six nuclear weapons.

AGREED FRAMEWORK. The U.S. government was disturbed by the removal and by IAEA reports that North Korea was withholding data, being uncooperative, and threatening to withdraw from the NPT. In response, the United States threatened to bring new economic sanctions against North Korea through the UN. The two countries eventually negotiated an agreement known as the Agreed Framework that called for North Korea to remain a party to the NPT, "freeze" its nuclear program, and dismantle nuclear reactors under IAEA supervision in exchange for the following concessions from the United States:

- Easing of economic sanctions
- Full diplomatic relations
- Two light-water nuclear reactors and 500,000 metric tons (3.7 million barrels) of oil
- Formal assurance that the United States would not threaten to use or use nuclear weapons against North Korea

The United States began shipping oil to North Korea, made preliminary arrangements for the light-water nuclear reactors, and began to phase out some economic sanctions. According to Niksch, North Korea "complained loudly" that U.S. efforts did not meet the intent of the Agreed Framework. Negotiations failed on assumption of full diplomatic relations.

In 2002 the Agreed Framework fell apart after the United States accused North Korea of operating since 1996 a secret program to develop nuclear weapons using highly enriched uranium instead of reprocessed plutonium. Niksch notes that James A. Kelly (1936–), the U.S. assistant secretary of state, claimed that North Korean officials told him about the highly enriched uranium program in October 2002. North Korea has repeatedly denied the claim. The United States immediately ceased oil shipments to North Korea; North Korea responded by expelling IAEA inspectors, withdrawing from the NPT, and restarting its plutonium reprocessing operations.

SIX-PARTY TALKS. In 2003 the United States and North Korea began a series of negotiations that included high-ranking officials from South Korea, China, Japan, and Russia. The so-called six-party talks were initiated after the United States refused to hold bilateral (two-party) meetings with North Korea. Many rounds were held in which virtually no progress was achieved in resolving the disputes at issue. Since the U.S. invasions of Afghanistan and Iraq in 2001 and 2003, respectively, North Korea has become increasingly concerned about a military strike from U.S. forces. In 2003 North Korean officials publicly announced that the country does have nuclear weapons. Subsequent announcements have included hostile and threatening rhetoric toward the United States. After the November 2005 six-party talks North Korea temporarily refused to meet again in protest of new accusations from the United States that North Korea has been conducting illegal activities, including drug trafficking and the counterfeiting of U.S. currency.

By the late 1990s North Korea had developed intercontinental ballistic missiles that were capable of reaching Alaska. According to Niksch, U.S. intelligence agencies believed that by 2003 nuclear warheads had been produced for the missiles. In July 2006 the world was stunned when North Korea test fired seven unarmed missiles toward the Sea of Japan to demonstrate their capabilities. One of the missiles was a Taepodong 2, which is thought to have a range of perhaps 1,860 miles (2,993 km). That missile failed after approximately forty seconds and fell into the sea. The other six missiles were short-range missiles.

Since 1999 North Korea had maintained a moratorium on the testing of long-range missiles following international outcry over such a test in 1998. Japan and South Korea, in particular, have expressed concern about North Korea's missile capabilities. Both nations host large U.S. military bases, which could be targets for the missiles in wartime. The timing of the July 2006 missile launches appears to have been politically motivated. Even though they were launched on July 5 in North Korea, it was still July 4 in the Western Hemisphere. U.S. officials called the missile launches "provocative behavior." The UN Security Council unanimously passed a resolution urging North Korea to resume six-party talks and prohibiting member nations from transferring to North Korea either money or technology that could support the development of WMDs. North Korea received further international condemnation in October 2006, when it conducted an underground test of a nuclear weapon. Two months later it returned to the six-party talks.

In October 2007 North Korea agreed to end its nuclear program in exchange for foreign economic and energy aid. It was supposed to turn over its declaration (i.e., documents detailing its program) by the end of the year. North Korea missed that deadline, but in the spring and summer of 2008 it turned over thousands of documents on the program and destroyed the cooling tower at its main reactor site. On June 28, 2008, President Bush lifted most of the sanctions that had been in place against North Korea since 1950 under the Trading with the Enemy Act. He also notified Congress of his intention to remove North Korea from the state sponsor of terrorism list. According to the

DOS, in "Background Note: North Korea" (August 2008, http://www.state.gov/r/pa/ei/bgn/2792.htm), the removal will take place after a verification program is established to verify the declarations made by the North Korean government.

U.S. Public Opinion

Frank Newport of the Gallup Organization reports in *Americans Favor Diplomacy with North Korea, Not Military Action* (July 13, 2006, http://www.gallup.com/poll/23689/Americans-Favor-Diplomacy-North-Korea-Military-Action.aspx) about a poll that was conducted days after the July 2006 missile launch to gauge American attitudes about how the U.S. government should handle North Korea. A majority (72%) of respondents preferred the use of diplomatic pressure and economic sanctions to get North Korea to stop testing and developing missiles capable of carrying nuclear warheads. Another 10% felt that nothing should be done. Nine percent opted for military action, such as air strikes and missile attacks, and 3% chose invasion with ground troops.

During the same poll, respondents were asked to categorize North Korea as one of the following: ally; friendly, but not an ally; unfriendly; or enemy. Nearly half (47%) of the respondents rated North Korea as an enemy. Just over one-third (34%) chose to describe the nation as unfriendly. Ten percent of poll participants judged North Korea to be "friendly, but not an ally," and 2% named the country an ally of the United States.

Newport notes that Americans were asked to rate the threat posed by North Korea to the United States. Only 20% of those asked considered North Korea an "immediate threat." A greater number (59%) rated the country as a "long-term threat," and 15% believed North Korea does not pose a threat to the United States. According to Newport, these percentages have remained consistent since the poll question was first asked in 2003. In other words, the missile launches of July 2006 appear to have had no discernible effect on American attitudes about the threat posed to U.S. national security by North Korea.

OTHER COUNTRIES OF CONCERN

Even though Iran and North Korea are considered the countries posing the most threat to U.S. national security, there are other countries of concern. These include three nations deemed state sponsors of terrorism: Cuba, Syria, and Sudan.

Cuba

The Republic of Cuba is a small island lying between the Caribbean Sea to the south and the Gulf of Mexico and the North Atlantic Ocean to the north. (See Figure 6.3.)

FIGURE 6.3

Map of Cuba, 2008

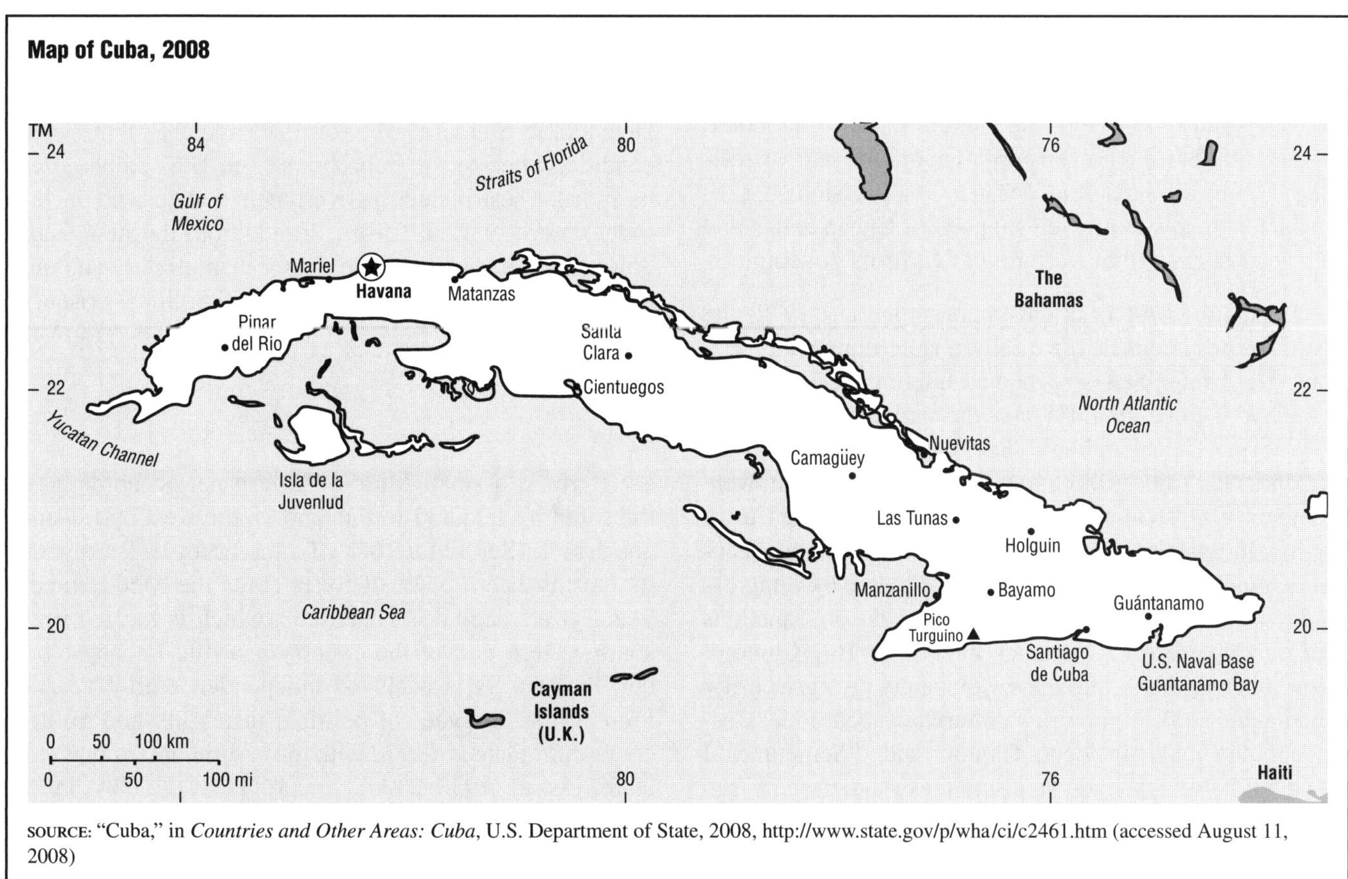

SOURCE: "Cuba," in *Countries and Other Areas: Cuba*, U.S. Department of State, 2008, http://www.state.gov/p/wha/ci/c2461.htm (accessed August 11, 2008)

Cuba is only 90 miles (145 km) southeast of Key West, Florida. It is a communist state that was ruled for nearly five decades by one man: Fidel Castro (1926–). In February 2008 he stepped down as Cuba's president due to ill health. His brother, Raúl Castro Ruz (1931–), officially became Cuba's leader.

Historically, Cuba enjoyed close economic and military ties to the former Soviet Union. The demise of the Soviet Union during the early 1990s sent Cuba into a sharp economic recession from which it has never recovered. According to the CIA, in *The World Factbook: Cuba* (September 4, 2008, https://www.cia.gov/library/publications/the-world-factbook/geos/cu.html), the standard of living for the average Cuban was less in 2008 than it was before the loss of Soviet aid.

Cuba and the United States have had a contentious relationship since Fidel Castro took power. In 1961 CIA-backed Cuban exiles attempted to invade Cuba and overthrow Castro. They were soundly defeated in a battle at the Bay of Pigs, a small bay located south of Matanzas along the southern coast of the island. Only a year later President John F. Kennedy (1917–1963) and the Soviet premier Nikita Khrushchev (1894–1971) faced off after U.S. intelligence agencies discovered that the Soviets had installed nuclear missile facilities in Cuba. After a suspenseful twelve-day diplomatic standoff, the Soviets backed down and agreed to dismantle the facilities. The United States implemented the first of many economic sanctions against Cuba. With only a handful of exceptions, American citizens were forbidden to travel to Cuba. The United States issued an open invitation to Cuban citizens wanting to flee to the United States—they could became eligible for citizenship after only a year of residency. Over the next four decades a succession of U.S. presidents openly expressed support for Cuban exiles and dissidents seeking the overthrow of Castro's government.

During the Carter administration in the late 1970s the two countries decided to partially restore diplomatic relations. The United States opened an Interests Section office in the Swiss embassy in Havana, the capital of Cuba. Then in 1996 the Cuban military shot down two U.S. civilian airplanes near Cuba, killing four people—all of whom were members of a Cuban-American group opposed to the Castro regime. In retaliation, President Clinton imposed new economic sanctions against Cuba that were passed by Congress in the Helms-Burton bill. In "Bill Clinton on Sanctions against Cuba: Amy Goodman Interviews Bill Clinton" (November 8, 2000, http://www.globalpolicy.org/security/sanction/cuba/00clintn.htm), an interview about Fidel Castro and the plane incident, Clinton said, "Sometimes I wonder if he shot them down just to make sure the embargo couldn't be lifted, because as long as he can blame the United States, then he doesn't have to answer to his own people for the failures of his economic policy."

In November 2001 Cuba was struck by Hurricane Michelle and suffered severe damage to its agricultural industry. In an unprecedented move, the United States sold shipments of food to Cuba as part of a humanitarian effort. There was talk in the United States of dropping the economic sanctions against Cuba. In the speech "Lift the United States Embargo on Cuba" (July 26, 2001, http://www.house.gov/paul/congrec/congrec2001/cr072601.htm), Representative Ron Paul (1935–) of Texas noted that "while sanctions may serve our patriotic fervor, they mostly harm innocent citizens and do nothing to displace the governments we claim as enemies." However, relaxing the sanctions was staunchly opposed by many conservatives in the U.S. government and members of the politically powerful Cuban exile movement centered in Miami, Florida.

In 2002 former president Carter was invited by Castro to visit Cuba for a series of meetings. It was the first visit by a high-ranking U.S. official since Castro took power. However, the Bush administration decided to take a hard line against Cuba. Immediately before Carter's visit, the administration accused Castro of cooperating with terrorist organizations in the development of WMDs. Cuba has been on the DOS's list of state sponsors of terrorism since 1982.

As of September 2008, the United States maintained strict sanctions against Cuba, but was cautiously optimistic that better relations may be possible in the future. These issues are discussed by Mark P. Sullivan of the CRS in *Cuba's Political Succession: From Fidel to Raúl Castro* (February 29, 2008, http://fas.org/sgp/crs/row/RS22742.pdf). Sullivan notes that the Cuban Liberty and Democratic Solidarity Act of 1996 requires that several conditions be met in Cuba before the U.S. embargo can be ended. These include a government that does not include Fidel Castro or Raúl Castro. In addition, the new Cuban government must be civilian, rather than military and must legalize all political activity, release all political prisoners, respect the human rights of its citizens, and reform the nation's justice system.

Syria

Syria is a small Middle Eastern nation bordered on the south by Iraq and Jordan and on the west by Lebanon and Israel. (See Figure 6.4.) To the north is Turkey, and the northwestern coast of Syria abuts the Mediterranean Sea. Syria's capital is Damascus, which is located in the southwestern part of the country near the Lebanese border. In 1946 Syria achieved independence after years of French rule. Decades of political instability and military coups culminated in 1970 with the assumption of power by Hafez Assad (1930–2000). According to the CIA, in *The World Factbook: Syria* (September 4, 2008, https://www.cia.gov/library/publications/the-world-factbook/geos/sy.html), Assad was a member of the Socialist Baath

FIGURE 6.4

Map of Syria, 2008

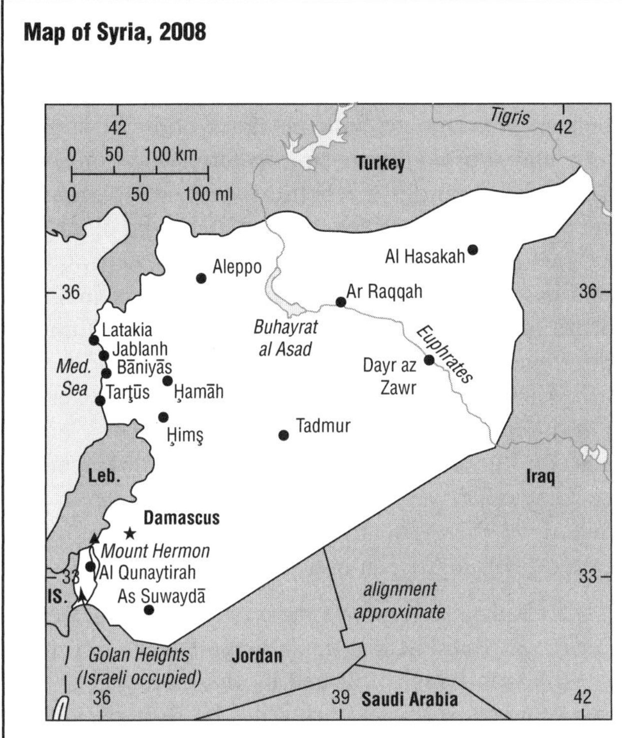

SOURCE: "Syria," in *Country Analysis Briefs: Sudan*, U.S. Department of Energy, Energy Information Administration, March 2008, http://www.eia.doe.gov/cabs/Syria/Background.html (accessed August 5, 2008)

Party—a pan-Arab organization. After his death in 2000 the presidency was turned over to his son, Bashar al-Assad (1965–). The CIA describes the Syrian government as a "republic under an authoritarian military-dominated regime." The official name of the country is the Syrian Arab Republic.

Syria and Israel have been enemies since the foundation of Israel in 1948, and have fought several wars. Most notable among them was the Six-Day War in 1967, during which Israel captured the Golan Heights. Israel has occupied this strategic piece of land along Syria's border with Israel ever since, deepening the divisions between the two countries. Syria has been on the U.S. list of state sponsors of terrorism since 1979, primarily for its support of groups that conduct terrorist activities against Israel. Alfred B. Prados of the CRS explains in *Syria: U.S. Relations and Bilateral Issues* (March 13, 2006, http://fpc.state.gov/documents/organization/64491.pdf) that Syria openly admits supporting Palestinian, Hamas, and Hezbollah attacks against Israeli occupation of disputed territories. Syria considers these attacks to be "legitimate resistance activity," rather than terrorism.

In 1976 Syria sent troops and intelligence personnel into neighboring Lebanon during the Lebanese civil war. According to Prados, up to forty thousand Syrian troops were in Lebanon by the late 1970s, and Syria began to wield considerable influence over Lebanese politics. An agreement reached with the Arab League in 1989 was supposed to sharply curtail Syrian involvement in Lebanon but was never fully implemented. In February 2005 Rafiq Hariri (1944–2005), the former Lebanese prime minister, was assassinated. Hariri had been openly criticizing Syria's military presence in Lebanon, and Syrian agents were suspected in his assassination. Two months later Syria withdrew its troops from Lebanon following intense pressure from the Lebanese people and the international community.

The United States has maintained economic sanctions against Syria since the 1970s. U.S.-Syrian relations have been particularly strained since the U.S. invasion of Iraq in 2003. U.S. officials have accused Syria of allowing, and perhaps facilitating, the passage of militia fighters and arms across its border into Iraq to aid the insurgency against U.S. troops. Syria has denied these claims. The Syrian government is primarily secular and views Islamic fundamentalism, such as that espoused by al Qaeda, as a threat to its own stability. However, a major issue of contention is Syria's continued support for Hezbollah, which maintains a large contingent of militia fighters in Lebanon. In July 2006 Hezbollah guerrillas crossed the border into Israel and kidnapped two Israeli soldiers, setting off a thirty-four-day armed conflict that left hundreds dead in Israel and Lebanon. A cease-fire negotiated by the UN went into effect in August 2006.

In September 2007 the Israeli air force destroyed a nuclear reactor under construction in northeastern Syria. The events that led up to the raid and its political ramifications are examined by Jeremy M. Sharp of the CRS in *Syria: Background and U.S. Relations* (May 1, 2008, http://assets.opencrs.com/rpts/RL33487_20080501.pdf). According to Sharp, the U.S. intelligence services believe Syria received help from North Korea in designing and building the reactor. Even though the Bush administration admits conferring with Israel about the Syrian reactor before the air strike, it denies that the United States okayed or participated in the raid. Syria angrily denounced Israel and the United States for the raid and has sworn revenge.

Sudan

Sudan is the largest country in Africa, approximately the size of the United States east of the Mississippi River. Sudan is in the north-central part of the African continent and lies due south of Egypt. (See Figure 6.5.) The capital of Sudan is Khartoum. The northeastern portion of the country is bounded by the Red Sea. Sudan has been an independent state since 1956; however, it has suffered from decades of civil war, social unrest, and political instability. According to the DOS, in "Background Note: Sudan" (July 2008, http://www.state.gov/r/pa/ei/bgn/5424.htm), the Sudanese population is extremely diverse and

FIGURE 6.5

Map of Sudan, 2007

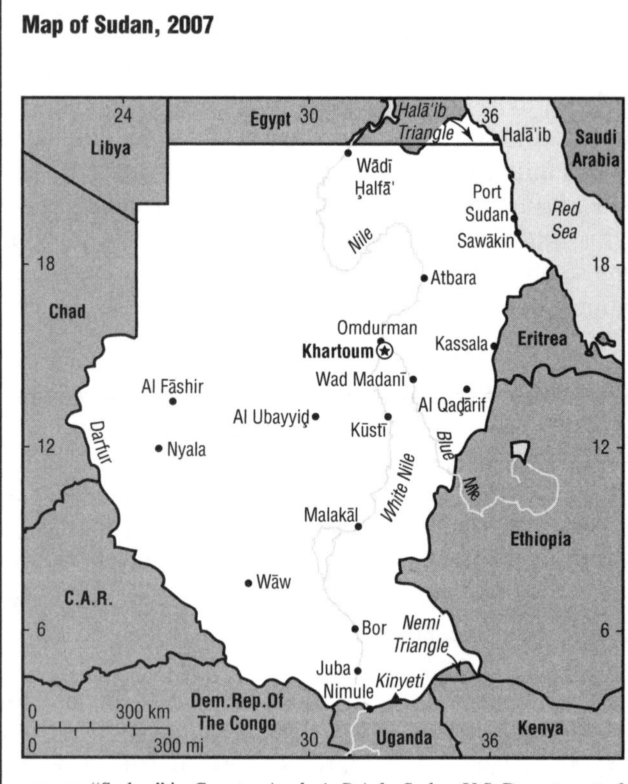

SOURCE: "Sudan," in *Country Analysis Briefs: Sudan*, U.S. Department of Energy, Energy Information Administration, April 2007, http://www.eia.doe.gov/emeu/cabs/Sudan/Background.html (accessed August 11, 2008)

includes hundreds of ethnic, tribal, and language groups. The two major groups are Arabic-speaking Muslims and black Africans. The northern part of the country contains most of the population and is urban in nature. The rural south is sparsely populated by a wide variety of tribal groups that follow many different traditional beliefs. The DOS estimates that more than two million people in southern Sudan have died as a result of civil war and approximately four million have been displaced from their homes. Sudan's total population was estimated at 39.4 million in 2007.

In 2002 an agreement was reached granting the southern rebels the right to self-determination. In January 2005 a Comprehensive Peace Agreement was signed that calls for a new Sudanese government based on power-sharing. National elections are expected to take place in 2009.

This agreement did not lead to peace throughout Sudan, however. During the successful negotiations between the Sudanese government and the main body of southern rebels, unrest broke out in the western region of Darfur. This rebellion within a rebellion was led by groups of farmers the DOS describes as "non-Arabized black African Muslims." The government's crackdown on these rebels has precipitated a humanitarian crisis in Darfur and has been criticized by the international community as attempted genocide. (Genocide is the eradication of an entire group of people based on their nationality, ethnicity, religion, or race.) In July 2007 the UN Security Council's Resolution 1769 authorized deployment of a peacekeeping force in Darfur. The troops have been supplied by the African Union, a cooperative venture between several African nations.

U.S.-Sudanese relations have been poor for decades. The rift was deepened by U.S. support for Israel during the 1967 Arab-Israeli War and by the murders of American diplomats in Sudan during the 1970s and 1980s. In 1989 General Omar Hassam Ahmed Bashir (1935–) overthrew the existing ruler and installed a government known as the National Islamic Front. According to the DOS, Bashir supported many terrorist organizations during the 1990s and provided a safe haven for notorious terrorists, such as Osama bin Laden (1957–) and Abu Nidal (1937–2002). In 1993 the United States designated Sudan as a state sponsor of terrorism. Throughout the remainder of the decade the United States imposed ever-stricter economic and trade sanctions against Sudan. In 1998 U.S. missile strikes were conducted against targets in Khartoum in retaliation for Sudanese involvement in the bombings of U.S. embassies in Kenya and Tanzania. Relations improved somewhat at the turn of the twenty-first century as Sudan began cooperating with the United States in its War on Terror. The DOS notes that the United States has been a major donor of humanitarian aid to Sudan, donating more than $1 billion in 2007. Future diplomatic relations will depend on the policies adopted by a future Sudanese government.

CHAPTER 7

PROLIFERATION OF WEAPONS

Proliferation means growth or multiplication. The proliferation of powerful weapons around the world is a source of great concern to U.S. national security. These weapons include conventional armaments such as military-type guns, bombs, and missiles, and the more lethal weapons of mass destruction (WMDs), which are based on nuclear, chemical, and biological technologies. U.S. goals for nonproliferation (or counterproliferation) include stopping the development of new weapons, reducing and safeguarding the stockpiles of existing weapons, and preventing the spread of WMD technology, particularly among enemies of the United States. The greatest threat to national security is believed to be the acquisition and use of WMDs by terrorists and rogue nations (nations that ignore international restrictions on weapons proliferation).

ARMS AROUND THE WORLD

Most nations of the world are heavily armed with conventional weapons. A handful of developed nations, including the United States, possess highly advanced conventional weapons that are enhanced by sophisticated technologies, such as laser guidance systems. The effectiveness of these weapons was demonstrated by the U.S. military in 1991 during the Persian Gulf War against Iraq. The United States has become a major supplier of conventional arms to its allies around the world. The Congressional Research Service (CRS) provides an annual report to Congress on the proliferation of conventional arms. In *Conventional Arms Transfers to Developing Nations, 1999–2006* (September 26, 2007, http://assets.opencrs.com/rpts/RL34187_20070926.pdf), Richard F. Grimmett of the CRS notes that the value of worldwide conventional arms transfer agreements between governments in 2006 was nearly $28.8 billion. This value was down slightly from $31.8 billion in 2005. In 2006 U.S. arms sales accounted for $10.3 billion, Russia had $8.1 billion in sales, and the United Kingdom had $3.1 billion in sales.

Grimmett lists in *U.S. Arms Sales: Agreements with and Deliveries to Major Clients, 1999–2006* (December 20, 2007, http://www.fas.org/sgp/crs/weapons/RL34291.pdf) the major clients for U.S. arms sales between 1999 and 2006. The top ten purchasers of delivered arms in 2006 were:

- Australia, $1.7 billion
- Israel, $1.5 billion
- Egypt, $1.2 billion
- Saudi Arabia, $1 billion
- Taiwan, $970 million
- Netherlands, $800 million
- Poland, $690 million
- South Korea, $610 million
- Japan, $560 million
- Greece, $440 million

Unconventional weapons are those that use nontraditional means to reap destruction and death, primarily nuclear technology or the release of chemical or biological agents. Small numbers of these weapons are capable of killing vast numbers of people; hence, they are called weapons of mass destruction. The proliferation of WMDs is governed by many international agreements that have been brokered by the United Nations (UN). Therefore, the United States is most concerned about the threat posed by WMDs in the hands of rogue nations and terrorists.

CONVENTIONAL WEAPON THREATS

In "Registry of Conventional Arms" (2008, http://disarmament2.un.org/cab/register.html), the UN divides major conventional weapons into seven categories: battle tanks, large-caliber artillery systems, combat aircraft, attack helicopters, warships (including submarines), armored combat vehicles, and missiles and missile launchers.

Most national militaries are equipped with many, if not all, of these weapons. Except for some missiles and missile launchers, the weapons listed are generally large in size and difficult to conceal from foreign intelligence services. As such, the extent of most national conventional weapons arsenals is fairly well known.

Missiles

Missiles are the latest generation of projectile weapons. Their evolution began in the 800s with the invention of gunpowder by the Chinese. Over the following centuries explosives technologies were employed on the battlefield in guns, cannons, and bombs. World War II (1939–1945) ushered in the modern missile age. During the early 1940s Germany developed the most sophisticated rocket program in the world. At its helm was a brilliant young man named Wernher von Braun (1912–1977). His team developed the rocket-powered Vergeltungswaffens (weapons of vengeance; they were called V weapons, for short). Thousands of V rockets rained down on England during the war. Following World War II the United States and the Soviet Union began researching the feasibility of attaching warheads to long-range rockets capable of traveling halfway round the world. These weapons could be equipped with conventional or nuclear warheads.

The Arms Control Association (ACA) is a U.S.-based nonprofit organization that supports arms control. According to the ACA, in the fact sheet "Worldwide Ballistic Missile Inventories" (September 2007, http://www.armscontrol.org/factsheets/missiles), thirty-two countries possessed ballistic missiles in 2007. Ballistic missiles are powered and guided during part of their flight. Then they enter a free-flight stage during which their trajectories are determined by natural forces, such as gravity and atmospheric effects. According to the ACA, the ranges of ballistic missiles are:

- Short range—less than 1,000 kilometers (km; 621 miles)
- Medium range—1,000 to 3,000 km (621 to 1,864 miles)
- Intermediate range—3,000 to 5,500 km (1,864 to 3,418 miles)
- Intercontinental—greater than 5,500 km (3,418 miles)

The ACA notes that only seven countries were believed to have intercontinental ballistic missiles in 2007. Those countries were the United States, China, France, Israel, Russia, the United Kingdom, and possibly North Korea.

In July 2006 North Korea fired seven unarmed missiles toward the Sea of Japan. One of the missiles is believed to have been an intermediate-range ballistic missile; however, it failed after approximately forty seconds and fell into the sea. The other six rockets were short-range missiles. U.S. intelligence agencies believe North Korea has possessed nuclear warheads for its missiles since 2003.

MAN-PORTABLE AIR DEFENSE SYSTEMS. Man-portable air defense systems (MANPADS) are more commonly called shoulder-fired antiaircraft missile systems (SAMS). They fire short-range surface-to-air missiles that are typically 4 to 6.5 feet (1.2 to 2 m) in length and only a few inches in diameter. Combined, a missile and its launcher can weigh less than 60 pounds (27 kg). Thus, a MANPADS can be carried and fired by a single individual and is easily transported and concealed. These qualities make them attractive weapons for terrorists and guerrilla fighters. However, MANPADS are difficult to aim with precision and shoot relatively slow-moving missiles. As such, they have limited effectiveness against most military aircraft.

In the fact sheet "MANPADS: Combating the Threat to Global Aviation from Man-Portable Air Defense Systems" (July 31, 2008, http://www.state.gov/t/pm/rls/fs/107632.htm), the U.S. Department of State (DOS) describes the U.S. government concerns about the threat posed by MANPADS to civil and commercial aircraft. According to the DOS, in 2002 rebels in Kenya fired two MANPADS at a civilian airliner in an attempt to shoot it down. The missiles missed the airliner, which was a Boeing 757 that had nearly three hundred people onboard. In the late 1990s in Africa three airliners were shot down by rebels using MANPADS, killing sixty-three people. In 2007 a cargo aircraft over Somalia was shot down with a MANPADS, killing the crew of eleven people. Figure 7.1 is a map compiled by the DOS showing the locations of MANPADS attacks on civilian aircraft since 1975. Most have occurred in central and southern Africa.

The DOS notes that U.S.-led efforts have resulted in the destruction of more than twenty-six thousand MANPADS around the world. Nearly six thousand of these units were in the government stockpile of Bosnia and Herzegovina. The United States has received commitments from dozens of countries to destroy thousands of obsolete or unneeded MANPADS to prevent them from falling into the hands of terrorists.

CONVENTIONAL WEAPONS CONTROLS

The Convention on Prohibitions or Restrictions on the Use of Certain Conventional Weapons Which May Be Deemed to Be Excessively Injurious or to Have Indiscriminate Effects (2008, http://www.un-documents.net/cpruccw.htm) entered into effect in 1983. It restricts certain conventional weapons considered to have particularly horrific effects. The Convention on Conventional Weapons (as it is commonly called) originally had three protocols that covered weapons producing fragments not detectable in the human body by x-rays; land mines, booby traps, and related devices; and incendiary weapons (weapons purposely designed to start fires or cause burns). In 1995 a fourth protocol was added to control the proliferation of

FIGURE 7.1

Countries in which MANPADS have been used against civil aircraft, 2008

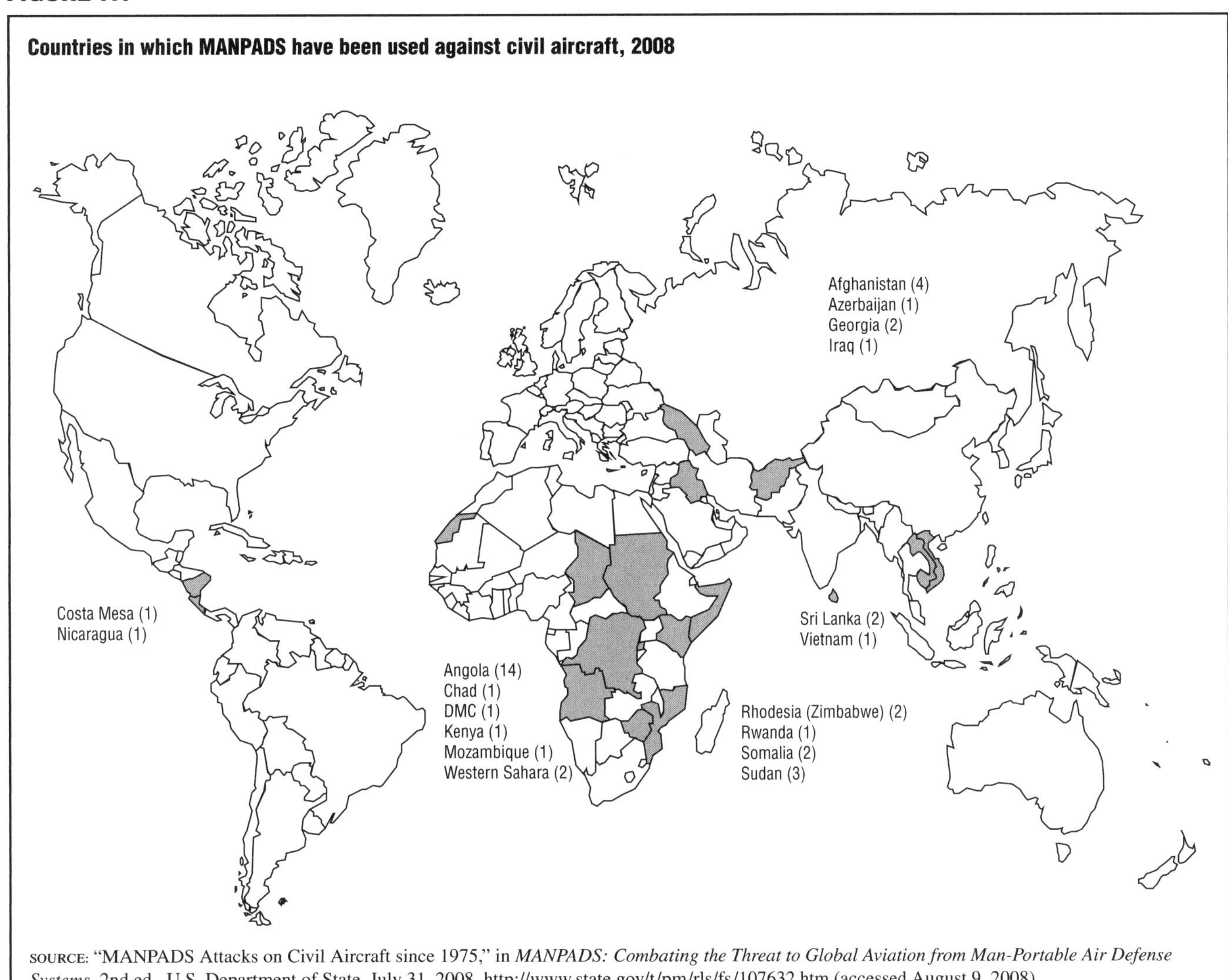

SOURCE: "MANPADS Attacks on Civil Aircraft since 1975," in *MANPADS: Combating the Threat to Global Aviation from Man-Portable Air Defense Systems*, 2nd ed., U.S. Department of State, July 31, 2008, http://www.state.gov/t/pm/rls/fs/107632.htm (accessed August 9, 2008)

laser weapons designed to permanently blind their victims. In 2003 a fifth protocol was added that requires bound parties to clear and destroy unexploded ordnances left over after a conflict has ended. As of September 2008, that protocol had not entered into force. A protocol goes into force six months after at least twenty nations have agreed to follow the protocol. Also, as of September 2008, the United States was a party to only the first and second protocols of the convention.

The Wassenaar Arrangement on Export Controls for Conventional Arms and Dual-Use Goods and Technologies (2008, http://www.wassenaar.org) is a multilateral agreement established in 1996 that concerns the export of conventional weapons and dual-use (military and civilian) technologies of a sensitive nature. The arrangement replaces the older Coordinating Committee for Multilateral Export Controls (CoCom), which had been in place since the 1940s. The sole purpose of CoCom was to prevent the export of weapons from Western nations to the Soviet Union and its allies. The end of the cold war in the early 1990s precipitated the new agreement for which the stated purpose is to promote "transparency and greater responsibility in transfers of conventional arms and dual-use goods and technologies, thus preventing destabilising accumulations. Participating States seek, through their national policies, to ensure that transfers of these items do not contribute to the development or enhancement of military capabilities which undermine these goals, and are not diverted to support such capabilities." The United States is a party to the Wassenaar Arrangement.

NUCLEAR WEAPONS

On August 6, 1945, a uranium-fueled bomb nicknamed Little Boy was dropped by a U.S. military plane onto Hiroshima, Japan. Three days later a plutonium-fueled bomb called Fat Man was dropped on Nagasaki, Japan, forcing a Japanese surrender and ending World War II.

U.S. atomic bombs had been developed by scientists engaged in the Manhattan Project—a top-secret program that included research and development facilities in Los Alamos, New Mexico; Oak Ridge, Tennessee; and Hanford, Washington. Even though the United States and the Soviet Union were wartime allies, Presidents Franklin D. Roosevelt (1882–1945) and Harry S. Truman (1884–1972) decided to keep the Manhattan Project a secret from the Soviets. It was thought this concealment would prolong the development of Soviet nuclear weapons that could one day threaten the United States. When the Soviets detonated their own atomic bomb in 1949, U.S. officials were stunned but soon discovered that some Manhattan Project scientists and conspirators had passed important research and development information to the Soviets.

A series of sensational trials were held during the early 1950s for the so-called atomic spies, and one pair—Julius Rosenberg (1918–1953) and Ethel Rosenberg (1915–1953)—were sent to the electric chair for espionage. For over three decades skeptics claimed the atomic spy trials were a product of anticommunist hysteria, which was common during the cold war. However, later findings from the Venona decryption project and declassified Soviet documents revealed the massive extent of espionage conducted during the Manhattan Project and seemed to validate the convictions of the Rosenbergs and other spies of the era.

One legacy of the cold war was the development and stockpiling of thousands of nuclear weapons by the United States and the Soviet Union. In *A Guide to the Nuclear Arms Treaties* (July 1999, http://www.lanl.gov/history/hbombon/pdf/00416713.pdf), David B. Thomson states that by 1950 the United States had approximately eight hundred nuclear warheads in its arsenal. In 1961 the Soviets conducted nuclear tests in the atmosphere. The United States responded with its own atmospheric tests. The rest of the world watched uneasily as the two great superpowers seemed to edge closer and closer to a nuclear showdown. A crucial event in the nuclear arms race occurred in 1962: the Cuban Missile Crisis. U.S. intelligence agencies discovered the Soviets had installed nuclear missile facilities in Cuba, only 90 miles (145 km) from the U.S. coast. President John F. Kennedy (1917–1963) confronted the Soviets. He imposed a naval blockade around Cuba and demanded that the nuclear facilities be removed. After a suspenseful twelve-day standoff the Soviets complied. It proved to be a turning point in the cold war, as the two nations began negotiating treaties on limiting the testing and proliferation of nuclear weapons.

Nuclear Club

By 1964 there were five nations in the so-called nuclear club: the United States, the Soviet Union, the United Kingdom, France, and China. Before the end of the decade an important multilateral nuclear treaty had been signed by dozens of nations. The Treaty on the Nonproliferation of Nuclear Weapons (NPT; 2000, http://www.un.org/events/npt2005/npttreaty.html) acknowledged "the devastation that would be visited upon all mankind by a nuclear war" and included the following provisions:

- No transfer of nuclear weapons or nuclear-related technical assistance from a nuclear state to a nonnuclear state
- No manufacture of nuclear weapons by nonnuclear states or acquisition of the weapons or associated technologies from nuclear states
- Acceptance by nuclear states of safeguards overseen and verified by the International Atomic Energy Agency (IAEA, an international agency established in 1957) to prevent conversion of peaceful nuclear energy projects to nuclear weapons development; these safeguards also apply to transfers of peaceful-purpose nuclear materials from nuclear states to nonnuclear states

NPT Outsiders

In the decades since the NPT was developed, several other nations have tested (or are believed to have tested) nuclear weapons and refused to join or comply with international agreements governing safeguards and verification procedures. These "rebel" members of the nuclear club are India, Israel, Pakistan, and North Korea. In regards to the NPT, these countries are not officially considered nuclear states. North Korea's nuclear program is described in detail in Chapter 6.

INDIA. In 1974 the world was stunned when India conducted its first test of a nuclear weapon. The United States had been sharing nuclear energy technology with India since the 1950s. It is believed that Indian scientists were able to use this peaceful-purpose technology to develop a weapons program. India has refused to sign the NPT, claiming that the treaty is "discriminatory." The U.S. response to India's test was the Nuclear Nonproliferation Act of 1978, which put strict restrictions on the transfer of any nuclear technology to nonnuclear-weapon states. At the international level the United States spearheaded the creation of the Nuclear Suppliers Group, a body designed to oversee nuclear transfers for peaceful purposes and ensure they are not converted to weapons purposes.

Paul K. Kerr of the CRS notes in *U.S. Nuclear Cooperation with India: Issues for Congress* (July 30, 2008, http://www.fas.org/sgp/crs/nuke/RL33016.pdf) that the United States was so angered by India's deception in 1974 that it refused to provide any "nuclear cooperation" to India for twenty-five years. In 2005 President George W. Bush (1946–) reversed this policy by announcing a new nuclear partnership between the two nations. This was followed by passage of the Henry J. Hyde United

States–India Peaceful Atomic Energy Cooperation Act of 2006. The United States intends to support India's "civilian nuclear energy" projects. The move is controversial because it will require loosening of U.S. laws governing nuclear technology exports. Kerr acknowledges criticism from observers that the new partnership "undercuts the basic bargain of the NPT." It is feared that the United States' bypassing of NPT restrictions will encourage other nuclear states, particularly China, to do likewise.

ISRAEL. In 1986 the *Sunday Times* of London claimed that Israel had been secretly developing nuclear weapons for several decades. The information and some related photographs were provided by the Israeli Mordechai Vanunu (1954–), who had worked at the Dimona nuclear reactor facility in the desert of southern Israel. Vanunu had traveled to England to expose the nuclear weapon activities at the facility. He was subsequently kidnapped by Israeli intelligence agents and returned to Israel, where he was convicted of treason and sentenced to eighteen years in prison. Vanunu's story is detailed by Olenka Frenkiel in "Israeli Nuclear 'Power' Exposed" (British Broadcasting Corporation, March 16, 2003). He was released from prison in 2004.

In the article "Nuclear Weapons" (January 8, 2007, http://www.fas.org/nuke/guide/israel/nuke/), the Federation of American Scientists (FAS) notes that U.S. officials suspected an Israeli nuclear weapons program was in operation as early as the 1960s but chose to remain silent for political reasons. Israel has steadfastly refused to confirm or deny that it operates such a program or has nuclear weapons. The FAS estimates that as of 2007 Israel possessed between one hundred and two hundred nuclear weapons in its stockpile.

PAKISTAN. Pakistan and India are neighbors and bitter rivals. They were once one territory under the rule of the British Empire. In 1947 the nation of India was created from the mostly Hindu eastern portion of the territory. The smaller and mostly Muslim nation of Pakistan emerged from the western portion. The two countries have clashed for decades over a disputed northern region called Kashmir. India, Pakistan, and China have conflicting claims on this region and have engaged in several wars over the dispute. India and Pakistan battled in 1947, 1965, and 1971. The last war resulted in the creation of an independent country—Bangladesh—from eastern Pakistani territory. That war, and India's nuclear test in 1974, spurred the development of a Pakistani nuclear weapons program. Pakistan conducted its first test of a nuclear weapon in 1998. The U.S. Department of Defense (DOD) reports in *Proliferation: Threat and Response* (January 2001, http://www.fas.org/irp/threat/prolif00.pdf) that Pakistan has refused to sign the NPT unless India follows suit.

A key figure in the Pakistani nuclear weapons program has been Abdul Qadeer Khan (1935–)—a European-trained scientist with expertise in uranium enrichment. He moved to Pakistan in the mid-1970s. The FAS states in "Pakistan's Nuclear Weapons" (December 11, 2002, http://www.fas.org/nuke/guide/pakistan/nuke/) that Khan "reportedly" used plans he had stolen from Europe to jump-start Pakistan's nuclear weapons program at a facility in Kahuta. The FAS also claims that Khan used a secret network of conspirators to acquire the materials and technologies needed for the program.

In *Pakistan-U.S. Relations* (August 25, 2008, http://www.fas.org/sgp/crs/row/RL33498.pdf), K. Alan Kronstadt of the CRS indicates that in late 2002 the Western press began linking Khan to the transfer of nuclear weapons technology to nonnuclear states. Even though Pakistan initially denied the reports, a U.S. government investigation subsequently revealed that Khan and other scientists had been conducting "independent proliferation activities." In February 2004 Khan made a public apology confessing to his involvement in a network that sold nuclear weapons technology and materials to Iran, Libya, and North Korea. Because Khan was a popular and well-respected figure in Pakistan, he received a presidential pardon for his role in the scandal. The former Pakistani president Pervez Musharraf (1943–) has repeatedly denied that his government had any knowledge of Khan's illicit nuclear activities.

The U.S. government's initial reaction to the Pakistani nuclear test in 1998 was to impose restrictions on nonhumanitarian aid to the country. These restrictions were eased over time and removed completely in late 2001, when Pakistan became a key ally in the United States' global War on Terror.

Nuclear Weapon Treaties

The lead scientists involved in developing the U.S. atomic bomb during World War II were deeply concerned about the proliferation of nuclear weapons. They convinced President Truman to call for international agreements on peaceful uses of atomic energy and limits on the development of atomic weapons. In 1946 the United States presented a proposal to the UN called the Baruch Plan (2006, http://www.atomicarchive.com/Docs/Deterrence/BaruchPlan.shtml), in which the stated U.S. position was: "The search of science for the absolute weapon has reached fruition in this country. But she stands ready to proscribe and destroy this instrument—to lift its use from death to life—if the world will join in a pact to that end." The Baruch Plan proposed strict UN oversight of all nuclear activities around the world to ensure that nuclear power would be used for peaceful purposes, rather than for weapons development. Suspicious of U.S. and UN intentions, the Soviet Union refused to agree to the plan.

Over the following decades the United States and the Soviet Union, along with other nations, did manage to agree on some limits on nuclear testing and weapons proliferation. In "Treaties and Agreements" (2008, http://

www.state.gov/t/ac/trt/), the DOS provides a list of nuclear weapons treaties and agreements to which the United States is a party. The following are just a few of the treaties cited in this list. The dates in parentheses denote when the treaties were ratified by the United States.

- Limited Test Ban Treaty (1963)—officially called the Treaty Banning Nuclear Weapon Tests in the Atmosphere, in Outer Space, and under Water, this treaty requires nuclear tests take place underground, where radiation and fallout can be prevented from spreading widely. Over one hundred nations are parties to the treaty.
- Nuclear Nonproliferation Treaty (1968)—prohibits the transfer of nuclear weapons, materials, and related technologies from nuclear states to nonnuclear states. It allows for verification procedures by the IAEA. Over 180 nations are party to the treaty.
- Threshold Test Ban Treaty (1990)—this treaty between the United States and Russia prohibits nuclear tests with a yield greater than 150 kilotons. Originally signed in 1974, its ratification was delayed for many years by technical issues related to verification techniques.
- Strategic Arms Limitation Talks (1972), Strategic Arms Reduction Treaty (1991), and Strategic Offensive Reductions Treaty (2002)—these treaties between the United States and the Soviet Union (later Russia) committed the two nations to limit, and then reduce, their enormous arsenals of nuclear weapons. The most recent treaty, Strategic Offensive Reductions Treaty, calls for a reduction to around two thousand deployed strategic nuclear warheads for each nation by the end of 2012. This treaty is also commonly known as the Moscow Treaty.

Another significant agreement was the Intermediate-Range Nuclear Forces Treaty (1988; http://www.state.gov/www/global/arms/treaties/inf1.html), which required the destruction of ground-launched missiles with ranges of 500 to 5,500 km (311 to 3,418 miles) and their associated launchers and support equipment.

U.S. Nuclear Stockpile

The U.S. Government Accountability Office (GAO) indicates in *Nuclear Weapons: Views on Proposals to Transform the Nuclear Weapons Complex* (April 26, 2006, http://www.gao.gov/new.items/d06606t.pdf) that the U.S. nuclear stockpile from the cold war contains many old and obsolete weapons systems that need to be replaced or destroyed. The stockpile includes many weapons that are, or soon will be, three decades old. The National Nuclear Security Administration is an agency within the U.S. Department of Energy (DOE) responsible for overseeing U.S. nuclear weapons facilities. These include four nuclear weapons production facilities in Texas, Tennessee, Missouri, and South Carolina; three national weapons laboratories in California and New Mexico; and the Nevada Test Site at which nuclear weapons were tested during the cold war.

Figure 7.2 shows the nation's nuclear weapons stockpile for various dates between 1990 and 2005 and projected for 2012 in accordance with the Moscow Treaty. There were just over four thousand nuclear weapons in the stockpile as of January 2005. That number is expected to be reduced to less than twenty-two hundred by 2012. Figure 7.3 shows the number of deployed delivery systems for strategic nuclear

FIGURE 7.2

U.S. stockpile of deployed strategic nuclear warheads, selected dates, 1990–2005 and projected for 2012

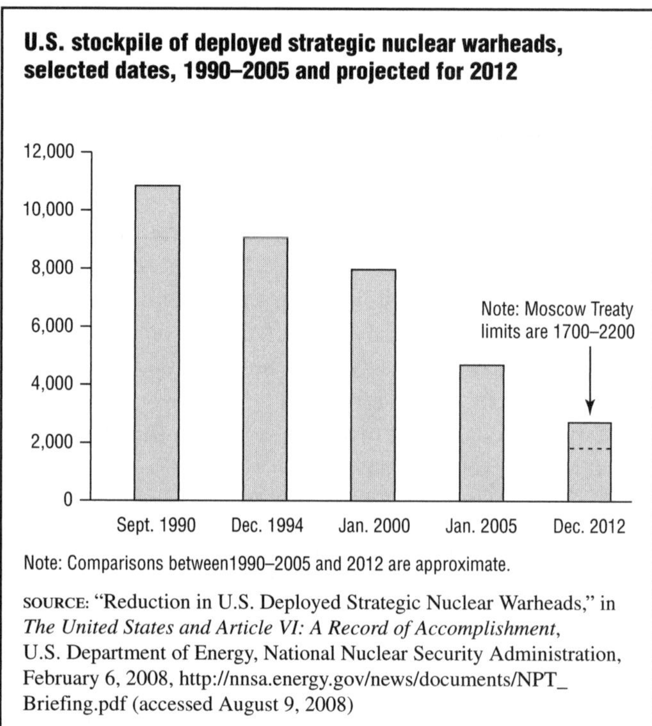

Note: Comparisons between1990–2005 and 2012 are approximate.

SOURCE: "Reduction in U.S. Deployed Strategic Nuclear Warheads," in *The United States and Article VI: A Record of Accomplishment*, U.S. Department of Energy, National Nuclear Security Administration, February 6, 2008, http://nnsa.energy.gov/news/documents/NPT_Briefing.pdf (accessed August 9, 2008)

FIGURE 7.3

U.S. stockpile of deployed delivery vehicles for strategic nuclear warheads, 1990–2012

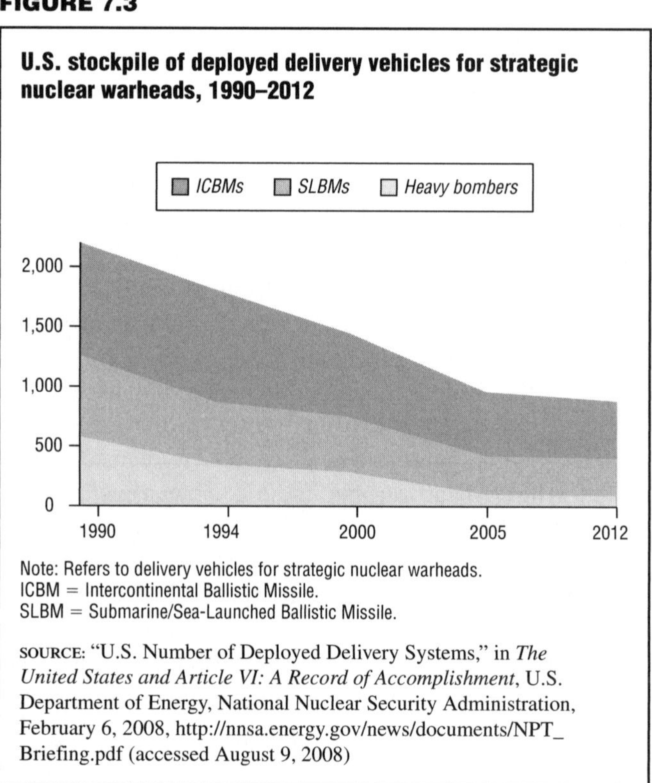

Note: Refers to delivery vehicles for strategic nuclear warheads.
ICBM = Intercontinental Ballistic Missile.
SLBM = Submarine/Sea-Launched Ballistic Missile.

SOURCE: "U.S. Number of Deployed Delivery Systems," in *The United States and Article VI: A Record of Accomplishment*, U.S. Department of Energy, National Nuclear Security Administration, February 6, 2008, http://nnsa.energy.gov/news/documents/NPT_Briefing.pdf (accessed August 9, 2008)

warheads in the U.S. stockpile between 1990 and 2005 and the projected number for 2012. Less than one thousand delivery systems are expected to be on hand by 2012.

Besides nuclear weapons, the government is also concerned about the security of the nation's nuclear reactors, particularly the small reactors that are operated for educational and research purposes. In January 2008 there were thirty-seven so-called research reactors in operation. (See Table 7.1.) The four reactors operated by the DOE are located at highly guarded government laboratories in Idaho, Tennessee, and New Mexico. Of more concern are the thirty-three research reactors regulated by the Nuclear Regulatory Commission (NRC) and located at universities and research institutions around the country. The GAO recommends in *Nuclear Security: Action May Be Needed to Reassess the Security of NRC-Licensed Research Reactors* (January 2008, http://www.gao.gov/new.items/d08403.pdf) that these reactors receive heightened security measures to protect them against theft of reactor fuel and/or sabotage by terrorists.

TABLE 7.1

Locations of operating U.S. research nuclear reactors, January 2008

Reactors	Location
DOE—4	
Advanced Test Reactor	INL, Idaho
High Flux Isotope Reactor	ORNL, Tennessee
Annular Core Research Reactor	SNL, New Mexico
Neutron Radiography Reactor	INL, Idaho
NRC—33	
National Institute of Standards and Technology	Gaithersburg, Maryland
University of Missouri, Columbia	Columbia, Missouri
Massachusetts Institute of Technology	Cambridge, Massachusetts
University of California, Davis	Sacramento, California
Rhode Island Nuclear Science Center	Narragansett, Rhode Island
Armed Forces Radiobiology Research Institute	Bethesda, Maryland
University of Massachusetts, Lowell	Lowell, Massachusetts
North Carolina State University	Raleigh, North Carolina
Oregon State University	Corvallis, Oregon
Pennsylvania State University	University Park, Pennsylvania
University of Texas	Austin, Texas
Texas A&M University	College Station, Texas
U.S. Geological Survey	Denver, Colorado
Washington State University	Pullman, Washington
University of Wisconsin	Madison, Wisconsin
Ohio State University	Columbus, Ohio
Dow Chemical Company	Midland, Michigan
Aerotest Operations, Inc.	San Ramon, California
University of California, Irvine	Irvine, California
Kansas State University	Manhattan, Kansas
University of Maryland	College Park, Maryland
Reed College	Portland, Oregon
Missouri University of Science and Technology	Rolla, Missouri
University of Arizona	Tucson, Arizona
University of Florida	Gainesville, Florida
General Electric Company	Sunol, California
University of Utah	Salt Lake City, Utah
Worcester Polytechnic Institute	Worcester, Massachusetts
Purdue University	West Lafayette, Indiana
Rennselaer Polytechnic Institute	Schenectady, New York
Idaho State University	Pocatello, Idaho
University of New Mexico	Albuquerque, New Mexico
Texas A&M University	College Station, Texas

*One megawatt is 1,000 kilowatts. On average, 1 kilowatt is the amount of power that is needed to operate a typical U.S. household for 1 hour.

SOURCE: Adapted from "Table 1. Location, Fuel Type and Power Level of Operating U.S. Research Reactors," in *Nuclear Security: Action May Be Needed to Reassess the Security of NRC-Licensed Research Reactors*, U.S. Government Accountability Office, January 2008, http://www.gao.gov/new.items/d08403.pdf (accessed August 5, 2008)

RADIOLOGICAL WEAPONS

Radiological weapons are different from nuclear weapons. The latter use nuclear reactions to create their destructive force. Radiological weapons rely on conventional explosives to disperse radioactive materials into the air. Radiological dispersal devices are commonly known as dirty bombs. Even though a dirty bomb does not have the destructive power of a nuclear bomb, it is an effective tool for creating terror. The detonation of a dirty bomb and the subsequent release of radiation could temporarily fool people into believing that a nuclear bomb has been detonated, leading to widespread panic.

The radioactive materials that can be used to manufacture a dirty bomb are widely used in industrial and medical equipment. Examples include low-level radioactive wastes, such as protective clothing and shoe covers, tools and equipment, discarded reactor parts and filters, rags, mops, reactor water treatment residues, luminous dials, and laboratory and medical supplies. Sealed radiological sources are small sealed containers containing a radionuclide in solid or powder form. U.S. law requires that all sealed radiological sources be safeguarded by the licensees that use them. The DOE is responsible for providing disposal for sources that are not needed any more. Table 7.2 provides a list of the toxic effects of some of the most common radiological materials. According to the GAO, in *Nuclear Security: DOE Needs Better Information to Guide Its Expanded Recovery of Sealed Radiological Sources* (September 2005, http://www.gao.gov/new.items/d05967.pdf), the sealed radiological sources considered most attractive to terrorists contain the radionuclides americium-241, cesium-137, plutonium-238, and strontium-90. A dirty bomb containing sufficient concentrations of one or several of these substances could cause radiation sickness in some victims exposed to the bomb.

CHEMICAL AND BIOLOGICAL WEAPONS

Chemical and biological weapons are considered WMDs because of the potentially lethal effects to many people that can be obtained with relatively small amounts of the substances. The use of chemical weapons during warfare is not new. Jonathan Tucker describes in *War of Nerves: Chemical Warfare from World War I to al-Qaeda* (2006) their use by German forces during World War I (1914–1918). In the spring of 1915 German troops had reached a stalemate in Belgium against the Allied forces of France, Britain, and Canada. Both sides were huddled in trenches that crisscrossed the countryside. On April 22 German troops simultaneously opened more than five thousand cylinders containing chlorine gas.

TABLE 7.2

Radiological warfare agents

Radioactive isotope	Respiratory absorption and retention	Gastrointestinal absorption and retention	Skin wound absorption	Primary toxicity
Americium-241	75% absorbed; 10% retained	Minimal, usually insoluble	Rapid in first few days	Skeletal deposition; marrow suppression; hepatic deposition
Cesium-137	Completely absorbed; follows potassium	Completely absorbed; follows potassium	Completely absorbed; follows potassium	Renal excretion; beta and gamma emissions
Cobalt-60	High absorption; limited retention	Less than 5% absorption	Unknown	Gamma emitter
Iodine-131	High absorption; limited retention	High absorption; limited	High absorption; limited retention	Thyroid ablation carcinoma
Plutonium-238 and Plutonium-239	Limited absorption; high retention	Minimal, usually insoluble	Limited absorption; may form nodules	Local effects from retention in lung
Polonium 210	Moderate absorption; moderate retention	Minimal	Moderate absorption	Spleen, kidney
Strontium-90	Limited retention	Moderate absorption	Unknown	Bone, follows calcium
Uranium-235 and Uranium-238	High absorption; high retention	High absorption	High absorption; skin irritant	Renal, urinary excretion

SOURCE: "Table 8. Radiological Warfare Agents," in *Homeland Security: First Responders' Ability to Detect and Model Hazardous Releases in Urban Areas Is Significantly Limited*, U.S. Government Accountability Office, June 2008, http://www.gao.gov/new.items/d08180.pdf (accessed July 24, 2008)

The wind blew the yellowish-green chlorine cloud across no-man's-land to the Allied trenches, where hundreds of soldiers were incapacitated almost immediately. The remainder of the troops fled in terror, many suffering from seared eyes and bronchial passages. At the time, Germany was a party to international treaties prohibiting the use of munitions to deliver chemical agents.

The horrors unleashed in the German attack led British forces to retaliate with chemical attacks of their own. Throughout the remainder of the war both sides employed toxic gases against the enemy with varying levels of success. The article "Gas Warfare" (January 15, 2000, http://www.worldwar1.com/arm006.htm) lists the chemical agents used during World War I. Public revulsion prevented the use of similar agents on the battlefield during World War II. They were employed by both sides during the Iran-Iraq War (1980–1988). In addition, the former Iraqi leader Saddam Hussein (1937–2006) was accused of using chemical weapons in 1988 against the minority Kurdish population in his own country.

In 1997 the Chemical Weapons Convention (CWC) went into effect. It prohibits the development, production, stockpiling, and use of chemical weapons and includes a verification regime to ensure that certain chemicals are produced or traded only for peaceful purposes. According to the Organization for the Prohibition of Chemical Weapons (2008, http://www.opcw.org/html/db/members_ratifyer.html), as of June 2008, there were 184 parties to the CWC, including the United States.

Chemical Agents as Weapons

Table 7.3 categorizes various hazardous chemicals by chemical type toxicity. According to the Central Intelligence Agency (CIA), in *Terrorist CBRN: Materials and Effects* (May 2003, https://www.cia.gov/library/reports/general-reports-1/CBRN_threat.pdf), terrorists have been experimenting with various toxic chemicals and planning dissemination methods that could be used in a chemical weapons attack. The chemical agents believed to be of greatest interest to terrorists are cyanide compounds (blood agents), mustard (a blister agent), and nerve agents, such as sarin, tabun, and VX. Videos recovered from terrorist training facilities in Afghanistan show dogs being killed in cyanide gas chambers. Cyanide compounds are easily available, because they have a variety of commercial uses. Mustard gas is not commercially available, but it is relatively easy to synthesize (produce) in the laboratory. Nerve agents are military-grade chemicals and thus extremely difficult for terrorists to obtain.

Even though these chemical agents are highly toxic, effective dissemination techniques have not yet been developed to make them strategically useful to terrorists. Airborne chemicals dissipate quickly unless they are in a confined space. They may be detectable by human senses before reaching a lethal concentration. For example, hydrogen cyanide and cyanogen chloride have distinctive odors. It is likely that potential victims would flee the area before being overcome by such gases.

Chemical Weapons Destruction

Several countries around the world are known to have developed chemical weapons at one time or another, including the United States. Figure 7.4 shows the original and current U.S. stockpile as of December 2007. More than one million items have already been destroyed. The largest remaining amounts were at the Pueblo Chemical Depot in Colorado (780,078 items) and the Anniston Army Depot in Alabama (446,712 items). The United States operates chemical weapon incinerators at four of the locations shown in Figure 7.4: Pine Bluff Arsenal, Annis-

TABLE 7.3

Chemical warfare agents

Class	Signs and symptoms	Name and symbol	Persistence	Rate of action	Eye and skin toxicity
Blister	First irritates cells, then poisons them; conjunctivitis (pink eye); reddened skin, blisters; nasal irritation; inflammation of throat and lungs	Ethyldichloroarsine (ED)	Moderate	Immediate irritation; delayed blistering	Vapor harmful on long exposure; liquid blisters
		Lewisite (L)	Days; rapid hydrolysis with humidity	Rapid	Severe eye damage; skin less so
		Methyldichloroarsine (MD)	Low	Rapid	Eye damage possible; blisters
		Mustard (H, HD)	Very high; days to weeks	Delayed hours to days	Eyes very susceptible; skin less so
		Nitrogen mustard (HN-1, -2, -3)	HN-1, -3, very high, days to weeks; HN-2, moderate	HN-1, -2, delayed 12 hours or more. HN-3, serious effects, same as HD; minor effects sooner	HN-1, eyes susceptible to low concentration, skin less so. HN-2 toxic to eyes; blisters skin. HN-3, eyes very susceptible; skin less so
		Phenyldichloroarsine (PD)	Low–moderate	Rapid	633 mg–min/m produces eye damage; less toxic to skin
		Phosgene oxime (CX)	Low, 2 hours in soil	Immediate effects on contact	Powerful irritant to eyes and nose; liquid corrosive to skin
Blood	Skin cherry red or 30% cyanosis (bluish discoloration from lack of oxygen); gasping for air; seizures before death	Arsine (SA)	Low	2 hours to 11 days	None
		Cyanogen chloride (CK)	Evaporates rapidly and disperses	Very rapid	Low; tears and irritation
		Hydrogen cyanide (AC)	Extremely volatile; 1–2 days	Very rapid	Moderate
Nerve	Salivation, lacrimation (tearing), urination, defecation, gastric disturbances, vomiting	Cyclosarin (GF)	Moderate	Very rapid	Very high
		Sarin (GB	Low; 1–2 days; evaporates with water	Very rapid	Very high
		Soman (GD)	Moderate; 1–2 days	Very rapid	Very high
		Tabun (GA)	Low; 1–2 days if heavy concentration	Very rapid	Very high
		VX	Very high; 1 week if heavy concentration; as volatile as oil	Rapid	Very high

SOURCE: "Table 6. Chemical Warfare Agents," in *Homeland Security: First Responders' Ability to Detect and Model Hazardous Releases in Urban Areas Is Significantly Limited*, U.S. Government Accountability Office, June 2008, http://www.gao.gov/new.items/d08180.pdf (accessed July 24, 2008). Non-government data from Analytic Services, Inc. and Edgewood Chemical Biological Center.

ton Army Depot, Deseret Chemical Depot, and Umatilla Chemical Depot. According to the GAO, in *Chemical Demilitarization: Additional Management Actions Needed to Meet Key Performance Goals of DOD's Chemical Demilitarization Program* (December 2007, http://www.gao.gov/new.items/d08134.pdf), the U.S. stockpile includes mustard gas and two nerve agents called GB (also known as sarin gas) and VX.

The GAO notes in *Cooperative Threat Reduction: DOD Needs More Reliable Data to Better Estimate the Cost and Schedule of the Shchuch'ye Facility* (May 2006, http://www.gao.gov/new.items/d06692.pdf) that Russia has the world's largest-known stockpile of chemical weapons, including 32,500 metric tons (35,800 short tons) of nerve agent and 7,500 metric tons (8,300 short tones) of blister agents. In 1992 Congress first authorized the DOD to assist the Russians in destroying the stockpile under the Cooperative Threat Reduction (CTR) program. The GAO reports that as of March 2006 the Russians had destroyed only about 3% of the stockpile, because only two destruction facilities had been completed. The remainder of the stockpile is supposed to be destroyed by 2012 to meet conditions of the CWC. It is estimated that Russia will need an additional $5.6 billion in funds to eliminate the entire stockpile. Canada, New Zealand, the European Union, and a number of European countries have committed funding to the destruction project.

The CTR program is managed by the DOD's Defense Threat Reduction Agency. Completion of the project is a high priority for the U.S. government because of the possibility of diversion and theft at the storage facilities.

Biological Agents as Weapons

Table 7.4 lists biological agents and diseases that could be used in a terrorist attack. The agents are divided into three categories. In *Terrorist CBRN*, the CIA explains that anthrax and botulism are the diseases likely of most interest to terrorists. Anthrax is a bacterial disease caused by the *Bacillus anthracis* bacteria, with onset one to six days after exposure. There are two common routes of exposure: inhalation and cutaneous (through the skin). Inhaled anthrax is generally fatal unless antibiotics are given within the first few hours after exposure. Cutaneous anthrax is easily treated and rarely fatal.

Shortly after the terrorist attacks of September 11, 2001, several envelopes containing high-grade anthrax spores were discovered at various locations in the eastern United States. Five people died of inhalation exposure and more than a dozen other people became sick but survived. The Federal Bureau of Investigation (FBI) suspected that the anthrax had originated at the U.S. Army Medical Research Institute in Fort Detrick, Maryland.

FIGURE 7.4

U.S. stockpile of chemical weapons, December 2007

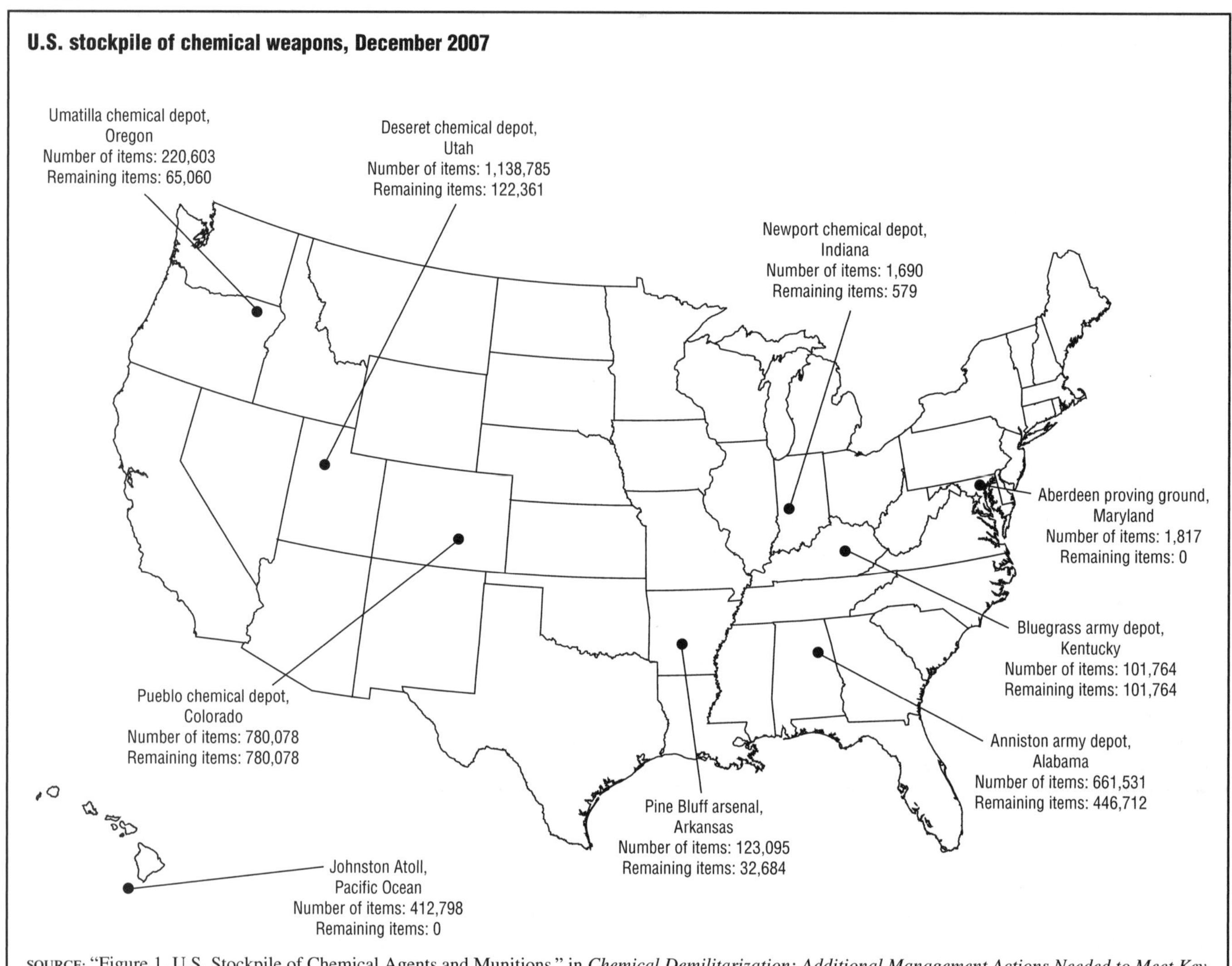

SOURCE: "Figure 1. U.S. Stockpile of Chemical Agents and Munitions," in *Chemical Demilitarization: Additional Management Actions Needed to Meet Key Performance Goals of DOD's Chemical Demilitarization Program*, U.S. Government Accountability Office, December 2007, http://www.gao.gov/new.items/d08134.pdf (accessed August 5, 2008)

The agency vigorously pursued one scientist from that facility, only to admit later that he was not the culprit. In July 2008 the FBI cleared the first suspect and paid him nearly $6 million to settle a lawsuit that the agency had violated his civil rights. A second scientist from the same facility, Bruce Ivins (1946–2008), was named the prime suspect in the case, but he committed suicide before being charged. As of September 2008, the FBI maintained that Ivins was responsible for the 2001 anthrax attack.

Botulism is caused by the ingestion or inhalation of the *Clostridium botulinum* bacteria. The CIA reports that recovered terrorist training manuals have included procedures for producing small quantities of botulinum toxin. The onset of symptoms from botulism usually occurs two to three days after exposure and includes severe gastrointestinal illnesses. Another biological agent of interest to terrorists is ricin. It is an extremely toxic agent that can be extracted from castor beans.

U.S. NONPROLIFERATION PROGRAMS

The breakup of the Soviet Union in the early 1990s into individual republics ended the cold war but produced new security concerns for the United States. In particular, the United States is worried about the safety of the enormous stockpile of WMDs that the Soviets accumulated. The new republics have struggled economically, producing fears that WMDs or related technologies might be sold on the black market and wind up in the hands of terrorists or rogue nations. Therefore, the security of the old Soviet stockpile is a major concern to U.S. national security.

Nunn-Lugar Program

In 1991 two senators of rival parties collaborated on an act intended to prevent the spread of WMDs from the former Soviet Union. The Nunn-Lugar Act was spearheaded by Senators Sam Nunn (1938–; D-GA) and Richard G. Lugar (1932–; R-IN). It provides funding for the destruction of missiles and chemical weapons and employment opportunities for former weapons scien-

TABLE 7.4

Biological warfare agents

Agent	Possible means of delivery	Time	Symptoms	Lethality	Stability
Bacterium					
Anthrax	Aerosol	Incubation 1–5 days; symptoms in 2–3 days	Fever, malaise, fatigue, cough, and mild chest discomfort, followed by severe respiratory distress	3–5 days; shock and death 24–36 hours after symptoms	Spores are highly stable
Brucellosis	Aerosol, expected to mimic a natural disease	Rate of action usually 6–60 days	Chills, sweats, headache, fatigue, joint and muscle pain, and anorexia	Weeks to months	Organisms are stable for several weeks in wet soil and food
Cholera	Sabotaged food and water supply; aerosol	Sudden onset after 1–5 days incubation	Initial vomiting and abdominal distention, with little or no fever or abdominal pain, followed rapidly by diarrhea	One or more weeks; low with treatment; high without treatment	Unstable in aerosols and pure water; more stable in polluted water
Plague	Contaminated fleas, causing bubonic type, or aerosol, causing pneumonic type	Rate of action 2–3 days; incubation 2– 6 days bubonic, 3–4 days pneumonic	High fever, chills, headache, spitting up blood, and toxemia, progressing rapidly to shortness of breath and cyanosis (bluish coloration of skin and membranes)	Very high	Extremely stable but highly transmissible
Q fever	Dust cloud from a line or point source	Onset may be sudden	Chills, headache, weakness, malaise, and severe sweats	Very low	Stable
Tularemia	Aerosol	Rate of action 3–5 days; incubation 1– 10 days	Fever, chills, headache, and malaise	2 weeks moderate	Not very stable
Typhoid	Sabotaged food and water supply	Rate of action 1–3 days; incubation 1– 10 days	Sustained fever, severe headaches, and malaise	Moderate if untreated	Stable
Typhus	Contaminated lice or fleas	Rate of action 6–15 days; onset often sudden, terminating after about 2 weeks of fever	Headaches, chills, prostration, fever, and general pain	High	Not very stable
Toxin					
Botulinum	Sabotaged food and water supply; aerosol	Rate of action 12–72 hours; incubation hours to days	Blurred vision; photophobia; skeletal muscle paralysis and progressive weakness that may culminate abruptly in respiratory failure	High	Stable
Ricin	Aerosol	Rate of action 6–72 hours	Rapid onset of nausea, vomiting, abdominal cramps, and severe diarrhea with vascular collapse	High	Stable
Virus					
Ebola	Aerosol; direct contact	Rate of action: sudden	Malaise, headache, vomiting, diarrhea	High: 7–16 days	Unstable
Marburg	Aerosol; direct contact	Rate of action 7–9 days	Malaise, headache, vomiting, diarrhea	High	Unstable
Smallpox	Airborne	Rate of action 2–4 days; incubation 7–17 days	Malaise, headache, vomiting, diarrhea, small blisters on skin, bleeding of mucous membranes	High	Stable
Venezuelan equine encephalitis	Airborne	Sudden rate of action; incubation 1–5 days	Headache, fever, dizziness, drowsiness or stupor, tremors or convulsions, muscular incoordination	Low	Unstable
Yellow fever	Aerosol	Sudden rate of action; incubation 3–6 days	Malaise, headache, vomiting, diarrhea	High	Unstable

SOURCE: "Table 7. Biological Warfare Agents," in *Homeland Security: First Responders' Ability to Detect and Model Hazardous Releases in Urban Areas Is Significantly Limited*, U.S. Government Accountability Office, June 2008, http://www.gao.gov/new.items/d08180.pdf (accessed July 24, 2008). Non-government data from Analytic Services, Inc. and Edgewood Chemical Biological Center.

tists. The act also resulted in the creation of the CTR program office within the Office of the Assistant to the Secretary of Defense for Nuclear, Chemical, and Biological Defense Programs. The CTR office's mission is to implement the Nunn-Lugar program to reduce WMDs subject to international arms control treaties.

In fiscal year (FY) 1992, when the Nunn-Lugar program was first instituted, $12.9 million was funded to the program; by FY 2007 the funding was $372 million. (See Figure 7.5.) In total, nearly $6.1 billion has been devoted to this program. According to Senator Lugar, in "The Nunn-Lugar Cooperative Threat Reduction Program" (2008, http://lugar.senate.gov/nunnlugar/index.cfm), the program has completely eliminated nuclear weapons from the Republics of Ukraine, Belarus, and Kazakhstan and created 580 jobs for former weapons scientists. More than twenty thousand weapons-related items have been destroyed, deactivated, or dismantled. (See Table 7.5.) By 2012 the program is expected to achieve more substantial reductions, representing a significant decrease in the CTR baseline inventory of these items.

Defense Threat Reduction Agency

In 1998 the Defense Threat Reduction Agency (DTRA) was established by the secretary of defense within the DOD. Joseph P. Harahan and Robert J. Bennett note in *Creating the Defense Threat Reduction Agency* (January 2002,

FIGURE 7.5

Annual funding for Nunn-Lugar program, fiscal years 1992–2007

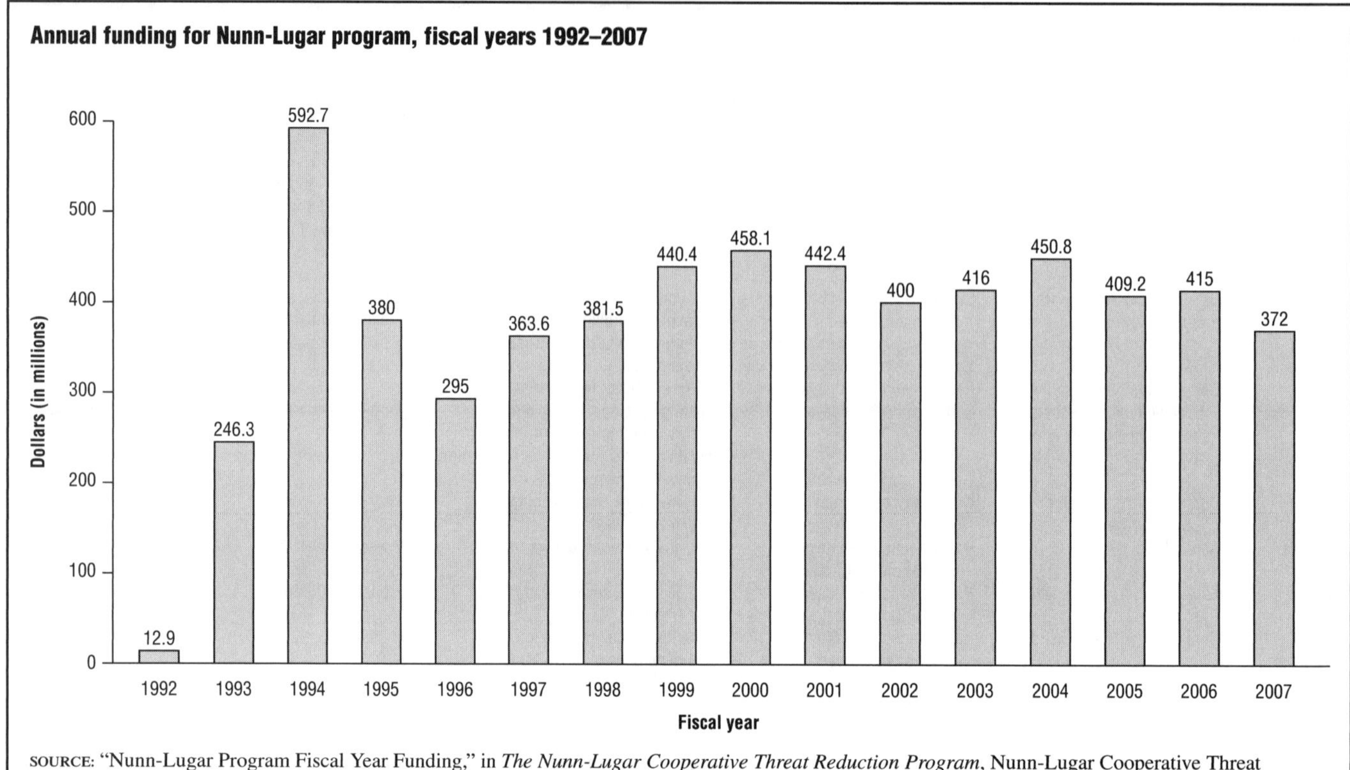

SOURCE: "Nunn-Lugar Program Fiscal Year Funding," in *The Nunn-Lugar Cooperative Threat Reduction Program*, Nunn-Lugar Cooperative Threat Reduction Program, undated, http://lugar.senate.gov/nunnlugar/index.cfm (accessed August 5, 2008)

TABLE 7.5

Goals and progress of Nunn-Lugar program, 2008–12

Soviet declared amounts		Reductions to date	Percent of 2012 targets	2012 targets
13,300	Warheads deactivated	7,292	79%	9,222
1,473	Intercontinental ballistic missiles (ICBM) destroyed	708	65%	1,078
831	ICBM silos eliminated	496	77%	645
442	ICBM mobile launchers destroyed	131	49%	267
48	Nuclear weapons carrying submarines destroyed	30	86%	35
936	Submarine launched ballistic missiles (SLBM) eliminated	631	91%	691
728	SLBM launchers eliminated	456	81%	564
906	Nuclear air-to-surface missiles destroyed	906	100%	906
233	Bombers eliminated	155	100%	155
194	Nuclear sites/holes sealed	194	100%	194
	Nuclear weapons transport train shipments	394	63%	620
	Nuclear weapons storage site security upgrades	16	67%	24
	Biological monitoring stations built and equipped	15	27%	55

Ukraine, Kazakhstan and Belarus are nuclear weapons free

SOURCE: "The Nunn-Lugar Scorecard," in *The Nunn-Lugar Cooperative Threat Reduction Program*, Nunn-Lugar Cooperative Threat Reduction Program, undated, http://lugar.senate.gov/nunnlugar/index.cfm (accessed August 5, 2008)

http://www.dtra.mil/about/media/historical_documents/books/DTRAHix.pdf) that the DTRA combined five existing components that had been devoted to various aspects of WMD control: the Defense Special Weapons Agency, the On-Site Inspection Agency, the Defense Technology Security Administration, the Chemical-Biological Defense Program, and the CTR. The DTRA is headquartered in Fort Belvoir, Virginia.

The DTRA takes a three-pronged approach to foreign WMD control (2008, http://www.dtra.mil/oe/index.cfm?More):

- Nonproliferation—prevent and limit WMD acquisition and development. This enterprise involves onsite inspections and the CTR program and is concentrated on the former republics of the Soviet Union.

TABLE 7.6

Status of arms control treaties and agreements as of January 2008

Treaty/agreement	Date signed	Signatories to date	Entry into force	Expiration date	Number of inspections to date
Chemical Weapons Convention (CWC)	Jan. 13, 1993	183 countries, including U.S. and Russia.	April 29, 1997	None	865 visits or inspections of Department of Defense (DoD) sites. 84 inspections of U.S. commercial industry facilities.
Comprehensive Test Ban Treaty (CTBT)	Sept. 24, 1996	177 countries, including all five permanent members of the U.N. Security Council; 140 countries have ratified.	TBD	None	None
Conventional Armed Forces in Europe (CFE) Treaty	Nov. 19, 1990	30 countries, including members of the North Atlantic Treaty Organization (NATO) and the former Warsaw Pact.	July 17, 1992	None	U.S. conducted 312 inspections and 169 reduction inspections. U.S hosted 153 escort missions and conducted over 810 liaison missions.
Adapted CFE Treaty	Nov. 19, 1999	30 countries, including members of NATO and the former Warsaw Pact	TBD	None	None
Cooperative Threat Reduction (CTR) Agreement (Nunn-Lugar)	June 17, 1992 Oct. 25, 1992 Oct. 22, 1992 Oct. 25, 1993	US/Russia US/Ukraine US/Belarus US/Kazakhstan	June 17, 1992 Oct. 25, 1992 Oct. 22, 1992 Oct. 25, 1993	June 17, 2000 Oct. 25, 1993 Oct. 22, 1992 Oct. 24, 1993	157 audits and examinations from 1995–2004
General Framework Agreement for Peace in Bosnia and Herze-Govina (Dayton Accords)	Article II — Jan. 26, 1996 Article IV — Jan. 14, 1996	6 parties: Federation of Bosnia and manufacturing facility Herze-Govina, Republika Srbska, Serbia, Montenegro and the Republic of Croatia. Four "assistants" including the U.S.	Jan. 26, 1996 Jan. 14, 1996	None	U.S. either led or participated in 23 inspections and 2 weapons manufacturing facility visits.
Mayak Fissile Material Storage Facility Agreement		U.S., Russia	TBD		The Fissile Material Storage Facility was completed in December 2003. Facility monitoring will begin after the signing of a transparency protocol agreement.
Intermediate Range Nuclear Forces (INF) Treaty	Dec. 8, 1987	U.S., USSR/Belarus, Kazakhstan, Russia, Ukraine	June 1, 1988	Inspections ceased May 31, 2001, after 13 years	U.S. conducted 511 inspections in Russia; Russians conducted 275 inspections in U.S. and Europe.
Peaceful Nuclear Explosions Treaty (PNET)	May 28, 1976 Protocol signed June 1, 1990	U.S., USSR/ Russia	Dec. 11, 1990	5 years with automatic extensions	U.S. peaceful nuclear explosions (PNEs) monitored: 0 Russian PNEs monitored: 0
Open Skies Treaty	March 24, 1992	34 countries including U.S.	Jan. 1, 2002	None	To date, U.S, has conducted 47 quota missions and escorted 12. Joint Trial Flights (JTFs)—over 125 since 1993.
Plutonium Production Reactor Agreement (PPRA)	Sept. 23, 1997	U.S., Russia	Sept. 23, 1997	None	U.S. conducted inaugural monitoring visit of Russian shutdown reactors in March 1999. Russia conducted their monitoring of shutdown U.S. reactors in June 1999.
Strategic Arms Reduction Treaty (START)	July 1, 1991	U.S., Russia, Ukraine, Belarus and Kazakhstan	Dec. 5, 1994	15 years with possible extensions	Through treaty year 10, December 2004, U.S. conducted 569 inspections and Russia conducted 389.
Threshold Test Ban Treaty (TTBT)	July 3, 1974 Verification protocol signed June 1, 1990	U.S., USSR/Russia	Dec. 11, 1990	5 years with automatic extensions	U.S. tests monitored: 2 Russian tests monitored: 0

SOURCE: Adapted from "DTRA Arms Control Inspections at-a-Glance," in *Fact Sheet*, U.S. Department of Defense, Defense Threat Reduction Agency, January 2008, http://www.dtra.mil/newsservices/fact_sheets/fs_includes/pdf/Arms_Control_Inspections.pdf (accessed August 5, 2008)

- Counterproliferation—this mission is described as "military activities to deter, identify, deny, and overcome our adversaries' development, acquisition, possession, and use of WMD." It is carried out by the Combat Support Directorate within the DTRA.
- Consequence management—this enterprise is devoted to mitigating the effects of WMD attacks or accidents. Emergency incidents are simulated to help government agencies train their response personnel.

Table 7.6 lists the status of DTRA arms control inspections under a variety of international agreements as of January 2008.

CHAPTER 8

AMERICAN CIVIL LIBERTIES AND THE WAR ON TERROR

Civil liberties (or civil rights) are individual rights designated by law. They are legal shields that protect citizens from abuses by their own government. Historically, times of war in the United States have produced situations in which the U.S. government has given national security concerns a higher priority than protection of the public's civil liberties. Most often, these transgressions have been instigated by the executive branch—the president and the departments and offices under his direct control. However, the framers of the U.S. Constitution included a system of checks and balances that allow individuals to challenge such transgressions in the courts. In addition, the Constitution's guarantee of freedom of speech allows the American press to publicize conflicts between the interests of national security and the protection of civil liberties. A debate over how best to balance these two important priorities has raged since the nation began and takes on new importance as the United States wages war once again.

HISTORICAL CONTEXT

In the United States the U.S. Constitution is considered the ultimate definer of Americans' civil rights. The original document, completed in 1789, included seven articles that outlined the structure and workings of the federal government. Over the next two years ten amendments known as the Bill of Rights were added to the Constitution. They were specifically designed to limit the power of the new government and ensure that certain individual rights are protected by law. An additional seventeen amendments have been enacted since that time.

Times of war in the United States have often produced contentious debates over the proper balance between protecting national security and protecting civil liberties. History shows that some civil rights have not been honored by the U.S. government when the nation was threatened, a condition known by the Latin term *Inter arma enim silent leges*, popularly translated as "In times of war, the laws fall silent." These civil liberty conflicts most often involve individual rights protected by the First, Fourth, and Fifth Amendments of the Constitution, which read as follows:

- First Amendment—"Congress shall make no law respecting an establishment of religion, or prohibiting the free exercise thereof; or abridging the freedom of speech, or of the press; or the right of the people peaceably to assemble, and to petition the government for a redress of grievances."
- Fourth Amendment—"The right of the people to be secure in their persons, houses, papers, and effects, against unreasonable searches and seizures, shall not be violated, and no warrants shall issue, but upon probable cause, supported by oath or affirmation, and particularly describing the place to be searched, and the persons or things to be seized."
- Fifth Amendment—"No person shall be held to answer for a capital, or otherwise infamous crime, unless on a presentment or indictment of a grand jury, except in cases arising in the land or naval forces, or in the militia, when in actual service in time of war or public danger; nor shall any person be subject for the same offense to be twice put in jeopardy of life or limb; nor shall be compelled in any criminal case to be a witness against himself, nor be deprived of life, liberty, or property, without due process of law; nor shall private property be taken for public use, without just compensation."

The rights to free speech and peaceable assembly guaranteed by the First Amendment receive exceptional attention when they are exercised during wartime by people opposed to the government's actions. The protections afforded under the Fourth and Fifth Amendments relate to judicial procedures, legal due process, and privacy issues. A right to privacy is not specifically spelled out in the Constitution but is believed to result inherently if the government operates in accordance with the articles of the Constitution and respects the Bill of Rights.

Civil War: Suspension of Habeus Corpus

During the Civil War (1861–1865) President Abraham Lincoln (1809–1865) suspended the writ of habeus corpus (a legal procedure in which a court can order that a prisoner held by the government be presented to the court for determination if the imprisonment is legal or not). Article One of the Constitution allows such a suspension "when in cases of rebellion or invasion the public safety may require it." Lincoln's action allowed Union troops to detain Southern sympathizers and anyone else deemed to be a threat to public safety and hold them indefinitely. In addition, military commissions tried and convicted civilian detainees accused of crimes. Thus, martial law went into effect, meaning that the military took over powers normally held by the civilian law enforcement system.

The consequences of the suspension were highly controversial and led to a legal battle in the U.S. Supreme Court after the war ended. In the 1866 case *Ex parte Milligan* (71 U.S. 2), the Court ruled that martial law cannot be imposed so long as civilian courts and governments are still in operation. In addition, any imposition of martial law must be confined to a limited area in which war is actually occurring. The Posse Comitatus Act of 1878 made it unlawful for the U.S. military to execute legal authority over civilians unless specifically authorized by the Constitution or an act of Congress. It should be noted that this prohibition does not apply to National Guard troops under state government command.

World War I: Free Speech?

The World War I era is associated with many serious conflicts between national security and civil liberties. Around the turn of the twentieth century a number of movements associated with labor rights, anarchy, and socialism became active in the United States. Some elements of these groups incited violence and were considered subversive (advocating the overthrow of the government). As such, the nation was in a wary mood when World War I erupted in Europe in 1914.

The United States' entry into the war in 1917 was accompanied by the passage of several federal laws aimed at squelching what the government considered anti-American activities. The Espionage Act of 1917 and the related Sedition Act of 1918 included a variety of provisions designed to prevent the passage of national security information to the enemy. The acts also made it illegal for anyone to obstruct military recruiting or enlistment. Most troubling to civil libertarians were provisions in the Sedition Act that made it illegal to say or write anything "disloyal" about the U.S. government, Constitution, flag, or military forces. The act also prohibited any expression of resistance to the United States or support for its enemies. In other words, acts of dissent (disagreement with the government) were forbidden during the course of the war.

The acts were used by the government against many socialists, anarchists, and other activists who had begun a vocal antiwar campaign. In 1919 the Supreme Court heard a case involving a socialist who had mailed circulars to recent military draftees urging them to defy the government and oppose the draft system. In *Schenck v. United States* (249 U.S. 47), the Court ruled in favor of the government and noted, "When a nation is at war many things that might be said in time of peace are such a hindrance to its effort that their utterance will not be endured so long as men fight and that no Court could regard them as protected by any constitutional right." Most of the provisions of the wartime acts were repealed during the 1920s.

World War II: Internment of Japanese-Americans

One of the most often referenced violations of American civil rights in wartime took place during World War II (1939–1945), when the U.S. government detained American citizens of Japanese descent. In 1942 President Franklin D. Roosevelt (1882–1945) signed Executive Order 9066 authorizing the removal and internment of all people of Japanese descent living in California and the western portions of Oregon and Washington. The military and civilian government decisions leading up to issuance of the executive order are described by Stetson Conn in "The Decision to Evacuate the Japanese from the Pacific Coast" (August 27, 1996, http://www.army.mil/cmh-pg/books/70-7_05.htm).

Conn notes that the military originally planned to forcibly evacuate only aliens (non-American citizens) who were Japanese, German, or Italian and lived near strategic areas along the Pacific coast. Ultimately, the plan evolved into forced internment of both aliens and American citizens of Japanese descent. This change was precipitated by a variety of factors, primarily widespread and persistent paranoia among the U.S. population that Japanese-American citizens had not been and would not be loyal to the United States. This feeling was aggravated by widely circulated, but false, rumors that traitors within the Japanese-American community had helped facilitate the surprise attack on Pearl Harbor in December 1941 and were engaging in acts of espionage to support a Japanese invasion of the U.S. mainland.

According to Our Documents, which is part of the National Archives and Records Administration, in "Executive Order 9066: Resulting in the Relocation of Japanese

(1942)" (2008, http://www.ourdocuments.gov/doc.php?flash=true&doc=74), approximately 122,000 people of Japanese descent, including children and elderly people, were detained under Executive Order 9066. The detainees were forced to leave their homes quickly and allowed to take only a minimum of possessions with them. They spent the duration of the war in internment camps throughout the Midwest and West (excluding the coastal states). These camps were surrounded by barbed wire and patrolled by armed guards. Following the war, the internees were released; however, many found it difficult to return to their previous homes and jobs.

In 1988 the Civil Liberties Act acknowledged that a "grave injustice" had been perpetrated on Japanese-Americans during World War II by the U.S. government and offered a payment of $20,000 to each internee as restitution.

Cold War: McCarthyism

McCarthyism describes a phenomenon that occurred in the United States when intense paranoia about communism created a social and political environment in which civil liberties were trampled in the interest of national security. The term is named after Senator Joseph R. McCarthy (1908–1957; R-WI), who served in the U.S. Senate from 1947 until his death in 1957. Even though the Soviet Union had been a U.S. ally during World War II, deep differences fostered a period of mutual distrust and animosity between the two nations after the war ended in 1945. In the United States many people believed the Soviets wanted to overthrow (subvert) the U.S. government and were being aided by American members of the Communist Party and sympathizers called fellow travelers.

Committees were formed within the U.S. House of Representatives and the Senate to investigate alleged communist activities by Americans. Two of the most prominent committees were the House Un-American Activities Committee (HUAC) and a Senate committee led by Senator McCarthy. The HUAC began meeting in 1938 and is most famous for its probe in the late 1940s through the mid-1950s into the political leanings of people in the entertainment industry, particularly in Hollywood. The committee held hearings and demanded that witnesses testify about their affiliations and the ties of their colleagues to the Communist Party. People who refused to cooperate were sent to prison or, at the very least, lost their job and reputation. Their names were put on a so-called blacklist, which meant that other companies in the industry were afraid to hire them.

McCarthy rose to prominence in U.S. politics after announcing in a 1950 speech that he had the names of dozens of communist sympathizers working within the U.S. Department of State (DOS). He began holding hearings similar to those of the HUAC and accusing fellow politicians of having communist sympathies. In "Censure of Senator Joseph McCarthy (1954)" (2008, http://usinfo.state.gov/infousa/government/overview/60.html), the DOS notes that McCarthy and his aides "made wild accusations, browbeat witnesses, destroyed reputations and threw mud at men."

The Fifth Amendment to the Constitution states that a person "shall [not] be compelled in any criminal case to be a witness against himself." Some witnesses seized on this provision, declaring their Fifth Amendment right as a reason for not answering committee questions. However, this legal maneuver often cost them their job. Investigations grew to include teachers and university professors around the country. Several states began requiring that all public employees take oaths swearing that they had not been and would not become members of any organization advocating the overthrow of the government and did not advocate such an organization. Employees who refused to take the oath were fired or otherwise punished.

In January 1954 McCarthy's hearings were televised for the first time. The DOS notes that "day after day the public watched McCarthy in action—bullying, harassing, never producing any hard evidence, and his support among people who thought he was 'right' on communism began to evaporate." The political tide turned against McCarthy, and in December 1954 the Senate passed a censure (official condemnation) of him for abusing his powers. The U.S. Supreme Court and state courts began ruling against the tactics that had been used on committee witnesses and government employees. In the 1956 case *Slochower v. Board of Higher Education of New York City* (350 U.S. 551), the Court found that New York City had acted illegally in firing a professor for using his Fifth Amendment right against self-incrimination to avoid committee questions. Many other rulings found that civil liberties had been violated during the anticommunist fervor.

Vietnam War: Domestic Surveillance

The 1960s and early 1970s were a time of domestic strife in the United States. Many groups and movements became active in protesting against the government for a host of reasons, including opposing the Vietnam War (1955–1975) and advocating the enforcement of civil rights for minorities and women. Political and social activism became a common means of expressing discontent in public. Even though some groups were openly subversive, many sought change through legal methods or civil disobedience (breaking civil laws in a nonviolent fashion, such as by trespassing or blocking traffic and refusing police orders to cease).

As described in Chapter 2, the nation's intelligence agencies conducted massive campaigns of domestic surveillance in the name of national security during this period. Many abuses of power and violations of civil liberties were later uncovered and publicly disclosed through federal investigations, such as those of the Subcommittee on Constitutional Rights (chaired by Senator Sam J. Ervin [1896–1985; D-NC]) and the Senate Select Committee to Study Governmental Operations with Respect to Intelligence Activities (chaired by Senator Frank Forrester Church III [1924–1984; D-ID]). Public distaste with domestic surveillance drove massive reforms within the intelligence community, including the Central Intelligence Agency, the Defense Intelligence Agency, and the Federal Bureau of Investigation (FBI).

THE WAR ON TERROR: NEW CONFLICTS ARISE

The United States enjoyed more than two decades of relative peace following the end of the Vietnam War in 1975. The disintegration of the Soviet Union during the early 1990s effectively ended the cold war. As a result, issues related to conflicts between civil liberties and national security became less prominent. This condition changed dramatically following the terrorist attacks of September 11, 2001 (9/11). The United States began a new war—the War on Terror—that has brought back many of the historic concerns about the protection of civil liberties during wartime. Once again, national security issues are weighed against constitutional rights and societal fears.

Because terrorism is associated by many Americans with people of the Middle East, U.S. citizens of Middle Eastern descent are subject to suspicions about their loyalty to the United States. In *Terrorism in the United States* (2008, http://www.gallup.com/poll/4909/Terrorism-United-States.aspx), the Gallup Organization reports on a number of polls that it conducted between 1995 and 2008. In July 2005 respondents were asked if they favored "requiring Arabs, including those who are U.S. citizens, to carry a special ID" as a means of preventing terrorist attacks in the United States. A slim majority (53%) of respondents expressed opposition to this idea. However, 46% of those asked favored implementing such a measure. A similar breakdown was obtained when pollsters asked if "special, more intensive" security procedures should be required for Arabs boarding airplanes in the United States. Slightly more than half (53%) of respondents favored this measure even though the question specified that the Arabs could be U.S. citizens.

In the same poll Gallup asked a number of other questions related to basic civil liberty issues. In general, respondents supported ID requirements (70% favorable) and the use of metal detectors (81% favorable) at the entrances to office buildings and other public places. Strong support also registered for implementing airport-like security measures in the United States' mass transit systems (78% favorable) and for requiring all Americans to carry a national identification card (66% favorable).

There was nearly universal disfavor (93% opposed) to a measure in which police officers could enter a home without a search warrant. Stiff opposition (75%) was also expressed for the idea of allowing the government to imprison and hold for years without trial a U.S. citizen suspected of terrorist activities. There was similar disfavor for allowing police officers to single out people at random on the street and search their belongings (70% opposed). Likewise, a large fraction (73%) were opposed to allowing law enforcement easier secret access to people's private communications. There was slightly less resolve against allowing government agents access to library records to determine what books patrons have checked out. Only 60% of respondents were opposed to this measure, whereas 37% favored it. Opinions were mixed on the issue of whether the police should be allowed to single out people at random on the street and ask for identification. This measure received nearly equal amounts of support (48%) and opposition (51%).

PATRIOT ACT

As described in Chapter 2, the Uniting and Strengthening America by Providing Appropriate Tools Required to Intercept and Obstruct Terrorism (USA PATRIOT) Act of 2001—known simply as the Patriot Act—was passed by Congress in response to the 9/11 terrorist attacks. Many of the provisions of the act deal with surveillance procedures and financial security enhancements that have implications on civil liberty issues.

Controversy Erupts

In "The USA PATRIOT Act: Preserving Life and Liberty" (2008, http://www.lifeandliberty.gov/highlights.htm), the U.S. Department of Justice (DOJ) claims that the Patriot Act of 2001 made only "modest, incremental changes" to existing law related to criminal activities. The DOJ notes that the act makes tools available to law enforcement for use in terrorism investigations that have been used for decades against other kinds of criminals, particularly suspected organized crime figures and drug traffickers. These tools include surveillance techniques (such as wiretapping) and legal maneuvers (such as streamlining the search warrant process). In addition, the Patriot Act allows federal agents to obtain business records relevant to national security investigations without going through the grand jury process to obtain a subpoena. Instead, the request is made through the Foreign Intelligence Surveillance Court (a federal court), which can grant permission if the government meets certain criteria. Other components of the act facilitate information sharing and cooperation between different government agencies, increase the penalties for terrorist-related crimes, and designate new criminal offenses, such as harboring people who have committed or plan to commit terrorist acts.

The Patriot Act was not considered that controversial when it was initially passed in October 2001. The act received overwhelming support in the House (passing 357 to 66) and in the Senate, where only one senator out of one hundred voted against it. (See Figure 8.1 and Figure 8.2.) The lone "nay" vote was cast by Senator Russell D. Feingold (1953–; D-WI). Feingold notes in "Civil Liberties" (2008, http://www.russfeingold.org/civil_liberties.php) that he supported nearly all the provisions of the act, but was deeply troubled by the civil liberty implications of a handful of provisions. The senator, who was reelected in 2004, fears that these provisions "may infringe on the rights of law-abiding citizens, while doing little [to] protect our country against terrorists."

The Patriot Act has been harshly criticized by others, including the American Civil Liberties Union (ACLU) and the Electronic Privacy Information Center (EPIC). Headquartered in New York City, the ACLU is a private nonprofit organization that is devoted to defending American civil liberties. In "National Security: Safe and Free at Home" (2008, http://www.aclu.org/natsec/index.html), it states that "illegal government spying, provisions of the Patriot Act and government-sponsored torture programs transcend the bounds of law and our most treasured values in the name of national security." EPIC is also a private organization. It calls itself a public interest research center and is based in Washington, D.C. EPIC is most concerned with emerging civil liberty and privacy issues that have arisen since the advent of electronic media. It maintains a Web site devoted to the Patriot Act (http://epic.org/privacy/terrorism/usapatriot/). EPIC claims that the 2001 act was passed so quickly in the aftermath of 9/11 that few traditional safeguards afforded by the Constitution were included to protect American civil liberties. Both organizations work to publicize what they consider to be civil liberty abuses committed by federal government agencies under the Patriot Act.

The 2001 Patriot Act included a provision that sixteen sections of the act would sunset (automatically expire) after four years unless Congress chose to renew them. In late 2005 intense debate began in Congress over whether those provisions should be renewed. In December 2005 the House voted 251 to 174 to renew the provisions with some modifications. (See Figure 8.3.) In March 2006 the USA PATRIOT Act Improvement and Reauthorization Act of 2005 also passed the Senate by a vote of 89 to 10. (See Figure 8.4.) The refurbished act made permanent fourteen of the original sixteen sunset provisions and placed new four-year sunset periods on the other two provisions (which concern surveillance techniques and the acquisition of business records). According to the DOJ, in the fact sheet "USA Patriot

FIGURE 8.1

House vote on the USA PATRIOT Act, October 24, 2001

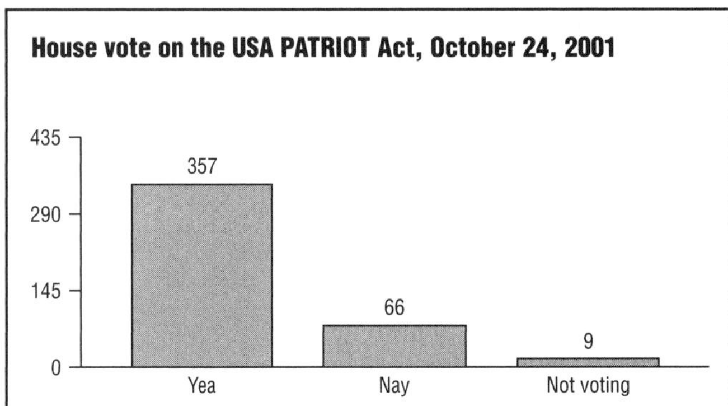

SOURCE: "House Vote on the USA PATRIOT Act, Vote #398—10/24/01," in *Passed by Congress*, U.S. Department of Justice, undated, http://www.lifeandliberty.gov/subs/p_congress.htm (accessed August 11, 2008)

FIGURE 8.2

Senate vote on the USA PATRIOT Act, October 25, 2001

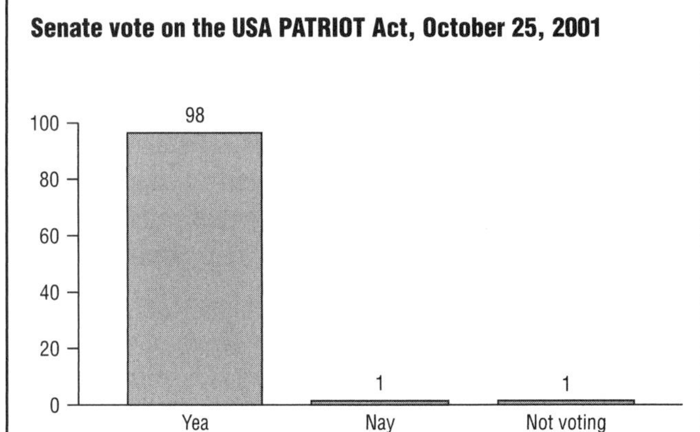

SOURCE: "Senate Vote on the USA PATRIOT Act, Vote #313—10/25/01," in *Passed by Congress*, U.S. Department of Justice, undated, http://www.lifeandliberty.gov/subs/p_congress.htm (accessed August 11, 2008)

FIGURE 8.3

House vote on the USA PATRIOT Improvement and Reauthorization Act of 2005, December 14, 2005

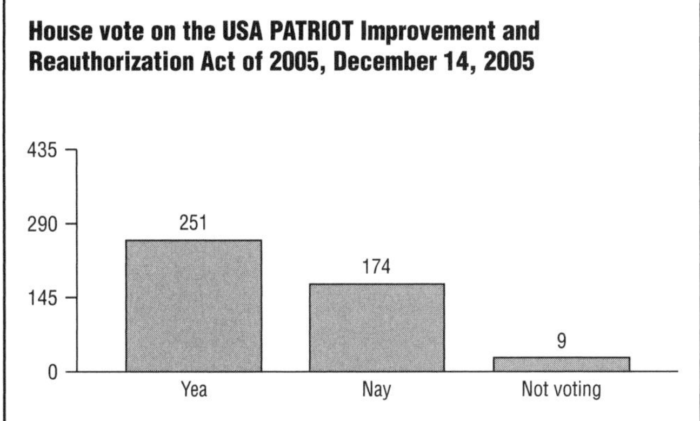

SOURCE: "House Vote on the USA PATRIOT Improvement and Reauthorization Act of 2005," in *Passed by Congress*, U.S. Department of Justice, undated, http://www.lifeandliberty.gov/subs/p_congress.htm (accessed August 11, 2008)

FIGURE 8.4

Senate vote on the USA PATRIOT Improvement and Reauthorization Act of 2005, March 2, 2006

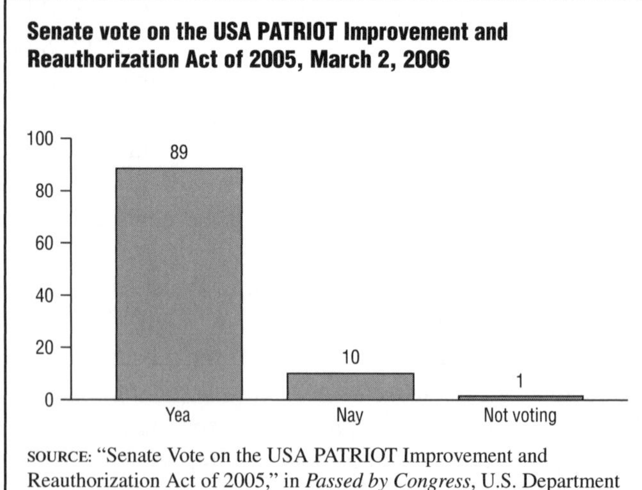

SOURCE: "Senate Vote on the USA PATRIOT Improvement and Reauthorization Act of 2005," in *Passed by Congress*, U.S. Department of Justice, undated, http://www.lifeandliberty.gov/subs/p_congress.htm (accessed August 11, 2008)

Act Improvement and Reauthorization Act of 2005" (March 2, 2006, http://www.usdoj.gov/opa/pr/2006/March/06_opa_113.html), Congress added "dozens of additional safeguards to protect Americans' privacy and civil liberties" as part of the reauthorization.

Some cities and municipalities and even states around the country have passed nonbinding resolutions expressing their opposition to certain provisions of the Patriot Act. The organization Bill of Rights Defense Committee (http://www.bordc.org/list.php) claims that as of September 22, 2008, 414 such resolutions had been passed. For example, in 2006 the mayor and city council of Las Vegas, Nevada, passed a resolution stating that "the City of Las Vegas affirms its strong opposition to terrorism, but also affirms that any efforts to end terrorism not be waged at the expense of the fundamental civil liberties, rights, and freedoms of the people of the City of Las Vegas, the United States, or the world" (May 3, 2006, http://www.bordc.org/detail.php?id=735). In particular, the resolution mentions concerns regarding the government collecting information on the political and religious activities of individuals when that information has no direct relation to a criminal investigation.

CONTROVERSY SURROUNDING ELECTRONIC SURVEILLANCE

The advent of the telephone and recording devices in the late 1800s introduced a new question to the debate over civil liberties: Does the use of equipment to intercept and record a private conversation constitute a "seizure" under the Fourth Amendment? In 1928 the Supreme Court ruled in *Olmstead v. United States* (277 U.S. 438) that the Fourth Amendment does not require a warrant for a wiretap placed on phone lines outside a suspect's residence. The case was decided on a narrow 5–4 vote, and the decision was highly controversial. Over the following decades Congress and the federal courts gradually chipped away at the legal precedent set in the 1928 case. In 1967 the decision was reversed by the Supreme Court in *Berger v. New York* (388 U.S. 41) and *Katz v. United States* (389 U.S. 347). Thus, judicial warrants became necessary to conduct electronic surveillance in criminal investigations. However, the gathering of intelligence related to national security has been treated differently by legal authorities.

In 1968 Congress passed the Omnibus Crime Control and Safe Streets Act, which authorized the use of electronic surveillance for certain classes of crimes so long as a judicial warrant is obtained. Section 2511 (3) of the act notes that the act does not limit "the constitutional power of the President to take such measures as he deems necessary" to obtain foreign intelligence information considered essential to national security, to protect national security information from falling into foreign hands, and to protect against hostile acts of a foreign power, overthrow of the government by force or other unlawful means, or any other "clear and present danger to the structure or existence of the Government." This section stipulates that information obtained via electronic surveillance conducted under the authority of the president pursuant to these powers can be used as evidence in a trial so long as the conduct is "reasonable." In general, this section was interpreted as meaning that the U.S. attorney general (operating under the authority of the president) could conduct warrantless electronic surveillance for national security purposes.

This interpretation was challenged in the 1972 Supreme Court case of *United States v. United States District Court* (407 U.S. 297). In this case the government had used taped phone conversations to indict three American defendants in the bombing of a Central Intelligence Agency office in Ann Arbor, Michigan. The electronic surveillance had been conducted without a warrant but at the direction of the U.S. attorney general. The U.S. District Court for the Eastern District of Michigan ruled that the warrantless surveillance violated the Fourth Amendment. The Supreme Court agreed, noting that "the freedoms of the Fourth Amendment cannot properly be guaranteed if domestic security surveillances are conducted solely within the discretion of the Executive Branch without the detached judgment of a neutral magistrate."

FOREIGN INTELLIGENCE SURVEILLANCE COURT

In 1978 Congress passed the Foreign Intelligence Surveillance Act (FISA), creating the Foreign Intelligence Surveillance Court (FISC). FISA stipulates that the government must obtain a special warrant from the

FISC before conducting specific intelligence-gathering activities related to national security within the United States. The original act related primarily to electronic surveillance. Subsequent amendments have allowed covert "physical searches," access to "certain business records," and the use of National Security Letters (NSLs). NSLs are letters used by intelligence agencies to request information (e.g., to request a suspect's credit card records from a financial institution). The recipient of an NSL does not have to comply with the request but must keep the request secret.

The creation of the FISC was driven by *United States v. United States District Court* and by a host of allegations that emerged during the early 1970s regarding spying by government intelligence agencies on U.S. citizens. These allegations were investigated by various government bodies, most notably the Senate Select Committee to Study Governmental Operations with Respect to Intelligence Activities. This committee found evidence that the executive branch of the federal government had abused its power by conducting domestic electronic surveillance that it claimed was in the interest of national security.

The FISC originally consisted of seven federal district court judges designated by the chief justice (the head of the judicial branch of the federal government who presides over the U.S. Supreme Court). The Patriot Act of 2001 changed this to eleven judges on the FISC. At least one of the judges must be a member of the U.S. District Court for the District of Columbia. The FISC is not in session regularly but convenes in Washington, D.C., when needed. Because the judges live at various locations around the country, they attend hearings on a rotating basis.

The workings of the FISC are described by the Federal Judicial Center (September 16, 2008, http://www.fjc.gov/history/home.nsf/page/fisc_bdy), an education and research agency for the federal courts. The process is as follows:

- A federal intelligence agency requests a warrant application
- The warrant application is drafted by attorneys at the National Security Agency (NSA)
- The application has to include certification from the U.S. attorney general that the target of the surveillance or search is a U.S. citizen or resident alien who "may be involved in the commission of a crime" or a foreign power or the agent of a foreign power
- The application is presented before the judges of the FISC
- If an application is denied, the government can appeal the decision to the Foreign Intelligence Surveillance Court of Review, which is presided over by three district or appeals court judges designated by the chief justice

According to the Federal Judicial Center, the Court of Review was first convened in 2002.

The FISC is often called a "secret" court, because much of its work is conducted in secrecy. The sensitive nature of national security matters means that the decisions of the court are based on classified information. FISA does require the U.S. attorney general to submit an annual report to Congress noting the number of applications filed with the FISC and the number of orders issued by the court. The Federation of American Scientists (2008, http://www.fas.org/irp/agency/doj/fisa/), a nonprofit organization, maintains copies of the annual reports. The first report covers 1979 and states that the FISC issued 207 orders that year granting the government authority to use electronic surveillance as part of national security investigations.

The latest available annual report indicates that the FISC reviewed 2,371 applications in 2007 for authority to conduct electronic surveillance and physical searches. All but one of the applications were approved. In addition, six applications were reviewed and approved by the FISC for access to certain business records for "foreign intelligence purposes." The report notes that the DOJ's Office of the Inspector General (OIG) had earlier in the year found inaccuracies in the NSL database. While the FBI reported that 12,583 NSL requests concerning 4,790 different Americans were made in 2006, this number is considered an estimate.

WIRETAPPING WITHOUT FISC APPROVAL

In "Bush Lets U.S. Spy on Callers without Courts" (*New York Times*, December 16, 2005), James Risen and Eric Lichtblau accuse the administration of George W. Bush (1946–) of conducting wiretap operations without FISC approval. Risen and Lichtblau allege that in early 2002 President Bush issued a secret executive order authorizing the NSA to bypass the FISC process for conducting domestic surveillance. Headquartered at Fort Meade, Maryland, the NSA oversees signals intelligence operations for the U.S. intelligence community. (Signals intelligence is the interception of signals, such as radio, for the purpose of intelligence gathering.)

Risen and Lichtblau estimate that the international phone calls and e-mails of "hundreds, perhaps thousands" of Americans had been monitored to search for links to international terrorism. They claim unnamed government officials told the *New York Times* in 2004 about the program because of concerns about its constitutionality. The newspaper said it delayed publishing the story for a year at the request of the White House because of concerns that the article would alert suspects they were under surveillance. Risen and Lichtblau report that the surveillance program had been credited by the government with uncovering several terrorist plots against targets in the United States and the United Kingdom.

President Bush allegedly based the program on his belief that a September 2001 congressional resolution granted him "broad powers" in the War on Terror to protect U.S. interests. Risen and Lichtblau claim that several members of Congress had been briefed about the monitoring program and at least one, Senator John D. Rockefeller IV (1937–; D-WV), had expressed concerns about it to the White House. Risen and Lichtblau note that it is puzzling why top officials decided to bypass the FISC process, considering that the FISC is believed to have granted nearly every request it has ever considered. Sources for the article note that it takes the FISC several hours to issue emergency approval for wiretaps and that the Bush administration considered this delay to be unacceptable. In addition, each FISC authorization requires information about specific surveillance targets, whereas the intelligence community is interested in monitoring many communications from a variety of sources at once.

According to Risen and Lichtblau, the program was suspended temporarily in mid-2004 because of concerns about its legality. Reportedly, the suspension was spurred by a complaint from the federal judge overseeing the FISC. The program was "revamped" and continued to operate.

Repercussions

Publicity about the warrantless surveillance program led to several repercussions for the Bush administration. One of the FISC judges resigned, reportedly to show his displeasure with the White House over the controversy. In January 2006 the ACLU filed a lawsuit against the NSA, claiming that the surveillance program violated the First and Fourth Amendments of the Constitution and that President Bush had exceeded his authority under the separation of powers principles of the Constitution. The lawsuit sought a court order to dismantle the program. In August 2006 Anna Diggs Taylor (1932–), a federal judge, granted that court order on the grounds that the surveillance program violated FISA and the Fourth Amendment. She also ruled that President Bush had exceeded his authority under the Constitution. The DOJ immediately filed an appeal, and top government officials defended the program, insisting that it is legal and necessary to combat terrorist attacks.

Lydia Saad of the Gallup Organization reports in *Public Opinion Mixed on Bush Anti-terrorism Agenda* (September 21, 2006,) http://www.gallup.com/poll/24625/Public-Opinion-Mixed-Bush-AntiTerrorism-Agenda.aspx) that in September 2006 Americans were split on whether the warrantless wiretapping was a right or wrong action by the Bush administration. Over half (55%) of the respondents felt it was right, whereas 42% thought it was wrong.

COLLECTING PHONE CALL DATA

In "NSA Has Massive Database of Americans' Phone Calls" (*USA Today*, May 11, 2006), Leslie Cauley reports that the NSA had been secretly collecting phone call data on tens of millions of Americans. Cauley alleges that the agency had been compiling a database of phone records to search for links to international terrorism. The database included information such as the calling and receiving phone numbers and the duration of calls. The program was reportedly begun shortly after 9/11. Cauley claims that the telecommunications companies AT&T, Verizon, and Bell South turned over phone call data to the NSA but that other companies—including Qwest—refused to do so because of legal concerns. The NSA did not obtain warrants for the information but simply asked (and may have paid) the companies to cooperate. According to Cauley, Qwest's lawyers asked the agency to process the request through the FISC, but the agency refused to do so.

Cauley's article led to media criticism of the phone companies for complying with the NSA request. However, the general public was largely ambivalent about the controversy. The Gallup Organization notes in *Civil Liberties* (2008, http://www.gallup.com/poll/5263/Civil-Liberties.aspx) that a poll on civil liberties was conducted only days after the story broke in *USA Today*. A slim majority of respondents (51%) expressed disapproval of the phone record collection program, whereas 43% approved.

Bell South and Verizon subsequently denied that they turned over records to the NSA. AT&T executives refused to confirm or deny the allegations but insisted that they had not endangered customer privacy. Leslie Cauley et al. retract in "Lawmakers: NSA Database Incomplete" (*USA Today*, June 30, 2006) part of Cauley's original story, noting that her sources could not confirm that Bell South and Verizon had cooperated with the NSA. Cauley et al. report that dozens of class-action lawsuits had been filed against the telecommunications companies linked to the story.

FOCUS ON NSLS

In March 2008 the OIG issued *A Review of the FBI's Use of National Security Letters: Assessment of Corrective Actions and Examination of NSL Usage in 2006* (http://www.usdoj.gov/oig/special/s0803b/final.pdf), which focuses on the FBI's use of NSLs during 2006. The report is unclassified, but redacted, meaning that parts of it are blacked out or omitted to protect national security interests. The FBI made 49,425 NSL requests in 2006. (See Figure 8.5.) This number was up slightly from 2005. Between 2003 and 2006 the FBI made a total of 192,499. In 2006 a majority (57%, or 11,517) of the NSL requests were for U.S. citizens. (See Figure 8.6.) This percentage was up from 39% in 2003.

The OIG notes that the FBI considers NSLs to be an "indispensable investigative tool in major terrorism and

FIGURE 8.5

FBI requests for National Security Letters, 2003–06

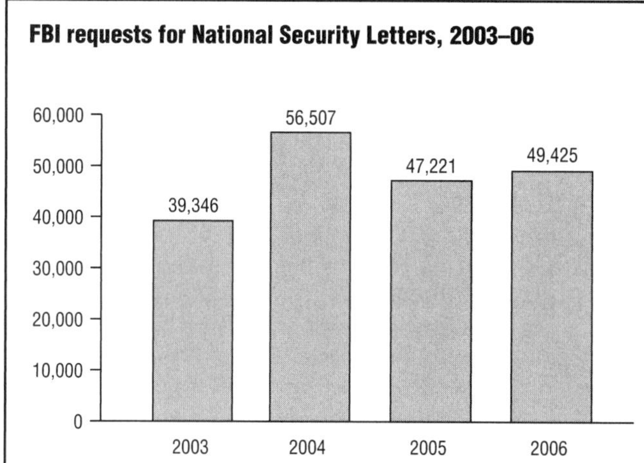

SOURCE: "Chart 4.5. NSL Requests (2003 through 2006)," in *A Review of the FBI's Use of National Security Letters: Assessment of Corrective Actions and Examination of NSL Usage in 2006*, U.S. Department of Justice, Office of the Inspector General, March 2008, http://www.usdoj.gov/oig/special/s0803b/final.pdf (accessed August 8, 2008)

FIGURE 8.6

FBI requests for National Security Letters, by citizenship of subject, 2003–06

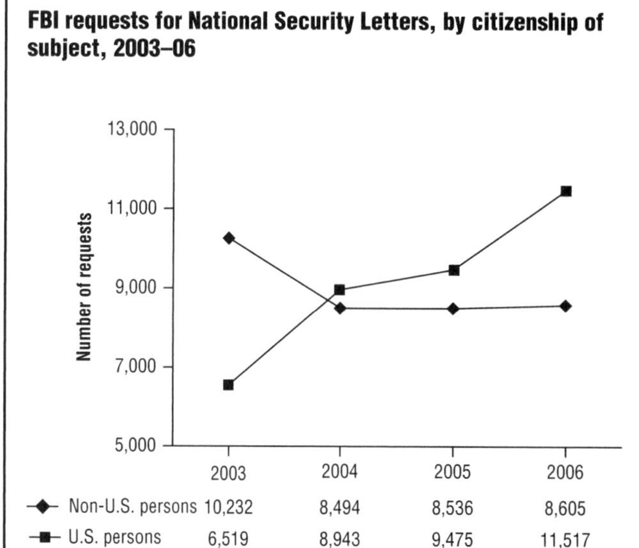

SOURCE: "Chart 4.6. NSL Requests Relating to U.S. Persons and Non-U.S. Persons (2003 through 2006)," in *A Review of the FBI's Use of National Security Letters: Assessment of Corrective Actions and Examination of NSL Usage in 2006*, U.S. Department of Justice, Office of the Inspector General, March 2008, http://www.usdoj.gov/oig/special/s0803b/final.pdf (accessed August 8, 2008)

espionage investigations." The NSLs requested in 2006 were used in counterterrorism and counterintelligence investigations to confirm the identities of suspects and explore their financial affairs.

THE FISA AMENDMENTS ACT OF 2008

Throughout 2007 and early 2008 lawmakers considered ways to amend FISA. This process is described in detail by Elizabeth B. Bazan of the Congressional Research Service, in *The Foreign Intelligence Surveillance Act: A Sketch of Selected Issues* (July 7, 2008, http://www.fas.org/sgp/crs/intel/RL34566.pdf). Bazan notes that in early August 2007 the director of national intelligence released a statement asking congressional leaders to amend FISA to include two critical changes: release the government from the requirement for a court order to gather foreign intelligence on foreign people located overseas and provide liability protection for companies that had furnished assistance to the government in foreign intelligence collection activities in the past.

In August 2007 the Protect America Act (PAA) was enacted into law. This short-term law was in effect only through February 2008. Its purpose was to allow the federal government to continue certain types of electronic surveillance while long-term changes to FISA were debated. The PAA specifically allowed surveillance that targeted foreign people located overseas. In other words, warrantless surveillance of people "reasonably believed to be located outside the United States" was allowed. Civil libertarians complained that American phone calls and e-mails could be unintentionally intercepted as part of the surveillance effort.

In July 2008 President Bush signed the FISA Amendments Act of 2008, which incorporated the provisions of the PAA. Critics complain that the law allows government surveillance without judicial oversight and gives immunity to the telecommunications companies that aided the government in its warrantless wiretapping program. The FISA Amendments Act of 2008 will sunset in 2012.

PUBLIC OPINION

The Gallup Organization notes in *Civil Liberties* that at various times from 2002 to 2005 it conducted polls to gauge American attitudes about balancing civil liberties against national security. In January 2002 the respondents were split evenly, with 47% expressing the view that the government should "take steps, even if civil liberties [are] violated," to prevent terrorist attacks in the United States. Only slightly more (49%) respondents said that government steps against terrorism should not violate civil liberties. This poll was conducted only four months after 9/11. Over time, public opinion has drifted toward greater protection of civil liberties. By August 2003 just over two-thirds (67%) of those asked were opposed to civil liberty violations as an acceptable measure in the fight against terrorism. Polls conducted in November 2003 and December 2005 showed little movement from this stance with 64% and 65%, respectively, in opposition.

Similar results were obtained in a Gallup poll conducted in May 2006 only days after allegations were published in *USA Today* regarding the government obtaining phone records of large numbers of Americans. Poll participants were asked to rate the actions of the Bush administration at fighting terrorism in terms of their effects on civil liberties. Forty-one percent of respondents felt the administration had gone "too far" in restricting people's civil liberties during the War on Terror. By comparison, only 11% agreed with this rating when the same question was asked in June 2002. At that time a majority of respondents (60%) felt the Bush administration's antiterror actions were "about right" in regards to restricting civil liberties. By May 2006 only 34% agreed with this assessment. Overall, the results indicated a growing discontent among Americans between 2002 and 2006 with the intrusion of the War on Terror on civil liberties in the United States.

The Angus Reid Global Monitor, an online information source, reports in "U.S. Upset with Bush on Terrorism, Civil Liberties" (January 6, 2008, http://www.angus-reid.com/polls/view/us_upset_with_bush_on_terrorism_civil_liberties/) that in December 2007 the polling company Harris Interactive asked Americans to rate the Bush administration on its performance at protecting civil liberties. A majority (57%) of respondents gave the administration a negative rating, whereas 33% gave it a positive rating.

CHAPTER 9

HUMAN RIGHTS AND THE WAR ON TERROR

While waging the War on Terror, U.S. military forces have captured many individuals who are classified as "enemy combatants." Historically, the United States has treated enemy soldiers in accordance with specific humanitarian standards and international agreements, such as the Geneva Conventions. Soon after the war in Afghanistan began in 2001, the administration of President George W. Bush (1946–) decided that most combatants fighting against the United States are not soldiers in the traditional sense but are war criminals. As such, they are not granted the protections against torture and humiliating treatment that are afforded prisoners of war (POWs) under international law. In addition, the Bush administration decided that detainees would be tried for their crimes by special U.S. military commissions (or tribunals) rather than by conventional courts-martial. These decisions have led to a long battle in U.S. courts over the legal status of detainees and a public debate about the power of the president in times of war.

There have been allegations in the media and by humanitarian organizations that detainees under U.S. control have been mistreated, tortured, and abused. A prisoner abuse scandal at the Abu Ghraib Detention Facility in Iraq made worldwide headlines and brought harsh criticism of the United States in the international community. The American public has watched uneasily as these events have unfolded. On the one hand, the public recognizes the life-and-death urgency of obtaining information from detainees about plans for future terrorist attacks against the United States. On the other hand, public opinion polls show a majority of Americans are opposed to torturing detainees to gain this information. However, this opposition is not overwhelming. Weighing the concerns of national security against the human rights of known or suspected terrorists clearly poses a difficult moral and ethical dilemma for the United States.

GENEVA CONVENTIONS

The Geneva Conventions are a series of international agreements related to humanitarian conduct during warfare. Their conception is linked to the birth of the International Committee of the Red Cross (ICRC). Both were inspired by the efforts of Jean-Henri Dunant (1828–1910), a businessman and author who lived in Geneva, Switzerland. In 1859 Dunant was traveling through Italy when he witnessed the battle of Solferino, a bloody conflict that was waged as part of the Second Italian War of Independence (1859) by French, Austrian, and Sardinian armies. The battle left 2,000 killed and over 20,000 wounded. Dunant was horrified by the lack of treatment afforded the wounded soldiers of the losing side. In 1862 he published the book *Un souvenir de Solferino* (*A Memory of Solferino*), in which he wrote about his observations and suggested that an international society be established and charged with recruiting trained volunteers to care for wounded soldiers during and after armed conflicts.

The First Geneva Convention

With the help of the Geneva Society for Public Welfare, Dunant convinced a dozen European nations to participate in a conference that ultimately led to an international treaty on the treatment of wounded soldiers during warfare. This became known as the First Geneva Convention. It granted neutrality on the battlefield to medical personnel working under the emblem of a red cross on a white background. Dunant's committee, originally called the International Committee for Relief to the Wounded, was renamed the International Committee of the Red Cross. In 1901 Dunant was a corecipient of the first-ever Nobel Peace Price.

According to the ICRC, in "From the Battle of Solferino to the Eve of the First World War" (December 28,

2004, http://www.icrc.org/web/eng/siteeng0.nsf/html/57JNVP), the First Geneva Convention was ratified (enacted into law) in 1864 by ten European governments: Belgium, Denmark, France, the Grand Duchy of Baden (later a part of Germany), Italy, the Netherlands, Norway, Spain, Sweden, and Switzerland.

The United States did not ratify the First Geneva Convention until 1882. The ratification was finally achieved largely due to the efforts of Clara Barton (1821–1912), who had volunteered as a nurse during the U.S. Civil War (1861–1865) and worked for many humanitarian causes. In 1878 she published the influential book *The Red Cross of the Geneva Convention: What It Is*, in which she urged U.S. legislators to ratify the Geneva Convention. Barton argued that the convention concerned "if not our safety, at least our honor, to signify our approval of those principals of humanity acknowledged by every other civilized nation." In 1881 the American Society of the Red Cross was founded and elected Barton as its first president. A year later the U.S. Senate unanimously ratified the First Geneva Convention.

Geneva Conventions Evolve

At the urging of the czar Nicholas II (1868–1918) of Russia, the First International Peace Conference was held in 1899 at The Hague in the Netherlands. More than two dozen nations participated, including the United States. Even though the conference was intended to negotiate arms control agreements, this goal was not achieved. A number of humanitarian agreements were signed but never ratified. In 1907 a Second International Peace Conference was held at The Hague in response to a proposal made by President Theodore Roosevelt (1858–1919). Again, many agreements were signed by the participants but not ratified by the signatories. However, these agreements laid the groundwork for international treaties that eventually extended the provisions of the First Geneva Convention to cover naval warfare (Second Geneva Convention), the treatment of POWs (Third Geneva Convention), and the treatment of civilians during warfare (Fourth Geneva Convention).

When World War I (1914–1918) was fought, the Geneva Conventions protecting POWs and civilians were not in force. The Third Geneva Convention was adopted in 1929. Its official title was the Convention Relative to the Treatment of Prisoners of War. The third convention was designed to carry out the intent and purpose of the provisions of the agreements reached at The Hague peace conferences. The United States ratified the convention in 1932, as did most other major nations with two exceptions: Russia and Japan. Both nations were subsequently accused of mistreating POWs during World War II (1939–1945). In general, historians agree that the United States treated POWs well in hopes that American POWs held in foreign lands would receive similar treatment.

Following World War II, many nations resolved to expand and modify the Geneva Conventions in response to atrocities committed during the war. In 1949 the modern framework of the four conventions was established. (See Table 9.1.) The United States has signed and ratified all four of the Geneva Conventions.

Since 1949 three protocols have been added to the conventions. As of September 2008, the United States had not ratified them.

Common Article 3

Each of the four Geneva Conventions contains a provision known as Article 3. According to M. Gandhi, in "Common Article 3 of Geneva Conventions, 1949 in the

TABLE 9.1

The Geneva Conventions

Part	Title	Treaty date	Ratified by U.S.	Scope
First Geneva Convention	Amelioration of the condition of the wounded in armies in the field	1949	1955	Concerns treatment of sick and wounded military forces and the neutrality of medical personnel assisting them
Second Geneva Convention	Amelioration of the condition of wounded, sick and shipwrecked members of armed forces at sea	1949	1955	Extends First Geneva Convention to naval warfare
Third Geneva Convention	Treatment of prisoners of war (POW)	1949	1955	Calls for humane treatment of POWs and all other combatants no longer active in hostilities
Fourth Geneva Convention	Protection of civilian persons in time of war	1949	1955	Governs the status and protection of civilian populations during wartime
Protocol I	Protection of victims of international armed conflicts	1977	No[a]	Protects people involved in battles for self-determination of their nations
Protocol II	Protection of victims of non-international armed conflicts	1977	No[a]	Protects people involved in internal national conflicts
Protocol III	Adoption of an additional distinctive emblem	2005	No[b]	Adds a new distinctive emblem called the red crystal

[a]The United States signed the protocol, but as of September 2006 had not ratified it. Other signatories that have not ratified the protocol are Iran, Morocco, and Pakistan.
[b]The United States signed the protocol, but as of September 2006 had not ratified it, nor had dozens of other signatories.

SOURCE: Created by Kim Masters Evans for Cengage Learning, Gale, 2008

Era of International Criminal Tribunals" (November 21, 2002, http://www.worldlii.org/int/journals/ISILYBIHRL/2001/11.html), this is called Common Article 3 because it is common to (appears in) all four conventions. Common Article 3 contains minimum humanitarian standards for the treatment during noninternational armed conflicts of "persons taking no active part in the hostilities." These people include civilians (noncombatants) and enemy soldiers who have surrendered or who can no longer fight because they are wounded, sick, or otherwise incapacitated or detained.

Common Article 3 prohibits "at any time and in any place whatsoever" all the following acts against these people:

- Violence, including torture, cruel treatment, mutilation, or murder
- Holding them as hostages
- Humiliating and degrading treatment or other "outrages upon personal dignity"
- Criminal punishments, including executions, passed without due legal process; this provision specifically requires that defendants receive "all the judicial guarantees which are recognized as indispensable by civilized peoples"

In addition, Common Article 3 requires that the wounded and sick be collected and given care and that a neutral international organization, such as the ICRC, be allowed to provide services to the parties involved in the armed conflict.

Even though Common Article 3 specifies that it applies to noninternational armed conflicts, in practice it has historically been deemed to represent the minimum humanitarian standards for all armed conflicts, including international ones.

UNITED NATIONS CONVENTION AGAINST TORTURE

The United Nations (UN) Convention against Torture and Other Cruel, Inhuman, or Degrading Treatment or Punishment entered into force in 1987. The United States signed the convention in 1984 and ratified it in 1994. The UN Office of the High Commissioner for Human Rights (UNHCHR; February 26, 2004, http://www.unhchr.ch/html/menu3/b/h_cat39.htm) explains that the convention defines torture as "any act by which severe pain or suffering, whether physical or mental, is intentionally inflicted on a person" for one of the following reasons:

- Obtaining information or a confession
- Punishment
- Intimidation or coercion
- Any reason based on discrimination of any kind

The convention covers torture inflicted by, instigated by, or with the consent or acquiescence of a public official or someone acting in an official capacity. Implementation of the convention is monitored by a ten-member Committee against Torture. Each ratifying party is required to report to the committee every four years. The committee also investigates complaints filed by individuals and by nations against other nations.

According to the UNHCHR (November 10, 2003, http://www.unhchr.ch/html/menu2/6/cat/treaties/opcat.htm), in 2002 an optional protocol to the convention was adopted that calls for "regular visits" by independent bodies to "places where people are deprived of their liberty" to ensure that torture and other treatments prohibited by the convention are not taking place. As of September 2008, the United States had neither signed nor ratified the optional protocol.

WAR CRIMES ACT OF 1996

The War Crimes Act of 1996 was signed by President Bill Clinton (1946–) in August 1996 and amended in 1997. The act applies to American victims or perpetrators (military or civilian) of war crimes. A war crime is defined by the act as conduct meeting any one of the following definitions:

- A "grave breach" of the Geneva Conventions (and any associated protocols) to which the United States is a party
- A violation of Common Article 3 of the Geneva Conventions
- An activity prohibited by the annex to the 1907 Hague peace conference (the text can be viewed at http://www.yale.edu/lawweb/avalon/lawofwar/hague04.htm)
- An activity prohibited by the Protocol on Prohibitions or Restrictions on the Use of Mines, Booby-Traps, and Other Devices (Geneva, May 1996) that purposely kills or seriously injures civilians (the text can be viewed at http://www1.umn.edu/humanrts/instree/1980d.htm)

The penalties for violating the War Crimes Act of 1996 include fines and imprisonment up to life in prison. The death penalty is allowed for perpetrators of war crimes in which victims are killed.

LEGAL ISSUES RELATED TO DETAINEES

The U.S. War on Terror is unique in U.S. history, because the enemy forces do not comprise soldiers officially fighting on behalf of other nations but individuals from various countries fighting for a common agenda or ideological purpose that the U.S. government defines as terrorism. When the United States launched the first military conflict in the War on Terror (Operation Enduring Freedom against Afghanistan in late 2001), President

Bush made the decision that terrorists captured during the course of the war would be regarded as enemy combatants.

Enemy Combatants

In "Guantanamo Detainee Processes" (October 2, 2007, http://www.defenselink.mil/news/Sep2005/d20050908process.pdf), the U.S. Department of Defense (DOD) defines an enemy combatant as "an individual who was part of or supporting Taliban or al Qaeda forces, or associated forces that are engaged in hostilities against the United States or its coalition partners. This includes any person who has committed a belligerent act or has directly supported hostilities in aid of enemy armed forces."

Once terrorists were declared enemy combatants, they left the realm of law enforcement and became legitimate targets of military action. In other words, terrorists could be killed outright by U.S. soldiers during the course of hostilities. Likewise, captured terrorists fell under military jurisdiction rather than law enforcement jurisdiction.

An important distinction in U.S. law is the difference between a lawful and unlawful enemy combatant. When the War on Terror began, the U.S. position was that lawful enemy combatants were uniformed members of an enemy nation's armed forces that adhered to a military hierarchy, bore their weapons openly, and conducted their operations in accordance with the laws and customs of warfare. Terrorists do not meet these criteria and as a result were deemed unlawful enemy combatants. The historical and legal basis for this distinction is described by Scott Reid in *Terrorists as Enemy Combatants: An Analysis of How the United States Applies the Law of Armed Conflict in the Global War on Terrorism* (February 9, 2004, http://fas.org/man/eprint/reid.pdf). Reid notes that "a nation must be expected to put uniforms on its troops in order to reap the benefits of lawful combatancy." These benefits include protections granted under the Geneva Conventions for POWs.

The Bush administration has maintained that captured unlawful enemy combatants are not POWs under the Geneva Conventions but war criminals. The logic behind this viewpoint is that the Geneva Conventions are international treaties signed and ratified by nation-states. Because terrorist groups such as al Qaeda are private organizations, they cannot be party to the conventions. Foreign individuals fighting against the United States without official sanction from their governments also cannot be party to the conventions.

Guantánamo Bay Detention Facility

Many of the enemy combatants captured during the War on Terror have been detained at a detention facility located at the U.S. Naval Base Guantánamo Bay in Cuba. (For a map of Cuba, see Figure 6.3 in Chapter 6.) This facility has been nicknamed Gitmo by the press and is often abbreviated as GTMO in U.S. military documents.

The initial screening of a captured individual is performed by military officials on the battlefield. The DOD states in "GTMO Detainee Processes" (November 14, 2005, http://www.defenselink.mil/news/Jan2006/d20060215detaineeprocesseschart.pdf) that these officials determine whether a captured individual is an enemy combatant, and if so, whether that person should be transferred to Guantánamo for incarceration.

Legal Rights under U.S. Law

The detention of terrorists as unlawful enemy combatants during wartime has triggered many court battles regarding their legal rights under U.S. law and the power of the executive branch (i.e., the president and the agencies under his control) over detainees. A chronological listing of the major milestones in this legal battle is provided in Table 9.2.

In *Ex Parte Quirin* (317 U.S. 1 [1942]), the U.S. Supreme Court decided that President Franklin D. Roosevelt (1882–1945) had the authority to convene a military tribunal to try eight civilian Germans who had entered the United States to commit sabotage during World War II. Six of the men were ultimately executed in the electric chair. The Court noted that "unlawful combatants" could be subjected to trial and punishment by military tribunals, rather than by civilian courts.

On September 18, 2001, Congress passed the Authorization for Use of Military Force (http://frwebgate.access.gpo.gov/cgi-bin/getdoc.cgi?dbname=107_cong_public_laws&docid=f:publ040.107.pdf), which states: "The President is authorized to use all necessary and appropriate force against those nations, organizations, or persons he determines

TABLE 9.2

Important milestones in U.S. policies regarding detainee treatment, 2001–08

Milestone	Date	Description
Authorization for use of military force	September 18, 2001	Public Law 107–40
Detention, treatment, and trial of certain non-citizens in the war against terrorism	November 13, 2001	Presidential military order
Hamdi v. Rumsfeld	June 28, 2004	Supreme Court case
Rasul v. Bush	June 28, 2004	Supreme Court case
Combatant status review tribunal process	July 7, 2004	Process established by U.S. Department of Defense
Detainee Treatment Act of 2005	December 30, 2005	Public Law 109–148
Hamdan v. Rumsfeld	June 29, 2006	Supreme Court case
Military Commissions Act	October 17, 2006	Public Law 109–366, Title X
Boumediene v. Bush	June 12, 2008	Supreme Court case

SOURCE: Created by Kim Masters Evans for Cengage Learning, Gale, 2008

planned, authorized, committed, or aided the terrorist attacks that occurred on September 11, 2001, or harbored such organizations or persons, in order to prevent any future acts of international terrorism against the United States by such nations, organizations or persons."

Two months later President Bush signed the military order "The Detention, Treatment, and Trial of Certain Non-citizens in the War against Terrorism" (November 13, 2001, http://www.whitehouse.gov/news/releases/2001/11/20011113-27.html), which granted him power to determine whether or not a captured person was a member of al Qaeda and had committed terrorist acts or harbored terrorists. It also stated that military commissions (or tribunals) would be used to try unlawful enemy combatants captured during the War on Terror.

***HAMDI V. RUMSFELD* AND *RASUL V. BUSH*.** In June 2004 the U.S. Supreme Court made two rulings regarding detainee legal rights. The first ruling, *Hamdi v. Rumsfeld* (542 U.S. 507), involved an American citizen named Yaser Esam Hamdi. Hamdi was captured in Afghanistan during 2001 by forces of the Northern Alliance, a rebel group working with the United States to overthrow the Taliban. Hamdi was accused of being part of a Taliban military unit. He was turned over to U.S. authorities, who labeled him an enemy combatant. Initially imprisoned at Guantánamo, Hamdi was transferred to a U.S. brig in 2002 after authorities learned that he was an American citizen. His father filed a petition for a writ of habeas corpus alleging that his son was being held illegally without access to legal counsel and without being formally charged with a crime, both of which violate the U.S. Constitution. The Supreme Court ruled in favor of Hamdi, finding that even though the military had the authority to detain him, he had the right as a U.S. citizen to contest his detention before a "neutral decision-maker." Months after the ruling, Hamdi was released without being charged. The Court did recognize the authority of the executive branch to hold detainees for the duration of the War on Terror.

The second ruling, *Rasul v. Bush* (542 U.S. 466), involved two Australians and twelve Kuwaitis who were being held as enemy combatants at Guantánamo. The detainees filed a petition in U.S. district court challenging the legality of their detention. They claimed they had never been charged with a crime, permitted to have legal counsel, or provided access to the courts. The district court considered the petition a request for habeas corpus and dismissed it, because this right has previously been deemed not to extend to aliens detained outside "United States sovereign territory." However, the U.S. Supreme Court overruled the district court, ruling that the Naval Base Guantánamo Bay is under the "complete jurisdiction and control" of the United States. The ruling precipitated the filing of dozens of habeas petitions on behalf of Guantánamo detainees.

On July 7, 2004, the DOD announced in the press release "Combatant Status Review Tribunal Order Issued" (http://www.defenselink.mil/releases/release.aspx?releaseid=7530) the creation of a Combatant Status Review Tribunal (CSRT) Process for detainees held at the Guantánamo Bay Detention Facility. The DOD described the CSRT "as a forum for detainees to contest their status as enemy combatants."

THE DETAINEE TREATMENT ACT OF 2005. In December 2005 the Detainee Treatment Act of 2005 was signed into law. A summary of the law is provided by Michael John Garcia of the Congressional Research Service (CRS) in *Boumediene v. Bush: Guantanamo Detainees' Right to Habeas Corpus* (June 18, 2008, http://fas.org/sgp/crs/natsec/RL34536.pdf). According to Garcia, the act eliminated the jurisdiction of federal courts to consider habeas claims by aliens that challenged their detention at Guantánamo. The U.S. Court of Appeals for the D.C. Circuit was granted sole jurisdiction over the review of determinations made by CSRTs or military commissions. In other words, the act made clear that alien combatants detained outside the United States do not have constitutional rights. It also stripped the courts of jurisdiction to hear habeas corpus claims from detainees.

***HAMDAN V. RUMSFELD*.** In June 2006 the Supreme Court ruled in *Hamdan v. Rumsfeld* (000 U.S. 05-184) that U.S. law does not allow military tribunals such as those created by President Bush's military order. The case centered on a Yemeni citizen named Salim Ahmed Hamdan, who was allegedly a chauffeur for Osama bin Laden (1957–) in Afghanistan. In 2001 Hamdan was captured during Operation Enduring Freedom and sent to the Guantánamo Bay Detention Facility. In 2004 he was officially charged with conspiracy to commit war crimes, murder, and terrorism. Hamdan's lawyers successfully argued that the president did not have the power under the Constitution to establish military commissions to try enemy combatants. Following the ruling, President Bush announced his intentions to work with Congress to set up a suitable legal process for detained enemy combatants.

On July 7, 2006, the DOD ordered all of its personnel to begin treating detainees in accordance with the Third Geneva Convention, which requires POWs to be afforded certain judicial guarantees (such as the right to challenge their detention). Days later, congressional hearings began on developing a constitutional process for trying detainees. One of the key issues was the handling of classified information during trial. The DOD officials testified that the court-martial process under the Uniform Code of Military Justice is not suitable for detainees, because it could require the release of intelligence information that could harm national security.

THE MILITARY COMMISSIONS ACT OF 2006. The Military Commissions Act of 2006 was the congressional response to

Hamden v. Rumsfeld. It established procedures for the use of military commissions to try alien unlawful enemy combatants who engaged in hostilities against the United States. The act is described in detail by Jennifer K. Elsea of the CRS in *The Military Commissions Act of 2006: Analysis of Procedural Rules and Comparison with Previous DOD Rules and the Uniform Code of Military Justice* (September 27, 2007, http://www.fas.org/sgp/crs/natsec/RL33688.pdf). Elsea explains that the act authorized the president to establish military commissions and allowed the DOD to create rules for the commissions that differed from the rules of the Uniform Code of Military Justice.

In March 2007 the Australian David Hicks was the first Guantánamo Bay detainee sentenced under the Military Commissions Act. Hicks had been detained since 2002 and had been charged with many serious crimes, including attempted murder and conducting terrorist acts for the Taliban in Afghanistan. He ultimately pleaded guilty to only one charge (providing material support for terrorism) and was turned over to Australia to serve the remaining nine months of his sentence.

BOUMEDIENE V. BUSH. In June 2008 the U.S. Supreme Court ruled in *Boumediene v. Bush* (000 U.S. 06-1195; combined with *Al Odah v. United States*) that alien enemy combatants detained at Guantánamo do have the constitutional privilege of habeas corpus. The ruling is described in detail by Garcia, who notes that the Court found unconstitutional the section of the Military Commissions Act that stripped the courts of jurisdiction to hear habeas corpus claims.

In "How Guantanamo Ruling Affects Detainees" (*Atlanta Journal-Constitution*, June 15, 2008), Carol J. Williams examines the effects of the ruling on the Guantánamo detainees. Williams reports that at the time of the Supreme Court ruling there were approximately 270 detainees at Guantánamo, 250 of which were being held without charge. Nineteen of the detainees had already been charged, and their trials were expected to proceed. Williams notes that lawyers for many of the uncharged detainees believed civilian judges will release the detainees due to lack of government evidence against them.

HAMDAN IS SENTENCED. In August 2008 Hamdan was found guilty of providing material support to terrorism. He was acquitted of a more serious conspiracy charge. Even though Hamdan faced a sentence of life in prison, he was sentenced to only sixty-six months in prison. Because he had already been detained for five years and one month, the judge ruled that Hamdan would serve only five additional months in prison. The sentence was deemed surprisingly light by many in the media. There was also widespread speculation about whether the DOD would, in fact, release Hamdan when his sentence was completed. The DOD has frequently insisted that it will not release any detainee who still poses a threat to U.S. national security. As of September 2008, the DOD had not issued an official statement on its intentions regarding Hamdan's release.

THE GUANTÁNAMO DETAINEE PROCESSES. Table 9.3 shows the official DOD list of legal processes for Guantánamo detainees in effect as of October 2007. Every detainee is eligible for an annual administrative review by DOD personnel to determine whether that individual should continue to be detained or not. These decisions are based on intelligence assessments performed as part of Detainee Operations about the detainee and the threat believed posed by that individual to U.S. national security. Every detainee is also subject to the CSRT process, which determines whether a detainee is designated an enemy combatant. Detainees who are not U.S. citizens are subject to commissions (i.e., military commissions or tribunals) that prosecute enemy combatants who have violated the laws of war.

TABLE 9.3

Legal processes for detainees at Guantánamo Bay (GTMO), October 2007

Process	Definition/purpose	Applies to	Responsibility
Admin review	Annual review to assess whether an individual should be released, transferred or should continue to be detained, based on threat or continued intelligence value.	All GTMO detainees.	Designated civilian official (Secretary of the Navy)
Combatant status review	Determine whether a person meets the criteria to be designated as an enemy combatant.*	All GTMO detainees.	Designated civilian official (Secretary of the Navy)
Commissions	Prosecute enemy combatants who violate the laws of war.	Non-U.S. citizens based upon the individual's participation in al Qaeda and acts of international terrorism.	Office of Military Commissions
Detainee operations	Detain enemy combatants to prevent them from continuing to fight against the U.S. and it allies.	All GTMO detainess.	Joint Task Force (JTF) GTMO

*Enemy combatant is defined as an individual who was part of or supporting Taliban or al Qaeda forces, or associated forces that are engaged in hostilities against the United States or its coalition partners. This includes any person who has committed a belligerent act or has directly supported hostilities in aid of enemy armed forces.

SOURCE: Adapted from "Guantanamo Detainee Processes" in *Guantanamo Detainee Processes*, U.S. Department of Defense, October 2, 2007, http://www.defenselink.mil/news/Sep2005/d20050908process.pdf (accessed August 8, 2008)

ABUSIVE TREATMENT OF DETAINEES

U.S. military operations in Afghanistan and Iraq have resulted in the capture of thousands of enemy combatants, both lawful and unlawful. Some of the methods used by the United States to detain, treat, and interrogate these prisoners have come under harsh criticism. One detention facility in particular became the focus of intense media attention because of disturbing allegations about mistreatment, torture, and abuse. This was the Abu Ghraib Detention Facility near Baghdad, Iraq.

Abu Ghraib

Abu Ghraib was already notorious in Iraq as the location of a prison run by the regime of Saddam Hussein (1937–2006) in which prisoners were routinely tortured and executed. Following the invasion of Iraq in March 2003, the U.S. military began using the facility to detain prisoners. These included both enemy combatants and common criminals. In January 2004 a soldier named Joseph Darby told his commanding officer at Abu Ghraib that fellow soldiers from the 372nd Military Police Company had been abusing prisoners. Darby's statements led the U.S. Army to launch an internal investigation. A few months later the abuses were reported to the public by the television news program *60 Minutes* and in the *New Yorker* magazine. These reports included many digital photos taken by soldiers at Abu Ghraib that showed prisoners posed in sexually explicit positions and enduring humiliating and abusive treatment. Many of the photos included smiling U.S. soldiers posing with the prisoners.

The photos caused an uproar around the world and inflamed anti-American sentiment, particularly among Muslim populations. A series of investigations was launched by U.S. officials. Eventually, the *Final Report of the Independent Panel to Review DoD Detention Operations* (August 2004, http://www.defenselink.mil/news/Aug2004/d20040824finalreport.pdf) was issued by the Independent Panel to Review DOD Detention Operations, a group created by the U.S. secretary of defense Donald Rumsfeld (1932–). The panel concluded that "acts of brutality and purposeless sadism" had been committed at the detention facility by both military police and military intelligence personnel. This "deviant behavior" on the part of U.S. personnel was blamed on "a failure of military leadership and discipline." Aggravating factors included severe overcrowding and understaffing (approximately ninety U.S. personnel were responsible for guarding up to seven thousand prisoners) and frequent attacks on the facility by local insurgents.

The panel found that the abuses depicted in the photographs were conducted primarily for the entertainment of the U.S. personnel involved and were not part of interrogation procedures. In fact, the victims in the photographs were not intelligence targets but civilian or criminal detainees. However, the panel noted that additional "egregious abuses" that were not photographed occurred during interrogation sessions. The lack of clear guidance on interrogation techniques was a major problem. Over the course of several months, U.S. personnel used various versions of interrogation techniques, some of which had only been officially approved for use on certain unlawful combatants at Guantánamo Bay with the specific permission of the secretary of defense.

As of September 2008, eleven U.S. soldiers had been convicted of crimes related to the abuse of detainees at Abu Ghraib. The harshest sentence handed out was ten years in prison. It was imposed on the alleged ringleader of the group, Charles Graner Jr., who was responsible for most of the abuse. In January 2008 the only officer charged in the case, Lieutenant Colonel Steven Jordan, was acquitted of all but one charge: failure to obey an order. He received a reprimand, but no jail time.

Interrogation Techniques

Confusion about appropriate interrogation techniques among U.S. military personnel in Afghanistan and Iraq was well documented in the panel's final report. Table 9.4 lists interrogation techniques that were approved by DOD officials at one point or another between 2002 and 2004 for use on unlawful enemy combatants at the Guantánamo Bay Detention Facility.

The techniques in use during much of 2002 came from the *U.S. Army Field Manual* dating from 1992. In December 2002 Rumsfeld approved additional, more intense, techniques for use under certain conditions and with his express approval on specific detainees at Guantánamo Bay. Many of these techniques lost their approval only a few weeks later in January 2003 after concerns were raised about their legality by military legal experts. U.S. officials later learned that the December 2002 list was widely circulated in Afghanistan and Iraq and some commanders mistakenly assumed it applied to detainees under all circumstances.

In April 2003 the list was revised again, reauthorizing two of the more intense techniques and authorizing three new techniques known as environmental manipulation (such as exposure to loud music), sleep adjustment (changing the regular sleeping hours of a detainee; this technique does not include sleep deprivation), and the false-flag technique (fooling a detainee into believing that he is being questioned by a representative from another country, typically a Muslim country).

In January 2006 a military jury found Lewis Welshofer Jr., a U.S. Army interrogator, guilty of negligent homicide and negligent dereliction of duty for the 2003 death of the Iraqi major general Abed Hamed Mowhoush. Welshofer allegedly put a sleeping bag over Mowhoush (who was bound and gagged) and sat on the Iraqi's chest during

TABLE 9.4

Department of Defense-approved interrogation techniques for Guantánamo Bay detainees, 2004

Interrogation techniques	FM 34–52 (1992) Jan 02–01 Dec 02	Secretary of Defense approved tiered system 02 Dec 02–15 Jan 03	FM 34–52 (1992) with some Cat I 16 Jan 03–15 Apr 03	Secretary of Defense memo 16 Apr 03–present
Direct questioning	X	X	X	X
Incentive/removal of incentive	X	X	X	X
Emotional love	X	X	X	X
Emotional hate	X	X	X	X
Fear up harsh	X	X	X	X
Fear up mild	X	X	X	X
Reduced fear	X	X	X	X
Pride and ego up	X	X	X	X
Pride and ego down	X	X	X	X
Futility	X	X	X	X
We know all	X	X	X	X
Establish your identity	X	X	X	X
Repetition approach	X	X	X	X
File and dossier	X	X	X	X
Mutt and Jeff				X*
Rapid fire	X	X	X	X
Silence	X	X	X	X
Change of scene	X	X	X	X
Yelling		X (Cat I)	X	
Deception		X (Cat I)		
Multiple interrogators		X (Cat I)	X	
Interrogator identity		X (Cat I)	X	
Stress positions, like standing		X (Cat II)		
False documents/reports		X (Cat II)		
Isolation for up to 30 days		X (Cat II)		X*
Deprivation of light/auditory stimuli		X (Cat II)		
Hooding (transportation & questioning)		X (Cat II)		
20-interrogations		X (Cat II)		
Removal of ALL comfort items, including religious items		X (Cat II)		
MRE-only diet		X (Cat II)		X*
Removal of clothing		X (Cat II)		
Forced grooming		X (Cat II)		
Exploiting individual phobias, e.g. dogs		X (Cat II)		
Mild, non-injurious physical contact, e.g. grabbing, poking or light pushing		X (Cat III)		
Environmental manipulation				X
Sleep adjustment				X
False flag				X

*Techniques require SOUTHCOM approval and SECDEF notification.
Notes: MRE=meal, ready to eat. FM=field manual. Cat=category.

SOURCE: "Evolution of Interrogation Techniques—GTMO," in *Final Report of the Independent Panel to Review DoD Detention Operations*, U.S. Department of Defense, August 2004, http://www.defenselink.mil/news/Aug2004/d20040824finalreport.pdf (accessed August 11, 2008)

questioning. An autopsy found the general died of suffocation. Welshofer was originally charged with murder but was acquitted of that charge. He was given a reprimand, fined $6,000, and ordered to undergo virtual house arrest for sixty days—a sentence that the article "Officer to Serve No Jail Time for Iraqi General's Death" (*USA Today*, January 23, 2006) said was "surprisingly light." During his trial the defense argued that Welshofer was under high pressure from his superiors to obtain information from Mowhoush but had no clear guidance on what interrogation techniques were unacceptable. The incident occurred at a U.S. military base nicknamed "Blacksmith Hotel" near Al-Qaim, Iraq.

FBI Report on Interrogation Techniques

In *A Review of the FBI's Involvement in and Observations of Detainee Interrogations in Guantanamo Bay, Afghanistan, and Iraq* (May 2008, http://www.usdoj.gov/oig/special/s0805/final.pdf), the U.S. Department of Justice's Office of the Inspector General (OIG) summarizes its findings regarding the observations and participation of Federal Bureau of Investigation (FBI) agents in detainee interrogations conducted at military facilities in Guantánamo Bay, Afghanistan, and Iraq between 2001 and 2004. The OIG reviewed relevant documents, interviewed over two hundred witnesses, and surveyed more than one thousand FBI agents as part of the investigation. The public version of the report is unclassified, but has been edited to censor certain information.

The OIG concludes that "the vast majority of FBI agents complied with FBI interview policies and separated themselves from interrogators who used non-FBI techniques." The OIG acknowledges that FBI agents witnessed interrogation techniques "that caused them concern." Questions and protests made by FBI agents in the field to the interrogators "sometimes resulted in friction between the FBI and the military." This was particularly true at Guantánamo Bay, where FBI agents reported serious concern about military interrogation techniques used against certain "high-value" detainees, including Muhammad Al-Qahtani (1979–). Al-Qahtani is believed to be involved in the planning of the 9/11 attacks. FBI agents complained that during late 2002 and early 2003 Al-Qahtani was subjected to many "aggressive techniques" including being put on a leash and forced to do dog tricks, held in "stress positions," having women's underwear put on his head, and ordered to pray to an idol shrine. The OIG found that FBI complaints to the DOD about the legality and effectiveness of these techniques were never officially addressed.

In total, more than two hundred FBI agents who served at Guantánamo reported witnessing or hearing about "harsh" interrogation techniques used by the military. Some of these techniques were in violation of DOD regulations effective at the time. A smaller unnamed number of FBI agents reported similar problems in Afghanistan. Over three hundred FBI agents reported observing or hearing about "harsh" interrogation techniques used by the military on detainees in Iraq. (See Table 9.5.) One hundred and twelve of the agents personally observed these techniques. However, the OIG notes that the "vast majority" of FBI agents stationed at Guantánamo Bay, Afghanistan, and Iraq reported neither observing or hearing about harsh interrogation techniques.

Redefining War Crimes?

In August 2006 Bush administration officials appeared before Congress and asked for clarification of how the Third Geneva Convention is to be applied under U.S. law to detainees. Specifically, the officials asked for a definition of what constitutes "outrages upon personal dignity, in particular, humiliating and degrading treatment" under Common Article 3, section (1)(c). Alberto Gonzales (1955–), the U.S. attorney general, asked Congress to establish a list of offenses that would be considered war crimes under the War Crimes Act of 1996 as violations of Common Article 3.

Some observers believe the Bush administration is worried that top U.S. officials could be charged under the War Crimes Act in light of the Supreme Court decision that detainees are covered by the Geneva Conventions. In "War Crimes Act Changes Would Reduce Threat of Prosecution" (*Washington Post*, August 9, 2006), R. Jeffrey Smith notes that the Bush administration has drafted amendments to the War Crimes Act that would omit the language barring "humiliating and degrading treatment."

Critics charge that President Bush and top administration officials have already committed war crimes. For example, Jeremy Brecher and Brendan Smith claim in "Senate Vote Advances President's Effort to Kill War Crimes Act" (*The Nation*, September 22, 2006) that the amendment to the War Crimes Act will be retroactive, meaning that past offenses will not be prosecutable. Brecher and Smith state that the amendment is designed solely to protect certain individuals (including the president) from charges of war crimes.

New Detainee Rules

In December 2005 Congress approved a 2006 DOD appropriations bill including an amendment outlawing the use of torture or cruel and inhuman treatment of detainees by military and civilian federal agencies. The Detainee Treatment Act of 2005 was proposed by Senator John McCain (1936–; R-AZ), who was a POW during the Vietnam War (1955–1975). It requires that military interrogators use only interrogation techniques listed in the *U.S. Army Field Manual*, which adheres to the requirements of the Third Geneva Convention for the treatment of POWs.

On September 5, 2006, the DOD issued Directive 2310.01E (http://www.dtic.mil/whs/directives/corres/pdf/231001p.pdf) regarding the DOD's Detainee Program. The directive concerns all detainee operations conducted by DOD personnel (military and civilian) and DOD contractors. It states that "all detainees shall be treated humanely and in accordance with U.S. law, the law of war, and applicable U.S. policy." Specifically, all detainees, regardless of legal status, are entitled to the protections of Common Article 3 of the Geneva Conventions. The directive also lists additional minimum standards of treatment for all detainees.

On September 6, 2006, the U.S. Army released a new version of the *U.S. Army Field Manual*, known as *FM 2-22.3 (FM 34-52) Human Intelligence Collector Operations* (http://www.army.mil/institution/armypublicaffairs/pdf/fm2-22-3.pdf). The new manual is nearly four hundred pages long and provides detailed guidance and instructions on conducting human intelligence (HUMINT) operations. Included in the fifth chapter of the manual is a section on interrogation, which notes that cruel, inhuman, and degrading treatment of detainees is prohibited. The manual states, "Use of torture is not only illegal but also it is a poor technique that yields unreliable results, may damage subsequent collection efforts, and can induce the source to say what he thinks the HUMINT collector wants to hear. Use of torture can also have many possible negative consequences at national and international levels." Specific prohibitions on the treatment of detainees are listed in Table 9.6.

TABLE 9.5

Survey of FBI agents who observed interrogation techniques in Iraq between March 2003 and December 2004

	Interrogation technique	Personally observed	Observations led me to believe	Detainee told me	Others described to me	None of the above
1	Depriving a detainee of food or water	—	—	1	2	284
2	Depriving a detainee of clothing	5	3	3	5	273
3	Depriving a detainee of sleep, or interrupting sleep by frequent cell relocations or other methods	10	6	7	28	234
4	Beating a detainee	—	3	7	4	274
5	Using water to prevent breathing by a detainee or to create the sensation of drowning	1	—	—	—	287
6	Using hands, rope, or anything else to choke or strangle a detainee	—	—	—	—	287
7	Threatening other action to cause physical pain, injury, disfigurement, or death	1	—	2	—	281
8	Other treatment or action causing significant physical pain or injury, or causing disfigurement or death	—	1	2	—	287
9	Placing a detainee on a hot surface or burning a detainee	—	3	4	—	281
10	Using shackles or other restraints in a prolonged manner	6	—	1	5	277
11	Requiring a detainee to maintain, or restraining a detainee in, a stressful or painful position	6	1	2	5	274
12	Forcing a detainee to perform demanding physical exercise	1	—	1	4	277
13	Using electrical shock on a detainee	—	—	1	2	283
14	Threatening to use electrical shock on a detainee	—	—	—	—	289
15	Intentionally delaying or denying detainee medical care	—	—	—	—	289
16	Hooding or blindfolding a detainee other than during transportation	22	3	—	1	260
17	Subjecting a detainee to extremely cold or hot room temperatures for extended periods	1	1	1	1	285
18	Subjecting a detainee to loud music	11	1	3	19	252
19	Subjecting a detainee to bright flashing lights or darkness	6	1	2	7	268
20	Isolating a detainee for an extended period	20	1	1	6	257
21	Using duct tape to restrain, gag, or punish a detainee	1	—	—	1	286
22	Using rapid response teams and/or forced cell extractions	2	3	1	9	275
23	Using a military working dog on or near a detainee other than during detainee transportation	1	—	—	3	285
24	Threatening to use military working dogs on or near a detainee	2	—	—	1	284
25	Using spiders, scorpions, snakes, or other animals on or near a detainee	—	—	—	—	288
26	Threatening to use spiders, scorpions, snakes, or other animals on a detainee	—	—	—	—	287
27	Disrespectful statements, handling, or actions involving the Koran	—	—	2	—	287
28	Shaving a detainee's facial or other hair to embarrass or humiliate a detainee	2	—	1	1	285
29	Placing a woman's clothing on a detainee	—	—	—	—	286
30	Touching a detainee or acting toward a detainee in a sexual manner	—	—	—	—	290
31	Holding detainee(s) who were not officially acknowledged or registered as such by the agency detaining the person.	1	2	—	4	280
32	Sending a detainee to another country for more aggressive interrogation	2	—	2	5	279
33	Threatening to send a detainee to another country for detention or more aggressive interrogation	6	—	—	2	278
34	Threatening to take action against a detainee's family	3	—	2	1	283
35	Other treatment or action causing severe emotional or psychological trauma to a detainee	—	—	—	—	290
36	Other religious or sexual harassment or humiliation of a detainee	1	—	—	—	287
37	Other treatment of a detainee that in your opinion was unprofessional, unduly harsh or aggressive, coercive, abusive, or unlawful	1	1	—	1	284
	Observation totals	**112**	**30**	**46**	**117**	**10,333**

SOURCE: "Table 10.1. Survey Results Concerning Interrogation Techniques Observed in Iraq," in *A Review of the FBI's Involvement in and Observations of Detainee Interrogations in Guantanamo Bay Afghanistan, and Iraq*, U.S. Department of Justice, Office of the Inspector General, May 2008, http://www.usdoj.gov/oig/special/s0805/final.pdf (accessed August 8, 2008)

Secret CIA Prisons Revealed

In "CIA Holds Terror Suspects in Secret Prisons" (*Washington Post*, November 5, 2005), Dana Priest accuses the Bush administration of operating secret overseas prisons for high-level detainees captured in the War on Terror. The prison system allegedly included facilities in several countries in eastern Europe and Thailand and was conducted with the cooperation of those governments. Priest claims that Central Intelligence Agency (CIA) interrogators were allowed to use "enhanced" interrogation techniques, such as waterboarding, that are prohibited by international law and the U.S. military. Waterboarding is an interrogation technique in which a prisoner is strapped to a board that is lowered into water in such a way that the prisoner believes he is going to drown.

On September 6, 2006, President Bush (http://www.whitehouse.gov/news/releases/2006/09/20060906-3.html) admitted in a speech that the CIA had been operating secret overseas prisons, but he denied that the detainees had been tortured, claiming they had been subjected to techniques that "were tough, and they were safe and lawful and necessary." All the detainees were believed to have been transferred to military control.

TABLE 9.6

List of detainee treatments specifically prohibited by U.S. Army Field Manual, 2006

Section 5-74
Specifically prohibited treatments under all circumstances:
Forcing an individual to perform or simulate sexual acts or to pose in a sexual manner.
Exposing an individual to outrageously lewd and sexually provocative behavior.
Intentionally damaging or destroying an individual's religious articles.
Section 5-75
Specifically prohibited treatments during interrogations:
Forcing the detainee to be naked, perform sexual acts, or pose in a sexual manner.
Placing hoods or sacks over the head of a detainee; using duct tape over the eyes.
Applying beatings, electric shock, burns, or other forms of physical pain.
"Waterboarding."
Using military working dogs.
Inducing hypothermia or heat injury.
Conducting mock executions.
Depriving the detainee of necessary food, water, or medical care.

SOURCE: Adapted from "Cruel, Inhuman or Degrading Treatment Prohibited," in *FM 2-22.3 (FM 34-52) Human Intelligence Collector Operations*, U.S. Army, September 6, 2006, http://www.army.mil/institution/armypublicaffairs/pdf/fm2-22-3.pdf (accessed August 11, 2008)

In July 2007 President Bush issued an executive order that CIA interrogations of terror suspects will be conducted in accordance with Common Article 3 of the Geneva Conventions. Later that year the director of the CIA admitted that videotapes of some detainee interrogations had been destroyed by the agency.

Amnesty International

The London-based Amnesty International (AI) is a private independent group that is concerned with protecting human rights around the world. It has been a vocal critic of U.S. policies toward detainees. In *Report 2006: The State of the World's Human Rights* (2006, http://www.amnestyusa.org/state-of-the-world-report/2006/page.do?id=1041003&n1=2&n2=18amp;&n3=782), the AI claims the United States is holding thousands of detainees without charge and operating secret detention facilities called "black sites" in various countries. The AI also accuses U.S. officials of practicing rendition (exporting U.S.-held detainees to countries known to practice torture). The AI insists that detainees at Guantánamo Bay are subjected to cruel, inhuman, or degrading treatment and that top U.S. officials "may have been responsible for war crimes and crimes against humanity."

In *Report 2008: The State of the World's Human Rights* (2008, http://thereport.amnesty.org/document/101), the AI claims that hundreds of detainees at Guantánamo Bay were being held without charges in inhumane conditions in 2007. The AI says many of the detainees are held for up to twenty-four hours per day in windowless cells and are suffering from physical and mental health problems due to their confinement. The organization also alleges that some of the detainees have complained during their CSRT hearings of being tortured, but the allegations have been deleted from the official transcripts of the hearings.

UN Criticisms

In May 2006 U.S. officials conducted an oral presentation before the UN Committee against Torture to present the United States' second required periodic report under the UN Convention against Torture and Other Cruel, Inhuman, or Degrading Treatment or Punishment. In "United States Presents Report to U.N. Anti-torture Committee" (May 5, 2006, http://www.globalsecurity.org/security/library/news/2006/05/sec-060505-usia03.htm), Vince Crawley reports the U.S. delegation claimed that "relatively few actual cases of abuse" had occurred, and that those cases had been addressed by authorities and did not represent widespread commission of torture by the United States in its War on Terror. U.S. officials noted that over 600 investigations had been performed into allegations of detainee abuse and over 250 Americans had been "held accountable." In addition, the delegation charged that many allegations of U.S. torture of detainees were unsupported and exaggerated to the point of being "absurd."

The Committee against Torture responded to the United States in *Consideration of Reports Submitted by State Parties under Article 19 of the Convention* (July 25, 2006). The committee acknowledged a handful of "positive aspects" in U.S. compliance with the convention but presented more than a dozen "concerns" about U.S. treatment of detainees. The major concerns relate to allegations of secret detention facilities that are not accessible to the ICRC, "enforced disappearances" of suspects, detainees being deprived of "fundamental legal safeguards," and detainee renditions (transfers) to countries believed to practice torture. The committee also noted that holding detainees indefinitely without charging them violates the convention and recommended that the Guantánamo Bay Detention Facility be closed as soon as possible.

In "United States Says U.N. Torture Report Ignored Crucial Data" (May 19, 2006, http://www.globalsecurity.org/security/library/news/2006/05/sec-060519-usia01.htm), the U.S. Department of State expressed disappointment in the committee report, complaining that it contained "numerous errors" and failed to acknowledge important information submitted by the U.S. delegation. The United States also accused the Committee against Terror of exceeding its authority for recommending closure of the Guantánamo Bay Detention Facility.

PUBLIC OPINION

Torture

Darren K. Carlson of the Gallup Organization reports in *Public Believes U.S. Government Has Tortured Prisoners*

(November 29, 2005, http://www.gallup.com/poll/20170/Public-Believes-US-Government-Has-Tortured-Prisoners.aspx) that in November 2005, 74% of Americans believed U.S. troops or government officials have tortured prisoners in Iraq or in other countries, whereas 20% believed torture has not taken place. Carlson notes that this poll was conducted only weeks after President Bush and Porter J. Goss (1938–), the chief of the CIA, assured the American public that prisoners in the War on Terror are not being tortured.

During the same poll respondents were asked whether they are willing to have the government torture known terrorists who know details about future terrorist attacks. Carlson notes in *Would Americans Fight Terrorism by Any Means Necessary?* (March 1, 2005, http://www.gallup.com/poll/15073/Would-Americans-Fight-Terrorism-Any-Means-Necessary.aspx) that this same question was asked by Gallup pollsters in October 2001 (only weeks after the September 11, 2001, terrorist attacks) and in January 2005. In all three polls, a majority of respondents opposed the use of torture to obtain vital information about future attacks. In November 2005, 56% of those asked had this viewpoint, compared to 38% who were willing to use torture.

In *War on Terrorism* (2008, http://www.gallup.com/poll/5257/War-Terrorism.aspx), the Gallup Organization indicates that in January 2005 people were asked about the appropriateness of using various interrogation techniques on prisoners suspected of knowing information about possible future attacks against the United States. Eighty-five percent thought it was wrong to permit female interrogators to have physical contact with Muslim men during religious observances that prohibit that kind of contact. Many people (82%) were also opposed to the use of waterboarding. Seventy-nine percent of those asked expressed disapproval for forcing naked prisoners into uncomfortable positions in cold rooms for several hours, and 69% were opposed to using dogs to threaten prisoners. There was less opposition to the idea of transporting prisoners to countries known to practice torture. Sixty-two percent of respondents felt this practice was wrong. The least objectionable of the interrogation techniques was sleep deprivation. Only 48% of respondents were opposed to depriving prisoners of sleep for several days.

The CIA and the Geneva Conventions

A Gallup poll conducted in September 2006 found that a majority of Americans (57%) believed the CIA should abide by the Geneva Convention standards when questioning suspects believed to have information about possible terror plots against the United States. (See Table 9.7.) Thirty-eight percent of respondents said the CIA should be able to use "more forceful interrogation techniques" than those permitted by the Geneva Conventions.

TABLE 9.7

Public opinion on whether the CIA should abide by the Geneva Conventions when questioning suspects about terror plots, September 2006

WHEN INTERROGATING PRISONERS, MEMBERS OF THE U.S. MILITARY ARE REQUIRED TO ABIDE BY THE GENEVA CONVENTION STANDARDS WHICH PROHIBIT THE HUMILIATING AND DEGRADING TREATMENT OF PRISONERS. WHEN THE CIA OR CENTRAL INTELLIGENCE AGENCY QUESTIONS SUSPECTS WHOM THEY BELIEVE TO HAVE INFORMATION ABOUT POSSIBLE TERROR PLOTS AGAINST THE UNITED STATES, DO YOU THINK—[FORM A: READ 1–2; FORM B: READ 2–1]—THEY SHOULD HAVE TO ABIDE BY THE SAME GENEVA CONVENTION STANDARDS THAT APPLY TO THE U.S. MILITARY, OR THEY SHOULD BE ABLE TO USE MORE FORCEFUL INTERROGATION TECHNIQUES THAN THE GENEVA CONVENTION STANDARDS THAT APPLY TO THE U.S. MILITARY?

Scale	%
They should have to abide by the same Geneva Convention standards that apply to the U.S. military	56.66
They should be able to use more forceful interrogation techniques than the Geneva Convention standards that apply to the U.S. military	38.36
Other/depends (vol.)	2.04
Don't know	2.62
Refused	0.31

(vol.) = Volunteered response.

SOURCE: Adapted from "Question qn19. When Interrogating Prisoners, Members of the U.S. Military Are Required to Abide by the Geneva Convention Standards Which Prohibit the Humiliating and Degrading Treatment of Prisoners. When the CIA or Central Intelligence Agency Questions Suspects Whom They Believe to Have Information about Possible Terror Plots against the United States, Do You Think—They Should Have to Abide by the Same Geneva Convention Standards That Apply to the U.S. Military, or They Should Be Able to Use More Forceful Interrogation Techniques Than the Geneva Convention Standards That Apply to the U.S. Military?" in *September Wave 1*, The Gallup Organization, September 2006, http://brain.gallup.com/documents/question.aspx?question=158580&Advanced=0&SearchConType=1&SearchTypeAll=interrogation (accessed August 8, 2008). Copyright © 2006 by The Gallup Organization. Reproduced by permission of The Gallup Organization.

Closing the Guantánamo Bay Detention Facility

In July 2007 Gallup asked poll participants their opinion about whether the United States should close the Guantánamo Bay Detention Facility. A majority (54%) of respondents said the facility should not be closed. (See Figure 9.1.) Another 33% favored closing the facility, and 13% were unsure or refused to answer.

FIGURE 9.1

Public opinion on whether the prison at Guantánamo Bay should be closed, July 2007

DO YOU THINK THE UNITED STATES SHOULD—OR SHOULD NOT—CLOSE THE PRISON AT THE GUANTANAMO BAY MILITARY BASE IN CUBA?

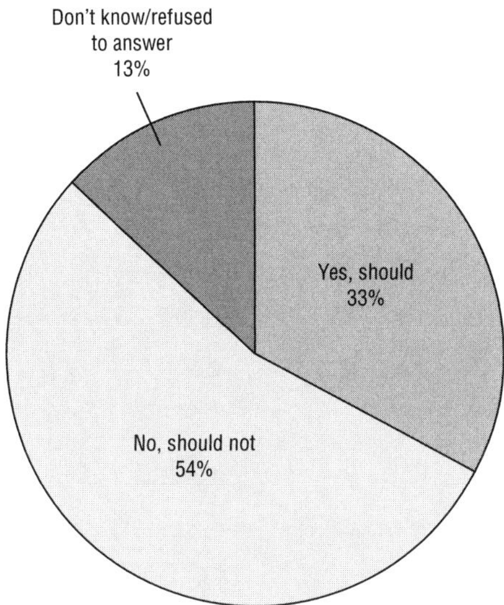

SOURCE: Adapted from "Question qn44. Do You Think the United States Should—or Should Not—Close the Prison at the Guantanamo Bay Military Base in Cuba?" in *July Wave 1*, The Gallup Organization, July 2007, http://brain.gallup.com/documents/questionnaire.aspx?STUDY=P0707023 (accessed August 8, 2008). Copyright © 2007 by The Gallup Organization. Reproduced by permission of The Gallup Organization.

CHAPTER 10

U.S. RELATIONS WITH THE ISLAMIC WORLD

Since the end of World War II (1939–1945) international terrorism has become a serious threat to U.S. national security. The vast majority of terrorist acts committed against Americans during this period were perpetrated by Muslims, or at least by people who claim to be acting in accordance with Islamic principles. This raises troubling issues about the nature and future of relations between the United States and Muslims around the world. Do terrorists who claim to be Muslims represent the true spirit of Islam, or are they rebels and rogues who have hijacked the religion for their own violent purposes? How deep are the political and cultural differences between the West and the Islamic world?

WHAT IS ISLAM?

Islam translates into English as "submission" and advocates submission to God by its followers. As described in Chapter 1, Muslims believe that Islam was introduced to Arabic tribes during the seventh century via messages from God revealed by the angel Gabriel to the prophet Muhammad (c. 570–632). Those messages were eventually written down to form the Koran, Islam's holy book.

Sharia is the body of Islamic law and is based on the Koran. It covers all aspects of life, rather than just matters of a legal nature. The Hadith are also important to Muslims. They are a collection of Muhammad's sayings and actions that help Muslims follow a way of life (called Sunna) modeled after the example of Muhammad and based on the Koran.

The Council for American Islamic Relations (CAIR) notes in "About Islam and American Muslims" (2008, http://www.cair.com/AboutIslam/IslamBasics.aspx) that there are five pillars of Islam:

- Declaration of faith—a person becomes a Muslim by declaring the following: "There is no deity but God, and Muhammad is the messenger of God"
- Obligatory prayers—Muslims are required to pray five times per day at set times
- Zakat—this is charitable giving to those in need
- Fasting—Muslims fast from sunrise to sunset during the Islamic lunar month called Ramadan if they are physically able to do so
- Hajj—this is a pilgrimage to Mecca, a sacred site in Saudi Arabia, that all Muslims are supposed to make at least once during their lifetime if they are physically and financially able to do so

Islam recognizes many prophets from the Judeo-Christian tradition, including Abraham (c. 1996–c. 1821 B.C.), Jacob (1838?–1689 B.C.), Moses (1392?–1272? B.C.), David (1000–c. 960 B.C.), and Solomon (985?–925? B.C.). Unlike Christians, Muslims believe that Jesus (4? B.C.–A.D. 29?) was a prophet rather than a divine messiah. Islam lacks a centralized leadership. There is no single religious leader (such as the pope in Roman Catholicism) who speaks on behalf of all Muslims. In fact, there is not even a structured hierarchy. Islam esteems many respected elders, learned men, and Islamic scholars, some of whom have titles such as mufti (judge) or sheikh (sheik). Prayer, worship, and other religious activities often take place at mosques, which are meeting places for Muslims.

The Diversity of Islam

Different people practice Islam in different ways around the world. While they agree on certain core tenets, they may diverge over many other aspects of their faith. In some cases they may disagree so strongly that one group will not recognize another as being Muslim at all.

In this, Islam is no different than any other active and widespread faith or ideology. For example, there are many differences among those who call themselves Christians. Furthermore, the form of government practiced in the United States is different from that found in the United Kingdom or Russia, but all three nations refer to themselves as democratic.

THE ISLAMIC WORLD

It is a common misconception among Americans that Muslims are Arabs from the Middle East. According to CAIR, in "About Islam and American Muslims," there are approximately 1.2 billion Muslims in the world, and less than 20% of them live in Arabic countries.

Figure 10.1 is a map created by the U.S. Government Accountability Office (GAO) that shows countries with "significant" Muslim populations. Table 10.1 is a GAO-provided list of the countries. Interestingly, India is not included in the list (or designated on the map as having a significant Muslim population). However, in "Background Note: India" (June 2008, http://www.state.gov/r/pa/ei/bgn/3454.htm), the U.S. Department of State (DOS) indicates that India's Muslim population is at least 138 million. Combining this statistic with data from Table 10.1 provides the following list of countries with the highest Muslim populations:

- Indonesia—213 million
- Pakistan—158 million
- India—138 million
- Bangladesh—120 million
- Egypt—73 million
- Turkey—70 million
- Iran—67 million
- Nigeria—64 million

Together, these eight countries account for approximately three-fourths of the world's total Muslim population.

FIGURE 10.1

Map of countries with significant Muslim populations, 2006

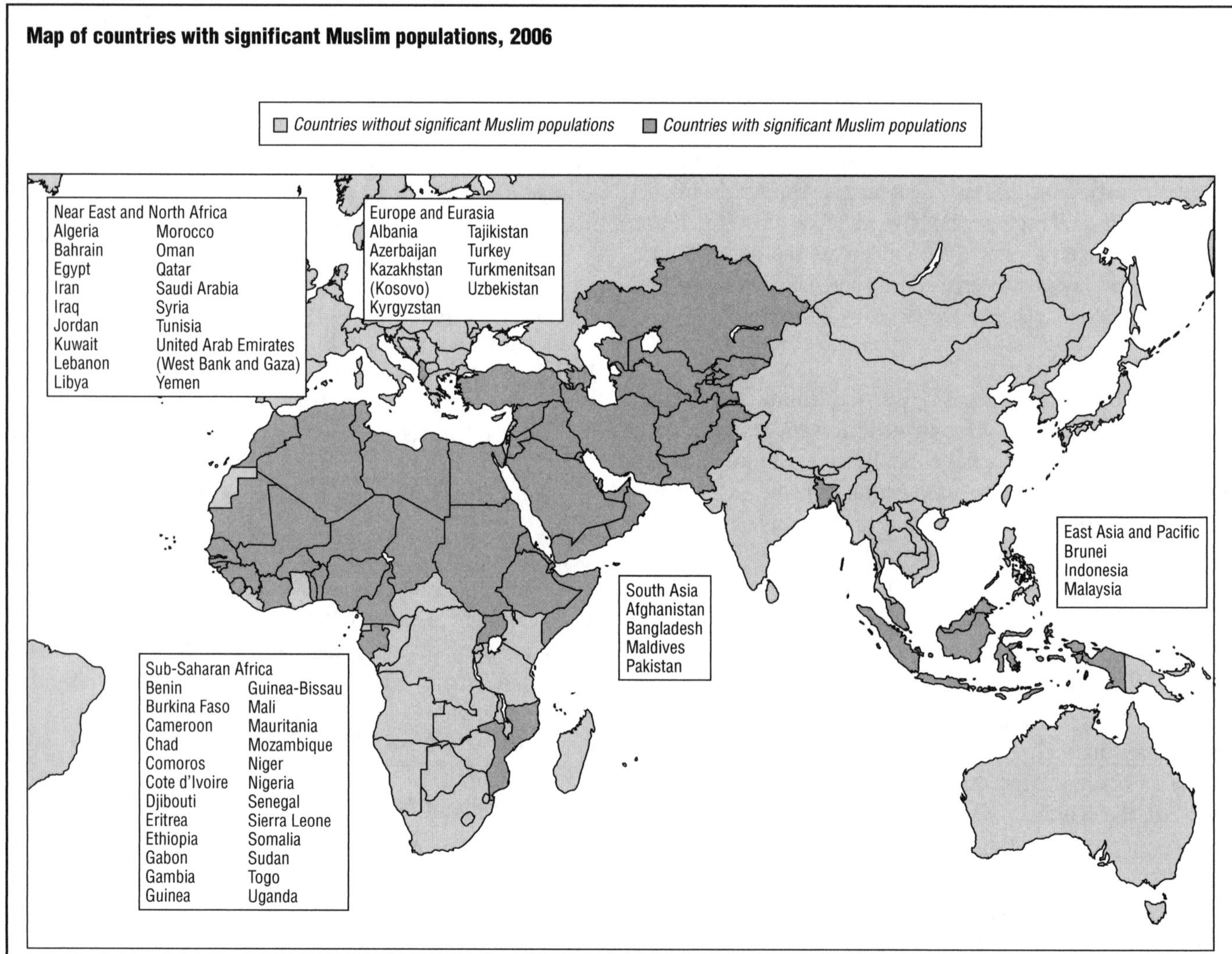

SOURCE: "Figure 1. Map of the Muslim World," in *U.S. Public Diplomacy: State Department Efforts to Engage Muslim Audiences Lack Certain Communication Elements and Face Significant Challenges*, U.S. Government Accountability Office, May 2006, http://www.gao.gov/new.items/d06535.pdf (accessed August 11, 2008)

TABLE 10.1

Countries and territories with significant Muslim populations, 2006

Region	Country	Population*	Percentage Muslim
Africa	Benin	7.5	20%
	Burkina Faso	13.9	50
	Cameroon	16.4	20
	Chad	9.8	51
	Comoros	0.7	98
	Cote d'Ivoire	17.3	35–40
	Djibouti	0.5	94
	Eritrea	4.6	>50
	Ethiopia	73.1	45–50
	Gabon	1.4	<1
	Gambia	1.6	90
	Guinea	9.5	85
	Guinea-Bissau	1.4	45
	Mali	12.3	90
	Mauritania	3.1	100
	Mozambique	19.4	18
	Niger	11.7	80
	Nigeria	128.8	50
	Senegal	11.1	94
	Sierra Leone	6.0	60
	Somalia	8.6	>50
	Sudan	40.2	70
	Togo	5.7	20
	Uganda	27.3	16
East Asia and Pacific	Brunei	0.4	67
	Indonesia	242.0	88
	Malaysia	24.0	60
Europe and Eurasia	Albania	3.6	70
	Azerbaijan	7.9	93
	Kazakhstan	15.2	47
	Kosovo	—	—
	Kyrgyzstan	5.1	75
	Tajikistan	7.2	90
	Turkey	69.7	100
	Turkmenistan	5.0	89
	Uzbekistan	26.9	88
Near East	Algeria	32.5	99
	Bahrain	0.7	100
	Egypt	77.5	94
	Iran	68.0	98
	Iraq	26.1	97
	Jordan	5.8	92
	Kuwait	2.3	85
	Lebanon	3.8	60
	Libya	5.8	97
	Morocco	32.7	99
	Oman	3.0	>75
	Qatar	0.9	95
	Saudi Arabia	26.4	100
	Syria	18.4	74
	Tunisia	10.1	98
	United Arab Emirates	2.6	96
	West Bank and Gaza	3.8	75
	Yemen	20.7	90
South Asia	Afghanistan	29.9	99
	Bangladesh	144.3	83
	Maldives	0.3	>50
	Pakistan	162.4	97

Note: As defined by the State Department's Bureau of Educational and Cultural Affairs.
*In millions.

SOURCE: "Appendix II. Countries and Territories with Significant Muslim Populations," in *U.S. Public Diplomacy: State Department Efforts to Engage Muslim Audiences Lack Certain Communication Elements and Face Significant Challenges*, U.S. Government Accountability Office, May 2006, http://www.gao.gov/new.items/d06535.pdf (accessed August 11, 2008)

FIGURE 10.2

Projected populations of 18- to 35-year-olds, by selected countries, 2010–20

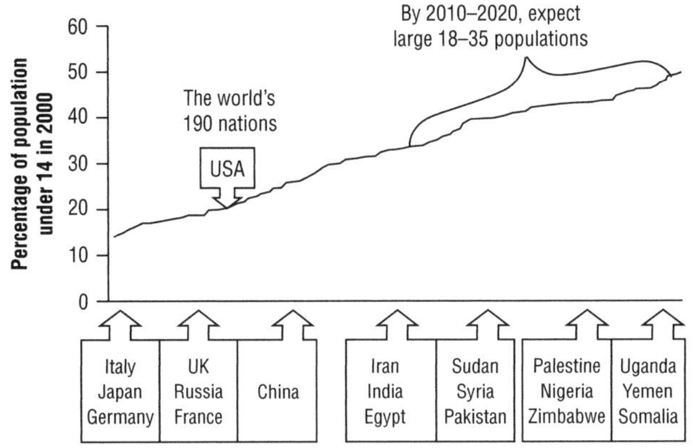

Percentage of population under 14 in 2000
60
50
40
30
20
10
0
By 2010–2020, expect large 18–35 populations
The world's 190 nations
USA
Italy Japan Germany
UK Russia France
China
Iran India Egypt
Sudan Syria Pakistan
Palestine Nigeria Zimbabwe
Uganda Yemen Somalia

SOURCE: "Illustration 3. By 2010+, 18–35 Cohorts in Unstable Countries," in *DIA Workforce of the Future: Creating the Future of the Defense Intelligence Agency*, U.S. Department of Defense, Defense Intelligence Agency, May 15, 2003, http://www.dia.mil/thisisdia/DIA_Workforce_of_the_Future.pdf (accessed August 11, 2008)

Many countries in the Islamic world are experiencing explosive population growth. Figure 10.2 is a chart prepared by the U.S. Department of Defense's (DOD) Defense Intelligence Agency. It ranks various countries in terms of the percentage of their population that was younger than fourteen as of 2000. During the 2010s these youngsters will be between eighteen and thirty-five years old—an age range commonly considered appropriate for military service and of particular concern to the DOD because of national security implications. As indicated in the chart, several countries considered "unstable" by the DOD will contain large numbers of people aged eighteen to thirty-five in the next decade. The list includes Egypt, India, Iran, Nigeria, Pakistan, Palestine, Somalia, Sudan, Syria, Uganda, and Yemen—all areas with significant Muslim populations.

HISTORICAL CONTEXT FOR U.S. RELATIONS

The roots of U.S.-Muslim relations trace back to medieval clashes between the Islamic world and the European kingdoms. The Middle Ages encompassed a period in history that began with the fall of the Roman Empire during the fifth century. At one time the Roman Empire covered a great swath of land from western Asia, across the Middle East, and west to Spain and Britain. A remnant—now known as the Byzantine Empire—survived along the eastern Mediterranean Sea and had its capital at Constantinople (modern-day Istanbul, Turkey).

The early centuries of the Middle Ages are called the Dark Ages because few known scientific and cultural achievements were made by Western societies during this time. This was not the case in the Islamic world (which began with the seventh-century establishment of Islam by the prophet Muhammad). Arab and Persian scholars made many important advancements in science and math, particularly algebra, geometry, chemistry, and astronomy. Some historians refer to the period between 750 and 1200 as the Islamic Golden Age.

Crusades

During the Middle Ages Catholic Church authorities wielded great power over the peoples of Europe. This was especially true of the popes—the supreme leaders of the Roman Catholic Church. Catholicism was the dominant religion of Europe throughout the Middle Ages. Medieval Europeans were politically divided among many competing kingdoms and tribal groups. However, they were often united by their shared religion. Such was the case in 1095, when the Byzantine emperor Alexius I Comnenus (c. 1048–1118) asked Pope Urban II (1042?–1099) for military assistance against the Islamic tribes that had recently captured Jerusalem—a city considered sacred by Christians, Jews, and Muslims. According to Paul Halsall, in "Medieval Sourcebook: Urban II—Speech at Clermont 1095" (January 1996, http://www.fordham.edu/halsall/source/urban2a.html), the pope called on Europeans to put aside their internal squabbles and march to the Holy Land to liberate Jerusalem from "a race from the kingdom of the Persians, an accursed race, a race wholly alienated from God."

The pope's speech initiated a wave of religious fervor across Europe. In 1096 armies of European knights and soldiers began the first of what would later be called the Crusades. In 1099 the European armies captured Jerusalem, only to lose it in 1187 to Muslim forces led by Saladin (1138–1193)—a renowned figure in Islamic history. In 1192 Saladin and King Richard I (1157–1199) of England signed a treaty agreeing that Jerusalem would remain under Muslim control but allow visits by Christian pilgrims. Crusaders captured the city again in 1229 only to lose it to the Muslims for the last time in 1244. Thus, for nearly two centuries European armies followed papal orders to fight for control of Muslim-held territory in Spain and the Middle East.

Within Western history and literature, the Crusades have become highly romanticized adventures that focus on the feats of King Richard I and the European knights. In the Islamic world, they are typically seen as a brutal invasion by European nations that foreshadows later colonial rule. Peter Ford reports in "Europe Cringes at Bush 'Crusade' against Terrorists" (*Christian Science Monitor*, September 19, 2001) that President George W. Bush (1946–) was chastised by Muslims after the September 11, 2001 (9/11), terrorist attacks for referring to U.S. retaliation as a "crusade" against terrorism. For Americans, it was a clue that events centuries old still resonate with many Muslim people.

Colonial Resentment

By the thirteenth century the Crusades were ending, and the Islamic world entered a new political age under the rule of the Ottoman Empire (named after Osman I [1259–1326], its first leader). The Ottomans eventually conquered the Byzantine Empire and controlled much of Eurasia. During the 1500s the Ottoman Empire reached the height of its geopolitical importance with territories around the Red, Black, and Mediterranean seas. It included much of modern-day Turkey and the Middle East and extended to the outskirts of modern-day Vienna, Austria, in Europe. A series of wars with European powers and the growth of nationalism within regions controlled by the empire gradually reduced its strength.

The death blow for the Ottoman Empire came during World War I (1914–1918), when it was defeated and dissolved by the Allies. The League of Nations placed Iraq and Palestine under the administration of Great Britain, and Syria and Lebanon were placed under France. All nations but Palestine eventually achieved their independence. The lack of an official homeland for the Palestinians became a major point of contention in the Middle East.

Even before the demise of the Ottoman Empire, most Muslim nations fell under European control at one time or another. Britain, France, and Italy all had colonies in the Middle East and/or North Africa during the 1800s and early 1900s. Even nations that were not colonized experienced some level of protection or influence by European powers, particularly Great Britain. The major exception is Saudi Arabia, which has been under continuous Muslim control for centuries.

By the 1950s most Muslim countries had achieved their independence. However, resentment about colonial rule and interference still play a major factor in Middle Eastern politics. Even though the United States did not exist at the time of the Crusades and was not a colonial power in the Middle East like its European allies, it must still contend with old grievances in the region. In "Roots of Rage" (*Time*, September 23, 2001), Lisa Beyer notes "the U.S. inherits the weight of centuries of Muslim bitterness over the Crusades and other military campaigns, plus decades of indignation over colonialism."

POLITICAL SYSTEMS

There are major differences in the political systems and values found in most Muslim-majority nations and in Western democracies such as the United States. These differences at times contribute to the difficulty of establishing and maintaining good relations between the United States and Muslims.

Most governments in Muslim countries interweave religion and politics. This reflects the fact that many followers of Islam feel that it should govern all aspects of society. They see it as a method for living life, governing nations, and maintaining law and order. These Muslims do not make the distinction between church and state that is common in Western nations. For example, Saudi Arabia uses the Koran and Sunna as its Constitution. Its legal system strictly adheres to the Sharia. According to the Saudi Network, in "Saudi Arabia—Constitution" (September 13, 2008, http://www.the-saudi.net/saudi-arabia/saudi-constitution.htm), the nation's rulers are believed to derive their power from the Koran. The government is a political system called a theocracy (it is considered divinely guided). Iran also has a strongly theocratic government. Since the 1979 Iranian Revolution an Islamic cleric has been the supreme leader and chief of state. As described in Chapter 6, Iran does have elections that determine the nation's president and legislative members. In 2005 Saudi Arabia conducted limited municipal elections; however, only men were allowed to vote. Some governments in the Middle East are more secular than others, with Turkey being considered the most secular nation in the region.

Many Muslim countries are ruled by autocrats (rulers with vast or unlimited power). These include kings in monarchies in which rule remains in the royal family. Examples include Saudi Arabia, Jordan, Morocco, Bahrain, and Kuwait. Other leaders have assumed and hold power through military means, for example, Libya. Several Islamic countries have less autocratic forms of government, including Indonesia and Egypt. Turkey is often heralded as the most democratic nation in the Muslim world. Formerly part of the Ottoman Empire, it evolved into a strong democracy after achieving independence.

Since the 9/11 attacks, the United States has made the spread of democracy among Muslims, and especially in the Middle East, an important priority. After invading Afghanistan in 2001 and Iraq in 2003, respectively, the United States helped devise new, democratic, constitutions for those nations. It has also pushed for democratic-style governments in other autocratic countries in the Middle East.

"WINNING HEARTS AND MINDS"

The U.S. government acknowledges that winning the War on Terror will require more than military and legal skills. Public opinion in the Islamic world is also a key factor. U.S. politicians and reporters often refer to the effort to make Muslim opinions more favorable toward the United States as "winning hearts and minds." There is no doubt that improving perceptions of the United States in the Islamic world (and the broader world) is a difficult task. In *Longitudes and Attitudes: Exploring the World after September 11* (2002), Thomas L. Friedman observes, "Since the end of the cold war anti-Americanism has overtaken soccer as the world's favorite sport."

Public Relations

For the U.S. government, the toughest public relations challenge has been trying to convince Muslims that the War on Terror is not a war on their religion. According to the article "In the President's Words: Respecting Islam" (April 29, 2003, http://www.whitehouse.gov/infocus/ramadan/islam.html), on September 19, 2001, President Bush said, "The face of terror is not the true faith of Islam. That's not what Islam is all about. Islam is peace. These terrorists don't represent peace. They represent evil and war." The president has often accused the terrorists of "hijacking" Islam for their own evil purposes. Despite these reassurances, many Muslims resent the strong link assumed in the West between Islam and terrorism.

As described in Chapter 2, the DOS conducts programs of public diplomacy in an attempt to influence the attitudes and behaviors of people around the world. Since 9/11, public diplomacy in the Middle East (or Near East, as it is also called) has taken on new emphasis.

As part of its public diplomacy programs, the U.S. government finances radio and television networks to counter what it considers misinformation disseminated about the United States by the state-run media in many Middle Eastern countries. Radio Sawa, an Arabic-language radio station that plays music and news stories, was launched in 2002. The Alhurra Satellite Television Network provides commercial-free Arabic-language news and feature stories throughout the Middle East. Radio Farda is a Persian-language station broadcast specifically for the Iranian audience and features music, news, and information programs. In 2003 the DOS provided millions of dollars for the new magazine *Hi* that was designed to reach the teenage populations of Arabic countries. Its sales were dismal, and the program was suspended in late 2005.

Middle Eastern youth, particularly boys, are the primary target of U.S. information campaigns. It is hoped that the information will help counteract the radical version of Islam that is associated with many Islamic religious schools called madrassas. These boarding schools are financed by wealthy Muslims and provide room and board for poor boys throughout the Islamic world. The educational studies are devoted almost exclusively to the Koran and Sharia. There are believed to be thousands of madrassas throughout the Middle East. The National Commission on Terrorist Attacks upon the United States notes in *The 9/11 Commission Report* (2004, http://www.9-11commission.gov/report/911Report.pdf) that as of 2004 there were 859 madrassas in Karachi, Pakistan, educating over 200,000 students and that some of these schools "have been used as incubators for violent extremism." The commission emphasizes the importance of an effective U.S. information campaign with this warning: "If the United States does not act aggressively to define itself in the Islamic world, the extremists will gladly do the job for us."

Foreign Aid

Another key element of U.S. public diplomacy is foreign aid. Providing food, money, and other aid to struggling countries has been a hallmark of U.S. foreign policy since the end of World War II. Under the Marshall Plan billions of dollars went to European countries to help them rebuild infrastructure and industries devastated during the war. The money helped ensure political stability, stave off communist interference, and create trading partners for the United States.

Muslim-majority countries have been the beneficiaries of U.S. foreign aid in the past. These programs received new emphasis when the War on Terror began in September 2001. Table 10.2 shows the fiscal year 2009 budget request of the U.S. Agency for International

TABLE 10.2

U.S. economic assistance requested for Near Eastern countries for fiscal year 2009

($ in thousands)	FY 2009 request
Total	5,524,133
Peace and security	4,320,699
Counter-terrorism	39,807
Combating weapons of mass destruction (WMD)	3,460
Stabilization operations and security sector reform	4,252,182
Transnational crime	500
Conflict mitigation and reconciliation	24,750
Governing justly and democratically	453,680
Rule of law and human rights	148,250
Good governance	112,580
Political competition and consensus-building	46,500
Civil society	146,350
Investing in people	253,621
Health	106,495
Education	143,326
Social services and protection for especially vulnerable people	3,800
Economic growth	488,583
Macroeconomic foundation for growth	201,428
Trade and investment	28,685
Financial sector	67,128
Infrastructure	1,000
Agriculture	71,450
Private sector competitiveness	80,552
Economic opportunity	4,950
Environment	33,390
Humanitarian assistance	7,000
Protection, assistance and solutions	6,000
Disaster readiness	1,000
Program support	550
Program support	550

FY = Fiscal Year.

SOURCE: Adapted from "Request by Program Area by Fiscal Year," in *Congressional Budget Justification: Foreign Operations, Fiscal Year 2009*, U.S. Department of State, U.S. Agency for International Development, February 2008, http://www.usaid.gov/policy/budget/cbj2009/101442.pdf (accessed August 9, 2008)

FIGURE 10.3

Map of Pakistan, December 2006

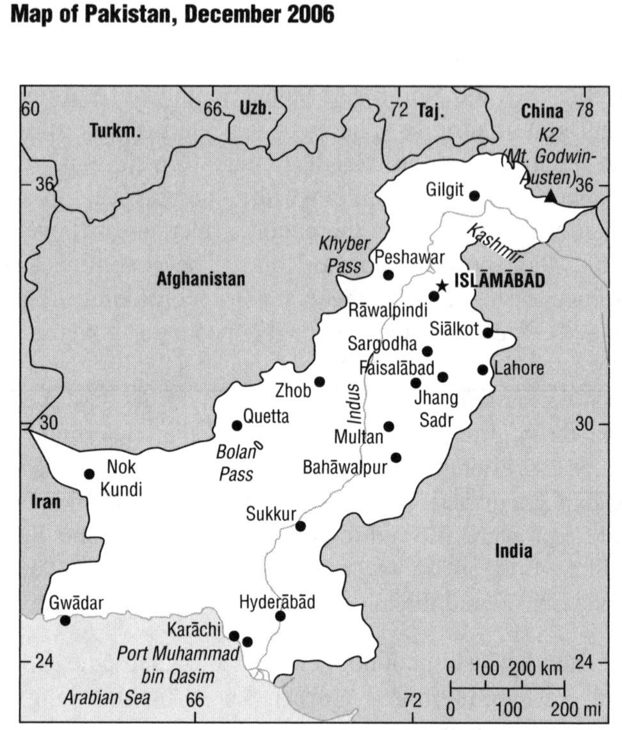

SOURCE: "Pakistan," in *Country Analysis Briefs: Pakistan*, U.S. Department of Energy, Energy Information Administration, December 2006, http://www.eia.doe.gov/cabs/Pakistan/Background.html (accessed August 5, 2008)

Development (USAID) for the Near East region (including Israel). USAID is the principal U.S. agency engaged in providing foreign economic assistance. It requested more than $5.5 billion in aid for nations in the Near East. Israel will be the largest aid recipient with nearly $2.6 billion. Egypt, a predominantly Muslim country, will be second with $1.5 billion. The remaining $2.4 billion will be spread among the remaining nations of the Near East, all of which are predominantly Muslim.

Pakistan is located in south-central Asia. (See Figure 10.3.) Its position next to Afghanistan makes it a key figure in the U.S. War on Terror. Between 2002 and 2008 the United States provided $10.9 billion in aid to Pakistan. (See Table 10.3.) An additional $996 million was requested for the fiscal year 2009 budget of the U.S. government. The vast majority of the aid provided between 2002 and 2008 was for security purposes. Nearly $7.9 billion were devoted to this purpose. The remaining amount ($3.1 billion) funded programs for children and economic development and provided food to the Pakistani people, the vast majority of which are Muslim.

Four Muslim-majority countries lying north of Afghanistan and Pakistan have also been the recipients of USAID assistance. Between 2002 and 2006 a USAID program dedicated to education helped finance school

TABLE 10.3

U.S. economic assistance to Pakistan, by program, fiscal years 2002–08 and requested for 2009

[Rounded to the nearest millions of dollars]

Program or account	FY2002	FY2003	FY2004	FY2005	FY2006	FY2007	FY2008 (est.)	FY2002–FY2008 Total	FY2009 (req.)
1206	—	—	—	—	23	14	16	**53**	[k]
CN	—	—	—	8	29	39	55	**131**	[k]
CSF[a]	1,169[e]	1,247	705	964	862	731[h]	[i]	**5,678**	[i]
FC	—	—	—	—	—	—	75	**75**	[k]
FMF	75	225	75	299	297	297	298	**1,566**	400
IMET	1	1	1	2	2	2	2	**11**	2
INCLE	91	31	32	32	38	21	22	**267**	32
NADR[b]	10	—	5	8	9	10	10	**52**	11
Total security-related	**1,346**	**1,504**	**818**	**1,313**	**1,260**	**1,114**	**486**	**7,891**	**445**
CSH	14	16	26	21	28	22	30	**137**	28
DA	10	35	49	29	38	95	30	**286**	—
ESF[c]	615	188	200	298	337	389	407	**2,434**	523
Food Aid[d]	5	28	13	32	55	—	—	**204**	—
Total economic-related	**669[f]**	**267**	**288**	**664**	**528[g]**	**506**	**467**	**3,105**	**551**
Grand total	**2,015**	**1,771**	**1,106**	**1,977**	**1,788**	**1,620**	**953[j]**	**10,946**	**996**

1206: Section 1206 of the National Defense Authorization Act for FY2006 (P.L. 109–163, global train and equip; Pentagon budget).
CN: Counternarcotics Funds (Pentagon budget).
CSF: Coalition Support Funds (Pentagon budget).
CSH: Child Survival and Health.
DA: Development Assistance.
ESF: Economic Support Fund.
FC: Section 1206 of the NDAA for FY2008 (P.L. 110–181, Pakistan Frontier Corp train and equip; Pentagon budget).
FMF: Foreign Military Financing.
IMET: International Military Education and Training.
INCLE: International Narcotics Control and Law Enforcement (includes border security).
NADR: Nonproliferation, Anti-Terrorism, Demining, and Related[b]

Notes:
[a]CSF is Pentagon funding to reimburse Pakistan for its support of U.S. military operations. It is not officially designated as foreign assistance, but is counted as such by many analysts.
[b]The great majority of NADR funds allocated for Pakistan are for anti-terrorism assistance.
[c]Congress authorized Pakistan to use the FY2003 and FY2004 ESF allocations to cancel a total of about $1.5 billion in concessional debt to the U.S. government. From FY2005–FY2007, $200 million per year in ESF was delivered in the form of "budget support" — cash transfers to Pakistan. Such funds will be "projectized" from FY2008 on.
[d]P.L.480 Title I (loans), P.L.480 Title II (grants), and Section 416(b) of the Agricultural Act of 1949, as amended (surplus agricultural commodity donations). Food aid totals do not include freight costs.
[e]Includes $220 million for peacekeeping operations reported by the State Department.
[f]Includes $25 million for emergency refugee and migration assistance.
[g]Although the Emergency Supplemental Appropriations Act, 2006 (P.L. 109–234) did not earmark international disaster and famine assistance funds for Pakistani earthquake relief, it allocated sufficient funds to meet the administration request of $70 million for this purpose; these are added to the total.
[h]Includes CSF payments (one pending) for support provided through August 2007. The Department of Defense Appropriations Act, 2007 (P.L. 109–289) and an emergency supplemental appropriations act (P.L. 110–28) appropriated a total of $1.1 billion for FY2007 CSF payments to "Pakistan, Jordan, and other key cooperating nations."
[i]Division L of the Consolidated Appropriations Act, 2008 (P.L. 110–161), appropriated $300 million for FY2008 CSF payments. The National Defense Authorization Act for FY2008 (P.L. 110–181) authorizes up to $1.2 billion in total CSF payments to "any key cooperating nation" in connection with U.S. military operations in Iraq or Afghanistan. To date, no CSF requests have been made for FY2009.
[j]Includes supplemental appropriations of $60 million for ESF and $7.5 million for diplomatic and consular operations in the FATA and along the Pakistan-Afghanistan border.
[k]This funding is "requirements-based" for "urgent and emergent threats and opportunities." Thus, there are no pre-allocation data.

SOURCE: K. Alan Kronstadt, "Table 1. Overt U.S. Aid and Military Reimbursements to Pakistan, FY2002–FY2009," in *Pakistan-U.S. Relations*, Congressional Research Service, May 30, 2008, http://ftp.fas.org/sgp/crs/row/RL33498.pdf (accessed August 9, 2008)

construction and renovation, teacher training, and related projects in Kyrgyzstan, Tajikistan, Turkmenistan, and Uzbekistan. (See Table 10.4.)

THE MIDDLE EAST PARTNERSHIP INITIATIVE. In 2002 the DOS created a new foreign aid program called the Middle East Partnership Initiative (MEPI). MEPI is described at length by the GAO in *Foreign Assistance: Middle East Partnership Initiative Offers Tool for Supporting Reform, but Project Monitoring Needs Improvement* (August 2005, http://www.gao.gov/new.items/d05711.pdf). According to the GAO, MEPI—which works with U.S. embassies and USAID—is designed to support four specific reform goals:

- Economic growth—enhance trade and global competitiveness, encourage domestic and foreign investment in business and industry, and facilitate entrepreneurship, particularly through the creation of small and medium businesses.
- Political stability—strengthen democracy by promoting democratic practices within governments, such as measures of accountability to the public and allowance of free speech by the press; another goal is enhancement of law and order and government institutions.
- Education improvement—provide greater access to educational opportunities (particularly among the female population); improve teacher training, curriculum, computer

TABLE 10.4

USAID (U.S. Agency for International Development) education program results for four Muslim-majority countries in central Asia, 2002–06

Type of program	Major program components	Regional impact (approximate numbers)
Increase access to education opportunities	• School and classroom construction and rehabilitation	• Rehabilitated 113 schools (Kyrgyzstan, Tajikistan, Uzbekistan)
	• School finance	• Piloted new school finance mechanism based on per capita funding formula to improve efficiency. Results include more efficient student/teacher ratios in pilot areas (Kyrgyzstan, Tajikistan, Uzbekistan).
Increase the quality of education	• Teacher training	• 8,142 primary and secondary school teachers trained in interactive, student-centered methods with mentoring and other follow-up support (Kyrgyzstan, Tajikistan, Uzbekistan, Turkmenistan).
	• Community and parental involvement	• 174 school community committees strengthened to support school quality improvements (Kyrgyzstan, Tajikistan, Uzbekistan).
	• Model school program	• 300 "Model Schools" model best practices in the use of new teaching methods, management practices and community involvement (Kyrgyzstan, Tajikistan, Uzbekistan, Turkmenistan).

SOURCE: "USAID/E&E Education Program Impact in Four Muslim Majority Central Asian Countries (2002–2006)," in *Country Reports on Terrorism, 2007*, U.S. Department of State, April 2008, http://www.state.gov/documents/organization/105904.pdf (accessed July 29, 2008)

access, and parental involvement in the school systems; and promote literacy and other practical skills.

- Women's issues—encourage the participation of women in the political process and reduce social, economic, cultural, and legal barriers that limit women's role in society.

According to MEPI (2008, http://www.mepi.state.gov/), the program has provided $480 million in funding since 2002 to over 450 projects in 17 nations and territories. Figure 10.4 shows the Middle Eastern countries that have benefited from MEPI projects.

FREEDOM OF SPEECH ISSUES

Freedom of speech is a highly regarded principle in Western democracies. As such, Western speakers and writers feel free to openly discuss matters of religion, including matters that relate to Islam. This has led to clashes with Muslims who hold many subjects within Islam to be so sacred or sensitive that they cannot be discussed in a manner deemed disrespectful. In addition, most Muslims consider it blasphemous to visually depict God or the prophet Muhammad in any media, including artwork.

In 1988 the Indian-born writer Salman Rushdie (1947–) published in England *The Satanic Verses*, which included dreamlike sequences involving Muhammad and the Koran. The book sparked outrage among many Muslims who felt it was blasphemous. Ayatollah Ruhollah Khomeini (1900–1989), the supreme leader of Iran, issued a fatwa (religious edict) calling on Muslims around the world to kill Rushdie. The author was forced to go into hiding. The incident severely strained Iran's relations with other nations, particularly Great Britain, which severed diplomatic ties with Iran. During the late 1990s moderates within the Iranian government downplayed the fatwa. However, Iran took a conservative turn in 2005. The article "Iran Adamant over Rushdie Fatwa" (BBC News, February 12, 2005) states that the fatwa against Rushdie was reaffirmed that same year by Iran's religious leaders.

The provocative ten-minute film *Submission* was released in 2004 in the Netherlands. It included several naked women with verses from the Koran written on their bodies. The film was a commentary on alleged mistreatment of women in Islamic society. Its release led to the murder several months later of its director, Theo van Gogh (1957–2004; a descendant of the painter Vincent van Gogh), by Mohammed Bouyeri (1978–), a man of Moroccan-Dutch descent affiliated with Islamic extremists. Toby Sterling reports in "Prosecutors: Van Gogh's Alleged Killer Cites Holy War" (*Seattle Times*, January 27, 2005) that the police arrested a dozen conspirators, all members of a terrorist group called the Hofstad network. The prosecutor called the crime "terrorism, inspired by an extreme interpretation of Islam."

Another freedom of speech furor erupted in 2005 after *Jyllands-Posten*, a newspaper in Denmark, published some comic strips featuring Muhammad as a character. One of the drawings depicted the Prophet wearing a turban with a bomb underneath it. Muslims reacted with anger. Dozens of people were killed in riots across the Middle East, and Scandinavian embassies and diplomatic offices in the region were attacked and set on fire. The newspaper received many bomb threats, and the comic strip artists had to go into hiding for fear of their lives. Several Muslim countries initiated an economic boycott of Danish goods. According to the article "Cartoons Row Hits Danish Exports" (BBC News, September 9, 2006), the boycott cut Denmark's exports to the Middle East by approximately half between February and June 2006, amounting to $170 million in lost revenue.

FIGURE 10.4

Countries included in the Middle East Partnership Initiative

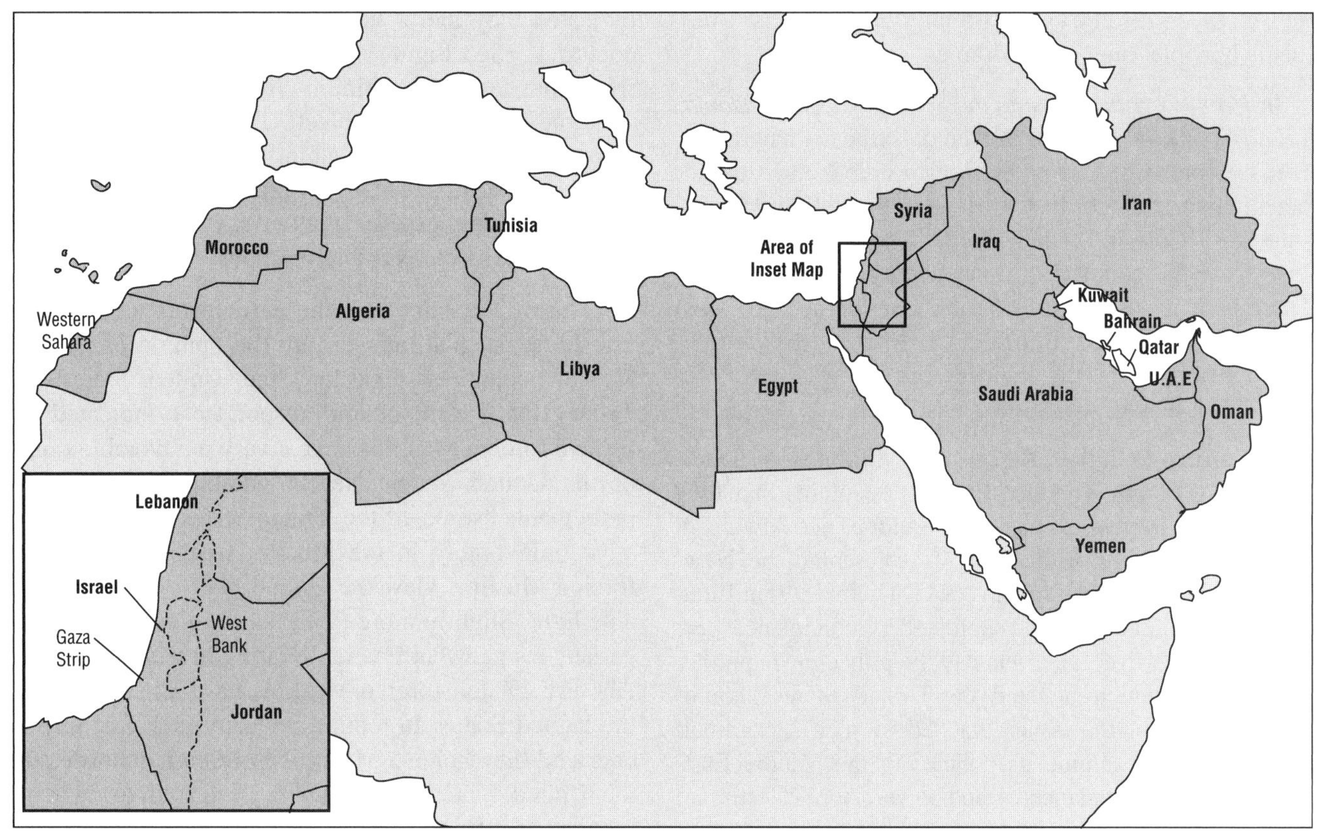

Boundary representation is not necessarily authoritative.
The West Bank and Gaza Strip are Israeli occupied, with interim status subject to Israeli-Palestinian negotiations–final status to be determined.

SOURCE: "Near Eastern Affairs," in *Middle East Partnership Initiative: Countries*, U.S. Department of State, Undated, http://mepi.state.gov/c10128.htm (accessed August 9, 2008)

The publication of the comics (or cartoons as they were called in Europe) and the resulting fury sparked a debate across Europe about the freedom of expression. Within a few months the newspaper issued a formal apology. However, in "Why I Published Those Cartoons" (*Washington Post*, February 19, 2006), Flemming Rose, the editor who had published the comics, defends his decision. He argues that the newspaper had a tradition of using satirical drawings to lampoon public figures, even religious ones. He rejected calls for self-censorship by the media to prevent insulting Muslims, noting "if a believer demands that I, as a nonbeliever, observe his taboos in the public domain, he is not asking for my respect, but for my submission. And that is incompatible with a secular democracy."

In September 2006 Pope Benedict XVI (1927–) angered Muslims when he quoted a text from the fourteenth century in which the Byzantine emperor Manuel II Paleologus (1350–1425) criticized Muhammad for spreading Islam by force. The comment drew a vehement backlash from Muslim leaders around the world, who demanded the pope apologize for being disrespectful. According to Ian Fisher, in "Pope Apologizes for Uproar over His Remarks" (*New York Times*, September 17, 2006), the incident may have sparked the killing of a nun in Somalia and attacks on several Christian churches in the Middle East. The pope issued a rare personal apology and insisted that the quoted text did not represent his own views on Islam.

CONDEMNING OR EXCUSING TERRORISM?

The most difficult issue in relations between the United States and Muslims is that some Muslims believe Islam justifies, or even requires, attacks against the United States and other Western nations. They see the United States, a powerful nation that has enormous direct and indirect influence over Muslims around the world, as a threat to Islam, and they have struck against it.

Most Muslims disagree with these views. They regard the terrorists as extremists who have misunderstood the true nature of Islam. At the same time, however, the reaction to terrorism by Islamic religious figures and the political leaders is not always as strong as Americans feel they should be. In "America Has to Face Reality" (*Newsweek*, October 13, 2001), Christopher Dickey calls it the "this is horrible, but..." syndrome.

In *Holy War, Inc.: Inside the Secret World of Osama bin Laden* (2001), Peter L. Bergen describes at length the terrorist exploits of Osama bin Laden (1957–) and the al Qaeda network. According to Bergen, the 2000 bombing of the USS *Cole* in Yemen elicited the following comments from the country's former deputy prime minister: "There was no justification for the *Cole* bombing. I was shocked and surprised. But the U.S. bears a great degree of responsibility for the incident for the way the U.S. deals with issues in the Middle East."

The article "Giuliani Rejects $10 Million from Saudi Prince" (CNN.com, October 13, 2001) explains that following the 9/11 terrorist attacks the Saudi prince Alwaleed bin Talal Abdulaziz Alsaud (1957–) presented the New York City mayor Rudy Giuliani (1944–) with a $10 million donation for relief efforts and expressed his condolences for the victims. However, later that day the prince made public statements in which he said the United States should "address some of the issues that led to such a criminal attack" and "re-examine its policies in the Middle East and adopt a more balanced stand toward the Palestinian cause." Giuliani angrily returned the prince's check and denounced the attempted linkage between the terrorist attacks and U.S. foreign policy.

In "Where's the Outrage?" (*USA Today*, September 12, 2006), Karen Hughes, the undersecretary of public diplomacy and public affairs for the DOS, laments the lack of worldwide "moral outrage" regarding terrorism and notes, "As I have traveled the world, I have met those who try to justify the violence based on policy differences, long-held grievances or a perceived threat from the West."

CAIR disputes the notion that prominent Muslims excuse terrorist attacks against the United States. In *Response to September 11, 2001, Attacks* (March 28, 2007, http://www.cair.com/Portals/0/pdf/September_11_statements.pdf), CAIR includes statements from dozens of Islamic scholars from around the world who have condemned terrorist attacks that kill innocent people. CAIR also published *Islamic Statements against Terrorism* (2005, http://www.cair.com/Portals/0/pdf/Condemnation_of_London_Bombings.pdf) after the July 7, 2005, bombings in London.

AMERICAN PUBLIC OPINION

In February 2007 the Gallup Organization conducted polls to gauge American attitudes about the Islamic world. Participants were asked to rate their opinion of Muslim countries as "very favorable," "somewhat favorable," "neither favorable nor unfavorable," "somewhat unfavorable," or "very unfavorable." Only 3% of respondents indicated they had a very favorable opinion of Muslim countries. (See Figure 10.5.) Another 23% expressed a somewhat favorable opinion. Just over one-third (34%) were neutral on the subject. Twenty-three percent of respondents had a somewhat unfavorable view of Muslim countries, and 12% had a very unfavorable opinion. Overall, 26% of those asked expressed favorable opinions, and 35% expressed unfavorable opinions.

During the same poll the participants were asked to use the same qualifiers to rate the opinion of people in Muslim countries regarding the United States. (See Table 10.5.) Half of the respondents indicated they believe foreign Muslims have a very unfavorable opinion of the United States. Nearly one-third (31%) of poll participants estimated the United States is viewed somewhat unfavorably in the Muslim world. Only 2% said foreign Muslims view the United States in a very favorable light. Slightly more (9%) believed the United States garners a somewhat favorable rating in Islamic countries. Another 4% felt foreign Muslims have a neutral view of the United States. In total, a majority (81%) of respondents said they believe Muslims in foreign countries view the United States unfavorably, compared to 11% who thought the United States is viewed favorably. These percentages have changed little since the question was first asked in March 2002.

Gallup also asked Americans why they believe Muslims have an "unfavorable view" of the United States. A majority (57%) of respondents believed this unfavorable view on the part of Muslims is based on misinformation provided by their media and governments. (See Figure 10.6.) Twenty-six percent thought U.S. actions have precipitated the unfavorable view. Another 13% thought both explanations or neither were to blame.

Knowledge about Muslim Opinions and Beliefs

During the February 2007 poll, participants were asked to indicate their level of knowledge about the opinions and beliefs of people who live in Muslim countries. Only 6% of those asked felt confident they have a great deal of knowledge about Muslim opinions and beliefs. (See Figure 10.7.) Another 37% felt confident they possess a moderate amount of knowledge. The largest component (43%) said they do not have much knowledge on the subject, and 14% admitted they know nothing at all about the opinions and beliefs of people in the Muslim world.

Table 10.6 illustrates the opinions of poll respondents about Muslim countries based on the respondents' self-

FIGURE 10.5

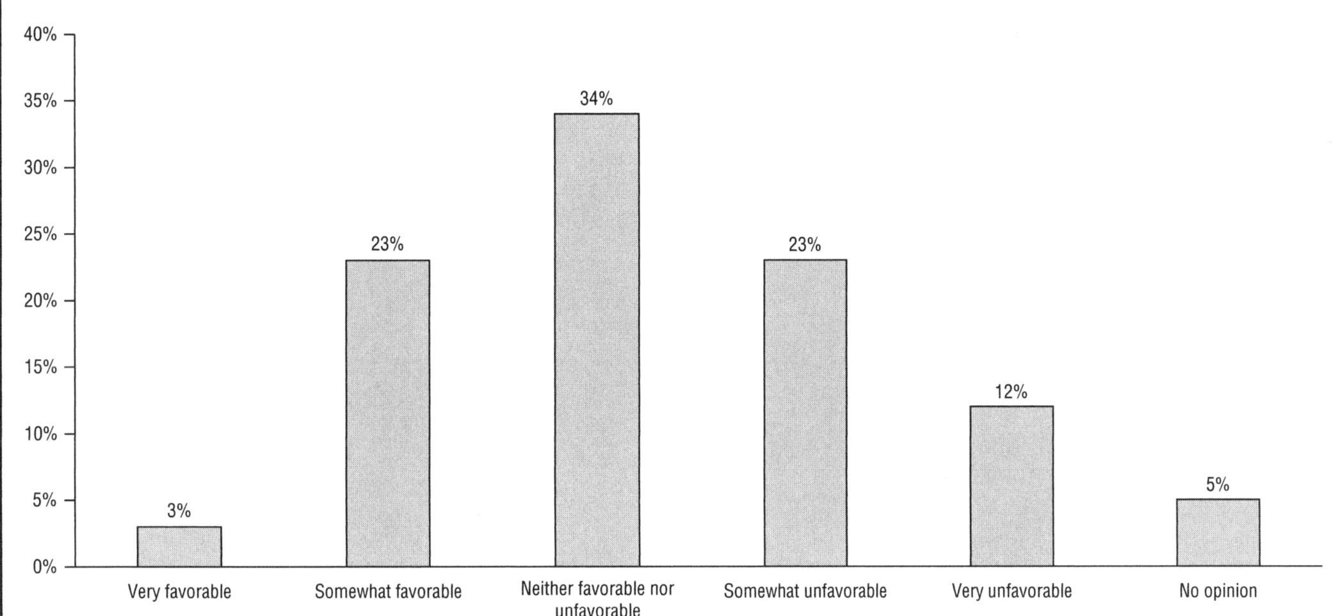

SOURCE: Adapted from Frank Newport and Dalia Mogahed, "In General, Please Tell Me Whether Your Opinion of Muslim Countries Is Very Favorable, Somewhat Favorable, Neither Favorable Nor Unfavorable, Somewhat Unfavorable, or Very Unfavorable?" in *Americans: People in Muslim Countries Have Negative Views of U.S.*, The Gallup Organization, February 2, 2007, http://www.gallup.com/poll/26350/Americans-People-Muslim-Countries-Negative-Views-US.aspx?version=print (accessed August 9, 2008). Copyright © 2007 by The Gallup Organization. Reproduced by permission of The Gallup Organization.

TABLE 10.5

Poll respondents' perceptions of the opinion people in Muslim countries have about the United States, February 2007

IN GENERAL, DO YOU THINK PEOPLE IN MUSLIM COUNTRIES HAVE A VERY FAVORABLE, SOMEWHAT FAVORABLE, NEITHER FAVORABLE NOR UNFAVORABLE, SOMEWHAT UNFAVORABLE, OR VERY UNFAVORABLE OPINION OF THE UNITED STATES?

	Very favorable	Somewhat favorable	Neither favorable nor unfavorable	Somewhat unfavorable	Very unfavorable	No opinion
2007 Jan 15–18	2%	9	4	31	50	4
2006 Mar 13–16	3%	9	4	33	49	3
2002 Mar 1–3	1%	8	7	35	47	2

SOURCE: Frank Newport and Dalia Mogahed, "In General, Do You Think People in Muslim Countries Have a Very Favorable, Somewhat Favorable, Neither Favorable Nor Unfavorable, Somewhat Unfavorable, or Very Unfavorable Opinion of the United States?" in *Americans: People in Muslim Countries Have Negative Views of U.S.*, The Gallup Organization, February 2, 2007, http://www.gallup.com/poll/26350/Americans-People-Muslim-Countries-Negative-Views-US.aspx?version=print (accessed August 9, 2008). Copyright © 2007 by The Gallup Organization. Reproduced by permission of The Gallup Organization.

reported knowledge about Muslim opinions and beliefs. People professing to have a great deal or moderate amount of knowledge about Muslim opinions and beliefs were split almost evenly between a favorable opinion (35%) and an unfavorable opinion (36%). Another 27% were neutral on the subject. By contrast, respondents who professed to have little knowledge about Muslim opinions and beliefs mostly had a neutral opinion about Muslim countries (43%). Twenty-one percent of them had a favorable opinion and 32% had an unfavorable opinion about Muslim countries.

Western and Muslim Worlds Coexisting

Frank Newport reports in *Complex but Hopeful Pattern of American Attitudes toward Muslims* (March 23, 2006, http://www.gallup.com/poll/22021/Complex-Hopeful-Pattern-American-Attitudes-Toward-Muslims.aspx) that in February 2006 Americans were asked to rate on a scale from one to five the amount of concern they believed Muslim (or Islamic) societies show for better coexistence between themselves and Western societies. A rating of one coincided with no concern, and a rating of five coincided with a lot of concern. Only 3% of respondents gave a five rating, meaning few believed Muslims definitely show a lot of concern about better coexistence. Seven percent were less firm in this opinion and gave a four rating. A much higher percentage (29%) chose a rating of three, indicating they believed Muslims show a moderate amount of concern for better coexistence.

FIGURE 10.6

Public opinion on the causes of the bad opinions Muslims have about the United States, February 2007

DO YOU THINK THAT THE UNFAVORABLE VIEWS MUSLIMS HAVE OF THE U.S. ARE—BASED MOSTLY ON WHAT THE U.S. HAS DONE (OR ARE) BASED MOSTLY ON MISINFORMATION PROVIDED BY THEIR MEDIA AND GOVERNMENT ABOUT WHAT THE U.S. HAS DONE?

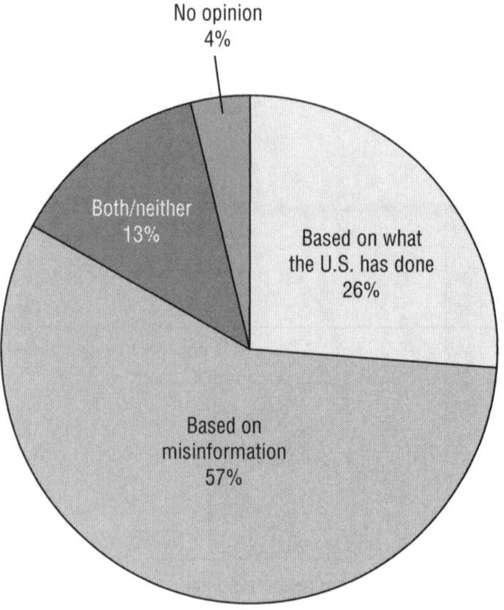

SOURCE: Adapted from Frank Newport and Dalia Mogahed, "Do You Think That the Unfavorable Views Muslims Have of the U.S. Are—[ROTATED: Based Mostly on What the U.S. Has Done (or Are) Based Mostly on Misinformation Provided by Their Media and Government about What the U.S. Has Done]?" in *Americans: People in Muslim Countries Have Negative Views of U.S.*, The Gallup Organization, February 2, 2007, http://www.gallup.com/poll/26350/Americans-People-Muslim-Countries-Negative-Views-US.aspx?version=print (accessed August 9, 2008). Copyright © 2007 by The Gallup Organization. Reproduced by permission of The Gallup Organization.

FIGURE 10.7

Poll respondents' level of knowledge about people who live in Muslim countries, February 2007

HOW MUCH WOULD YOU SAY YOU KNOW ABOUT THE OPINIONS AND BELIEFS OF PEOPLE WHO LIVE IN MUSLIM COUNTRIES—A GREAT DEAL, A MODERATE AMOUNT, NOT MUCH, OR NOT AT ALL?

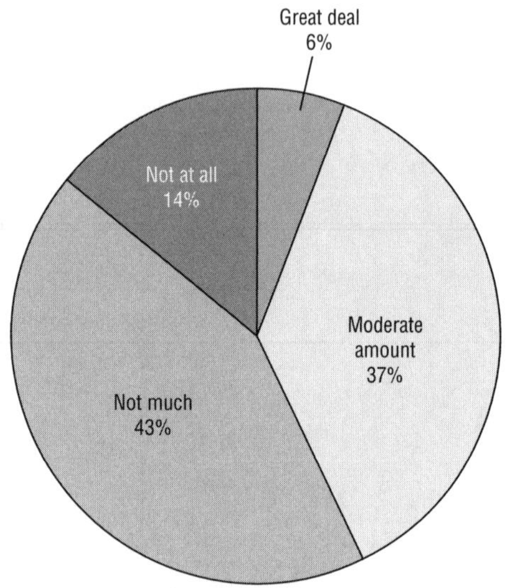

SOURCE: Adapted from Frank Newport and Dalia Mogahed, "How Much Would You Say You Know about the Opinions and Beliefs of People Who Live in Muslim Countries—a Great Deal, a Moderate Amount, Not Much, or Not at All?" in *Americans: People in Muslim Countries Have Negative Views of U.S.*, The Gallup Organization, February 2, 2007, http://www.gallup.com/poll/26350/Americans-People-Muslim-Countries-Negative-Views-US.aspx?version=print (accessed August 9, 2008). Copyright © 2008 by The Gallup Organization. Reproduced by permission of The Gallup Organization.

Slightly more than one-third (34%) of respondents gave a rating of two. Finally, 24% of poll participants chose a rating of one. In other words, they believed Islamic societies show no concern about better coexistence.

Overall, the poll results indicate that 58% of those asked believed Muslims show little to no concern for better coexistence, and only 10% felt Muslims show a lot or nearly a lot of concern. A solid component (29%) chose a middle-ground answer.

Newport indicates that the participants were asked to use the same rating system to rate their own personal level of concern for a "better understanding" between the Western and Muslim cultures. Only 5% of those asked indicated they felt no concern about improving understanding between the two worlds. A slightly higher percentage (6%) chose a two rating, coinciding with a small level of concern. Twenty-two percent of poll participants rated their level of concern at the three (or midrange) level. A larger component (31%) gave a higher rating of four. More than one-third (34%) of the people said they felt a lot of concern about obtaining a better understanding between the Western and Muslim cultures.

TABLE 10.6

Poll respondents' opinion of Muslim countries based on respondents' level of knowledge about Muslims, February 2007

	Great deal/ Moderate amount %	Not much %	Nothing %
Favorable opinion	35	21	13
Neither favorable nor unfavorable opinion	27	43	29
Unfavorable opinion	36	32	43
Don't know	2	4	15

SOURCE: Frank Newport and Dalia Mogahed, "Opinion of Muslim Countries, by Self-Reported Knowledge of the Opinions and Beliefs of People Who Live in Muslim Countries," in *Americans: People in Muslim Countries Have Negative Views of U.S.*, The Gallup Organization, February 2, 2007, http://www.gallup.com/poll/26350/Americans-People-Muslim-Countries-Negative-Views-US.aspx?version=print (accessed August 9, 2008). Copyright © 2008 by The Gallup Organization. Reproduced by permission of The Gallup Organization.

When viewed in total, the results indicate a relatively high level of concern in this area. A solid majority (65%) said the issue concerns them a lot or a moderately high amount. Only 11% indicated little to no concern. Finally, 22% expressed a moderate amount of concern.

Improving Relations between the Western and Muslim Worlds

Newport notes that Americans were also asked to name things that each society could do to improve relations between the Western and Muslim worlds. First, the participants were asked about what the Islamic world could do to improve relations with the West. A fifth (20%) of the people named "improve communication" as an important step toward better relations. The second most often named activity dealt with stopping, lessening, or controlling terrorism, which was named by 15% of poll participants. Twelve percent thought better understanding each others' beliefs would improve relations, and 10% said Muslims could work to better understand Westerners' beliefs. Together, these four activities were named by more than half (57%) of all the people taking part in the poll.

When asked what Western societies could do to improve relations with the Muslim world, 18% of respondents said Westerners should try harder to understand Muslim beliefs. Another 14% indicated that improved education and more cultural intermixing would be good for relations. A smaller percentage (9%) expressed the belief that working together was the answer to better relations.

Muslim-Americans

The United States has a relatively small population of Muslims. CAIR estimates in "About Islam and American Muslims" that the Islamic-American population is about seven million. In its July 30, 2007, issue, *Newsweek* included a special feature titled "Islam in America." The feature notes that "Muslim Americans represent the most affluent, integrated, politically engaged Muslim community in the Western World." However, the Muslim-American community does face suspicion from fellow Americans about the link between Islam and terrorism. According to a July 2007 poll conducted for *Newsweek* by Princeton Survey Research Associates International (2008, http://www.pollingreport.com/terror.htm), 32% of Americans thought Muslim-Americans are "less loyal" to the United States than they are to Islam. Forty percent believed Muslim-Americans are "equally loyal" to the United States and Islam. Another 9% believed Muslim-Americans are "more loyal" to the United States.

Newsweek also finds that Americans worry about Islamic radicalization within the United States. Thirty-eight percent of poll respondents were "somewhat worried" and 16% were "very worried" about this possibility. A quarter were "not too worried" and 18% were "not at all worried" about radicalization within the U.S. Muslim community.

IMPORTANT NAMES AND ADDRESSES

American Civil Liberties Union
125 Broad St., Eighteenth Fl.
New York, NY 10004
(212) 549-2585
1-888-567-2258
E-mail: membership@aclu.org
URL: http://www.aclu.org/

Amnesty International USA
5 Penn Plaza
New York, NY 10001
(212) 807-8400
FAX: (212) 627-1451
E-mail: aimember@aiusa.org
URL: http://www.amnestyusa.org/

Centers for Disease Control and Prevention
1600 Clifton Rd.
Atlanta, GA 30333
1-800-232-4636
E-mail: cdcinfo@cdc.gov
URL: http://www.cdc.gov/

Central Intelligence Agency
Office of Public Affairs
Washington, DC 20505
(703) 482-0623
FAX: (703) 482-1739
URL: http://www.cia.gov/

Congressional Research Service Library of Congress
101 Independence Ave. SE
Washington, DC 20540-7500
URL: http://www.loc.gov/crsinfo/

Council on American Islamic Relations
453 New Jersey Ave. SE
Washington, DC 20003
(202) 488-8787
FAX: (202) 488-0833
E-mail: info@cair.com
URL: http://www.cair.com/

Defense Personnel Security Research Center
99 Pacific St., Ste. 455-E
Monterey, CA 93940
(831) 657-3000
URL: http://www.fas.org/sgp/othergov/perserec.html

Defense Threat Reduction Agency
8725 John J. Kingman Rd., Stop 6201
Fort Belvoir, VA 22060-5264
(703) 767-5870
1-800-701-5096
FAX: (703) 767-4450
E-mail: dtra.publicaffairs@dtra.mil
URL: http://www.dtra.mil/

Electronic Privacy Information Center
1718 Connecticut Ave. NW, Ste. 200
Washington, DC 20009
(202) 483-1140
FAX: (202) 483-1248
URL: http://www.epic.org/

Federal Bureau of Investigation
J. Edgar Hoover Bldg.
935 Pennsylvania Ave. NW
Washington, DC 20535-0001
(202) 324-3000
URL: http://www.fbi.gov/

Federal Emergency Management Agency
500 C St. SW
Washington, DC 20472
1-800-621-3362
URL: http://www.fema.gov/

Federation of American Scientists
1725 DeSales St. NW, Sixth Fl.
Washington, DC 20036
(202) 546-3300
FAX: (202) 675-1010
E-mail: fas@fas.org
URL: http://www.fas.org/

Government Accountability Office
441 G St. NW
Washington, DC 20548
(202) 512-3000
E-mail: contact@gao.gov
URL: http://www.gao.gov/

International Atomic Energy Agency
PO Box 100, Wagramer Strasse 5
A-1400
Vienna, Austria
011-43-1-2600-0
FAX: 011-43-1-2600-7
E-mail: Official.Mail@iaea.org
URL: http://www.iaea.org/

International Committee of the Red Cross
19 avenue de la Paix
CH 1202
Geneva, Switzerland
011-41-22-734-60-01
FAX: 011-41-22-733-20-57
URL: http://www.icrc.org/eng

Joint Chiefs of Staff
Public Affairs Office
9999 Joint Staff Pentagon
Washington, DC 20318-9999
URL: http://www.dtic.mil/jcs

National Center for Policy Analysis
601 Pennsylvania Ave. NW, Ste. 900, South Bldg.
Washington, DC 20004
(202) 220-3082
FAX: (202) 220-3096
URL: http://www.ncpa.org/

National Guard Bureau
1411 Jefferson Davis Hwy.
Arlington, VA 22202-3231
(703) 607-2584
E-mail: webmaster@ngb.ang.af.mil
URL: http://www.ngb.army.mil/

National Security Agency
(301) 688-6524
E-mail: nsapao@nsa.gov
URL: http://www.nsa.gov/home_html.cfm

North Atlantic Treaty Organization
Blvd. Leopold III1110
Brussels, Belgium
E-mail: natodoc@hq.nato.int
URL: http://www.nato.int/

Office of the Director of National Intelligence
Washington, DC 20511
(703) 733-8600
URL: http://www.dni.gov/

Office of the National Counterintelligence Executive
National Counterintelligence Executive
CS5, Rm. 300
Washington, DC 20505
(703) 733-8600
FAX: (703) 682-4510
URL: http://www.ncix.gov/

Transportation Security Administration
601 S. Twelfth St.
Arlington, VA 22202-4220
1-866-289-9673
E-mail: TSA-ContactCenter@dhs.gov
URL: http://www.tsa.gov/

United Nations
First Avenue at Forty-sixth St.
New York, NY 10017
URL: http://www.un.org/

U.S. Agency for International Development
Ronald Reagan Bldg.
Washington, DC 20523-1000
(202) 712-4320
FAX: (202) 216-3524
URL: http://www.usaid.gov/

U.S. Air Force
Office of the Secretary of the Air Force
Public Affairs Resource Library
1690 Air Force Pentagon, Rm. 4A120
Washington, DC 20330-1690
URL: http://www.af.mil/

U.S. Army
Office of the Chief of Public Affairs
1500 Army Pentagon
Washington, DC 20310-1500
(703) 692-2000
URL: http://www.army.mil/

U.S. Citizenship and Immigration Services
20 Massachusetts Ave. NW
Washington, DC 20529
1-800-375-5283
URL: http://www.uscis.gov/graphics/index.htm

U.S. Coast Guard
2100 Second St. SW
Washington, DC 20593
URL: http://www.uscg.mil/

U.S. Customs and Border Protection
1300 Pennsylvania Ave. NW
Washington, DC 20229
(202) 354-1770
URL: http://www.cbp.gov/

U.S. Department of Defense
1400 Defense Pentagon
Washington, DC 20301-1400
(703) 545-6700
URL: http://www.defenselink.mil/

U.S. Department of Energy
1000 Independence Ave. SW
Washington, DC 20585
(202) 586-5000
1-800-342-5363
FAX: (202) 586-4403
URL: http://www.doe.gov/

U.S. Department of Homeland Security
Washington, DC 20528
(202) 282-8000
URL: http://www.dhs.gov/

U.S. Department of Justice
950 Pennsylvania Ave. NW
Washington, DC 20530-0001
(202) 514-2000
E-mail: AskDOJ@usdoj.gov
URL: http://www.usdoj.gov/

U.S. Department of State
2201 C St. NW
Washington, DC 20520
(202) 647-4000
URL: http://www.state.gov/

U.S. Department of the Treasury
1500 Pennsylvania Ave. NW
Washington, DC 20220
(202) 622-2000
FAX: (202) 622-6415
URL: http://www.ustreas.gov/

U.S. House of Representatives Permanent Select Committee on Intelligence
H-405 U.S. Capitol Bldg.
Washington, DC 20515-6415
(202) 225-7690
1-877-858-9040
FAX: (202) 226-5068
E-mail: intelligence.hpsci@mail.house.gov
URL: http://intelligence.house.gov/

U.S. Marine Corps
Director of Public Affairs
2 Navy Annex
Washington, DC 20380-1775
(703) 614-1034
FAX: (703) 614-2358
URL: http://www.usmc.mil/

U.S. Navy
Office of Information
1200 Navy Pentagon, Rm. 4B463
Washington, DC 20350-1200
(703) 697-9020
FAX: (703) 697-8921
URL: http://www.navy.mil/

U.S. Senate Select Committee on Intelligence
211 Hart Senate Office Bldg.
Washington, DC 20510
(202) 224-1700
URL: http://intelligence.senate.gov/

White House
1600 Pennsylvania Ave. NW
Washington, DC 20500
(202) 456-1414
FAX: (202) 456-2461
E-mail: comments@whitehouse.gov
URL: http://www.whitehouse.gov/

RESOURCES

Several government agencies and organizations provided resources for this book. The U.S. Government Accountability Office (GAO) is the investigative arm of Congress and posts its many publications online. GAO reports on national security, weapons of mass destruction, and federal government agencies and spending were invaluable. The Congressional Research Service (CRS) is a division of the Library of Congress and publishes regularly updated reports on U.S. policies and laws and other issues of interest to members of Congress. CRS reports on foreign policy and civil and human rights were a major source of information for this book.

Other government agencies and offices consulted during the compilation of this book include: Broadcasting Board of Governors, Central Intelligence Agency, Federal Bureau of Investigation, the Library of Congress, Majority Staff of the U.S. Congressional Committee on Homeland Security, National Counterterrorism Center, Nunn-Lugar Cooperative Threat Reduction Program, U.S. Agency for International Development, U.S. Department of Defense, U.S. Department of Energy, U.S. Department of Homeland Security, U.S. Department of Justice, U.S. Department of State, U.S. Department of the Treasury, and the White House. The latter provided national strategy and planning documents, budgetary information, and the text of presidential speeches and executive orders.

Commissions appointed by U.S. presidents have produced reports on topics related to national security. These include the *Report to the President of the United States* (March 2005) by the Commission on the Intelligence Capabilities of the United States Regarding Weapons of Mass Destruction and the *9/11 Commission Report* by the National Commission on Terrorist Attacks upon the United States.

The Central Intelligence Agency's *World Factbook* provides a wealth of information about countries around the world and is updated frequently. Other valuable resources in the intelligence community were the National Counterintelligence Executive and the Office of the Director of National Intelligence.

The following news organizations, outlets, and educational publications were useful for providing timely features about national security: *Atlanta Journal-Constitution*, Associated Press, BBC News, CBC News, CNN.com, FOXNews .com, National Geographic, *Newsday*, *Newsweek*, *New York Times*, Public Broadcasting Service, *Seattle Times*, *Sunday Times* (London), *Time*, *USA Today*, and *Washington Post*.

Private domestic or international organizations that provided information for this book included the American Civil Liberties Union, Amnesty International, the Council on American Islamic Relations, the Defense Personnel Security Research Center, the Electronic Privacy Information Center, the Federation of American Scientists, the International Committee of the Red Cross, and the National Center for Policy Analysis. As always, much thanks to the Gallup Organization for its insightful articles and poll results.

INDEX

Page references in italics refer to photographs. References with the letter t *following them indicate the presence of a table. The letter* f *indicates a figure. If more than one table or figure appears on a particular page, the exact item number for the table or figure being referenced is provided.*

D

E

I

J

K

L

M

U

V

W

Y

Z